FOR THE ENCOURAGEMENT OF LEARNING

# For the Encouragement of Learning

## The Origins of Canadian Copyright Law

MYRA TAWFIK

UNIVERSITY OF TORONTO PRESS
Toronto Buffalo London

© University of Toronto Press 2023
Toronto  Buffalo  London
utorontopress.com
Printed in the USA

ISBN 978-1-4875-4524-6 (cloth)
ISBN 978-1-4875-4526-0 (PDF)
ISBN 978-1-4875-4525-3 (EPUB)

Studies in Book and Print Culture

---

**Library and Archives Canada Cataloguing in Publication**

Title: For the encouragement of learning : the origins of Canadian copyright
    law / Myra Tawfik.
Names: Tawfik, Myra J., author.
Series: Studies in book and print culture.
Description: Series statement: Studies in book and print culture | Includes
    bibliographical references and index.
Identifiers: Canadiana (print) 20220479038 | Canadiana (ebook) 20220479054 |
    ISBN 9781487545246 (cloth) | ISBN 9781487545260 (PDF) |
    ISBN 9781487545253 (EPUB)
Subjects: LCSH: Copyright – Canada – History.
Classification: LCC KE2799 .T39 2023 | LCC KF2995 .T39 2023 kfmod |
    DDC 346.7104/82 – dc23

---

We wish to acknowledge the land on which the University of Toronto Press
operates. This land is the traditional territory of the Wendat, the Anishnaabeg,
the Haudenosaunee, the Métis, and the Mississaugas of the Credit First Nation.

This book has been published with the help of a grant from the Federation
for the Humanities and Social Sciences, through the Awards to Scholarly
Publications Program, using funds provided by the Social Sciences and
Humanities Research Council of Canada.

University of Toronto Press acknowledges the financial support of the
Government of Canada, the Canada Council for the Arts, and the Ontario Arts
Council, an agency of the Government of Ontario, for its publishing activities.

*To Ian
for everything he taught me*

# Contents

# Acknowledgments

This book has taken more than fifteen years to research and write – literally half my academic career – and it took a village to bring it to fruition. Over the years, I have benefited from the research assistance of dozens of law students who devoted their summers to poring over nineteenth-century materials, providing me with their findings on arcane aspects of law, labouring over footnotes and citations, helping with translations, and lifting me up with their enthusiasm for the project. I remember each one of them with profound gratitude.

I would like to acknowledge the financial backing and other support I received from the Faculty of Law at the University of Windsor. My early research was also bolstered by a University of Windsor Humanities Research Group Fellowship and a grant from the Osgoode Society for Canadian Legal History. A visiting scholarship from the American Antiquarian Society Library enabled me to spend a month on site in Worcester, Massachusetts.

I am thankful for all the exceptional assistance I received from archivists and librarians at the American Antiquarian Society Library, Bibliothèque et Archives nationales du Québec, Library and Archives Canada, and the University of Windsor's Paul Martin Law Library and Leddy Library. My research was also greatly facilitated by digitized archival documents and other online resources, a boon for equitable access to essential research material. There is no doubt that the level of detail contained in this book would have been impossible without the availability of online materials and the ability to conduct keyword searches. The digital collections on which I relied most heavily were the Canadiana Collections from the Canadian Research Knowledge Network, especially canadiana.ca and heritage.canadiana.ca; Bibliothèque et Archives nationales du Québec collections numériques; University of Alberta Digital Historical Collections, especially the CIHM and Digital Archive

Collections; the HathiTrust Digital Library; and the Internet Archive. I also frequently consulted the online Dictionary of Canadian Biography and Les Manuels Scolaires Québécois database at Université Laval.

The legal historians at the Osgoode Society for Canadian Legal History provided constructive feedback on the first chapters and were generous with their insights and expertise on the history of law in Canada. One of the most unexpected and wondrous consequences of this research was my introduction to the work of book historians and to the community of scholars from the Canadian Association for the Study of Book Culture, the Society for the History of Authorship, Reading, and Publishing, and the Bibliographical Society of Canada. These scholars welcomed me from the start and have been a continuous source of inspiration. I have benefited immensely from their research and would especially like to acknowledge the editors and contributors of the *History of the Book in Canada* project for their rich compendium of material on Canada's book and print culture.

Many copyright colleagues provided me with references, avenues of pursuit, and words of encouragement. They will never know just how much their collegial support sustained me through periods of doubt. I will always be indebted to Meera Nair for urging me to remain steadfast and to write the book I wanted write. In this regard, I would also like to acknowledge Bita Amani, Pascale Chapdelaine, Michael Everton, Ysolde Gendreau, Philip Girard, Maureen Irish, Ariel Katz, Pierre-Emmanuel Moyse, and Teresa Scassa.

I am extremely grateful to my indefatigable team of chapter reviewers: Janet Friskney, Leslie Howsam, and Marcia Valiante. I could not have asked for a better mix of experts in law and book history to read draft chapters, provide insightful commentary, and offer keen editorial advice. Leslie Howsam deserves a special mention for the many ways she contributed to this book through her mentorship, encouragement and wise counsel. She managed to transform a legal scholar into a book historian, and I am forever in her debt.

My family had to endure many years of single-minded purpose with all the sacrifices this entails. Some voluntarily rolled up their sleeves to help with the research or to read and comment on chapters. I am saddened that some of them are no longer here to see this project at its end. I will always be grateful for their belief in me.

When all is said and done, however, none of this would have been possible without my partner Ian Coffin, who accompanied me on this journey with unflagging good humour and equanimity. He was my champion and fiercest supporter. I am heartbroken that he did not live long enough to see the published manuscript. This book is dedicated to him.

# Abbreviations

AAS — American Antiquarian Society Library
APS — American Philosophical Society
BAnQ — Bibliothèque et Archives nationales du Québec
BCSS — British and Canadian School Society
BFSS — British and Foreign School Society
CEWW — The Database of Canada's Early Women Writers (Project director: Dr. Carole Gerson)
DCB — Dictionary of Canadian Biography
HBC — Patricia Fleming, Yvan Lamonde, Gilles Gallichan, Fiona Black eds., *History of the Book in Canada*, volume 1 (Beginnings to 1840) and volume 2 (1840–1918). (Toronto: University of Toronto Press, 2004 and 2005)
JLP — Joseph Lancaster Papers, American Antiquarian Society Library
LAC — Library and Archives Canada
ManScol — Les Manuels Scolaires Québécois database (Project director: Dr. Paul Aubin)

FOR THE ENCOURAGEMENT OF LEARNING

# Introduction

Copyright's history matters. It matters in its own right – as history – but it also plays an important role in contextualizing contemporary copyright law and policy. Law evolves in historical increments. In the British common law tradition, to which most of Canada adheres, reliance on precedent in judicial decision-making means that the past remains integral to current legal thought. Indeed, it is not unusual for twenty-first-century judges to refer to nineteenth-century legislation or judicial decisions. And it is not unusual for today's judges to reflect on the history and normative tradition of a particular body of law in order to interpret its modern applications. This is especially true in relation to copyright, which is susceptible to multiple and varied interpretations regarding its policy objectives.

Copyright is an elusive construct. Its nature and purpose have been obscured by attempts to capture its foundational policy in one broad organizing principle. Contemporary legal discourse describes the law in terms of the dichotomy between two Western copyright traditions – the British (and American) "copyright" tradition and the Continental European "droit d'auteur" tradition. Assumptions are made about *droit d'auteur* versus copyright jurisdictions based on particular interpretations and subjective assessments of the law's fundamental purpose. How lawmakers view copyright's predominant orientation will influence the way in which the law is drafted and interpreted. At the most simplistic level, the *droit d'auteur* tradition upholds the primacy of the "author" or "creator" as the focus of legislative attention, and advances personality theories of the law. In contrast, the British tradition views copyright in economic terms and situates it within property conceptions of the law. As such, commercial actors, like printers and publishers, are central to legislative consideration. Copyright is designed to support the intermediaries, the cultural industries, that give material form to and disseminate the works of authors and other creators. Yet even within this so-called copyright tradition there are variations and important distinctions. American copyright law, although originally transplanted from the British, has its own characteristics, which tend towards a third interested party, the user of copyright works, as the focus of policy concern. Under this framework, the primary goal of copyright is to encourage learning by providing authors and publishers with exclusive rights only for the duration necessary to achieve that public policy objective.

There is no question that creators and cultural industries are integral to the law both in policy and in practice. This is true in both *droit d'auteur* and copyright countries. Indeed, both authors and "proprietors" are expressly recognized as copyright holders in the statutes themselves. However, the copyright paradigm would be incomplete if we failed to recognize the centrality of those who *use* and who learn from copyright works; the law must also safeguard the spaces that must remain outside proprietary capture by the copyright holder.

The research that became this book began because Canadian courts have been advancing competing views of Canada's copyright tradition. Some, like Justice Gonthier of the Supreme Court of Canada and Justice Décary of the Federal Court of Appeal, postulate that Canadian law follows the *droit d'auteur* civil law school or at least an amalgam of civil law and British common law traditions. To Justice Décary, "[t]he use of the word 'copyright' in the English version of the Act has obscured the fact that what the Act fundamentally seeks to protect is 'le droit d'auteur.'"[1] In Justice Gonthier's view, "it is important to recall that Canadian copyright law derives from multiple sources and draws on both common law tradition and continental civil law concepts."[2] Others, like Justice Binnie of the Supreme Court of Canada, assert that Canadian law falls exclusively within the British copyright tradition: "It is not altogether helpful that in the French and English version of the Act the terms 'copyright' and 'droit d'auteur' are treated as equivalent."[3] In his view, "Canadian copyright law has traditionally been more concerned with economic than moral rights ... The economic rights are based on a conception of artistic and literary works essentially as articles of commerce. (Indeed, the initial Copyright Act, 1709 (UK) ... was passed to assuage the concerns of printers, not authors)."[4]

---

1   *Tele-Direct (Publications) Inc. v. American Business Information Inc.*, [1998] 2 F.C 22 (FCA).
2   *Théberge v. Galerie d'art du Petit Champlain inc.* 2002 SCC 34, para. 116.
3   *Théberge v. Galerie d'art du Petit Champlain inc.* 2002 SCC 34, para. 12.
4   *Théberge v. Galerie d'art du Petit Champlain inc.* 2002 SCC 34, para. 62.

These judges are all saying different things about the nature of the law based on their belief that copyright must be anchored in the primacy of one interest – either creators or industry – over the others. Yet they have provided no authoritative basis for these assertions, including evidence drawn from history. As the following chapters demonstrate, history tells us that copyright is an integrated system that functions precisely *because* it encompasses the rights, interests, and responsibilities of creators, industry, and users to achieve overarching public policy goals that transcend the self-interested motivations of each of these groups. Indeed, even though it means something quite different to copyright scholars to say that Canadian law owes its origins to British, French, or American legal traditions, the central preoccupation in all these jurisdictions was quite similar. Copyright's complexity, its ambiguity, which continues to challenge us today, is that it is more nuanced than the superficial distinctions between *droit d'auteur* and copyright would suggest.

There is a dearth of research on Canadian copyright history, in contrast to the rich body of scholarship that has explored American, British, and French copyright histories, these jurisdictions being the most relevant to Canada. This book aims to redress that deficiency by teasing out, from the historical record, the genesis of Canada's own copyright story. Can the nineteenth-century origins of the law help contemporary scholars, jurists, and policy-makers more effectively distil copyright's *raison d'être*? What is Canada's copyright history?

As this book demonstrates, copyright's earliest focus was on advancing literacy and learning by providing incentives to authors to disseminate their works. These authors were teachers, and the works they were producing were schoolbooks. Indeed, the people who populated the early British North American copyright landscape were education reformers, politicians, and teachers united in the goal of advancing provincial education policy. The policy concerns related to ensuring learners would have access to the latest knowledge and ideas disseminated through the medium of print. As the nineteenth century progressed, British North America became mired in the geopolitical gamesmanship between the United Kingdom and the United States over unauthorized foreign reprints entering colonial markets. As a nation-building imperative began to take shape, copyright policy shifted, especially in the largest and most economically developed region, the Province of Canada, to encompass both education and cultural policy. Thus began Canada's preoccupation with fostering and protecting its cultural industries.

Uncovering Canada's copyright roots and discovering Canada's copyright origin story offers scholars of intellectual property a deeper appreciation of the earliest drivers of legal policy. However, the study of copyright history is inherently a multidisciplinary exercise, and the law must be situated within a larger frame of reference. One cannot interrogate Canadian copyright history without recognizing the law's connection to a given society's book and print culture. This book therefore contributes to the growing scholarly treatment of copyright at the intersection of legal history and the rich and diverse scholarly discipline of book history. Indeed, the research methodology in this book is decidedly cross-disciplinary and offers a roadmap for future research in both law and book history. The capaciousness of the footnotes and citations is deliberate so that this book can serve as a reference work for scholars.

Canada's copyright story is a colonial one in that British North America and, later, the Dominion of Canada were British colonies throughout the nineteenth century and therefore restricted in their legislative autonomy. In this way, Canada's copyright history differs from that of the United States and the United Kingdom. Canada's colonial identity shaped its copyright story in a distinctive way. It is also a settler history constructed by white male settlers to British North America, French- or English-speaking, Catholic or Protestant. As a body of law, copyright was introduced by the educated and politically active elites from both groups, and its frame of reference remained predominantly that of the two ruling classes. It is therefore a history that does not include women except in the very few cases of women writers registering their copyright, a practice that belies the fact that the statutes of the period assumed that only men could be authors. It also does not recognize the contributions of Indigenous peoples or religious or racialized minorities to colonial book and print culture, let alone the ways in which the law itself perpetuates the systemic exclusion of certain communities and certain types of creative expression. It is, nevertheless, a story of accommodation of differences – at least between the English and the French in Lower Canada and, later, in the Province of Canada. There was a willingness (albeit often uneasy) to foster the educational and cultural aspirations of both populations as each sought an identity separate from the British Empire and, in the case of French Canada, an identity distinct from that of English Canada. Copyright was one of the agents of their respective political and cultural emancipations in the face of Empire and led to an alignment of interests and a certain shared understanding.

The decades discussed in this book span two distinct and significant periods in Canada's copyright history. The first period began with Lower Canada's first attempt at legislating on copyright in 1824 and culminated in the first instance of direct British interference in colonial copyright affairs in 1842. This eighteen-year span represents a significant moment in Canada's copyright history in that it was within this period that many of the British North American provinces first began to consider enacting copyright laws. The research reveals that these early provincial legislatures were driven by considerations of education policy and the imperative of encouraging literacy and learning. This was a singular and halcyon period of legislative freedom as the British North American provinces were left free to determine their own copyright laws. This period is discussed in chapters 1 to 7.

The second period, which spans from 1842 to 1924, was marked by British intrusion into colonial copyright affairs, beginning with the enactment of the UK Copyright Act 1842. Britain's actions in relation to the circulation of books within its colonies were felt most strongly by the largest and most developed province, the Province of Canada, which sought to legislate in support of its own socio-economic and cultural aspirations while at the same time satisfying British copyright interests. More specifically, the copyright events that occurred from 1842 to 1850 in the Province of Canada represent a defining moment in shaping Canada's copyright narrative. Thereafter, the predominant discourse became increasingly about promoting a strong printing and publishing industry to support an emerging national cultural identity. This period is discussed in chapters 8 to 10. Although the focus of these chapters is on events that occurred prior to Canadian Confederation in 1867, the final chapter illustrates how they influenced Canadian copyright law and policy leading up to 1924, when a new period in Canada's copyright history began.

By studying these two pivotal periods, this book fills a temporal gap that connects with and complements existing multidisciplinary scholarship on post-Confederation copyright law. Tracking copyright developments in British North America from 1824 to 1867 uncovers the foundation upon which Canada's copyright policy was constructed. Ultimately, the principles that animated British North American copyright law remain relevant to this day, as the overarching themes of education, learning, access to knowledge, and cultural identity resonate with us still.

Some words about terminology: This book is primarily concerned with the colonies in British North America from 1793 to Confederation in 1867. Lower Canada was the most important province in Canada's early copyright story. Lower Canada existed from 1793 to 1840 and was roughly what we now know as the province of Quebec. The other British North American colonies under review are Upper Canada

(Ontario), New Brunswick, Nova Scotia, and, to a much lesser extent, Prince Edward Island and Newfoundland. In 1840, Lower Canada was united with Upper Canada to form the Province of Canada. At Confederation, the Province of Canada along with the provinces of New Brunswick and Nova Scotia joined to form the Dominion of Canada. The Province of Canada was dissolved, and the provinces of Quebec and Ontario were created. Because of these changing circumstances, choosing the correct terminology to describe the jurisdictions is a challenge. I have attempted to remain true to their historical designations, which means that depending on the temporal stage under discussion, the term Lower Canada gives way to Canada (East) in the Province of Canada. Upper Canada becomes Canada (West) in the Province of Canada.

In relation to Lower Canada, I refer to French Canadians as francophone Lower Canadians or *Canadiens*. I use this term in a non-political sense to mean the francophone, Catholic population, including those who were sympathetic to the British. The English population of Lower Canada is referred to as anglophone or English-speaking Lower Canadians. In the legislature, the Parti Canadien and, after 1826, the Parti Patriote represented the interests of the *Canadiens* and their desire for greater sociopolitical autonomy within the framework of the British parliamentary system. I use the terms Parti Canadien and, later, Parti Patriote, to include their anglophone allies.

I refer to Canada or Canadians to designate post-Confederation residents of the Dominion of Canada or to speak more generally in terms of Canada and Canadians today. Otherwise, I refer to residents of the Province of Canada as French Canadian or English Canadian. In the final chapter, to distinguish the population living in the Province of Canada from Canadians after Confederation, I refer to the former as provincial Canadians.

The time span of this book covers Great Britain (England, Scotland, and Wales) (1707–1801), the United Kingdom of Great Britain and Ireland (1801–1922) and, to a lesser extent, the United Kingdom of Great Britain and Northern Ireland (1922–present). I use the term Great Britain in those chapters that discuss the history of the law prior to 1801. I use the term United Kingdom to mean the jurisdiction that encompassed England, Wales, Scotland, and Ireland prior to 1922. Throughout the book, I use the terms "Britain" and "British" without distinguishing between Great Britain and the United Kingdom.

The various settlements in British North America were designated as "provinces" by the British. I refer to the various British North American jurisdictions interchangeably as provinces or colonies but tend to describe them as "colonies" when reference is being made to their relationship with the British. I use the term "province" more frequently especially when the discussion relates to the internal actions of the jurisdiction or within British North America. The provinces operated under bicameral parliamentary systems. The legislative branch consisted of an elected House of Assembly and an appointed Legislative Council. I use Assembly (or House of Assembly) and Legislative Council separately to refer to those specific bodies. I use the terms "legislature" or "Parliament" to refer to the legislative branch more generally.

Finally, quotations from French sources have been reproduced in their original language. I have provided English translations in the relevant footnotes. Any errors in translation are my own.

# Chapter One

# Contextualizing Colonial Copyright in Nineteenth-Century British North America

On 23 January 1832, the Standing Committee on Education and Schools of the House of Assembly of Lower Canada issued a report recommending "the introduction of a Bill securing Copyright."[1] The committee's chair, the Scottish-born John Neilson, was the most important printer, publisher, and bookseller of his day in British North America. He was also a highly regarded politician who, as later chapters will show, enjoys the distinction of being the architect of Canada's first intellectual property laws.[2]

That same day, the Assembly's representative for the district of Belle-chasse, Augustin-Norbert Morin, acting on the committee's recommendation, introduced a "Bill for the protection of Copyrights."[3] The young lawyer and journalist was a relative newcomer to the Lower Canadian legislature.[4] Nevertheless, even at this early stage of his political career, Morin had involved himself in matters relating to the book trade, most notably in appealing on behalf of Ludger Duvernay, a Montreal printer, publisher, and journalist who had been imprisoned for libel,[5] and in

---

1   First Report of the Standing Committee on Education and Schools, 23 January 1832, 2 Will. 4, Appendix to the XLIst volume of the Journals of the House of Assembly of the Province of Lower Canada, Appendix I.i.

2   See the entry for John Neilson (1773–1848) in *Dictionary of Canadian Biography* (hereafter DCB). On his life and political activities, see especially Francis J. Audet, "John Neilson"; Bateson, "John Neilson of Lower Canada (1818–1828)"; Hagerman, "John Neilson"; and Neilson, "John Neilson: Constitutionalism." On the Neilson printing, publishing, bookselling business, see Alston, "Canada's First Bookseller's Catalogue"; and Tomlinson, *L'Imprimerie Neilson*; Hare and Wallot, "Le livre au Québec."

3   Journals of the House of Assembly of Lower Canada, 2 Will. 4 (1831–32), 303.

4   On Augustin-Norbert Morin (1803–1865), see his entry in DCB. See also Paradis, *Augustin-Norbert Morin.*

5   Journals of the House of Assembly of Lower Canada, 2 Will. 4 (1831–32), 426. Morin and Duvernay were both involved in the French-language newspaper *La Minerve*, which

securing financial assistance for the posthumous publication of Jacques Labrie's *Histoire du Canada*.[6]

The Lower Canadian legislature enjoyed the constitutional authority to enact its own copyright laws pursuant to the Constitutional Act 1791, which gave general legislative powers to an elected House of Assembly and an appointed Legislative Council to enact laws for the peace, welfare, and good government of the province.[7] This bicameral legislative process was not fundamentally different from current parliamentary practice. A Bill, which was a draft of proposed legislation, was introduced into the Assembly and given first reading. Often, the Bill would then be referred to an Assembly committee for further consideration.[8] A second reading of the Bill followed, during which a more thorough debate was conducted. The final stage was the third reading of the Bill, at which point the legislature decided whether to enact it. If passed, the legislation was then referred to the Upper House, the Legislative Council, which could return it with amendments or pass it as drafted. Once passed by both Houses, the legislation still required Royal Assent – approval by the British Crown – before becoming law.

Lower Canadian parliamentary politics were especially complex. The former French colony of New France had been ceded to the British in 1763, and thereafter, most of the members elected to the Assembly were Catholic francophones or *Canadiens*, who represented the interests of the majority of the population.[9] In contrast, the members appointed to

---

    Morin founded in 1826. Morin sold the paper to Duvernay a year later but remained involved in the editorial aspects. See correspondence between Morin and Duvernay, Bibliothèque et Archives nationales du Québec (BAnQ) – Fonds Ludger-Duvernay, P-680.

6  Jacques Labrie (1784–1831) was a member of the Assembly from 1827 until his death in 1831. See his entry in DCB. The legislature had agreed to allocate £500 for the purchase of copies of the book once published. See Journals of the House of Assembly of Lower-Canada 1831, 2 Will. 4 (1831–32), 120.

7  *An Act to repeal certain parts of an Act passed in the fourteenth year of His Majesty's Reign, intituled, "An Act for making more effectual provision for the Government of the Province of Quebec in North America" and for making further provision for the Government of the said Province*, 1791, 31 Geo. 3, c. 31 (UK). ("The Constitutional Act").

8  Depending on the matter in question, committees could either be smaller special or select committees or larger standing committees. In cases involving legislative enactments, consideration of the Bill was often delegated to a committee consisting of all the members of the Assembly or a Committee of the Whole House. See, generally, O'Brien, "Pre-Confederation Parliamentary Procedure."

9  The 1831 Lower Canadian census showed 412,717 Roman Catholics, 34,620 Church of England, 15,069 Church of Scotland, 7,801 Presbyterians, 7,081 Methodists, 2,461 Baptists, 107 Jews, 5,577 Others, and 67,755 Not Given. Total population 553,134. See Canada, *Censuses of Canada, 1665 to 1871*, 109.

serve on the Legislative Council were drawn from the English-speaking and predominantly Protestant community, whose loyalty was to the British imperial administration. This meant that the two legislative branches were often at odds, and it was frequently the case that legislation that had been passed by the Assembly never made it through the Legislative Council. Governor of Lower Canada Sir James Kempt described the dysfunction in a letter to Sir Robert Hay, Under-Secretary of State for the Colonies:

> The Government has no Representative in the Assembly to take part in the discussion that take place in that House … The Consequence of this is that Acts on Popular Subjects are sometimes passed by the Assembly, that are at variance with British Statutes; or with the King's Instructions to the Governor; or an Infringement of the Rights of the Crown.
>
> In all such Cases, however, the Legislative Council (which is chiefly composed of Protestant Members connected with the Government) does effectually interpose by withholding its assent to the Bills … but this gives rise to angry feelings in the latter body, and Bills sent down from the Council to the Assembly meet the same Fate there: – mutual jealousy and distrust are thus engendered between the two Branches of the Legislature, the Papists get excited, and Measures of great Public Importance are sometimes lost, for want of that Cordiality and good Understanding which ought to exist between the Legislative Bodies.[10]

Given this antagonistic relationship, it is noteworthy that the 1832 Copyright Bill moved swiftly through the Assembly and was approved without amendment by the Legislative Council. It was given Royal Assent roughly a month from the time of its introduction, and on 25 February 1832 *An Act for the Protection of Copy Rights* ("the 1832 Act") became law in Lower Canada.[11] It was the first copyright act in British North America and the archetype of pre-Confederation copyright.[12] This Lower Canadian statute was also the legislative antecedent of the

---

10   Sir James Kempt to Sir Robert Hay, 3 January 1830, LAC Fonds James Kempt, MG 24 H-1830, vol. 7, image 51, pp. 9–10.

11   *An Act for the Protection of Copy Rights* 1832, 2 Will. 4, c. 53 (Lower Canada). French title: *Acte pour protéger la propriété littéraire.*

12   Nova Scotia was the next to enact a copyright statute in 1839. New Brunswick had tried and failed in 1838. Upper Canada did not enact a copyright statute until it united with Lower Canada. See further in chapter 7.

first post-Confederation copyright statute, the Dominion of Canada's *An Act Respecting Copyrights* of 1868.[13]

This first British North American copyright statute did not arise in isolation. Lower Canada was a British colony, and its actions on copyright must therefore be situated within a larger colonial context. This necessitates an examination of the legal status of the United Kingdom's copyright law in its North American colonies.

**Reception of British Copyright Law in British North America**

In 1709, the British Parliament at Westminster enacted the world's first copyright statute, *An Act for the Encouragement of Learning, by Vesting the Copies of Printed Books in the Authors or Purchasers of such Copies, during the Times therein mentioned.*[14] Known more commonly as the Statute of Anne, this piece of legislation, which came into force in 1710, did not automatically form part of the domestic law of the British North American colonies. Instead, its applicability would have been determined under the doctrine of reception of laws, which established the rules as to whether British laws, both statutory and judge-made "common law," applied in a colony and at what date.[15]

Reception rules differed between colonies that had been settled by the British and those, like Lower Canada, that had been ceded through conquest. In the former case, British law automatically applied unless the law in question was ill-suited to local conditions. In the latter case, the opposite rule prevailed: the laws of the conquering nation did not automatically apply to the conquered nation; they had to be expressly or tacitly deemed to apply. In the case of Lower Canada, the imperial Parliament had established in 1774 that the "laws of Canada" that had been in force pre-conquest would continue to apply, except in criminal law matters.[16] Copyright should logically have been considered part of the "laws of Canada" for reception purposes, except that no such law

---

13  *An Act Respecting Copyrights*, 1868, 31 Vict., c. 54. (The "Copyright Act of 1868"). French title: *Acte concernant la propriété littéraire et artistique.*

14  *An Act for the Encouragement of Learning, by Vesting the Copies of Printed Books in the Authors or Purchasers of such Copies, during the Times therein mentioned*, 1710, 8 Anne, c. 10. The statute was passed in 1709 but took effect in April 1710.

15  On reception of laws in British North America see Hogg, *Constitutional Law of Canada*; Blackstone, *Commentaries on the Laws of England*; Girard, "British Justice"; Côté, "The Reception of English Law."

16  *An act for making more effectual provision for the government of the Province of Quebec in North America*, 1774, 14 Geo. 3, c. 83 (UK) (The Quebec Act 1774).

existed in France, and therefore not in New France, prior to 1774. This created the situation that, as nineteenth-century publisher Samuel Edward Dawson put it, "the right of copy does not therefore appear in our Civil Code, because our laws date from a period anterior to the [French] Revolution."[17] The first French copyright statute dates to 1793, thirty years after the colony became British.[18]

However, prior to 1793, French printers and publishers enjoyed a form of protection known as Royal grants of printing privileges.[19] There is some indication that France extended these printing privileges to its colonies as long as there was a printing press and a printer within the jurisdiction.[20] But as historian Aegidius Fauteux reported, "there was never a printing shop in Canada under the fleur-de-lys."[21] The absence of printing capabilities meant that the French system of printing privileges, the precursor of copyright, was inapplicable in that part of New France that would become Lower Canada.[22]

It was only in the wake of British rule that William Brown and his partner Thomas Gilmore set up the first press in Quebec City in 1764. Upon Brown's death, the business passed to his nephew Samuel

---

17   Dawson, *Copyright in Books*, 11. Early legal texts on the law applicable in New France are silent on the question of printing privileges or other forms of protection for printed books. See, for example, Doutre and Lareau, *Le droit civil canadien*.

18   *Décret de la convention nationale du dix-neuf juillet 1793 relatif aux droits de propriété des auteurs d'écrits en tout genre, des compositeurs de musique, des peintres et des dessinateurs.*

19   On French printing privileges prior to the French Revolution, see, for example, McLeod, *Licensing Loyalty*. See also Pfister, "Author and Work in the French Print Privileges System."

20   The traditional position was that the French had forbidden printing in its colonies. See Galarneau, "Samuel Neilson (1800–1837)": "La France n'a pas permis l'entrée de l'imprimerie au Canada" (79) [France did not permit the establishment of the press in Canada]. However, recent scholarship is more nuanced on this point, suggesting that the French authorities would have permitted printing in New France provided that there was a printer *in situ*. François Melançon chronicles one example of a French printer obtaining permission to travel to New France, but there is no record to show that he in fact arrived or set up a print establishment. See François Melançon, "Print and Manuscript in French Canada under the Ancien Régime," in Howsam and James Raven, eds., *Books Between Europe and the Americas*. See, as well, Banks, "Communications and 'Imperial Overstretch.'" Banks provides the example of bookseller and printer Denis Braud of New Orleans, who purchased a press and obtained a permit to print in Louisiana in 1764.

21   Fauteux, *The Introduction of Printing into Canada*.

22   The French had colonized a large swath of North America, and New France covered territory that later became part of the United States and Canada. It included what we know now as Quebec (Lower Canada) and Ontario (Upper Canada).

Neilson, who, upon his death in 1793, left it to his sixteen-year-old brother, John, who would later figure so prominently in the history of Lower Canadian copyright law.[23] However, the arrival of the printing press in Lower Canada did not automatically bring with it the reception of the Statute of Anne, since British legislation would only be received if it was expressly or tacitly deemed to apply. The language of the Statute of Anne made it clear that it was intended to operate exclusively within Great Britain and was not the law in Lower Canada. Indeed, in his legal treatise on the laws of Lower Canada, Montreal notary Nicolas-Benjamin Doucet confirmed that the Statute of Anne did not extend to the province.[24]

This was also the outcome in Upper Canada, which had been part of the territory of New France at the time of cession to the British. The Constitutional Act 1791 that created the provinces of Lower Canada and Upper Canada had provided that French civil law would apply to both provinces unless changed by their respective legislatures. Upper Canada acted on this authority and legislated to receive the "laws of England" as at 1792, in other words after the enactment of the Statute of Anne.[25] However, the principle remained that reception was not automatic. The fact that the territorial reach of Britain's copyright legislation was expressly limited to England and Scotland meant that the Statute of Anne did not have force of law in Upper Canada either.

The other British North American provinces were settled rather than ceded territories for reception purposes. In these cases, the rule was that British laws were automatically received into domestic law at a specified date unless ill-suited to the conditions in the provinces. New Brunswick set its reception date at 1660, therefore to a period prior to the enactment of the Statute of Anne. It therefore did not receive the statute into its law. The other provinces all received British law at dates that succeeded the enactment of the Statute of Anne.[26] However,

---

23   On the Brown and Gilmore publishing firm, see entries in DCB under Thomas Gilmore or William Brown. The partnership between Brown and Gilmore was dissolved in 1774.

24   Doucet, *Fundamental Principles of the Laws of Canada*, 215.

25   *An Act to repeal certain parts of an Act passed in the Fourteenth Year of his Majesty's Reign, entitled "An act for making more effectual Provision for the Government of the province of Quebec, in North-America, and to introduce the English Law, as the Rule of Decision in all Matters of Controversy relative to Property and Civil Rights."* Statutes of Upper Canada, 1792, 32 Geo. 3, c. 1.

26   Nova Scotia received British laws in 1758, the date of its first legislative assembly. New Brunswick declared its reception date to be 1660, the date of the English Restoration. Prince Edward Island is either 1758 or 1773. See Hogg, *Constitutional Law of Canada*.

because of its local nature, the British copyright statute was unsuited to colonial conditions and was not automatically received. Writing about the laws in Nova Scotia in 1833, Halifax lawyer Beamish Murdoch referred to the Statute of Anne as law in the "mother country" exclusively.[27]

Although the Statute of Anne never formed part of the laws of the British North American provinces, Lower Canadian authors, and indeed British North Americans in general, were not in a legal vacuum in respect of their writings prior to the passage of domestic legislation. First, even though the Statute of Anne did not automatically apply in British North America, colonial authors could nevertheless avail themselves of its benefits within the United Kingdom. Second, the British North American provinces recognized some form of legal protection outside of statute. Although the extent of this "common law" entitlement is unclear, at minimum it conferred exclusive rights upon authors to authorize the first publication of their manuscripts. Finally, individuals could exercise their constitutional right of petition to request of the provincial legislature the grant of exclusive printing privileges or financial aids for printing. However, we will see that none of these options was sufficiently robust to fully address the public policy interests of the provinces in relation to book production. This militated in favour of domestic copyright legislation.

### Securing a British Copyright: The Statute of Anne 1710 and Its Amendment in 1814

Although the Statute of Anne was not automatically received into the various British North American colonies as *their* copyright law, nothing prevented colonial authors from benefiting from British copyright protection as long as their works were first published in Great Britain or, after 1801, in the United Kingdom, and as long as they complied with the other statutory formalities.[28] How useful or desirable an option this was, however, remained another question entirely. Although the statute did not require that authors be resident in the jurisdiction at the time of publication, it was impractical, if not impossible, for most British North

---

27   Murdoch, *Epitome of the Laws of Nova Scotia*, vol. 3, 6–7.

28   First publication in the United Kingdom was the essential requirement for protection. However, the actual printing did not have to occur there. The Statute of Anne rewarded publishers, namely those who undertook the financial risks of bringing the book to market.

American authors to avail themselves of its benefits.[29] These authors would have had to seek out a British publisher from afar and without an established network in the United Kingdom. In addition, adherence to the statutory formalities was costly and cumbersome, requiring registration of title with the Stationers' Company, the payment of a fee, and a deposit of copies of the work for distribution to certain university libraries.[30] Importantly, infringements of a British copyright would have had to have occurred in that country and be enforced through its courts. The Statute of Anne, therefore, had little to recommend to colonial authors in the early nineteenth century, especially those whose primary market for their writings was not England, Scotland, or Ireland.

Little changed in this regard when the Statute of Anne was amended, in 1814, to prohibit the printing, reprinting, or importing of a British copyright work for sale or hire "in any Part of the British Dominions," which included British North America.[31] Even though a British copyright could now be enforced in the courts of the colony in which the infringement had occurred, the statute remained uninviting for many British North American authors, especially for francophone Lower Canadians. Copyright protection remained predicated upon first publication in the United Kingdom. The law did not extend to works first published in the colonies. The risks inherent in publishing at so great a distance remained a significant deterrent. A colonial author needed

---

29  Prior to 1854, non-resident British subjects and foreign authors were given the benefit of British copyright protection upon first publication in the United Kingdom. The situation changed when the House of Lords revisited the issue and declared that foreign authors had to be resident in the United Kingdom at the time of first publication (*Jefferys v. Boosey* (1854) 4 H.L.C 815). See Drone, *A Treatise on the Law of Property*; and Nowell-Smith, *International Copyright Law*.

30  See section 5 of the Statute of Anne, which provided for a mandatory deposit to designated libraries in England and Scotland. In 1814, this number was expanded from nine to eleven copies to include deposits to libraries in Ireland. To fulfil this obligation, publishers were required to send, at their own expense, copies of published books to the enumerated libraries. This deposit requirement was controversial. Publishers and others in the book trade complained repeatedly about this unjust "tax," which discouraged them from publishing and impeded "the encouragement of learning." The libraries argued, in return, that the mandatory deposit "encouraged learning." See Feather, "Publishers and Politicians," 49; and Barrington-Partridge, *The History of the Legal Deposit of Books*.

31  *An Act to amend the several Acts for the Encouragement of Learning, by securing the Copies and Copyright of Printed Books, to the Authors of such Books or their Assigns* 54 Geo. 3, c. 156 (1814) at section 4. See also Bently, "The 'Extraordinary Multiplicity,'" 172–3. Bently explains that little is known about the motives behind extending the reach of the statute to the colonies.

sufficient funds to finance the costs of printing and publishing; that, or the wherewithal to find a British publisher willing to take the financial risk if the work in question was of interest to British readers. These difficulties were exacerbated for the *Canadiens*. Even if they found it politically palatable to engage in this way with the British, they would have confronted linguistic barriers and the absence of social or business connections in the United Kingdom. As lawyer and politician Dominique Mondelet related to Alexis de Tocqueville during the latter's visit to North America, "presque toute la richesse et le commerce est dans la main des Anglais. Ils ont leur famille et leurs relations en Angleterre et trouvent des facilités que nous n'avons pas."[32]

Indeed, the records of the Stationers' Company, the guild of British printers, publishers, and booksellers that acted as the registrar of copyright, demonstrate that only a few British North American authors availed themselves of copyright protection under the Statute of Anne. The Stationers' records evince a number of copyright registrations for works of Canadiana – poems, religious and political tracts, songs, and travelogues on Canadian themes were popular during this period – but most of these had been written by British residents on brief sojourns in North America.[33] Copyright registrations for works composed by British North American authors, whether born in the colonies or permanent residents, were much fewer in number.[34] Of the handful of cases between 1814 and 1832, all the authors save one were British immigrants who enjoyed a strong, ongoing connection with the United Kingdom, and most were in that country at the time of publication.[35]

---

32   Vallée, *Tocqueville au Bas-Canada*, 58. [Almost all of the wealth and commerce remains in the hands of the English. They have their families and relations in England and find an ease that we don't have.] On Dominique Mondelet (1799–1863), see DCB.

33   Robin Myers, *Records of the Worshipful Company of Stationers*. Accessed on Microfilm.

34   My survey of the Stationers' records spanned the period from the enactment of the 1814 UK Act and ended with the passage of the 1832 Act of Lower Canada. It does not give a true measure of copyright practices in the other British North American provinces. It also does not study British copyright registrations by Lower Canadians after the passage of the 1832 Act. A more comprehensive review of this kind is beyond the scope of this book but would be an important area for further research.

35   Two authors were from Lower Canada, four from Upper Canada, and one each from Nova Scotia and New Brunswick. Other than those discussed in this chapter, the other authors were as follows: Lower Canada – Samuel Simpson Wood, the rector of St-James Church in Trois-Rivières, who published *An Apology for the Colonial Clergy of Great Britain specially for those of Lower and Upper Canada* with the London firm of Hatchard & Son. Copyright was registered by the publisher in 1828 (Records of Stationers' Company, Reel 14, 99). Upper Canada – Charles Stuart published *An*

Examples include Scottish-born author Ann Cuthbert Knight, who lived in Montreal for a year before returning briefly to Scotland in 1811. In 1815 she returned to Lower Canada permanently, but not before publishing *A Year in Canada and other Poems* with the London firm of Baldwin, Cradock and Co., which registered its copyright as the proprietor on 13 March 1816.[36] Similarly, in 1826, Upper Canada's solicitor general Henry John Boulton registered his copyright as author in *A Short Sketch of the Province of Upper Canada, for the Information of the Labouring Poor throughout England*.[37] Boulton was in England around the time of publication, conducting business on behalf of the Welland Canal Company. John Inglis, the Bishop of Nova Scotia, was on a visit to London when *A Charge Delivered to the Clergy of His Diocese* was published by J.G. & F. Rivington, which registered its copyright in October 1831.[38]

Joseph Bouchette was the only *Canadien* to engage with the British copyright system during this period. As Surveyor General of Lower Canada, he had cultivated an amicable relationship with the British authorities, and his publishing endeavours were greatly facilitated by his professional network.[39] In 1829, Bouchette travelled to England to

---

*Emigrant's Guide to Upper Canada* (London: Longman, 1820), with copyright in the author (Records of Stationers' Company, reel 11, 475); Edward Allen Talbot published *Five Years Residence in the Canadas: Including a Tour through Part of The United States of America, in the Year 1823*, 2 vols. (London: Longman, 1824), with copyright in the author (Records of Stationers' Company, reel 13, 309), William Dunlop, *Statistical Sketches of Upper Canada* (London: John Murray, 1832) (reel 15, 421); Thomas Baillie, *An Account of the Province of New Brunswick: Including a Description of the Settlements, Institutions, and Climate of that Important Province, with Advice to Emigrants* (London: J.G. & F. Rivington, 1832), copyright held by publisher (Records of Stationers' Company, reel 15, 238). Baillie appears to have been the only author who was not physically in the United Kingdom at the time of publication.

36  Records of Stationers' Company, reel 10, 34. Ann Cuthbert Knight Fleming (1788–1860) was a schoolteacher and author. See her entry in DCB as well as in Canada's Early Women Writers database (CEWW). In 1845, Fleming registered copyright in the Province of Canada for *Progressive Exercises on the English Language* (Montreal: Lovell & Gibson, 1845), as discussed in chapter 9.

37  Henry John Boulton, *A Short Sketch of the Province of Upper Canada, for the Information of the Labouring Poor throughout England* (London: John Murray, 1826). Records of Stationers' Company, reel 13, 376. On Henry John Boulton (1790–1870), see his entry at DCB.

38  John Inglis, *A Charge Delivered to the Clergy of His Diocese* (London: J.G. & F. Rivington, 1831). Records of Stationers' Company, reel 15, 64.

39  Joseph Bouchette (1774–1841) held the position of Surveyor General from the early 1800s until that office was abolished in 1840. He was appointed at the behest of Lieutenant-Governor Robert Shore Milnes, after whom he named one of his sons. See entry for Bouchette in DCB. See also Parizeau, "Joseph Bouchette: L'homme et le haut fonctionnaire"; Gilles Boileau, "L'histoire de la fameuse carte de Joseph Bouchette," 36–8.

supervise the publication of his monumental works: *The British Domin-ions in North America, or a Topographical and Statistical Description of the Provinces of Lower & Upper Canada, New Brunswick, Nova Scotia, the Is-lands of Newfoundland, Prince Edward and Cape Breton, including consider-ations on Land-granting and Emigration – To which are annexed, statistical Tables and Tables of Distances etc . ("The British Dominions")* (2 volumes) and *A Topographical Dictionary of the Province of Lower Canada. ("Topo-graphical Dictionary")*.[40] On 1 June 1832, London publisher Longman and Co, registered its copyright in both publications.[41]

Given the complexities inherent in printing maps and other engrav-ings, it would not have been unusual for Bouchette to have published his works in England rather than Lower Canada.[42] London printers and publishers were highly skilled in their craft. In fact, Bouchette had trav-elled to England once before to oversee the publication of a *Topograph-ical Description of the Province of Lower Canada: with Remarks upon Upper Canada, and on the Relative Connexion of both Provinces with the United States of America*.[43] What was different about his later sojourn in London was that copyright was secured in his books, something that had not been done for the earlier publication.

The circumstances surrounding the copyright registrations by Bou-chette's London publishers offer insights into book financing and

---

40   Joseph Bouchette, *The British Dominions in North America, or a Topographical and Sta-tistical Description of the Provinces of Lower & Upper Canada, New Brunswick, Nova Sco-tia, the Islands of Newfoundland, Prince Edward and Cape Breton, including considerations on Land-granting and Emigration – To which are annexed, statistical Tables and Tables of Distances etc.*, 2 vols. (London: Longman and Co., 1832); and Joseph Bouchette, *A Topographical Dictionary of the Province of Lower Canada* (London: Longman and Co., 1832). See State Papers – Lower Canada, 63 Victoria A. 1900 in Brymner, *Report on Canadian Archives*. Bouchette had obtained a series of leaves of absence from Gov-ernor James Kempt. Aspects of the trip were documented by his son Robert Shore Milnes Bouchette, who accompanied his parents to England. See R. Bouchette, *Mémoires*. Bouchette did not return to Lower Canada until 1834.

41   Records of Stationers' Company, reel 15. Published in quarto format, these three volumes were handsomely produced and were dedicated to his "Excellent Majesty William IV." Longman & Co. had secured their copyright over the 1832 editions, published in 3 volumes. However, the firm of Colburn & Bentley had first pub-lished the works in two volumes, in 1831, as had Longman, who published what would seem to be a sub-edition that same year. In his memoirs, Robert Bouchette alluded only to the 1831 Longman edition.

42   Winearls, "The Printing and Publishing of Maps."

43   J. Bouchette, *Topographical Description of the Province of Lower Canada*. This book was published in both English and French, ensuring a broad readership in the United Kingdom and British North America.

publishing practices of the day. Books were commonly published at the expense of the author, who solicited subscriptions to defray the printing costs.[44] Indeed, Bouchette's agreement with his publishers was to this effect.[45] However, the printing and engraving costs for these publications were extremely high – so exorbitant, in fact, that the Lower Canadian Assembly later admonished him for succumbing to such extravagance: "practical and colonial interests would have been better consulted if his publication had been made in a manner so as by its moderate price to come within the reach of all such Inhabitants of the Province."[46] Bouchette had obtained commitments from subscribers, including the Lower Canadian legislature, which had purchased 100 copies, but these were not sufficient to satisfy his printing debt.[47] The total publication costs were in excess of £3,300, and Bouchette still owed £1,805 13s 11d. Longman & Co had thus claimed the copyright as security for the debt. In his petition to the Assembly in 1833, Bouchette explained that he had assigned his copyright to his publishers, with rights reverting to him once his debt had been discharged: "By my Bond, I have assigned over to the Printer the property in the printed

---

44  Subscription publishing was the most common form of book financing at the time. Subscriptions were advance commitments to purchase the book once published and were usually solicited through a printer or publisher. The author was generally responsible for all the printing and publishing costs. Subscription publishing will be discussed in later chapters.

45  The records of the firm of Colburn & Bentley show an agreement with Bouchette for advertising and publishing "at author's risk.'" Archives of Richard Bentley & Son, microfilm reel 35, 25. The subscription list dated 18 November 1831 identified seventeen subscribers for a total of thirty-nine copies. The Bentley Archives, microfilm reel 51, 126. The Longman records are, unfortunately, silent on the nature of their agreement with Bouchette. There is only a one-page ledger entry for *Bouchette's Canada* that relates to the advertising and publication of the three-volume copyrighted set in 1832. See Archives of the House of Longman, microfilm reel 11, 419.

46  Journals of the House of Assembly of Lower Canada, 3 Will. 4 (1833), 381. The Assembly also inquired as to why Bouchette did not produce the works in both English and French, as he had with his 1815 publication; to which he replied that there was no market in England for the French works and the production costs would have doubled. These costs would not have been offset by any increase in Lower Canadian sales. See also Morgan, *Bibliotheca Canadensis*, where he says, "His works were printed and published in Eng., on a scale of magnificence which rendered them costly to the author, and too expensive for general circulation" (42).

47  *An Act to Authorize the purchase of a certain number of the Topographical Map and Statistical Tables to be Published by Joseph Bouchette, Esq*, 1829, 9 Geo. 4, c. 68. Provision was made for the distribution of the 100 copies by virtue of *An Act to provide for the distribution of certain copies of the Topographical Map and Statistical Tables published by Joseph Bouchette Esquire*, 1832, 2 Will. 4, c. 52.

work, provided he shall not dispose of any to pay himself, for less than £2 16s Sterling, per Copy. He has moreover, the right of reprinting the work for his own benefit, if he be not paid by 1834; he would accept of £200 Sterling, per annum … and would remit me the work."[48]

It appears that Bouchette never satisfied the debt despite the numerous requests for financial assistance he made to the Lower Canadian Assembly and to the legislatures of the other British North American provinces he had discussed in the book. His pleas met with a mixed response, and even when they succeeded, the support remained inadequate.[49] Bouchette's prodigality aside, high printing and publishing costs were a prevailing public policy concern, for they created barriers to the dissemination of knowledge. As we will see, it was this concern that would ultimately drive Lower Canada's copyright policy. Joseph Bouchette's experience also demonstrates that the tensions between the francophone population in Lower Canada and the British and colonial administrations discouraged all but an intrepid few from publishing in the United Kingdom and obtaining copyright there. Bouchette's close connections with the British administration had enhanced his ability to publish his books in London, but he paid a price for it back home. His loyalty to the British Crown, as well as the length of his various stays abroad and the great expense attendant to his publication, were much maligned in the Assembly and criticized in the press.[50] Bouchette's numerous requests to the Assembly for financial support were met with parsimony by his political detractors, and his financial circumstances would remain precarious throughout his life.[51] While Bouchette's case

---

48  *Continuation of the Appendix to the XLIInd volume of the Journals of the House of Assembly of the Province of Lower Canada, Session 1832–3*, 7 February 1833, 3 Will. 4, 73–4. The financial statement accompanying the petition reads "Mortgage, by Bond, embracing the Copyright of the work as Security." Bouchette retained an interest in the work upon the full satisfaction of the printing debt through the reprinting and sale of the work by Longman.

49  Between 1832 and 1835, Bouchette petitioned the assemblies of Lower Canada, Upper Canada, Nova Scotia, New Brunswick, and Prince Edward Island.

50  See for example, *La Minerve*, Monday, 1 March 1830, reproducing the Assembly's debate over Bouchette's request for financial aid; and Thursday, 1 May 1827, letter from Junius. See also Boileau, "L'histoire de la fameuse carte de Joseph Bouchette"; and Parizeau, "Joseph Bouchette."

51  Besides being indebted to Longman & Co., Bouchette had incurred considerable expense in publishing his *Topographical Description* in 1815. In 1814 he had been awarded £1,500 by the House of Assembly to cover the publishing costs, but this commitment was never honoured during his lifetime. His heirs would not receive satisfaction on the debt until 1875.

is the most extreme illustration of the difficulties colonial authors faced in publishing their books in the UK and securing their copyright there, the truth remained that a British copyright offered little advantage for most British North American authors, even allowing for the expanded geographic scope of protection brought about by the amendment to the Statute of Anne in 1814.

### Recognition of a Non-statutory or Common Law Right in Published Works

In 1882, Montreal printer and publisher Samuel Dawson asked: "Does copyright exist by Common Law, *fortified and extended by statute*? Or is copyright a *creation of the Statute Law*?" He mused: "In Lower Canada this is a theoretical question; but in Ontario and in the Lower Provinces it might be a practical one. For the Common Law of England passed into these latter provinces; and if copyright exists at Common Law, damages might be claimed in addition to the penalties under the statutes."[52]

This fundamental question of whether there existed a common law of copyright or whether copyright was entirely a creature of statute was very much a live issue in jurisdictions that followed the British common law tradition. In 1774 the British House of Lords in *Donaldson v. Becket* sought to resolve this point, but the reasons for the decision were not clear and the rationale behind the judgment continues to this day to be fiercely debated in scholarly circles.[53] The Lords established that there was no common law of copyright under British law, but did the court hold that there had never been a common law of copyright, so that only legislation could provide rights for authors or publishers, or were they of the view that there was a pre-existing common law of copyright that could be abrogated by statute? If the former, then copyright was a statutory privilege granted for limited times and for particular public purposes rather than an inherent right vested in authors. At the very least, *Donaldson* held that if common law rights existed at all, then the Statute of Anne had altered them by circumscribing the duration of copyright in published works. Authors and publishers were limited to the statutory term of protection; their rights were not perpetual. However, it

---

52  Dawson, *Copyright in Books*, 11 (emphasis Dawson).
53  *Donaldson v. Becket*, Hansard, 1st ser. 17 (1774): 953–1003. For scholarly discussions on the interpretive difficulties, see Deazley, "The Myth of Copyright at Common Law"; and Gómez-Arostegui, "What Is the Point of Copyright History."

remained an open question whether the Statute of Anne eliminated other common law rights, especially the ability of authors and publishers to claim monetary damages in addition to the remedies available by statute. This issue was resolved in 1798 in *Beckford v. Hood*, where the court held that authors and publishers retained common law rights to sue for damages even in circumstances where they had failed to comply with the statutory registration formalities.[54]

However, this British jurisprudence on the question of common law copyright did not automatically apply in British North America, for the same reasons that the Statute of Anne had not been received as law in the individual provinces. Therefore, as Samuel Dawson suggested, the question of whether some body of law outside of statute provided a recourse to authors and publishers remained a live one in British North America and, indeed, in the Dominion of Canada after Confederation.[55] The issue was more theoretical than practical since it had never been tested before the courts. Nevertheless, the existing historical record suggests how British North American legal experts viewed the question. Writing in 1833 about the laws of Nova Scotia, lawyer Beamish Murdoch stated that an author enjoyed, at common law, "an exclusive and permanent property in the copyright of his works; without his permission no one can legally publish copies of his composition."[56] This perpetual copyright could be derogated from by statute but since "[n]o statute has been passed here on the subject; accordingly the right is perpetual as at common law, and the author ... may, by bringing his action

---

54  *Beckford v. Hood* (1798) 7 D. & E. 620. In contrast, the Supreme Court of the United States ruled in *Wheaton v. Peters* 33 U.S 591 (1834) that American authors of unpublished works retained a perpetual common law right to authorize first publication but, once published, the terms of the copyright statute prevailed, including its mandatory registration formalities. See Abrams, "The Historic Foundation of American Copyright Law."

55  The recognition of common law rights was theoretically possible well into Confederation since the question was never judicially decided and the relevant statutes were silent on the issue. It wasn't until *An Act to amend and consolidate the Law relating to Copyright* 11 & 12 Geo. 5 c. 24, which was assented to in 1921, amended in 1923 by virtue of *An Act to Amend the Copyright Act* 13 & 14 Geo. 5, and proclaimed into force in 1924 ("Copyright Act 1921") that any doubt as to the subsistence of common law rights was resolved. Section 44 denied any rights outside of statute: "No person shall be entitled to copyright or any similar right ... otherwise than under and in accordance with the provisions of this Act." French title: *Loi modifiant et codifiant la législation concernant le droit d'auteur*. A similar provision is retained in Canada's current copyright statute, the *Copyright Act* R.S.C 1985 c. C-42, at section 89. French title: *Loi sur le droit d'auteur*.

56  Murdoch, *Epitome of the Laws of Nova Scotia*, 6.

of damages, obtain redress for any invasion of his interest."[57] Presumably, once copyright legislation was passed in Nova Scotia in 1839, it altered whatever common law rights operated within the province. Murdoch expressed the view that a statute could limit the duration of copyright, and he specifically referenced the law in the United Kingdom on this point. Murdoch's opinion on whether a statute would displace the availability of monetary damages at common law is not clear from the passage, although he might well have endorsed the British position under *Beckford* that common law remedies subsisted. In addition, although Murdoch was writing only about the law in Nova Scotia, one can nevertheless surmise that his opinion on the subject may have been shared by legal experts in the other common law provinces of Upper Canada, New Brunswick, Prince Edward Island, and Newfoundland.

Lower Canada was the only jurisdiction that did not adhere to the British common law. What rights, if any, might have been recognized in published works in that jurisdiction prior to the passage of the 1832 Act? There are indications that some Lower Canadian authors believed that in the absence of statute they enjoyed legally enforceable rights over their published works. For example, in a letter dated 18 March 1809, from author Jean-Baptiste Boucher to his printer John Neilson in anticipation of the release of a new edition of his *Recueil de cantiques à l'usage des missions, des retraites et des catéchismes*, Boucher wrote: "This edition will probably be the last of which I will be the publisher, and *to you alone I give and transfer as author the right I have in the work*" (emphasis added).[58] In another example, from 1831, the *Quebec Mercury* reported the following about publisher H.H. Cunningham's publication of the work of author John Howard Willis: "We learn that the copy right of this volume was purchased from the author, by the publisher, Mr. Cunningham of Montreal, and that it is the first instance in this province in which a bookseller has ventured upon such a speculation."[59]

These two cases are examined more closely in a later chapter. The question at hand is, what rights might the law have recognized in Boucher and Willis that could be transferred to their printers and publishers? While it is likely that they enjoyed rights in their manuscripts prior to publication, did they also benefit from rights in their published works in the absence of statute? Boucher assumed that he

---

57  Murdoch, *Epitome of the Laws of Nova Scotia*, 7.
58  Letter from Jean-Baptiste Boucher to John Neilson, LAC, Neilson Collection, vol. 2, reel 15769, 113 (Laprairie, 18 March 1809).
59  *Quebec Mercury*, 11 January 1831. A similar announcement appeared in *Halifax Monthly*, 1 February 1831, vol. 1, no. 9.

still had claims over his published work, given that at the time of his letter, he was preparing the fifth edition of the *Recueil de cantiques*. He clearly intended to transfer to Neilson whatever rights or entitlements he believed he had as an author. The same applied in Willis's case in that most of the essays had already been released in serial form by the time Cunningham acquired "the copyright" from the author.[60] Both Boucher and Willis considered that they had some legally recognized rights in their publications that they could dispose of as they saw fit.

Lawyer and jurist Denis-Benjamin Viger held a similar view of the state of the law. In his opinion, Lower Canada recognized "copyright" outside of statute. Writing to his friend John Neilson in 1824, he advised that "le droit de propriété littéraire ... à en outre été reconnu et consacré par les décisions des Cours aussi bien que par les opinions des Jurisconsultes et le principe en est généralement admis: – *Il n'y a point de doute sur ce sujet*" (emphasis added).[61] Viger does not specify which decisions of which courts and which opinions of which eminent jurists, nor does he clarify the extent of the legal protection. Nevertheless, he was emphatic that the civil law in Lower Canada protected literary property – there was no doubt on the subject.

Viger's remarks were related to a matter involving the *Quebec Gazette*, a newspaper that John Neilson had established in 1764. The *Gazette*, which at the time of the dispute was in the hands of John Neilson's son Samuel and his business partner William Cowan, also acted as the official organ for government announcements. In 1823 the British authorities replaced Neilson & Cowan as their authorized printers and appointed printer John Charlton Fisher in their stead. Fisher began to

---

60   Although it is arguable that the published book was a different publication since it consisted of both previously published and unpublished content. However, in the preface, Willis refers to the previously published content as "republished." See Willis, *Scraps and Sketches*.

61   Denis-Benjamin Viger to John Neilson, 26 June 1824, LAC, Neilson Collection, vol. 4, 382–5. "[T]he right of literary property ... has been recognized ... by court decisions and the opinions of jurists and the principle is generally admitted – there is no doubt on this subject.] *Le droit de propriété littéraire* would have been the French equivalent of copyright in Lower Canada. The French title of the 1832 Copyright Act was *Acte pour protéger la propriété littéraire*. Viger may have been using the term "propriété littéraire" in its broader sense to encompass both the rights in published works (copyright) and the author's right in the manuscript, but this is doubtful given the context. For a study of the nature of authorial rights and literary property prior to the statutory copyright period, see Willinsky, *The Intellectual Properties of Learning*.

print the official records in a publication also titled the *Quebec Gazette*.[62] John Neilson was investigating whether there was any legal recourse to prevent Fisher from adopting the same title for his publication. Viger's comments make it clear that he believed there *was* legal recourse outside of statute that applied to published works, since his advice related to a newspaper of long standing. He suggested that this inchoate right in literary property could be enforced by a claim for damages for reputational harm similar to the *action d'injure*, a recourse derived from Roman law and recognized in Lower Canada.[63] Viger's opinion about the law in Lower Canada mirrored that of Beamish Murdoch in respect of Nova Scotia, although their sources of law differed. Viger applied Franco-Roman civil law, instead of the English common law, to conclude that outside of statute, authors had claims in damages for infringements of their rights in their publications.

Lower Canadian Attorney General James Stuart took a very different view when, in 1830, he provided a legal opinion to the effect that authors, printers, and publishers did not enjoy any exclusive rights over their published works in the absence of copyright legislation: "as yet no Legislative Provision has been made in this Province for conferring on, or securing to, authors or compilers, a copy right in their respective Productions."[64] Stuart's interpretation of the state of affairs in Lower Canada is palpably different from Viger's. It also represents a significant departure from Beamish Murdoch's assessesment of the law in Nova Scotia. Stuart's opinion that published works were afforded no legal protection at all in Lower Canada would have heightened the need for copyright legislation in that province. Even in situations

---

62   In 1823, Governor Dalhousie terminated Samuel Neilson's appointment as King's Printer of the *Quebec Gazette*. See entries in DCB for Fisher and Neilson. See also LAC, Neilson Collection, vol. 28, *Correspondence and Manuscripts Submitted to the Quebec Gazette 1795–1845* including a letter dated 10 February 1823 from lawyer Andrew Stuart, who, like Viger, advised Neilson that he would have a remedy in damages or an injunction against a new paper using the same title, although he did not provide the foundation for the cause of action. Neilson & Cowan initiated a lawsuit claiming exclusive rights over the title but were unsuccessful. They also took their claim to the papers, saying that the title had become their private property. See *Quebec Mercury*, Friday, 12 October 1823.

63   The *action d'injure* was recognized in Lower Canada in decisions such as *Boucher v. Casgrain* KBQ 1810; *Fraser v. Peltier* KBQ 1816; and *Smith v. Binet* KBQ 1821. See also Reiter, "From Shaved Horses to Aggressive Churchwardens."

64   Letter from James Stuart to Lt-Col. Yorke, Secretary to James Kempt from Quebec, 12 May 1830. LAC, Civil Secretary's Correspondence Quebec, Lower Canada, and Canada East, 1760–1863, 28. See entry for James Stuart (1780–1853) in DCB.

where provinces perhaps recognized some residual common law rights for published works, the uncertainty surrounding the extent of those rights would have militated in favour of legislative intervention.

## The Right of Petition

The right of colonists to petition the legislature for grants, remedies, or redress for individual or collective grievances was recognized parliamentary practice throughout British North America.[65] Indeed, as we will see throughout this book, it was a series of printing and publishing petitions that led to the introduction of copyright legislation in Lower Canada, and similar patterns occurred in the other provinces. Petitions were, however, not an entirely effective means of obtaining legislative grants or concessions. There was no guarantee that they would successfully pass every stage of the process. Each petition had to be introduced by a member of the Assembly and then referred to a committee for consideration. If the request resulted in a financial allocation, the decision would be implemented either by specific legislative enactment or by referral to a committee of supply or another budgetary committee. In practice, petitions often stalled before a final decision was reached and would either disappear entirely or would have to be reintroduced in subsequent sessions, often meeting the same fate. In addition, because they were assessed on a case-by-case basis, there was no consistency as to whether and under what terms they would be granted.

Joseph Bouchette's petitions to the legislatures of Lower Canada, Upper Canada, Nova Scotia, New Brunswick, and Prince Edward Island for the purchase of copies of his three-volume *British Dominions* and *Topographical Dictionary* offer a valuable illustration of the vagaries of the process in a transcolonial context. We have already seen that Lower Canada agreed to purchase 100 copies. Prince Edward Island subscribed for six copies, but it took three years for Bouchette's petition to make its way through the legislative process.[66] Nova Scotia's

---

65   On the right of petition in the British parliamentary tradition, see for example Huzzey, "Petitions, Parliament and Political Culture." In terms of nineteenth-century Canadian practice, see Bourinot, *Parliamentary Procedure and Practice.* In relation to book and printing petitions, see Laurence, "Never Been a Very Promising Speculation." In the context of printing petitions in the United Kingdom, see Seville, *The Internationalisation of Copyright Law.*

66   *Journal of the House of Assembly of Prince Edward Island* (Charlottetown: J.D. Haszard). Introduced during the 1833 session (3 Will. 4) it was deferred (at 81). It was reintroduced in 1834 session (4 Will. 4), and six copies were ordered to be

Assembly also responded favourably to Bouchette and agreed to purchase five copies of the books. However, it appears that the money was never actually disbursed.[67] Similarly, Bouchette's sole petition to the New Brunswick legislature requesting the "purchase of a number of books" stalled in the Assembly after it was introduced.[68]

The prehistory of copyright in British North America demonstrates the inadequacy of the status quo in addressing the needs and interests of colonial authors, printers, publishers, and readers. Individual petitions to the legislature were unpredictable and precarious. Any rights that might have existed outside of statute were vague and uncertain. Finally, the availability of the Statute of Anne left much to be desired for colonists because British copyright law served British interests. Colonial aspirations could only be met through the enactment of local legislation. It was, therefore, to this end that Lower Canada's House of Assembly directed its attention in the early decades of the nineteenth century. The next chapter discusses the legislative precedents to which Lower Canadian lawmakers turned for inspiration, as well as the policy that informed their approach.

---

purchased (at 39). The necessary resolutions to complete the transaction were only approved in the subsequent session (1835 5 Will. 4, 17).

67 Journal and Proceedings of the House of Assembly for the Province of Nova Scotia (Halifax: R. Nugent). The petition was introduced in the 1833 session (at 403) and was referred to the Committee of Supply with the direction to purchase five copies during the 1834 session (at 643), but the records end there and it is not clear that Bouchette ever received his money. See as well Laurence, "Never Been a Very Promising Speculation."

68 Journal of the House of Assembly of the Province of New Brunswick, from January to March 1833 (Fredericton: J. Simpson, 1833), 22.

# Chapter Two

# How Copyright Laws Originate: The Anglo-American Copyright Tradition

Despite Lower Canada's former status as a French colony, French copyright law played no role in the Assembly's deliberations.[1] Instead, Lower Canada's copyright history was shaped by the two countries that exerted influence over the province, one through conquest (the United Kingdom), the other through geopolitical propinquity (the United States). It was ultimately the American copyright tradition that shaped the way Lower Canadian parliamentarians understood the nature and purpose of the law.

**The Statute of Anne 1710:** *An Act for the Encouragement of Learning*

The Statute of Anne was the world's first statutory scheme to regulate the printing and publishing of books. The present-day legal debate, discussed in the introductory chapter and exemplified by the competing comments of Justice Binnie on the one hand and Justices Gonthier and Décary on the other, exists in large measure because of ambiguities in the Statute of Anne. The statute's preamble identified its purpose:

Whereas Printers, Booksellers, and other Persons, have of late frequently taken the Liberty of Printing, Reprinting, and Publishing, or causing to be

---

1 As this book will demonstrate, any influence of the French *droit d'auteur* on the development of Canadian law did not arise until the early twentieth century. In 1931, Canada enacted a moral rights provision in its copyright legislation. Moral rights are more commonly recognized in Continental European civil law jurisdictions, such as France, than in those, like Canada, that follow the British copyright tradition. See Adeney, "Moral Rights in Canada." On the particularities of Canadian conceptions of *droit d'auteur* versus copyright in historical context, see Gendreau, "De l'importance d'être constant"; and Tawfik, "Copyright as *droit d'auteur*." See also, more generally, Hayhurst, "Intellectual Property Laws in Canada."

Printed, Reprinted, and Published Books, and other Writings, without the Consent of the Authors or Proprietors of such Books and Writings, to their very great Detriment, and too often to the Ruin of them and their Families: For Preventing therefore such Practices for the future, and for the Encouragement of Learned Men to Compose and Write useful Books ...

The preamble suggests that copyright was intended as a "publisher's right" in that it concerned itself with the interests of the book trade in preventing unscrupulous printing and publishing practices, although it recognized that the impact of unauthorized reprints was felt by authors as well. There is no doubt that British printers and publishers were the most dominant lobbyists for the Statute of Anne.[2] They had little incentive to invest in the cost of bringing a book to market if they could be easily undercut by competitors' cheaper reprints. At the time the legislation was enacted, the British book trade was a flourishing industry organized around the Stationers' Company, a trade guild established in London in the fifteenth century.[3] Until the late seventeenth century, the guild enjoyed grants of exclusive and (often) perpetual printing privileges as the mainstay of their early business model. However, by the latter half of the seventeenth century, as beliefs in individual liberty, freedom of choice, and freedom of the press intensified, the idea that the Stationers could control all the printing and publishing in the country became untenable for British society.[4] This system of exclusivity came to an end in 1694, when the legislation granting them their monopoly was allowed to lapse.[5]

The Statute of Anne was promulgated out of the ashes of this history. Having lost their status, their financial security, and their considerable political power, the Stationers sought an alternative form of exclusivity from the British Parliament. During this same period, a nascent authorial class in Britain was agitating for legal recognition of their intellectual efforts.[6] They succeeded in their advocacy: the Statute of Anne vested initial copyright ownership in authors rather than in the book

---

2  See for example, Birrell, *Seven Lectures on the Law*; Patterson, *Copyright in Historical Perspective*; and Feather, *Publishing, Piracy and Politics*.

3  On the Stationers' Company, see Myers and Harris, *The Stationers' Company*.

4  For example, John Milton, *Areopagitica* (London: 1644), which was an influential polemic against the exclusive licensing system and in favour of a free press. See also Rose, "The Public Sphere and the Emergence of Copyright."

5  *Act for Preventing Abuses in Printing Seditious, Treasonable, and Unlicensed Books and Pamphlets, and for Regulating of Printing and Printing Presses*, 3 & 4 Car. II, c. 33.

6  British authors and philosophers like Jonathan Swift and Daniel Defoe argued vigorously for legislative protection. See Deazley, *On the Origin of the Right to Copy*.

trade. Printers and publishers fell under the broad category of "proprietors," who could only derive their rights as assignees of the author. The fact that authors emerged as central figures in this statutory construct was reinforced when the Statute of Anne was amended in 1814 to fix the duration of copyright to the life of the "author."[7]

However, focusing solely on the interests of authors and publishers under the statutory regime does not provide a complete picture of the nature and purpose of copyright law, especially when one considers the British North American context. Lower Canada was at the very earliest stages of industrial and cultural development when it first began to consider questions of copyright. Its printing and publishing industries were small; the most prominent enterprises were located in the major centres along the St Lawrence River – Quebec City, Trois-Rivières, and Montreal. Lower Canadian printers, publishers, and booksellers relied heavily on importing books, printing government tracts, and private printing.[8] They were often stationers as well, selling notebooks and other paper products, writing instruments, and school supplies. At least one early printer also manufactured paper for sale, as imported paper was expensive and increased printing costs.[9] There is no evidence of undercutting or other sharp practices among these early printers that would explain the need for statutory protection. The absence of a "courtesy of the trade" system between Lower Canadian printers and publishers to address problems of unfair trade practices outside of statute is another indication that the book trade was not at the forefront of legislative consideration. In the United States, where copyright did not extend to the works of foreign authors, some American publishers agreed among themselves to guarantee exclusive publishing rights to

---

7   The 1814 UK Act at section 4 provided that if the author was alive at the expiry of the initial term of twenty-eight years, the copyright would subsist for the remainder of the author's life.

8   On early Lower Canadian printing and publishing, the book trade, and the development of a reading culture in Lower Canada, see Lamonde, *Histoire sociale des idées au Québec*; Gallichan, *Livre et politique au Bas-Canada*; Lamonde and Montreuil, *Lire au Québec au XIXè siècle*; Galarneau, and Lemire, *Livre et lecture au Québec*; and Wallot, "Frontière ou fragment du système Atlantique." For insight into the early Canadian book trade more generally, see Fleming et al., *HBC*, vols. 1 and 2; and Parker, *The Beginnings of the Book Trade in Canada*.

9   James Brown opened the first paper mill in Lower Canada in 1807, producing paper from discarded rags and other fabrics. He procured these paper-making supplies through advertisements inserted in the books he printed: "Cash given for clean linen and cotton rags, and old ropes, and anything made of hemp, flax or cotton by James Brown, at the St. Andrew's Paper-Mill or at his book store, Montreal." See Gagnon, *Essai de bibliographie canadienne*, citing the advertisement at 157.

any publisher who asserted a claim over a legally unprotected book. Some British North American printers and publishers acted as agents for American publishers who engaged in trade courtesy; however, there is nothing to indicate that Lower Canadian printers and publishers adopted similar arrangements among themselves.[10]

John Neilson, who chaired the Standing Committee on Education and Schools when it recommended the introduction of a copyright law for Lower Canada, was the most prominent British North American printer, publisher, and bookseller of his time, yet he never took up the cause of copyright as a publisher's issue, nor did any of his competitors.[11] Most telling is the correspondence from Augustin-Norbert Morin to his friend, Montreal printer and publisher Ludger Duvernay, about Assembly activities during the period of the passage of the 1832 Act. Morin related details of parliamentary business but made no mention of the copyright bill he had introduced in the Assembly or of its successful passage.[12] The question of copyright was not top of mind for Lower Canadian printers, publishers, and booksellers. The need to regulate the book trade was not a determining factor in the decision to legislate on copyright. The same can be said about Lower Canadian authors. There is no evidence that they were clamouring for redress from unauthorized reprinting or other unauthorized uses of their works. While the number of books authored by Lower Canadians and published domestically grew steadily after the turn of the century, there are only very scant indications of concern about "piracy" in the public records. Even if there was grumbling about unethical conduct by some, it did not reach a pitch loud enough for action to be taken on that basis. Land surveyor Jacques Viger, later to become the first mayor of the City

---

10  On British North American printers and publishers and the American courtesy system, see Parker, *The Beginnings of the Book Trade in Canada*. On courtesy of the trade in the United States see Spoo, *Without Copyrights*; and Everton, *The Grand Chorus of Complaint*. The case of H.H. Cunningham and his agreement with J.H. Willis as a possible example of Lower Canadian courtesy of the trade is explored in chapter 6.

11  When Neilson entered politics in 1818, he abandoned any direct involvement with publishing. In 1822, he left the business to his son Samuel Neilson, who carried on in partnership with William Cowan. There is only one reference to copyright in the John Neilson papers prior to 1832, and it was only a passing reference by Andrew Stuart to John Neilson, 18 November 1822. Canada: Sessional Papers of the Dominion of Canada, session 1914, vol. 25 (Ottawa, 1914), Sessional Paper no. 29b, 129.

12  Augustin-Norbert Morin to Ludger Duvernay, BAnQ (Vieux-Montréal), Fonds Ludger Duvernay. In fact, none of the correspondence Duvernay received from 1815 to 1832 makes mention of copyright at all. Ironically, he was one of the first printers and publishers to take advantage of the new law (see chapter 6).

of Montreal, alleged that one of his maps had been copied and published without attribution by Joseph Bouchette in his *Topographical Description 1815*.[13] At the time, there were also persistent rumours – later discounted – that Bouchette had plagiarized from German entrepreneur William Berczy.[14] These hints of opprobrium over the copying of another author's work did not instigate legislative action.

Reprinting, adapting, and translating the works of others without their permission was a common practice and was not generally considered unethical or unlawful.[15] Education historian Paul Aubin writes that by the end of the 1830s, 19.3 per cent of French-language schoolbooks circulating in Lower Canada were local reprints of works authored and published in France.[16] With regard to English-language reprints, "[t]he English-language market in Lower Canada was more dependent on foreign works than the French. Of 30 titles published in the province for Anglophones, 56.6 per cent were reprints from England; a few titles came from the United States."[17] Joseph-François Perrault, who as we will see was an important figure in both education and copyright reform, routinely translated schoolbooks and other didactic works into French for use in his schools. During this period, unauthorized translations were not viewed as infringing activities, since they were not direct reproductions of the original work. As an American court explained in *Stowe v. Thomas* (1853), in which it dismissed Harriet Beecher Stowe's claim of infringement related to an unauthorized translation of *Uncle Tom's Cabin*:

> [a]ll that now remains is the copyright of her book; the exclusive right to print, reprint and vend it, and those only can be called infringers of her rights, or pirates of her property, who are guilty of printing, publishing,

---

13   As Surveyor General, Bouchette would have been Viger's supervisor and may therefore have believed he was entitled to claim his subordinate's work as his own, assuming that he had in fact knowingly reproduced Viger's map. However, Viger certainly felt aggrieved. In a note written around April 1811, Viger alleged that a certain Lieutenant Gray to whom he had submitted his map had copied it and that this copy had been reproduced and published by Bouchette without Viger's name attached. See Fernand Ouellet, "Inventaire de la Saberdache de Jacques Viger," 88. See also entry for Jacques Viger (1787–1858) in DCB.

14   See Parizeau, "Joseph Bouchette: l'homme et le haut fonctionnaire."

15   Marcel Trudel cites numerous examples of Voltaire's works being reproduced or adapted in Lower Canadian newspapers throughout the first half of the nineteenth century. Trudel, *L'influence de Voltaire au Canada*.

16   Aubin, "Books of Instruction," in *HBC* vol. 1, 256–9.

17   Aubin, "Books of Instruction," in *HBC* vol. 1, 258.

importing or vending without her license, "copies of her book." A translation may, in loose phraseology, be called a transcript or copy of her thoughts or conceptions, but in no correct sense can it be called a copy of her book.[18]

The freedom to adapt foreign works to local conditions and to translate English-language works into French was especially important for Lower Canada. Indeed, there are no recorded instances of a foreign author suing in respect of Lower Canadian reprints or translations of their publications. Moreover, Lower Canadian newspapers of the day offer no evidence that this was an issue of concern. There is, however, this one cryptic remark by French social commentator, Isidore Lebrun, on the reason for the enactment of the Lower Canadian Act in 1832: "On a refait des grammaires, des traités d'arithmétique, de géographie etc...mais sans les améliorer: c'est sans doute à cause de ces plagiats que la législature vient d'adopter en faveur de la propriété littéraire, un bill qui, autrement, semblerait être une anomalie avec l'état présent du Bas-Canada."[19] The suggestion here is that the practice of reprinting the works of others without permission and without improving on them led the legislature to step in at a time when the Lower Canadian Parliament would not otherwise have had any reason to intervene. We will return to Lebrun and his statement in chapter 5, but for the moment it is sufficient to understand that he was only hypothesizing. We will see that copyright law in Lower Canada did not emerge to address concerns about "piracy." Disquiet over the impact of unauthorized reprinting would grow later in the century, especially as it pertained to American reprinting of British copyright works, but we are not, at this stage, concerned with that fractious time, to which we will return in the final chapters.

Although Lower Canada was the most populous of the British North American colonies, its population was still relatively small,

---

18  *Stowe v. Thomas* 23 F. Cas. 201 (1853), 208. See too Reese, "Innocent Infringement in US Copyright Law," 133. By the 1850s, opinion in Europe had changed. In 1852, the United Kingdom and France agreed to reciprocal protection for translations under the *Convention between Her Majesty and the French Republic for the Establishment of International Copyright* (signed at Paris, 3 November 1851, ratified 8 January 1852) Parliamentary Papers 1851, Paper No. 1432, LIV., 103.

19  Isidore Lebrun (1786–1860), *Tableau statistique et politique des deux Canadas*, 201–2. ["They remade grammars, arithmetic and geography books etc. but without improving them. It is undoubtedly as a result of these plagiarisms that the legislature has just adopted a bill in favour of literary property that would, otherwise, appear to be an anomaly given the present state of Lower Canada."]

with roughly 250,000 inhabitants in 1806, growing to 553,134 by 1831.[20] It was also a society with a limited readership, as literacy rates were low.[21] Politically and socially, it was divided along linguistic and religious lines that inhibited attempts to create an effective public education infrastructure.[22] Although the early nineteenth century saw the beginnings of a print culture and the emergence of newspapers, literary reviews, and other print materials, those who read them were but a small minority of educated francophone and anglophone elites. Yet within thirty years of its establishment, the House of Assembly, already consumed with significant issues of colonial governance – including navigating the British legal and parliamentary systems and reconciling two distinct cultures – nevertheless directed its attention to enacting a copyright law. Why would a colonial society at such an early stage of development see fit to concern itself with copyright if printers, publishers, and authors were not agitating for redress?

The rationale for enacting this first Canadian copyright statute must be sought outside of orthodox policy objectives, which provide only a truncated version of the interests at play. The primary mischief the law was designed to correct did not relate to rewarding authors for their creativity or to providing publishers with financial security for their investments in book production. A different policy objective predominated in Lower Canada that, upon close examination, was also central to both British and American constructions of the law: the encouragement of learning.

## The Statute of Anne and the Diffusion of Knowledge

Book historian Robert Darnton has characterized the life cycle of the printed book as "a communications circuit that runs from the author to the publisher (if the bookseller does not assume that role), the printer, the shipper, the bookseller, and the reader. The reader completes the circuit because he influences the author both before and after the act of

---

20   See Canada, *Censuses of Canada, 1665 to 1871*, 109.

21   New scholarship on literacy has called into question some of the assumptions about the illiteracy levels of Lower Canadians. See for example, Michel Verrette, *L'alpha-bétisation au Québec*. Regardless of whether the rates are exaggerated, Lower Canadian politicians considered illiteracy to be a serious social problem to be addressed through public schooling.

22   See Jolois, *Joseph-François Perrault*; Curtis, *Ruling by Schooling Quebec*; and Wilson, Stamp, and Audet, *Canadian Education*.

composition. Authors are readers themselves."[23] Darnton did not consider the legal dimension in his approach, but I argue in this book that, from its inception, copyright necessarily became a part of the circuit of communication that is the book – both defined by it and, in turn, defining it. The dialogic relationship between author, publisher, and reader situates the law within a broader policy paradigm that encompasses more than merely the rights of authors or of publishers – it is ultimately the reader, the learner, the "user" of copyright works, who completes the circuit.[24] Indeed, a careful assessment of the history of the Statute of Anne demonstrates that the world's first Copyright Act was designed to advance the public interest in the dissemination of knowledge. The title itself would suggest this purpose: *An Act for the Encouragement of Learning*. Surely, any initiative to advance learning must address itself, at least in part, to the "learner" – or the "reader" or "user" – or any other term that can be used to describe the recipient of the knowledge communicated through books and other print material. As copyright scholar Ronan Deazley has argued:

> A statutory phenomenon, copyright was fundamentally concerned with the reading public, with the encouragement and spread of education, and with the continued production of useful books. In allocating the right to exclusively publish a given literary work, the eighteenth-century parliamentarians were not concerned primarily with the rights of the individual, but acted in the furtherance of these much broader social goals. The pre-eminence of the common good as the organizing principle upon which to found a system of copyright regulation is revealed. This element of the public interest, overlooked or perhaps ignored in other historical tales of the origin of copyright, once lay at its very core.[25]

---

23  Darnton, "What Is the History of Books?," 111. Darnton's model has been critiqued, refined, and amended over the years, including by Darnton himself, but remains a useful starting point from which consider the role of copyright in the cycle of book production. For further discussion of the study of book history and Darnton's communications circuit, see, generally, Howsam, *The Cambridge Companion*.

24  In relation to copyright and its dialogic interaction with authors, industry, and users, see Craig, *Copyright, Communication, and Culture*. On the concept of user rights in copyright law see, for example, Chapdelaine, *Copyright User Rights*; and Vaver, "Copyright Defences as User Rights." See also the Supreme Court of Canada in *CCH Canadian Ltd. v. Law Society of Upper Canada*, 2004 SCC 13.

25  Deazley, *On the Origin of the Right to Copy*, 226. See also Rose, "Nine-Tenths of the Law."

Some scholars caution against minimizing the importance of both publishers and authors in the construction of copyright law,[26] yet the status of the "learner" in the *Act for the Encouragement of Learning* must not be overlooked. There is ample material in the historical record to support the proposition that eighteenth-century British parliamentarians legislated with a view to encouraging the spread of ideas and knowledge. The Statute of Anne was a product of the Western Enlightenment and served the ideal of human progress through the acquisition of knowledge and the exercise of critical inquiry.[27] Scholars have probed the connections between the Enlightenment, the birth of the "professional author," and copyright law.[28] However, more consideration must be given to the relationship between copyright law and Enlightenment values surrounding the diffusion of knowledge, especially "useful" or practical knowledge.[29] The emergence of the first copyright laws must therefore be studied in light of the political, philosophical, social, and cultural upheavals that overtook Britain, Europe and, later, North America during the eighteenth and nineteenth centuries. Eurocentric and reflecting the biases of white Western privilege, the culture of knowledge characteristic of this period manifested itself in the emergence and proliferation of agencies through which ideas could be disseminated.[30] This period witnessed the rise of a lively and active transatlantic public lecture circuit and the beginnings of subscription, specialized, and circulating libraries.[31] Learned societies were

---

26   Feather, "Review of the *Origin of the Right to Copy*."

27   On the British Enlightenment and print culture see, for example, Porter, *Enlightenment*; Sher, *The Enlightenment and the Book*; and St Clair, *The Reading Nation*.

28   See Woodmansee and Jaszi, *Copyright and the Construction of Authorship*; and Saunders, *Authorship and Copyright*.

29   Hesse, "Enlightenment Epistemology"; Hesse, "The Rise of Intellectual Property"; Rose, "Nine-Tenths of the Law," 76. Rose states that "the establishment of the author as the owner and the establishment of the rights of the public at large were both Enlightenment products, embedded in Enlightenment modes of thought." See also Alexander, "*Sayre v. Moore (1785)*." On the meaning of "useful knowledge" during this period, see Rauch, *Useful Knowledge*; Burns, "From 'Polite Learning' to 'Useful Knowledge'"; and Koropchak, *The Love of Learning in the Industrial Age*.

30   For scholarship critical of this period for its systemic exclusion of women, racialized groups, and religious minorities, see, generally, Conrad, "Enlightenment in Global History." On issues of gender, race, and religion, see, for example, Taylor and Knott, *Women, Gender, and Enlightenment*; and Chisick, "On the Margins of the Enlightenment." In relation to copyright specifically, see Bannerman, *International Copyright and Access to Knowledge*.

31   Myers, Harris and Mandelbrote, *Libraries and the Book Trade*; Buschman and Leckie, *The Library as Place*. See also HBC, vol. 1, esp. ch. 7 on social networks and libraries.

established to provide forums for the exchange of scientific and scholarly discoveries.[32] Mechanics' Societies, intended for the edification of working-class adults, offered public lectures and sponsored scientific demonstrations along with technical education. These types of associations played an important role in advancing knowledge and ideas in British North America. As literature scholar Heather Murray described them, "these first societies (for men only) focused on debate, discussion, and essay reading in the period prior to 1840. They often provided public cultural amenities such as lecture series and *conversazioni*, and sometimes they attempted to establish library collections."[33] These associations were perceived as the tangible manifestations of a cultured society. An editorial commentary announcing the establishment of the Literary and Historical Society of Quebec in 1824 suggested that "the number and importance of the Institutions or Societies, in any country, afford a very sure criterion, whereby we may judge of the progress it is making in civilization, and of its remoteness from barbarism."[34]

The eighteenth and nineteenth centuries also saw a profound reassessment of class privilege and a growing recognition that universal public education was a human right. Education reformers and poverty activists began to establish free schools for the children of the poorer socio-economic classes and to lobby for state-funded public schools. Among them was a London teacher, Joseph Lancaster, whose monitorial system of education proved extremely popular throughout North America and who played an instrumental role in bringing copyright law to Lower Canada, as we will see in the next chapters. There were also economic and practical dimensions to this desire to instruct the masses. Industrialization required skilled and educated workers. Finally, education was a powerful political and ideological tool to advance imperialistic and colonial structures and to establish the English language and British modes of thought as universal.[35]

---

32  See generally, Murray, *Come, Bright Improvement!*; Oleson and Brown, *The Pursuit of Knowledge*; and Roderick and Stephens, "The Role of Nineteenth-Century Provincial Literary and Philosophical Societies."

33  Murray, "Readers and Society," HBC, vol. 1, 172–82 at 176.

34  Nickless, "On Literary and Historical Societies," 111. On the history of the early literary societies in Lower Canada, see Bernatchez, "La société littéraire et historique de Québec."

35  In relation to the politics of education in Lower Canada, see Curtis, *Ruling by Schooling*. On the politics of colonialism and racism in education during the same period, see Catherine Larochelle, *L'école du racisme*. See also Howsam, "What the Victorian Empire Learned"; Walsh, "Education and the 'Universalist' Idiom of Empire."

As literacy and learning increased, so did the demand for materials to satisfy a growing number of readers. The eighteenth and nineteenth centuries saw an explosion of print materials and the development of a print culture that privileged the printed word over other modes of communication. The centrality of book production within this burgeoning print culture cannot be underestimated. The book was the pre-eminent mass medium of its day – the material object through which the widest diffusion of knowledge could occur. American historian Richard Sher posits that "books were the basic building blocks of the Enlightenment."[36] Copyright law emerged within this environment, and one may well characterize it as *the law of the book* in that its purpose was to encourage the production and circulation of knowledge in print.

The Statute of Anne was a number of years in the making, draft upon draft evincing the difficulties early parliamentarians encountered in their efforts to satisfy a number of interests, including those of the greater good in the circulation of ideas.[37] This broad social policy objective had not been met by the previous licensing system, which had been abused by London printers, publishers, and booksellers. The final statutory text reflected the tenor of the times and attempted to redress these past wrongs. Instead of privileging publishers, the legislation sought to break their monopoly. It is true that the book trade played its part in shaping the law. However, publishers frequently advanced their claims before Parliament or the courts in the name of the public interest in learning instead of the commercial and regulatory needs of their industry.[38] Whether these arguments were proffered with genuine conviction is an open question. At the very least, they were made because they needed to be made at the time. The public discourse over copyright had to be cast in broad social policy terms for the British Parliament to intervene.[39]

It is also true that ideas about the natural rights of authors permeated the copyright discourse at the time. The theoretical foundation of copyright as a form of authorial property is rooted in Lockean conceptions

---

36   Sher, *The Enlightenment and the Book*, 597. See also, Febvre and Martin, *L'apparition du livre*.

37   Ronan Deazley provides a detailed exposé of the circumstances and events that led to the final enactment of the Statute of Anne, in *On the Origin of the Right to Copy*.

38   Kaplan, *An Unhurried View of Copyright*; Deazley, *On the Origin of the Right to Copy*.

39   See, in this regard, Alexander, *Copyright Law and the Public Interest*.

of ownership over one's creative labour[40] or else on Hegelian notions of property in the tangible manifestations of one's personality.[41] Whatever the philosophical underpinning, justifying copyright in this way meant protecting authors against piracy or the unauthorized reprinting of their works, which undermined both their economic interests and their reputational integrity.[42] Nevertheless, the arguments in support of authorial rights were also frequently couched in terms of the broader public interest. Access to knowledge was the ultimate justification for the grant of exclusivity. Samuel Johnson, the eighteenth-century British essayist and lexicographer, exemplified this view when he opined:

> There seems ... to be in authors ... a right, as it were, of creation which should from its nature be perpetual; but the consent of nations is against it; and indeed *reason and the interests of learning* are against it; for were it to be perpetual, no book however useful, could be universally diffused amongst mankind should the proprietor take it into his head to restrain circulation. No book could have the advantage of being edited with notes, however necessary for its elucidation, should the proprietor perversely oppose it. *For the general good of the world*, therefore, whatever valuable work has once been created by an author, and issued out by him, should be understood as no longer in his power, but *as belonging to the publick*; at the same time, the author is entitled to an adequate reward. This he should have by an exclusive right to his work for a considerable number of years. [emphasis added][43]

Whatever the rights of authors or publishers, "reason and the interests of learning" demanded that their monopoly lapse after a certain period in time. Whether characterized as a social contract between the author and the public for a period of exclusivity over a work in exchange for its eventual release into the public domain, or whether justified on other

---

40   The idea that authors had natural rights over their intellectual labours emerged out of the writings of the English philosopher John Locke (1632–1704). On the relationship between Locke and copyright, see, for example, Peter Jaszi, and Martha Woodmansee, eds., *The Construction of Authorship*; and David Saunders, *Authorship and Copyright*. For an access to learning approach to Locke, see Willinsky, "When the Law Advances Access to Learning."

41   Derived from the work of German Enlightenment philosopher Georg Hegel (1770–1831) and his theories of personality rights. See Drahos, *A Philosophy of Intellectual Property*; and Radin, "Property and Personhood."

42   Rose, *Authors and Owners*; Sherman and Bently, *The Making of Intellectual Property Law*; May and Sell, *Intellectual Property Rights*; Feather, "From Rights in Copies to Copyright," 455. See also Rose, "The Author as Proprietor."

43   Boswell, *Life of Johnson*, 220 (entry dated 1773).

utilitarian grounds, the early history of copyright makes it clear that the law was as much designed around the interests of readers and learners as it was around authors and publishers.

Copyright users were recognized through a variety of statutory markers.[44] The phrase "for the encouragement of learning" in the title of the statute stressed its ultimate objective. In addition, the use of the word *vesting*, as in *An Act for the Encouragement of Learning by Vesting ...,* suggested that copyright was a new form of legal recognition granted by the state rather than a pre-existing natural right that was confirmed by legislation.[45] As a statutory privilege, the law could be modified, amended, or repealed at the will of Parliament if it failed in its policy objectives. More importantly, the Statute of Anne imposed a fixed duration of protection of fourteen years with the possibility of an additional fourteen years for the author if still living at the expiration of the initial term. The shift from perpetual rights to limited duration was significant in that it established a public domain for published books once the copyright expired. This public domain ensured the affordability of print material, in that the prices of books declined as the copyright came to an end.[46] It also provided for the circulation of new ideas and creative expressions, as these works could be adapted and enhanced without constraint. In addition, printers and publishers could no longer rely on the steady income generated from their exclusive print repertoires but would have to seek out new authors, as well as new readers, to satisfy their production capabilities, given that their copyright interests were finite. The durational limit of protection under the Act was strengthened with the decision in *Donaldson v. Becket,* discussed in the previous chapter, that ended any claims to a vestigial subsistence of perpetual copyright in published works. Rights in published works would lapse at the end of the statutory term. Book historian William St Clair has argued that because of this judgment, Britain became a "reading nation" due to the proliferation of new books.[47]

---

44   See Deazley, *On the Origin of the Right to Copy*; Rose, "Nine-Tenths of the Law," 76. See, as well, Alexander, *Copyright Law and the Public Interest*; and Khong, "The Historical Law." Though John Feather has referred to these features as mere "window dressing": see his "The Book Trade in Politics:"

45   In 1801, the term "securing" replaced "vesting" in *An Act for the further Encouragement of Learning, in the United Kingdom of Great Britain and Ireland, by securing the Copies and Copyright of printed Books to the Authors of such Books, or their Assigns for the Time herein mentioned,* 1801, 41 Geo. III, c.107.

46   St Clair, *The Reading Nation.*

47   St Clair, *The Reading Nation.* Trevor Ross argues that the Statute of Anne and the *Donaldson* decision encouraged the circulation of ideas and created a public literary tradition. Ross, "Copyright and the Invention of Tradition."

The Statute of Anne offered other measures to facilitate greater access to print material. For example, it established a complaint mechanism for anyone who felt that a bookseller or printer was selling a book at a "high or unreasonable price"[48] as well as a mandatory deposit of a certain number of copies of each book to designated university libraries to build their collections.[49] In addition, the statute permitted the importation and sale of books in Greek, Latin, or any other foreign language that were printed overseas. In this way, the popular works of classical antiquity would circulate unhindered.[50] These statutory devices and the jurisprudence that supported them advanced the broad social purpose of encouraging learning by placing restrictions on the depth and breadth of the copyright monopoly. Similar limits found their way into the copyright laws of the New World in North America, where the emphasis on fostering learning was more pronounced.

**Copyright in the United States: To Promote the Progress of Science**

As was the case in the British North American colonies, the Statute of Anne was not received in pre-revolutionary America, in that it did not automatically become the law of the land. Nevertheless, it served as a close legislative model for the various state and later federal copyright enactments. This transplanted British copyright law was adapted to suit local contexts. Legal scholar Oren Bracha explains: "By the late nineteenth century, American copyright law was different from the original Statute of Anne regime far beyond the degree betrayed by the simple comparison of statutory texts."[51]

By virtue of Article 1, section 8, clause 8, of the Constitution of the United States, the federal Congress was given the power "[t]o promote the Progress of Science and useful Arts, by securing for limited Times to Authors and Inventors the exclusive Right to their respective Writings and Discoveries." The subject of much scholarly discussion, the constitutional clause brought both copyright (progress of science) and patent

---

48   Section 4 of the Statute of Anne.

49   Section 5 of the Statute of Anne required copies for nine universities and institutions of higher learning throughout England and Scotland. With the unification of Great Britain and Ireland, the deposit was increased to eleven copies. See *Copyright Act*, 1801, 41 Geo. 3, c. 107.

50   Section 7 of the Statute of Anne. The provision was repealed after printer Samuel Buckley argued that the clause gave rights to foreign publishers and booksellers to the detriment of the British book trade. See Deazley, *On the Origin of the Right to Copy*.

51   Bracha, "The Adventures of the Statute of Anne," 1430.

(useful arts) under its purview.[52] At the time, the term *science* was understood as *knowledge*.[53] Thus, the clause directed Congress to encourage the spread of (the progress of) knowledge by granting to authors the exclusive rights to their writings for a limited time. George Washington in his first address to Congress cast the constitutional authority over copyright on those terms: "There is nothing which can better deserve your patronage than the promotion of science and literature. Knowledge is, in every country, the surest basis of public happiness."[54]

In 1790, the first US Federal Copyright Act, *An Act for the Encouragement of Learning, by securing the copies of maps, charts and books to the authors and proprietors of such copies, during the times therein mentioned,* was enacted pursuant to this constitutional mandate.[55] Its title echoed that of the Statute of Anne but with two significant differences. First, the scope of protected material extended to maps and charts in addition to books. Second, the title referred to *securing* copies rather than *vesting* copies in authors and proprietors, which might lead to the conclusion that American lawmakers viewed copyright as an inherent, pre-existing right rather than as a privilege defined by statute. It is not clear, however, that this textual deviation from its antecedent was deliberate. In 1834, in *Wheaton v. Peters,* the use of the term *securing* instead of *vesting* was determined by the US Supreme Court to be of no consequence.[56] The Court took the view that "Congress ... by this act, instead of sanctioning an existing right, as contended for, created it."[57]

The first American statute contained most of the same anti-monopolistic pro-learner or -user features found in the Statute of Anne, but with sharper delineation.[58] Indeed, the copyright law of the United States is

---

52   For the early history, see, for example, "Proceedings in Congress During the Years 1789 and 1790"; Donner, "The Copyright Clause of the US Constitution"; Ochoa and Rose, "The Anti-Monopoly Origins"; and Oliar, "Making Sense of the Intellectual Property Clause."

53   Pollack, "What Is Congress Supposed to Promote?" The word "science" in French continues to signify knowledge.

54   Speech to both Houses of Congress delivered on 8 January 1790. See Sparks, ed., *The Writings of George Washington,* 9.

55   *An Act for the Encouragement of Learning, by securing the copies of maps, charts and book to the authors and proprietors of such copies during the times therein mentioned,* 1790, 1 Statutes at Large 124.

56   *Wheaton v. Peters,* 33 US 591 (1834).

57   *Wheaton v. Peters,* 33 US 591 (1834) 661.

58   One notable absence was a provision enabling complaints for usurious book prices, similar to the one enacted in the Statute of Anne in 1710, which was subsequently repealed in 1739. In addition, the American statute did not provide for the deposit of books in university libraries. Instead, there was a deposit with the Secretary of State.

still one of the most user-oriented of its kind.[59] Literary scholar Meredith McGill points out that for early Americans "the notion that an individual author had a natural right to his printed text ... was fundamentally incompatible with the political philosophy that associated the depersonalization of print with a kind of selfless publicity, the exercise of civic virtue. *Perpetual* private ownership and control over printed texts was unacceptable in a culture that regarded the free circulation of texts as the sign and guarantor of liberty."[60] Copyright would be of limited duration and would be granted only upon the completion of formal requirements, including registration of title with the district court. According to the court in *Wheaton v. Peters*, these registration obligations were mandatory; works that did not comply with the statutory formalities belonged in the public domain. British copyright law was more permissive; the absence of registration did not prevent a claim at common law for damages for copyright infringement.[61]

The statute limited eligibility for copyright to American citizens and permanent residents, thereby excluding foreign authors from its purview. To further reinforce this, section 5 of the Act declared that the importation, reprinting, or republication in the United States of books originally printed or published elsewhere by non-citizens were lawful activities. This provision was derived from the Statute of Anne, which had provided for the unconstrained importation of texts in Greek and Latin, but the American version was much broader in scope. It enabled the importation of any foreign book regardless of its language – which became a source of considerable international friction. This legislative measure facilitated the mass production of cheap American reprints of the works of foreign authors, especially British authors, who found themselves without any recourse. For the Americans, affordable books were essential for social and political growth. As one United States senator explained in a speech to Congress in 1838, "the multiplication of cheap editions of useful books, brought within the reaches of all classes, serves to promote that general diffusion of knowledge and intelligence, on which depends so essentially the preservation and

---

59  See for example, Patterson and Lindberg, *The Nature of Copyright*; McGill, *American Literature and the Culture of Reprinting*; Khan, *The Democratization of Invention*; and Dallon, "The Problem with Congress and Copyright Law."

60  McGill, *American Literature and the Culture of Reprinting*, 48 (emphasis McGill). See also Gross, "Building a National Literature."

61  *Beckford v. Hood* (1798). Although opinion in the United States was mixed on the impact of the copyright statute on common law remedial rights. See Ginsburg, "The US Experience with Copyright Formalities," 311.

support of our free institutions."[62] Meredith McGill suggests that "foreign authors' disenfranchisement under American law was not inconsistent but integral to many Americans' understanding of the nature and scope of domestic copyright protection."[63] This American copyright strategy may have been consistent with how the country saw its economic, political, social, and cultural development, but it had a destructive impact on British North America, as later chapters will illustrate.

This brief foray into British and American law and policy underscores the fact that, whatever tensions existed then, and continue to exist in the construction of copyright as it mediates among the interests of authors, publishers, and readers, the law was ultimately an integrated system to further the transmission of knowledge in print form. Authors and publishers were the means of fulfilling a larger legislative intent; they were not the ends in themselves. To interpret copyright law otherwise would be to fundamentally misunderstand its emergence in the United Kingdom and the way in which it was transplanted into North America.

The British and American copyright experiences informed British North American thinking on the law, and it is against this dual backdrop that Canada's early copyright history must be assessed. This comparative perspective deepens our understanding of Canada's own copyright legacy; it also situates that history within a much larger Anglo-American paradigm that emphasized the acquisition of knowledge as essential for human progress. Writing in 1880, Quebec civil law jurist Pierre-Basile Mignault distinguished literary property from other forms of property:

Quelle est la nature de ces droits? Est-ce un droit de propriété ordinaire? Il est évident que non, car le livre n'est qu'un ensemble d'idées et ... les idées, étant une chose toute spirituelle, ne peuvent être regardées comme la propriété de leur auteur ... L'auteur écrit pour ainsi dire avec la collaboration de la société ... Néanmoins, comme l'écrivain n'est pas le seul

---

62   Cited in Khan, *The Democratization of Invention*, 225. The quote is attributed to Senator John Ruggles (1789–1874), and the same sentiment is expressed in early Congressional debates on the first copyright and patent laws. Congressional reports referred to literature and science as "essential to the preservation of a Free Constitution" or advanced the view that "the promotion of science and literature will contribute to the security of a free Government." See "Proceedings in Congress During the Years 1789 and 1790," 255–6.

63   McGill, *American Literature and the Culture of Reprinting*, 82.

créateur de ses œuvres, il n'est que juste, qu'après une récompense rai-
sonnable, il les rende à la société, en reconnaissance des services qu'il en
a reçus.[64]

Mignault argued that because the author drew inspiration from society, the work must be returned to the public after a reasonable term
of exclusivity. Montreal printer and publisher Samuel Dawson, in his
1882 work *Copyright in Books*, argued similarly that "those who enjoy
the fruit of [the author's] labour should pay for the privilege; but I
am arguing against the demand to enclose in perpetuity the common
ground of intellectual life."[65] The "common ground of intellectual life"
demanded that copyright be limited in duration and closely circumscribed in scope. The public interest in education and learning was a
more prominent policy consideration than has generally been allowed,
and, as this book demonstrates, it resonated especially strongly in nineteenth-century British North America. Indeed, the "encouragement of
learning" had a very specific meaning for Lower Canada as it strug-
gled to advance itself economically, culturally, and politically, and it
is significant that the first "Canadian" Copyright Act was introduced
as result of a recommendation of the Assembly's Standing Committee
on Education and Schools. The education portfolio overwhelmed the
Lower Canadian parliamentary agenda in the early part of the nineteenth century, and the relationship between public education, the encouragement of learning, and copyright law can be traced to Lower
Canada's very first attempts to establish a legislative framework for the
printing and publishing of books in the province. These efforts, which
arose between 1824 and 1827, are the subject of the next chapter.

---

64  Mignault, "La propriété littéraire," 292. [What is the nature of these rights? Are they
    ordinary property rights? It is obviously not the case because a book is only a col-
    lection of ideas and … ideas, being entirely intangible things, cannot be regarded as
    the author's property … In effect, the author writes with the collaboration of society
    … However, because the author is not the sole creator of the works, it is only right
    that, after reasonable compensation, the work is handed over to society, in recogni-
    tion of the services rendered to the author.].
65  Dawson, *Copyright in Books*, 35. Dawson also argued that there was nothing sacred
    about literary property. On Mignault's and Dawson's views on copyright, see also
    Moyse, "Canadian Colonial Copyright."

# Chapter Three

# Dr François Blanchet and the Quest for Copyright in Lower Canada, 1824–1827

On 9 February 1824, a Bill for the Encouragement of Learning by securing the Copies of Maps, Charts and Books, to the Authors and Proprietors of such Copies during the Times therein mentioned was introduced into the Assembly of Lower Canada by François Blanchet, the member from Hertford, Quebec.[1] Although we will see that petitions were the ultimate catalysts for the enactment of the Lower Canadian copyright statute in 1832, this initial attempt to secure copyright in the province was not prompted by an individual request. Blanchet appears to have initiated this first copyright bill of his own accord.

The Journal of the Assembly for the legislative session 1823–4 records that the Bill passed first reading, but it never proceeded beyond that initial stage due to the adjournment of the legislature. Revived and given second reading, it was referred to a Committee of the Whole House, where it once again died.[2] It was once again revived by a motion that passed by a vote of seventeen to six, and there it sat.[3] Parliament was prorogued on 9 March of that year, and the Bill fell with it. No further evidence has survived regarding this failed first attempt at enacting a copyright law. During this period, the practice of parliamentary reporting was rudimentary at best. Absent a system of official record-keeping, public awareness of the legislature's activities depended upon the goodwill and commitment of the few newspaper reporters with

---

1  Indexed under Private and Public Bills. French title: *Bill pour encourager les sciences en assurant les copies des cartes, plans et livres aux auteurs et propriétaires de ces copies, durant le tems y mentionné.* Identified in the margins as: Bill to secure Copy-rights to Authors / *Bill pour assurer le droit de copie aux auteurs,* Journals of the House of Assembly of Lower Canada, 1823–24, 4–5 Geo. 4.

2  Journals of the House of Assembly of Lower Canada, 1823–24, 4–5 Geo. 4, 213, 225.

3  Journals of the House of Assembly of Lower Canada, 1823–24, 4–5 Geo. 4, 249 (20 February 1824).

the time, resources, and inclination to sit through the lengthy daily sessions, or upon those legislators who troubled to pass along their speeches and notes to the press.[4] These newspaper reports were often inconsistent and susceptible to error; generally, they provided only very basic procedural information.[5] Thus, newspaper references to the 1824 Bill reported only its introduction and its progress through the House without providing any substantive details.[6] François Blanchet was among those who sought, unsuccessfully, to introduce systematic, reliable, and independent legislative reporting to Lower Canada.[7]

To compound the gaps in the historical record, few of Blanchet's papers remain, and none make reference to copyright. Moreover, a review of the Journals of the House of Assembly from its inception in 1793 to 1824 indicates that prior to Blanchet's Bill, the Assembly had been involved in only a smattering of files that touched on matters relating to printing and publishing. Among the first tasks of the newly established House of Assembly was to provide for a king's printer to print the official legislative records, as well as an official translator.[8] A few years later, in 1805, the House resolved to set aside funds for the French translation and printing of the four-volume *Precedents of Proceedings in the House of Commons* by John Hatsell, first published in London in 1785.[9] Neither of these legislative issues

---

4  For further discussion on early parliamentary reporting, see Nish, *Debates of the Legislative Assembly of United Canada*, vol. 1; Gallichan, "Les débats parlementaires du Québec."

5  *La Minerve*, 22 February 1827, outlined the difficulties in receiving the legislative debates in time to publish them. In the 5 March 1827 edition, the editor repeated the frustration, this time apologizing for the unavoidable errors made by a young reporter. Similar problems in establishing systematic parliamentary reporting arose in the other British North American provinces.

6  See for example, *Le Canadien*, 18 February 1824, 3; or Ludger Duvernay's *Le Constitutionnel: Gazette Politique et Littéraire*, 24 February 1824, 1.

7  See generally, Gallichan, "Les débats parlementaires," 410. See also Gallichan, *Livre et politique*.

8  *An Act to Provide for the publication of certain Laws and for the Printing and distributing of certain Persons, for the purpose of public information, all Laws that have been or shall be passed in the Legislature of this Province under the present Constitution*, 1793, 33 Geo. 3, c.1.

9  Journals of the House of Assembly of Lower Canada, 1805, 45 Geo. 3, 470 (Hatsell's 1796 edition to be translated and 200 copies printed "provided that the expenses of translating and printing … do not exceed the sum of Seven Hundred Pounds Current Money of this Province"). The Assembly authorized the disbursement in 1806 (Journals of the House of Assembly of Lower Canada, 1806, 46 Geo. 3, 268). The Assembly was divided on the question of whether to support French translations on principle. A competing motion regarding the translation of Hatsell to the effect that "[t]his House ought not to encourage the study of any language by translation of English books, in preference to the Language of the Empire" (at 270), was defeated by a vote of eight to five. Issues surrounding the availability of books in the French language will be discussed in later chapters.

sparked discussions on copyright law in the Assembly. Nor did Joseph Bouchette's numerous petitions in respect of the publication of his maps and statistical tables, which began flowing to the legislature in 1814 and continued to do so with regularity well into the 1830s. It will be recalled from chapter 1 that Bouchette had appealed to the legislature for financial relief for his printing debts. The absence of a more extensive official record to explain why the Lower Canadian legislature first put copyright on its agenda in 1824 is unfortunate. However, insights into the Assembly's actions can be gleaned by exploring François Blanchet's life and career and the sociopolitical context of early nineteenth-century Lower Canada.

### François Blanchet and the Lower Canadian Enlightenment

The circulation of books and other print materials in Lower Canada brought with it the diffusion of progressive and democratic ideas. The works of the major figures of the French Enlightenment – Montesquieu, Voltaire, Rousseau – had already been circulating in New France during the French regime; British rule now brought with it exposure to the works of leading British, Scottish, and American thinkers.[10] Imported books in French and English on a multitude of subjects were available for sale in the bookshops of Montreal and Quebec, including John Neilson's shop at 3 Mountain Street (*Côte de la Montagne*).[11] In addition, news and social commentary from abroad were routinely reported in the various newspapers that began to proliferate in both French and English; these became the primary vehicles for political and social debate.[12] This period also saw the establishment of reading rooms, circulating libraries, and specialty libraries in the major Lower Canadian centres.[13] The library of the House of Assembly, founded in 1801, was well-stocked with a variety of legal materials originating primarily, but not exclusively, in the other British North American provinces, the United Kingdom, France, and the United States. Its collection extended to works of philosophy, economics, and political theory.[14]

---

10   See Trudel, *L'influence de Voltaire au Canada*; Lemire, *La vie littéraire au Québec*; Yvan Lamonde, *Histoire sociale*.

11   See, generally, Alston, "Canada's First Booksellers' Catalogue"; Gallichan, *Livre et politique*; Rotundo, "Les catalogues et leur contribution"; Monette, "L'offre de titres littéraires"; and Wallot, "Frontière ou fragment du système Atlantique."

12   See Eamon, *Imprinting Britain*; Laurence, "The Newspaper Press in Quebec and Lower Canada."

13   Gallichan, *Livre et politique*; Ducharme, "L'offre de titres littéraires"; Lamonde, and Rotundo, "The Book Trade and Bookstores"; Gallichan, "Parliamentary and Professional Libraries."

14   For example, in 1810–11 the House of Assembly ordered copies of the Journals of the House of Commons of Great Britain, its Parliamentary Debates, and Statutes at

The early nineteenth century also saw the emergence of a professional class of doctors, lawyers, and notaries, especially among the *Canadiens*. These individuals were well-read and had been exposed to the influx of social and political ideas emanating from Great Britain, Europe, and the United States. These people were increasingly attracted to political life and sought elected office to advance their progressive beliefs.[15] In Parliament, they rallied under the banner of the Parti Canadien, the political party established in 1806 to represent the interests of *Canadiens* in the legislature. François Blanchet was a leading figure among this group of cosmopolitan politicians, whose world views were informed by the wave of liberal thinking that had spread from Europe to North America.[16] His background and experiences made him exceptionally well-suited to advance progressive ideas in his public and professional capacities.

Born in 1776 into a comfortable farming family in Saint-Pierre-de-la-Rivière-du-Sud, Blanchet studied at the Petit Séminaire de Québec from 1790 to 1794. In 1795, he began medical studies under the tutelage of influential Quebec physician Dr James Fisher, who taught him English and encouraged him to further his medical education at Columbia College in New York.[17] Blanchet attended medical school from 1799 to

---

Large and Private Acts passed since 1800, as well as the Laws of the United States and the Journals of the Assemblies of the other British North American provinces and those of the British colonies of Jamaica and Barbados. It also purchased John Locke's *On Government*, a French translation of Jeremy Bentham's *Principles of Legislation*, *Oeuvres* of Dumoulin, and David Hume's *Essay on Taxation*. Journals of the House of Assembly of Lower Canada, 1810–11, 15 Geo. 3, 566–9. Blanchet served on one of the first committees tasked with recommending books for the Assembly Library.

15  See Lamonde, *Histoire sociale*; Jolois, *Joseph- François Perrault.*

16  On Blanchet (1776–1830), see Castonguay and Limoges, *François Blanchet*; and Bernier, "François Blanchet et le mouvement reformiste." See as well the entry for Blanchet in DCB.

17  Blanchet's proficiency in English included writing scholarly papers in that language. As Blanchet wrote to Benjamin Smith Barton (1766–1815) on 25 November 1800: "Je crois que j'aurai un mémoire sur l'aurore boréale pour votre volume de transactions philosophiques. Je crois que je pourrai l'écrire en anglois, car j'ai découvert ces jours passés que je puis écrire l'anglois." [I think that I will have a memorial on the aurora borealis for your volume of philosophical transactions. I think I could write it in English because I have, these last days, discovered that I can write in English.] Blanchet was presumably referring to the *Transactions of the American Philosophical Society*. Benjamin Smith Barton Papers, American Philosophical Society, Section 1: Correspondence. Barton, a physician and botanist, was a member of the American Philosophical Society and became its Vice-President in 1802.

1801 and during that time involved himself in American intellectual life. From New York, he ordered scientific books and international newspapers through the intermediary of John Neilson, with whom he corresponded regularly and with whom he would later serve in the Lower Canadian House of Assembly.[18]

Blanchet's studies led him to the works of John Locke, whom he described as a man of rare sagacity and genius.[19] Blanchet was also introduced to the writings of the leading scientists of the Scottish Enlightenment, likely through his professors, especially Dr Samuel Latham Mitchill, who played an instrumental role in steering Blanchet's early career.[20] In January 1801, Blanchet was elected a member of the august American Philosophical Society Held at Philadelphia for Promoting Useful Knowledge (APS).[21] Established in 1768, its first president was Benjamin Franklin. At the time of Blanchet's election, it was led by Thomas Jefferson, then Vice President of the United States. Blanchet was also elected a member of the Society Instituted in the State of New York for the Promotion of Agriculture, Arts and Manufactures, which was founded in 1791 by Dr Mitchell, among others.[22] These affiliations mattered. Blanchet announced his APS membership in John Neilson's *Quebec Gazette* in 1801.[23] In his petition for a licence to practise medicine in Lower Canada in 1801, he identified himself as "Francis Blanchet MD Member of the Philosophical Society of Philadelphia and of the Agricultural Society of the State of New York."[24] Blanchet would

18   LAC, Neilson Collection. See as well Castonguay, and Limoges, *François Blanchet*, 50.

19   Blanchet, *Discours préliminaire*, reproduced in Castonguay and Limoges, *François Blanchet*, 114. On Locke's influence on Lower Canadian political life, see Ajzenstat, *The Canadian Founding*.

20   According to Castonguay and Limoges, *François Blanchet*, most of the faculty at Columbia had studied medicine at the University of Edinburgh at the height of the Scottish Enlightenment. This included Dr Samuel Latham Mitchill (1764–1831), who was a politician as well as a doctor and lawyer.

21   The minutes of the meeting of the society held on 16 January 1801 record Blanchet's election. See Castonguay and Limoges, *François Blanchet*. See also the entry "Francis Blanchet of Quebec" in the *Transactions of the American Philosophical Society* for 1802 as a foreign member (1802), vol. 5, xiii.

22   Founded in New York City, the society moved to Albany in 1797. In 1804 it became the Society for the Promotion of Useful Arts. See Hobbins, "Shaping a Provincial Learned Society."

23   See Castonguay, and Limoges, *François Blanchet*, 52.

24   Petition to Governor Robert Shore Milnes, 22 June 1801. LAC, Civil Secretary and Provincial Secretary, Application for Licenses, Bonds & Certificates 1763–1867, Quebec, Lower Canada and Canada East, reel H-1733, vol. 47, 153.

later become a member of the Quebec Agricultural Society in 1818 and a member of the Société pour l'encouragement des arts et sciences established in 1827.[25]

Under Mitchell's mentorship, the young Blanchet was encouraged to write scientific articles for publication in scholarly journals – in other words, to contribute to the advancement of "useful knowledge.'"[26] His most significant scholarly achievement was his book titled *Recherche sur la médecine, ou l'application de la chimie à la médecine*, the first scientific treatise by a Lower Canadian–born author.[27] He wrote the book while at Columbia College, and it was printed and published in 1800 by Imprimerie Parisot, a New York–based French publishing house.[28] The introductory essay, *Discours préliminaire*, provides a glimpse into Blanchet's sociopolitical orientation. His views were liberal and secular, consistent with the prevailing intellectual culture among the young and rising professional class in Lower Canada and deeply influenced by the spread of Enlightenment thinking in North America.[29] Blanchet had considerable ambitions for this work, which he intended principally for the European market although he had also made arrangements, through John Neilson, to sell the book by subscription in Lower

---

25  Joseph Bouchette was the first president. The *société* merged with the Literary and Historical Society of Quebec in 1829. On the history of the early literary societies in Lower Canada, see Bernatchez, "La société littéraire et historique de Québec."

26  Between 1800 and 1801, Blanchet published four papers in *Medical Repository*, which was a scientific journal that Mitchill edited, and at least three more in *American Review and Literary Journal*. For a bibliography of Blanchet's scientific and other writings see Castonguay and Limoges, *François Blanchet*.

27  François Blanchet, *Recherche sur la médecine*. Blanchet dedicated the work to Dr James Fisher.

28  Not much is known about Claude Parisot (or Parizotte) and his New York printing enterprise. McKay, in *A Register*, shows him carrying on business at various addresses from 1793 to 1802.

29  According to Castonguay and Limoges, "le texte de Blanchet, son 'Discours préliminaire' notamment, doit être reconnu comme l'une des expressions les plus nettes de la pénétration de la pensée des Lumières en Amérique, aux États-Unis comme au Bas-Canada." [Blanchet's text, especially his *Discours préliminaire*, must be recognized as one of the clearest expressions of the penetration of Enlightenment thinking in North America – in the United States and in Lower Canada.] Castonguay, and Limoges, *François Blanchet*, 11. In this prefatory text, Blanchet sets out the philosophical framework for his scientific theories, citing with admiration Locke's *Essay Concerning Human Understanding* and the work of leading figures of the Scottish Enlightenment.

Canada.[30] While there is no evidence that Blanchet ever considered securing his copyright in the United States, he would have been ineligible in any case because the law only protected authors who were citizens or permanent residents. The copyright records for 1800 do not reveal a registration by Blanchet or Imprimerie Parisot.[31]

By the time Blanchet returned to Quebec City, in the summer of 1801, he was a published author, a scientist, and a member of an active network of learned individuals advancing the liberal ideas of the day – ideas that would animate Blanchet's actions throughout his political career. Not surprisingly, given his early exposure to American liberalism, Blanchet was one of the first to vigorously argue against replicating the class structures and hierarchies of old Europe in Lower Canada.[32] He played a key role in advancing what cultural historian Yvan Lamonde refers to as "l'américanité du Québec," that is, the shared values and sensibilities that ran throughout the eastern half of North America during this period.[33] As Blanchet's biographers, Claude Castonguay and Camille Limoges, have noted: "les travaux de Blanchet au cours de ces années 1799–1801 témoignent éloquemment de la circulation des discours savants – et des personnes – dans un réseau en voie de constitution qui embrasse le nord-est des États-Unis et le Bas-Canada."[34]

In 1806 Blanchet co-founded the nationalist newspaper *Le Canadien*, the prospectus for which was an impassioned plea for freedom of the press.[35] The paper advocated for greater self-determination for

---

30   The list of subscribers can be found in LAC, Neilson Collection. In Blanchet's letters to Neilson he expressed the hope that the new ideas contained in his book would be well-received by the European scientific community. Unfortunately, according to Castonguay and Limoges, Blanchet's treatise did not receive the accolades for which he had hoped. Blanchet also asked Benjamin Smith Barton for comments on his book. See letter François Blanchet to Barton, 25 November 1800, Benjamin Smith Barton Papers, APS: "J'espère que vous m'avez fait l'honneur de lire mon petit ouvrage avec attention et j'attends beaucoup d'un juge aussi éclairé et aussi impartial que vous. " [I hope that you have done me the honour of reading attentively my small work and I expect a lot from such an enlightened and impartial judge such as yourself.]. Barton's reply is not in the archives.

31   Wills and Galbreath, *Federal Copyright Records*.

32   See François Blanchet's 1824 polemic, *Appel au Parlement impérial*.

33   See Yvan Lamonde, *Allégeances et dépendances*; and Bouchard and Lamonde, *Québécois et Américains*.

34   Castonguay, and Limoges, *François Blanchet*, 105. [Blanchet's works in the years 1799–1801 eloquently attest to the circulation of scholarly lectures – and individuals – through a developing network that encompassed the northeastern United States and Lower Canada.]

35   The prospectus is reproduced in Lamonde, and Corbo, *Le rouge et le bleu*.

*Canadiens* (its motto was "nos institutions, notre langue, nos droits") and was critical of the British administration. In 1810, the Governor of Lower Canada moved against its founders and Blanchet was briefly imprisoned for sedition. After his release, he divested himself of ownership of the paper and turned his full attention to effecting his reforms through the legislature. He was first elected to the House of Assembly in 1810, and served there, with one interruption, until his death in 1830.[36] During his tenure, Blanchet would be one of the driving forces behind a number of democratizing initiatives. His belief in the power of print and its role in political reform included attempts to have the activities of the House of Assembly open to public scrutiny. In 1819, he questioned the legislature's printing costs and the lack of transparency in the bidding process for securing printing contracts.[37] In 1823, he sought without success to provide newspaper reporters with open access to the proceedings and bills of the House. In 1825, he suggested, again unsuccessfully, that a committee be formed to study the best way to publicize the deliberations of the House of Assembly.[38]

Blanchet's agitations for political reforms were matched by his commitment to the encouragement of learning and the diffusion of knowledge. Almost immediately upon setting up his medical practice in Quebec City, he began to offer chemistry classes from his home.[39] He devoted himself throughout his life to the furtherance of the medical profession and especially to medical education.[40] However, his dedication to the advancement of knowledge extended beyond his chosen profession. As a member of the Assembly, he chaired a committee to look at the bequest of James McGill to establish McGill College,[41] and he promoted the founding of a museum of natural history.[42] He served on numerous committees reviewing petitions for funding from literary and scientific associations, including the Literary and Historical Society of Quebec. However, the

---

36   Blanchet lost his seat in 1816 but regained it in 1818.

37   Gallichan, *Livre et politique*.

38   Gallichan, *Livre et politique*.

39   See Castonguay, and Limoges, *François Blanchet*. See also Leblond, "Pioneers of Medical Teaching."

40   Blanchet taught science and medicine at the Quebec Medical Dispensary and later at the Emigrant Hospital of Quebec. During his tenure in the House of Assembly, he was instrumental in the establishment of the first hospitals and the provision of basic health care, including setting up a Vaccine Board. On Blanchet's medical career, see Abbott, *History of Medecine*. See also Tunis, "Medical Education and Medical Licensing."

41   See Journals of the House of Assembly of Lower Canada, 1816, 56 Geo. 3.

42   See Gagnon, "Pierre Chasseur."

legacy for which he is most remembered was his commitment to bringing public elementary education to Lower Canada: "Mais c'est surtout par ses efforts pour l'éducation de la jeunesse canadienne qu'il s'est élevé un trophée que couvriront de fleurs toutes les générations à venir."[43]

François Blanchet was a learned man, and all his life he sought to foster learning throughout the province. His championing of copyright was part and parcel of this same commitment to the advancement of knowledge, and his actions can be situated within a broader set of policy goals fundamental to a developing society like Lower Canada. First, the timing of Blanchet's Bill is consistent with the view at the time that copyright and patent laws were closely connected as policy instruments for the diffusion of useful knowledge. His second and more fundamental legislative preoccupation was the inadequacy of the public education system and the dearth of schoolbooks to support it.

## The Publisher and the Scientist: The Genesis of Patent and Copyright Laws in Lower Canada

Blanchet's copyright Bill was introduced just days after Lower Canada's first Patent Act was passed by both legislative houses.[44] Spearheaded by John Neilson, the patent statute was a close copy of the US Patent Act of 1793.[45] It is curious that Blanchet was not involved in the patent file. As a scientist, he would certainly have been knowledgeable about patent laws. The APS, of which he was a member, functioned as a patent office, and its scholarly journal frequently contained material relating to patents.[46] Furthermore, as a member of the Assembly, Blanchet sat on a number of committees reviewing petitions from Lower Canadian inventors seeking exclusive rights over their new discoveries.[47]

---

43   Remarks of Dr François-Xavier Tessier (1799–1835) at a meeting of the Société de Médecine de Québec in memory of Blanchet not long after his death in 1830. François-Xavier Tessier, "A la mémoire du docteur François Blanchet " *L'Observateur* 25, no. 1 (1830): 393. [But it is above all through these efforts for the education of Canadian youth that a memorial has been built which all the generations to come will cover with flowers.]

44   *An Act to Promote the Progress of Useful Arts in this Province*, 1824, 4 Geo. 4, c. 25 (in force 9 March 1824). The legislation was passed by both houses on 2 February 1824. Blanchet introduced the copyright bill on 9 February 1824.

45   *Patent Act of 1793*, Ch. 11, 1 Stat. 318–323 (21 February 1793).

46   See, for example, *Transactions of the American Philosophical Society*, vols. 4–6 (1799–1809).

47   Petitions of E.N. Lambert Dumont (1815), Jean Baptiste Perrault (1819), and Timothy Hebbard (1819).

Instead, it was a printer, publisher, and bookseller who brought the patent legislation forward. Neilson's initiative on patents is not as incongruous as might appear on the surface, however. Among his many attributes, Neilson was an inventor of new agricultural products and processes.[48] This would explain his interest in supporting this type of legislation. However, it does seem surprising that Neilson played no part in copyright law or policy at this stage, given his central role in the Lower Canadian book trade and the fact that he was to figure prominently in the enactment of the 1832 Copyright Act.

It may well be that John Neilson had exerted some influence over Blanchet's actions. We know that the two men were friends of long standing from the time of Blanchet's student days in New York. Historian Jacques Bernier referred to Neilson as Blanchet's mentor.[49] The two men had also, by this time, served together in the Assembly for roughly six years. It appears more likely, however, that Blanchet was the prime mover. As already mentioned, there is no evidence that Neilson took any special interest in copyright law despite his being, by profession, someone who would be directly affected by this type of legislation.[50] Nor is there any suggestion that he was concerned about any unscrupulous printing and publishing practices by his Lower Canadian competitors. As a member of the Assembly during the first copyright period, between 1824 and 1831, Neilson was not involved in any actions related to copyright. It was only after Blanchet's death that he took stewardship of the Education Committee, which then recommended the introduction of the 1832 Act.

Regardless of who led the initiative, the fact that this first copyright Bill was dealt with in the same legislative session as the first patent Bill was not a coincidence. Today, we consider patents and copyright as separate and distinct forms of intellectual property, but these two bodies of law were more closely connected at their inception. Both patents and copyright were intended to encourage the tangible manifestations of intellectual effort, be it in the form of machines or books. The early nineteenth century was a period of flux in terms of how best to classify and organize the legal regimes we now know as copyright law and patent law. In Britain, a number of suggestions were put forward

---

48   See Neilson entry in DCB. See also Hagerman, "John Neilson."

49   Bernier, "François Blanchet et le mouvement réformiste."

50   The Neilson archives at LAC (Neilson Collection) contain only one written reference to copyright prior to 1824, this being a letter from Andrew Stuart to Neilson advising of his desire to reserve his copyright in a pamphlet that was to be printed in the United States. LAC, Neilson Collection, vol. 4, 62.

to conceptualize both bodies of law within one organizing principle.[51] In line with this, it was not unusual for individuals to use the terms patents and copyright interchangeably and to ask for copyright in inventions or patents for books.[52] Only later in the century would these legislative schemes become more distinct. This nexus between patent and copyright was more than just a conceptual abstraction. We tend to forget that nineteenth-century societies placed great store in the circulation of "useful" knowledge. It was through the medium of print that new ideas and information were communicated to the reading public. In an address to officially open the Pictou Academy in 1816, Nova Scotian author and educator Thomas McCulloch explained: "In tracing the progress of education, the effects resulting from the invention of letters and the art of printing ought not to be overlooked. By these means, the information of past ages is transmitted to the present and every additional discovery and invention communicated with ease to the various sections of civilized society."[53]

Nowhere is the interplay between patents and copyright more apparent than in the American context. As we have seen, the constitutional power given to Congress over intellectual property referred to "science" (or knowledge) and "useful arts" (or patents) in a single clause. Initially, acting on a number of petitions from inventors and authors, Congress introduced one Bill to address both forms of legal protection.[54] In other words, the earliest text combined legal protections for copyright and patent in one statute. However, delays and postponements greatly increased the urgency in attending to the copyright file as "several gentlemen had lately published the fruits of their industry and application, and were every hour in danger of having them surreptitiously printed."[55] Since the patent file was proving more problematic, the two were severed. As it turned out, the US Congress passed the Patent Act

---

51   According to Brad Sherman, one option under consideration was "to do away with a copyright-patents-designs style approach and to divide productions into 'two great classifications – works (whatever their intention) addressed to the tastes, passions, and existing circumstances of the age, and those adapted to all the fluctuations of society." Sherman, "Remembering and Forgetting," 4.

52   A number of North American authors requested patents for their writings, including, in British North America, Joseph-François Perrault, Joseph Lancaster, and William Phillips. These petitions will be explored further in subsequent chapters.

53   As cited in Parker, *The Beginnings of the Book Trade*, 25.

54   A Bill to Promote the Progress of Science and Useful Arts, by securing to Authors and Inventors the Exclusive Right to their Respective Writings and Discoveries. See "Proceedings in Congress during the Years 1798 and 1790."

55   "Proceedings in Congress during the Years 1789 and 1790," 258.

first (7 April 1790), but it was soon followed by the Copyright Act 1790 (31 May 1790). A similar pattern arose in Lower Canada as legislative considerations of patent and copyright occurred in tandem.

The First Patent Act: *An Act to Promote the Progress of Useful Arts in This Province*, 4 Geo. 4, c. 25 (1824)

To better understand Blanchet's copyright initiative, it is instructive to examine the circumstances surrounding the introduction of the first Patent Act in Lower Canada.[56] Industrialist and politician George Waters Allsopp first proposed the establishment of a patent office to John Neilson in 1821.[57] No action having been taken, he followed up two years later, urging Neilson to introduce a patent law for the province. He argued that the current system of individual petitions to the Assembly was burdensome, time-consuming, and so uncertain as to discourage inventors from pursuing their ideas and discoveries:

> I would be happy to learn of you if you have thought further of what I proposed ... two years past respection [*sic*] the introduction of a Law to establish an office for registering Patents for improvements and discoveries whether it be machining or even simple discoveries and advantageous to agriculture, mechanics, navigation, medicine ... in order to give encouragement to the Inventors with out [*sic*] the tedious process of occupying the Legislature – and such as is established both in England and the United States ... I do not mean turnpikes or bridges which are a kind of Taxation but what every man may claim for useful inventions – Should the invention not reap the benefit he may expect in that case the individual only would be the sufferer as its usefulness only would stamp its value. I do not think such a measure would meet with opposition and might be easily carried thro' at the same Time it would encourage those who are deterred from carrying forward with their discoveries from the apprehension of the difficulties attending Enactments.[58]

---

56  For a more complete exploration of early Canadian patent law, see Asher, "The Development of the Patent System."

57  See entry for Allsopp (1769–1837) in DCB. Allsopp was a member of the Assembly from 1814 to 1820, during which time he sat on a number of Special Committees reviewing petitions for exclusive rights over inventions, including the petition of E.N. Lambert Dumont (1815), on whose committee he served with Blanchet.

58  Letter from Allsop to Neilson, 10 November 1823, LAC, Neilson Collection, reel C-15769, no. 317–318 (1822–24).

Allsopp's comments offer insights from which to draw similar conclusions about the motivations behind the introduction of copyright law. First, he argued that it was time to pass a law of general application given the growing number of petitions cluttering the legislative agenda. However, the Assembly's burdened docket was only part of the problem. Of greater concern was that the cumbersome process deterred inventors from "carrying forward their discoveries," thereby ensuring that only those inventors with the patience and fortitude to withstand the vagaries of the legislative process would bring their inventions to market. This left numerous useful innovations to wallow unprotected in obscurity. Indeed, prior to the 1823–4 session, ten petitions were made to the Assembly for exclusive rights over new or improved products or processes ranging from bridges to chimney brushes to kitchen stoves. Only two of these were successful, and even then, in the case of Jean-Baptiste Bédard, it took two successive parliamentary sessions to complete the process. His petition, to build a bridge based on his invention, was introduced on 29 March 1806, but it wasn't until 16 April 1807 that he was granted fourteen years of exclusivity.[59] Two other petitions were denied. The majority of them – six in total – had not been fully resolved by the end of the legislative session. A more efficient and expeditious process was needed, one that would not only alleviate the burden on the legislature but also provide certainty and expediency to inventors seeking to put their inventions to good use.

During the 1823–4 parliamentary session, presumably with Allsopp's urgings in mind, John Neilson introduced two petitions to the Assembly – that of Charles Laurier, and that of Noah Cushing and William Thurber. Provincial surveyor Laurier was petitioning for an exclusive privilege to build and use his invention – a Terrestrial Log/*Loch Terrestre* designed to measure distances and roads.[60] The Cushing and Thurber petition requested exclusive rights over the inventions of a churn and a fulling and washing machine.[61] Neilson was appointed to chair the special committee to which the petitions were referred; that committee was

---

59  *Act to grant to Jean Baptiste Bedard the exclusive Right and Privilege of erecting Bridges in this Province, according to the models therein mentioned*, 1807, 47 Geo. 3, c. 15. The Act gave Bédard rights for fourteen years although he had requested twenty-five. John Bragg, who also invented a particular method of constructing bridges, was the other successful petitioner. He was also given rights for fourteen years.

60  Journals of the House of Assembly of Lower Canada, 1823, 4 Geo. 4, p. 33. For Charles Laurier's patent, see also LAC, Wilfrid Laurier Fonds, Family Papers, vol. 1027. Laurier was the grandfather of Sir Wilfrid Laurier, Canada's seventh prime minister.

61  Journals of the House of Assembly of Lower Canada, 1823, 4 Geo. 4, 36.

given additional instructions by the Assembly to inquire "if it is expedient to provide by Legislative Enactments for promoting the progress of useful Arts in this Province and the enregistering of Patents of useful Inventions."[62] The province's Patent Act became law on 9 March 1824.

Enacting a patent law was not just about addressing the interests of inventors. The stakes were important for the province as well. Colonial governments were constrained in their ability to raise funds to support their various activities. Laws that would place the risk in the hands of individual enterprise and private industry were to be preferred, for then the government would not have to subsidize individual projects that later failed or proved costly. Similar concerns prevailed on the issue of copyright. One need only think back to the Assembly's censure of Joseph Bouchette's extravagant expenditures to understand why Lower Canadian politicians would have preferred not to involve the public purse in the business of providing financial support for speculative publishing undertakings. With limited resources available to them, they were sensitive to the need to wean petitioners off government aid.

With this background in mind, it is easy enough to grasp why Blanchet's actions on copyright followed so closely on the heels of the successful Patent Act. As a man of science and a man of letters, Blanchet would have recognized that if the time was right for Lower Canada to promote the progress of useful arts through a patent law, then the time was also right to encourage learning through copyright. However, it is insufficient to describe the genesis of copyright law exclusively in terms of the emergence of intellectual property laws in the province. More fundamental policy interests drove Blanchet's efforts. Lower Canadian politicians were preoccupied with establishing a system of public education, especially for children in francophone rural areas, and ensuring a ready supply of affordable schoolbooks.

## The Politics of Education in Lower Canada

In its first decade, the Lower Canadian legislature set about building the province's economic, social, and political infrastructures. A key area for social reform revolved around the development of a public education system for the province. There were a number of reasons for this dedicated interest in universal education among liberal-minded Lower Canadian politicians. Belief in the value of education was steeped in the progressive ideals of the day: it was generally agreed that education and learning should no longer be the exclusive preserve of the upper

---

62  Journals of the House of Assembly of Lower Canada, 1823, 4 Geo. 4, 75.

reaches of society.[63] Also, the discourse of the times was permeated by utilitarian sentiments: education should be *useful* in that boys and girls should each be taught the respective skills necessary to better their situation so that they could contribute to the province's industrial progress. Universal education served a fundamental political purpose as well: a literate and informed population would govern itself based on democratic principles. As literary scholar George Parker noted, in British North America "it was an axiom that better education brought social and economic progress, and that schools were absolutely necessary if responsible government were to triumph."[64]

The sociopolitical realities of Lower Canada lent a sense of urgency to this aspect of the educational mission. Education was a profoundly political question for the Assembly and its francophone political leaders. The linguistic, cultural, and religious survival of the *Canadiens* depended on an educated and engaged citizenry, especially given the increasing levels of immigration from the United Kingdom and the United States. As John Neilson related to Alexis de Tocqueville during the latter's tour of North America: "Il y a quatre ans notre Chambre des communes aperçut clairement que si la population canadienne ne s'éclairait pas, elle finirait par se trouver entièrement absorbée par une population étrangère qui s'élevait à côté et au milieu d'elle. On fit des exhortations, on donna des encouragements, on forma des fonds, on nomma enfin des inspecteurs des écoles."[65] Speaker of the Assembly Louis-Joseph Papineau echoed this concern. He worried that the *Canadiens* would be denied opportunities to rise within the ranks of government because of their limited education. Without change, English Lower-Canadians and the imperial authorities would continue to dominate governmental decision-making. Education provided entry into the arenas of political power. As he expressed it:

Si pour d'autres peuples l'éducation est utile … elle est une nécessité pour nous en particulier, elle est une instante nécessité. Nous ne sommes amis

---

63   "[T]he demands of a frontier society contributed to a leveling process that tended to eliminate class distinctions and to create a demand for universal education." Wilson, Stamp, and Audet, *Canadian Education*, 38.

64   Parker, *The Beginnings of the Book Trade*, 116.

65   De Tocqueville, *Regards sur le Bas-Canada*, 174. [It has been four years since our House of Assembly saw clearly that if the *Canadiens* did not educate themselves, they would become completely absorbed by a foreign population that was growing alongside and among them. We offered exhortations, gave incentives, established funds, named school inspectors.]. See also Curtis, "Tocqueville and Lower Canadian Educational Networks."

de la liberté et des droits de notre pays, nous ne sommes capables de les conserver, qu'à proportion que nous serons amis de l'instruction, et attentifs à la faire parvenir dans toutes les classes de la société. Nous recevons journellement une émigration nombreuse des deux pays où l'on a fait le plus pour l'éducation du people, la Grande Bretagne et les États-Unis d'Amérique. Les trois quarts et plus de nos administrateurs viennent de ces pays; leurs prédilections et leurs préférences seraient toujours actives contre les nôtres, s'ils pouvaient prétexter avec quelque plausibilité, qu'ils ne trouvent personne parmi ses habitans [*sic*], dignes de partager avec eux les soins du gouvernement.[66]

In 1801, the year Blanchet returned to Lower Canada from New York, Lower Canada's first Education Act was passed. *An Act for the Establishment of Free Schools and the Advancement of Learning in this Province* provided for the centralization of authority in the hands of the Royal Institution for the Advancement of Learning (the "Royal Institution"), which would oversee the establishment and maintenance of schools throughout the province.[67] The legislation proved to be ineffectual for a number of reasons, most notably because of the suspicion among the francophone population that it was intended to advance English Protestantism within the province, although the Royal Institution had established both Catholic and Protestant schools.[68] Empowering the francophone population to engage more fully in public life and in their own governance required an education system that was responsive to their particular linguistic, religious, and cultural needs. In 1814, a

---

66   As cited in Lamonde, and Claude Larin, *Louis-Joseph Papineau*, 189. An address delivered on 5 May 1831. [If for other peoples education is useful ... it is a necessity for us in particular, it is an immediate necessity. We can only be friends of freedom and rights in our country to the extent that we are friends of education and attentive to the need to make it accessible to every class of society. On a daily basis, we receive numerous emigrants from two countries that have done the most to educate their people, Great Britain and the United States of America. Over three quarters of our administrators come from those countries; their predilections and preferences will always prevail if they could argue, with some plausibility, that they cannot find anyone among the local population worthy enough to share the work of government.].

67   *An Act for the Establishment of Free Schools and the Advancement of Learning in this Province*, 1801, 41 Geo. 3, c. 17.

68   On the schools established by the Royal Institution. see Curtis, *Ruling by Schooling*; and Kominek, "The Royal Institution." Kominek argues that even if the legislation was benign, the administration of the schools was controlled by Protestant groups with proselytizing missions.

resolution of the House declared that the 1801 Education Act was "insufficient for attaining to the instruction of youth, in what relates to the Country Parishes."[69] A year later, an Assembly committee was established to inquire into the state of education. Chaired by François Blanchet, that committee recommended the province-wide adoption of Joseph Lancaster's system of monitorial schooling as a "method of extending elementary education which is not attended by much expense."[70]

Blanchet belonged to a network of social reformers that included John Neilson and education activist Joseph-François Perrault. They, like many of their contemporaries, were admirers of the system of monitorial or mutual instruction developed by the British pedagogue Joseph Lancaster, who developed his pioneering method while working with poor children in London. It relied on using older students as "monitors" to instruct younger children in the rudiments of reading, writing, and arithmetic. This system offered a cost-effective way to educate children and train new teachers and had broad appeal in the developing societies of North America as a means of providing affordable mass education.

In 1808, Neilson's *Quebec Gazette* published a summary of Lancaster's method.[71] Two years later, this same paper reported on the success of Lancaster's system in New York with the comment that it "would be well worth the attention of some intelligent person of fair character, to make a similar attempt in this province."[72] Somewhere around 1813 or 1814, the first Lancasterian schools opened in Montreal and Quebec City.[73] Neilson, Blanchet, and Perrault were involved in the direction and financing of the school at Quebec City,

---

69   Journals of the House of Assembly of Lower Canada, 1814, 54 Geo. 3, 50.

70   See report of the Committee to Enquire into the State and Progress of Education as resulting from the Act of the 41st Geo. III Chapter 17, which provides for the establishment of Free Schools and the advancement of Learning in this Province, Journals of the House of Assembly of Lower Canada, 1815, 55 Geo. 3, 610.

71   See Jolois, *Joseph-François Perrault*, 100.

72   Spragge, "Monitorial Schools," 38.

73   The Quebec Free School was established by Rev. Thaddeus Osgood under the auspices of the British and Foreign School Society (BFSS), which was the principal vehicle for the promotion of Lancasterian schools throughout the UK and beyond. It closed three years later for want of funds. There is some indication that James Edwards was the first to open a Lancasterian School in Montreal as early as 1813, also with support from the BFSS. See "Proceedings of the Royal Lancasterian Institution for 1812," 681.

which failed a few years later due to lack of funding.[74] In 1822 and 1823, two new Lancasterian Schools were established, in Montreal and Quebec, through the agency of the British and Canadian School Society (BCSS). Joseph-François Perrault was the president of the Quebec BCSS and played an instrumental role in the establishment of monitorial schools in that city; that included founding his own boys' and girls' French-language schools, which employed a modified form of Lancasterian teaching of his own devising.[75] Lancaster's system was never officially adopted by the province, but it remained popular among education reformers like Blanchet, Neilson, and Perrault. This meant that when Joseph Lancaster came to live in Montreal in 1829, he easily became part of this closely connected network. As later chapters will show, these same individuals, with Lancaster at the forefront, would play pivotal roles in bringing copyright law to Lower Canada. For that seminal copyright moment to occur, however, more groundwork on public education would be necessary. The same year that Lancaster arrived in the province, the legislature enacted the 1829 Trustees School Act. This statute marked a turning point in Lower Canadian education history.[76] This piece of legislation was the first successful attempt to establish a publicly supported and managed system of elementary education. It did not, however, correct a related and equally pressing problem, namely the dearth of affordable schoolbooks to support the province's educational mission.

**Education and Schoolbooks in Lower Canada in the First Half of the Nineteenth Century**

The shortage of schoolbooks was an ongoing concern for Lower Canadian education advocates. Unlike the elite private institutions based

---

74  Neilson and Blanchet were members of the Committee of Subscribers to Osgood's Quebec Free School (Neilson was the president). According to Jolois, *Joseph-François Perrault*, Perrault had been elected to the executive committee of the Quebec Free School, but declined to serve, promising his financial and personal support instead. According to Bruce Curtis, "Perrault was partly responsible for John Neilson's enthusiasm for monitorial schooling and Neilson occupied an important position in colonial educational networks before he broke definitively with the patriote party in 1834." "Tocqueville," 120.

75  See Jolois, *Joseph-François Perrault*.

76  *An Act for the Encouragement of Elementary Education*, 1829, 9 Geo. 4, c. 46. The legislation provided for boards of elected trustees with the power to establish schools and hire teachers in communities throughout the province.

largely in urban areas, schools for poorer children, whether in the cities or the countryside, were vastly under-supplied. French-language schoolbooks were especially scarce. Even Lancasterian monitorial schools, which used lesson cards or single large sheets to teach basic reading, writing, and arithmetic, could not do without schoolbooks entirely. As Paul Aubin observed, the fact that Joseph-François Perrault wrote "coup sur coup trois abécédaries en 1830 démontrant ainsi que, tout utiles qu'ils soient, ces outils [cartes sur les murs] ne sauraient être que des apports au livre."[77]

The vast majority of schoolbooks circulating in Lower Canada were British, American, and French books, some imported and others reprinted locally.[78] However, imported books were expensive and the vagaries of cross-Atlantic transportation and the inauspicious climate that prevented year-round shipments inhibited their circulation throughout British North America. Import duties on books from France and the United States were especially high, but even the reduced duty on British imports placed a significant financial burden on importers and booksellers.[79] In her study of colonial book prices using Scotland as her basis of comparison, book historian Fiona Black concluded that on the whole, British North Americans paid 25 per cent more for books than their Scottish counterparts, although there were some exceptions where book prices were either the same or less.[80] Nineteenth-century Montreal bookseller Édouard-Raymond Fabre estimated that books imported from France cost twice as much in Lower Canada than they did in their country of origin.

> Les droits d'entrée dans la colonie équivalent à cinquante pour cent de la valeur du prix d'achat; de plus, il faut compter vingt pour cent pour les frais de transport, vingt-cinq pour cent pour faire passer l'argent en France. À ces divers coûts, s'ajoutent les frais d'assurance évalués à quinze

---

77   P. Aubin, *300 ans de manuels scolaires au Québec*, 46. [The fact that Joseph-François Perrault wrote three spellers in quick succession in 1830 shows how these tools [the lesson sheets], as useful as they were, could only be supplements to schoolbooks.]

78   See for example, Galarneau, and Lemire, *Livre et lecture*; and Curtis, *Ruling by Schooling*.

79   During this period, the import duty was 30 per cent *ad valorem* on foreign books entering British possessions.

80   The imported editions were usually exported already bound rather than in sheets, which also increased their cost. See Black, "Book Availability in Canada." The situation in Lower Canada was a bit harder to gauge since the currency was a bit different, but there is no doubt that the prices of imported books were beyond the means of most Lower Canadians. See also Black, "Importation and Book Availability."

pour cent de la valeur de la merchandise. Si l'on ajoute quinze pour cent comme profit avoué, il faut conclure que le volume français se vend à Montréal près du double de son prix en librarie parisienne.[81]

Church officials often sought relief from import duties for religious books, including Sunday School books, and were routinely granted dispensation by imperial officials.[82] Fabre complained that the Lower Canadian clergy were undercutting him because they were able to procure religious texts from France duty free. He went so far as to ask at least one of his French distributors to refuse to sell directly to members of the Church.[83] However, the relief from duties afforded to religious books did not extend to schoolbooks. For example, in 1830, H.W. Miller of Georgeville in the Eastern Townships wrote to Governor Kempt asking that the Rev. John Reid from Stanstead be allowed to import schoolbooks duty free. The reply from the Civil Secretary was the following: "I have submitted to H.E Sir J. K your letter of 17th Inst representing the difficulties of procuring School Books in this Province and requesting that Rev'd John Reid of Stanstead be permitted to import some free of duty and H.E desires me to inform you that it is not in his power to grant the authority for this purpose that you desire."[84]

In addition to selling imported editions of popular schoolbooks, Lower Canadian booksellers sold locally reprinted editions of foreign works. In 1800, John Neilson produced the first Lower Canadian edition of French cleric and grammatician Charles-François L'Homond's *Élémens de la grammaire française*. Other popular schoolbooks included Jean Palairet's *Nouvelle méthode pour apprendre à bien lire*, first issued in 1821 by La Nouvelle Imprimerie in Quebec City and reproduced

---

81   Roy, *Édouard Raymond Fabre*, 74. [Import duties in the colony amount to 50% of the purchase price to which one must add 20% for transportation costs and 25% for currency exchange in France. To these costs must be added insurance of 15% of the value of the merchandise. If you add 15% profit, one must conclude that a French book sold in Montreal sells for over double the price of the same book in a Parisian bookstore.]

82   For example, C. Brewster was permitted to import Sunday school books duty free for use in the American Presbyterian Sunday School. LAC Civil Secretary Letter Books Lower Canada, 1819–1833, 4 November 1830, vol. 10, 125.

83   Undated letter to Frères Gaume (Paris) from the firm of Fabre & Perrault. Roy, *Édouard Raymond Fabre*, 99. The Fabre and Perrault partnership operated between 1828 and 1835, so presumably the letter was sent during that period.

84   LAC, Civil Secretary Letter Books Lower Canada 1819–1833, 28 September 1830, vol. 9, 217.

numerous times once the work was recommended for use in the Catholic schools run by the Royal Institution.[85] For English-language schools, local versions of Lindley Murray's *The English Spelling Book*, *The English Reader*, and *The English Grammar* were great favourites.[86] Similarly, William Mavor's *The English Spelling Book* was frequently reprinted throughout British North America.[87]

Despite these efforts, the availability of schoolbooks was still insufficient to satisfy the growing demand. Allowing that English schools had better access to a wider variety of schoolbooks than did the French schools, some parts of the province, especially outside the major cities and among poorer communities, remained chronically underserved. In the case of Royal Institution schools, the Bishop of Quebec often paid for schoolbooks from his personal funds. Some people raised the possibility of selling schoolbooks to those who could afford them in order to fund the supply for those who could not. In 1827, the schoolmaster at Williamston, in Beauharnois, wrote to the Reverend Joseph Langley Mills, secretary of the Royal Institution:

> Among the number of Children under my care, there are seventeen whose parents are so very poor that they cannot furnish the books necessary. I therefore make bold to enquire if any books may be expected from the Institution for children of such description. If not, I should like to know what books you recommend & some means will be found to procure them. The schoolmaster now established in the Parish of St. Constant wishes to be informed also.[88]

---

85   See Kominek, "Royal Institution."

86   The first Lower Canadian edition of *The English Spelling Book* was produced in 1811. See Lindley Murray, *The English Spelling Book* (Montreal: N. Mower, 1811). According to Aubin, "Books of Instruction," "reprinting only grew over the course of the next decades and, all told, between 1824 and 1865, [Murray's] seven English manuals were reprinted a total of twenty-five times." According to Lyda Fens-de Zeeuw, Murray assigned his copyright in his various publications to his British publishers for the United Kingdom. His brother exercised his rights in the United States. Fens-de Zeeuw, "Lindley Murray." The status of these British North American reprints is unclear. Under British copyright law, the Lower Canadian reprint would presumably have been infringing unless permission had been obtained from the copyright holder.

87   First published in 1801 in London, the book was issued "with a liberal allowance to schools," according to the title page. William Fordyce Mavor was born in Scotland in 1758 and died in 1837.

88   Kominek, "Royal Institution," 121. Joseph Langley Mills (1788–1832), a Church of England clergyman, was appointed secretary of the Royal Institution in 1819. See his entry in DCB.

Mills took the matter up with the rector of the Christ Church Cathedral in Montreal:

> I believe I mentioned to you … a letter from Mr. Mcleod, in which he complains that the poor children who are taught gratis, amounting to one half the school, are without the means of purchasing the necessary books. The Royal Institution have unfortunately no funds at their disposal, from which they could be supplied, but I was directed by the Bishop to request, that you would select books to the value of £4 from your repository, for the use of this School, & charge them to His Lordship's account. The Master might perhaps be able to sell some of the Books in which case the proceeds should be applied towards the formation of a fund for supplying the school with books.[89]

In 1824, around the same time that François Blanchet introduced his first copyright Bill to the Assembly, the Reverend Robert Raby Burrage of the Royal Grammar School in Quebec City testified before the Special Committee to Enquire on the State of Education in This Province and raised the problems associated with the provision of schoolbooks to the rural poor:[90]

> Schools in the country … have been all along very imperfectly supplied with Books … This must have operated very materially in retarding education. Masters who have little else than a small salary to depend on are unwilling, and parents are either unwilling or unable, to purchase the books that are necessary for their childrens' progress; hence they depend upon any books which they may by chance have or be able at little or no expense to procure. But, that Education may go on well; and that the Scholars may make the best use of their time, it is above all things necessary that the same books should be used throughout the School, and that each boy should have his own supply.[91]

---

89  Kominek, "Royal Institution," 122.

90  Journals of the House of Assembly of Lower Canada, 1823–1824, 4–5 Geo. 4, 17. John Neilson was a member of this committee.

91  The committee's report can be found at Appendix Y of the Appendix to the XXX-IIIrd volume of the Journals of the House of Assembly of Lower Canada, 1824, 4–5 Geo. 4. Five teachers and school administrators testified on questions related to the problems with schooling, but the committee did not solicit responses about schoolbooks specifically. Joseph-François Perrault appeared on behalf of the Société d'éducation de Québec and did not raise the issue of schoolbooks in his testimony. Burrage was the only one to refer to the question of schoolbook supply.

Burrage requested that the Assembly intervene:

> As the want of proper and necessary Books has been found so material a
> cause in retarding Education, it would be well perhaps for the House of
> Assembly to consider whether they could not do something for the Coun-
> try in this respect – They might order the publication of several thousand
> Copies of Elementary Books which should be selected as proper for Coun-
> try Schools, and the distribution of them where they are most wanted
> would serve the cause of Education very much … I am inclined to lay
> particular stress on this as a matter of great moment, because the last time
> I examined the Scholars of the Pointe Levi School, I saw only one book of
> Arithmetic and one for repetitions and lessons in reading. How ten twelve
> or more boys could advance in their Education with such a lamentable
> deficiency of School-books, I cannot conceive; and if this is the case so
> near Town, what must it be in distant Parishes? If Parents find so much
> difficulty in paying the money which the Master is allowed to exact, they
> would find still more difficulty in paying the Expenses of books. This they
> certainly do, and in this very important point, the Legislature, if it saw
> proper, could be of great service to the Country.[92]

Burrage's suggestion that the Assembly order the publication and distribution of elementary schoolbooks at its expense was not formally
considered by the legislature, but the concerns he raised may well have
had some impact on those legislators who were already invested in the
question and who later turned to copyright as a solution.

Schoolbook procurement was not the only problem, however. Questions were also raised about the appropriateness of the content of
imported schoolbooks. In some cases, Lower Canadian printers and
publishers reprinted versions of popular foreign texts but adapted
them to suit the needs of the local community. For example, in their
1832 reprint of French pedagogue Moustalon's *Abrégé de mythologie à
l'usage des maisons d'éducation* in 1832, Neilson & Cowan advised that it
had made some small modifications to the text to make it more useful
for Lower Canadian teachers:

> L'Abrégé de Mythologie … est peut-être le meilleur et le plus satisfaisant
> de tous ceux qu'on a jusqu'à present rédigés en français pour l'usage
> de la jeunesse. Les éditeurs ont donc cru rendre service aux maisons

---

92   Appendix Y of the Appendix to the XXXIIIrd volume of the Journals of the House of
Assembly of Lower Canada, 1824, 4–5 Geo. 4.

d'éducation du pays, en réimprimant cette partie du Lycée de M. Moustalon, avec quelques légers changemens [*sic*], dont l'utilité sera facilement
sentie par tous les Instituteurs.[93]

The unsuitability of foreign books led Lower Canadian teachers to
take matters in hand. Jean Antoine Bouthillier's *Traité d'arithmétique à
l'usage des écoles*, printed by John Neilson in 1809, was the first schoolbook by a Lower Canadian to be printed locally. In the preface, the author described the hardship resulting from the scarcity of schoolbooks
on arithmetic in that students had to copy the mathematical principles
and rules by hand in their notebooks. Bouthillier also noted that foreign books were not adapted to the weights and measurements used in
Lower Canada. These factors, he explained, led him to write his own.
A few years later, the schoolmaster at the British and Canadian School
at Quebec, William Morris, inserted this prefatory remark in his *Accountant's Guide for Elementary Schools in Canada*: "Having encountered
many difficulties during ten years as a Teacher in Quebec for want of
a proper initiating book of arithmetic, I was induced to compile the
following work."[94] In *The British North American Arithmetic*, printed and
published by Walton & Gaylord in 1833, the publishers included a preface explaining that "the public generally, and school teachers in particular, have long felt the need of using books prepared particularly for
our own schools, instead of those written for the United States, or for
foreign countries."[95] This book on arithmetic was different; its full title
proclaimed that it was "prepared expressly for the British Provinces."
Walton & Gaylord were expressing a common concern among English-speaking communities throughout British North America. Foreign
schoolbooks could not adequately speak to local conditions, or values.
American schoolbooks were especially frowned upon because they encouraged anti-British sentiments and promoted republicanism.[96] In a
letter to Governor Dalhousie in 1823, Reverend Mills opined that the

---

93   Moustalon, *Abrégé de mythologie. Avertissement* dated Québec, 20 October 1832, after
     the title page. [The *Abrégé de mythologie* is perhaps the best and most satisfactory of
     all the books for youth that have been issued in French. The publishers have there-
     fore thought to provide a service to the schools in this country by reprinting this
     part of the Lycée of Mr. Moustalon, with some slight changes, whose usefulness will
     easily be recognized by all instructors.]
94   Morris, *The Accountant's Guide*.
95   *The British North American Arithmetic*.
96   This was a more common complaint in Upper Canada and in the Eastern Town-
     ships in Lower Canada. See chapter 7 for more on the use of American schoolbooks
     in Upper Canada.

only way to prevent American schoolbooks from being used was "by furnishing books of a more desirable kind at an equal or lower price and providing also for their being procured with equal readiness."[97] François Blanchet's 1824 initiative on copyright must therefore be understood in this broader context. Universal education demanded readily available, affordable and appropriate schoolbooks in both French and English. Copyright was a response to this policy imperative because it encouraged local authors to write books for local readers and offered an economic incentive for local printers and publishers to print, publish, and distribute them. However, for reasons that are unclear from the official records, Blanchet's first copyright Bill did not proceed beyond second reading and did not resurface in the next parliamentary session. In 1826, Blanchet tried again, this time armed with a petition from a constituent seeking legislative support for his book on teaching English as a second language.

### The Petition of Hamilton Leslie for a Premium or Reward for a New System of Teaching

On 27 January 1826, Blanchet introduced the petition of Hamilton Leslie of Quebec, who claimed that after having long viewed "with regret the vast difficulty experienced by Students in the acquisition of Languages," he had developed a pedagogical method that would result in foreign language proficiency in record time.[98] He asked the legislature to "grant him such premium or reward for his labour as may encourage the exertions of others, and contribute to the advancement of Science, and that the Petitioner may without delay publish his Work and put in general practice a system which must be honourable to the Country and beneficial in its consequences both to the rising generation and to the adults."[99]

The petition was referred to a five-member committee, which Blanchet chaired. This was a group well-qualified to deliberate on Leslie's request as most of them were very actively engaged in advancing education and learning in the province. Jean-Thomas Taschereau and Joseph-Rémi Vallières de St-Réal had served with Blanchet on the 1815 Committee to

---

97   As cited by Kominek, "Royal Institution," 113. This passage is contained in a letter from Mills to Civil Secretary A.W. Cochran petitioning Governor Dalhousie to fund the transportation of textbooks to the Eastern Townships. Cochran refused the request.

98   Journals of the House of Assembly of Lower Canada, 6 Geo. 4 (1826), 33.

99   Journals of the House of Assembly of Lower Canada, 6 Geo. 4 (1826), 34.

Enquire into the State and Progress of Education and were involved in the administration of the Royal Institution. Amable Berthelot spent much of his political life on questions of education. *Le Canadien* newspaper described him as someone who believed that public instruction was the basis for a free and democratic society.[100] The studious bibliophile also played an instrumental role in facilitating public access to the Parliamentary Library and was reputed to have a personal library of 1,500 books.

Hamilton Leslie was born in Ireland around 1795. Classically educated, he was proficient in a number of languages, including Greek and Latin.[101] He arrived in Quebec City around 1820 and began working as a land surveyor and a teacher.[102] The Quebec Directory for 1822 identified him as: "Leslie, Hamilton – commercial and mathematical teacher, near the Cape."[103] The 1825 baptismal certificate of his daughter recorded him as a schoolmaster.[104] However, Leslie's professional life extended beyond land surveying and teaching. He and François Blanchet were well acquainted; Leslie was one of Blanchet's medical students. Blanchet's letters in support of Leslie's application for a medical licence confirm their close working relationship. The first of these, dated Quebec, 3 September 1825, read: "This is to certify that Mr. Hamilton Leslie of the city of Quebec has studied the profession of medicine ... under my inspection from the fifteenth day of April 1824 to the third day of September 1825 during which time he has conducted himself with undeviating assiduity and attention."[105] The second, dated Quebec, 4

---

100   *Le Canadien*, 14 July 1824, 3. As Gallichan described him: "Amable Berthelot qui avait parrainé cette reforme du règlement de la bibliothèque était reconnu comme un député qui voyait dans 'l'instruction du peuple cette grande base d'un gouvernement libre.'" [Amable Berthelot, who sponsored this reform of the library, was recognized as a legislator who saw in "the education of the people the basis of a free government."] Gallichan, *Livre et politique*, 260. See also Curtis, *Ruling by Schooling*. For more on Berthelot (1777–1847), see his entry in DCB.

101   Author's correspondence with David Wilson, Hamilton Leslie's great-great-grandson. Wilson explained that Leslie was likely classically educated at one of the Royal Schools near Moy in Ireland.

102   LAC, Register of Commissions for Notaries, Advocates, and Land Surveyors, Land Surveyor for the City of Quebec, District of Quebec, 7 September 1820, reel H-1418, 10400–90.

103   Gleason, *The Quebec Directory for 1822*, 83.

104   Correspondence with David Wilson. Records of the Anglican Cathedral Holy Trinity Church, Quebec (1825).

105   LAC, Civil Secretary and Provincial Secretary Applications for Licenses, Bonds, and Certificates, Quebec, Lower Canada, and Canada East, reel H-1733, 1100. Leslie's petition for a medical licence, dated 30 August 1825, stated that he had engaged in "a long period of study, partly in Dublin and partly in Quebec." He was licensed on 14 March 1826. See Armour, *The Montreal Almanack*, 71.

March 1826, certified that Leslie "has continued his Medical Studies with me from the third of September last, until this date, during which period he has deligently [sic] attended lectures on Anatomy at the Emigrant Hospital and has dissected also himself."[106]

It seems likely that Blanchet had a hand in encouraging Leslie's petition to the legislature. Its introduction in the Assembly occurred while Leslie was under Blanchet's tutelage. Leslie's promise of a cost-effective and expeditious way of teaching foreign languages would have been enticing to Blanchet and his Assembly colleagues; many francophone politicians recognized the necessity of bilingualism:[107] "Je dirai qu'il y a une nécessité absolue pour les Canadiens d'adopter avec le temps la langue anglaise, seul moyen de dissiper la répugnance et les soupçons que la diversité de langue entretiendra toujours entre deux peoples réunis par les circonstances et forcés de vivre ensemble."[108]

Blanchet understood the benefits implicitly. His facility in both languages would have assisted him throughout his political and professional careers. Indeed, Leslie was not the only Lower Canadian to set himself the task of simplifying foreign-language instruction. Joseph-François Perrault had also directed himself to the question of English-language teaching. In his search for a suitable book on the subject for the Quebec Free School, Perrault lamented on the prohibitive cost, insufficient quantity, and unsuitability of the books on offer in the bookshops of Quebec:

> Je me suis empressé à chercher par la ville des livres élémentaires pour enseigner cette langue, et j'ai eu le malheur de n'en point trouver en assez grande quantité et encore étoient-ils [sic] à des prix exhorbitants [sic] et chargés de préceptes et de remarques si fatiguantes pour des enfans

---

106   Armour, *The Montreal Almanack*, 1098. Not long after his licensure, Leslie returned to Dublin to establish his medical practice. He died there on 31 May 1858.

107   The newspapers often contained advertisements from individuals offering English- or French-language instruction. See, for example, the announcement in French in the *Quebec Mercury* by an Englishman who had studied at the University of Paris and who offered his services to teach children English. *Quebec Mercury*, 1 September 1820, 30.

108   As per Pierre-Louis Panet, Member of the Assembly, in 1792, quoted in Blanchet and Beaudoin, *Jacques Viger*, 86. [I would say that it is essential for the *Canadiens* to adopt the English language over time as the only way to eliminate the repugnance and suspicion that a diversity of languages engenders in two peoples united by circumstance and forced to live together.] According to Louis-Philippe Audet, the British policy on language was not one of compulsion: "It did not occur to the English either to force or to persuade the Canadians to give up their language. It was hoped, none the less, that they would make the necessary effort to learn English." See Wilson, Stamp, and Audet, *Canadian Education*, 145.

[*sic*], que je me suis determiné à faire quelque chose de plus simple par moi-même pour leur faciliter la connoissance [*sic*] de cette langue.[109]

To remedy the situation, he wrote *Nouvelle méthode pour apprendre la langue angloise avec facilité, expédition et économie, introduite dans l'École Gratuite à Québec*. In developing his method, Perrault was influenced by the pioneering work of Irish educator James Hamilton, whom he heard speak in Quebec.[110] Hamilton had toured Lower Canada in 1822 to lecture on his system of foreign-language teaching.[111] Is it possible that Hamilton Leslie was also in attendance and, like Perrault, found in Hamilton's address the inspiration for his own teaching method?

Leslie's system of instruction was ambitious. He claimed that individuals could be taught to speak English proficiently in the span of three months:

> That the Petitioner conscious of the desire felt in the Country by the French population for a knowledge of English, and persuaded of the vast utility of such knowledge to the Province in general, has brought his ideas on the subject into form as respects the English Language, by which those whose native Tongue is French, and who can read and write, may acquire the practical use of the former in the space of three months with very little labour or study.[112]

However, as things stood, his students laboured under difficulty because they had to share his single manuscript copy. Without the financial resources to print and publish his method of instruction, it was impossible to teach larger groups and achieve the most beneficial results. He therefore cast his request of the Assembly in the following terms:

> The Petitioner prays that the House may take his case into consideration and grant him such premium or reward for his labour as may encourage

---

109 Joseph-François Perrault, *Nouvelle méthode*, Introduction. [I searched the city for elementary books to teach this language [English] but I was unable to find any in large enough quantities or that were not being sold at exorbitant prices and they were full of precepts and remarks so tedious for children that I was determined to do something simpler myself to facilitate their knowledge of that language.]

110 Perrault reported: "L'hiver dernier j'avois [sic] assisté aux lectures d'un certain Mr. Hamilton." [Last winter I attended the lectures of a certain Mr Hamilton.] See Perrault, *Nouvelle méthode*, Introduction.

111 In Hamilton's words: "In 1822, I went to Montreal, and thence to Quebec, and succeeded tolerably well in both places." Hamilton, *The History, Principles, Practice, and Results*, 13.

112 Journals of the House of Assembly of Lower Canada, 6 Geo. 4, 33 (1826).

the exertions of others, and contribute to the advancement of Science, and that the Petitioner may without delay publish his Work and put in general practice a system which must be honourable to the Country and beneficial in its consequences both to the rising generation and to the adults.[113]

Leslie sought a "premium or reward for his labour" to enable him to print copies of his manuscript, arguing that a financial award would encourage others to write useful books. He did not specifically request an exclusive printing privilege. This is to be contrasted with the contemporaneous petitions of inventors who came before the Assembly for exclusive rights to manufacture and sell their inventions for a certain number of years. These types of requests suggest that the petitioners already had the financing and manufacturing capabilities to produce, use, and sell their inventions; that, or the grant of exclusive rights provided sufficient incentive for investors to finance their ventures. As we see throughout this book, this was not how manuscripts were approached. The chief obstacle to the circulation of knowledge in print was the expense involved in producing books, especially front-end costs of printing. Printers and publishers were loath to assume any financial risk, and authors were often unable to cover these expenses themselves. Indeed, most petitioners to the Assembly sought grants or subsidies to cover the costs of printing their books rather than exclusive rights over their publications.

Hamilton Leslie's petition was referred to a special committee. The proceedings confirm how closely intertwined patents and copyright were in the minds of Lower Canadian politicians. The committee called a number of witnesses, and the questions they were asked were akin to what we would recognize today as a patent examination. The novelty and inventive merits of Leslie's method of instruction were scrutinized. Leslie himself was asked whether he had "invented a Method of teaching Language which was never practised before," to which he replied in the affirmative. He was also asked whether he had communicated his system to anyone – a patent-like question of disclosure that might have vitiated the novelty of the invention. Leslie replied: "I may have mentioned it, but I have not explained or entered into the merits of the System." Two of Leslie's students were called to testify as well. Prosper Métot, who was qualifying to become a lawyer, affirmed that Leslie's system was new. William Blumhart, a medical student, agreed when asked the leading question: "Did you find that his new Method

---

113   Journals of the House of Assembly of Lower Canada, 6 Geo. 4, 34.

of teaching the English Language is more easy and expeditious than the usual Method?" An analysis of the merits of a process or method of doing something was customary for inventions but unusual in respect of books, which were usually assessed on whether they provided useful knowledge, not on whether they disclosed a new or inventive idea. As nineteenth-century legal theorist Eaton S. Drone explained: "The material enquiry ... is not whether a production has literary or scientific merit, but whether it may be regarded as a material addition to useful knowledge, a source of general information. If it be of substantial importance, and have a material value in this respect, the law does not inquire into the degree of its usefulness or of its merits."[114]

Notwithstanding the special committee's patent-like line of questioning, the boundaries between copyright and patents were beginning to crystallize, and matters involving books and other writings were consigned to copyright. The committee's final recommendation was that Leslie be granted "the Privilege of printing his Method" and that a Bill be introduced "to secure to every person a Copyright."[115] On 21 February 1826, François Blanchet was given leave to introduce a Bill for the Encouragement of Learning by securing the Copies of Maps, Charts and Books to the Authors and Proprietors of such Copies during the time therein mentioned *Bill pour encourager les sciences en assurant les copies des cartes, plans et livres aux auteurs et propriétaires de ces copies durant le tems y mentionné.*[116] After second reading, the Bill was referred to a Committee of the Whole House, which reported that it "had made some progress" and was given leave to sit again on 6 March 1826.[117] This was the last entry. On 29 March 1826, Governor Dalhousie prorogued Parliament and this copyright Bill, like its predecessor, died with the session of the legislature. Hamilton Leslie's manuscript was never published. He and his family returned to Ireland later that same year.

### One Final Attempt: The Parliamentary Session of 1827

One final unsuccessful attempt to legislate on copyright occurred during the 1827 Parliamentary session. Although Blanchet remained active on a number of education files, it was his colleague Denis-Benjamin Viger who

---

114   Drone, *A Treatise on the Law of Property*, 210.
115   Journals of the House of Assembly of Lower Canada, 1826, 7 Geo. 4, 95.
116   Journals of the House of Assembly of Lower Canada, 1826, 7 Geo. 4, 129.
117   Journals of the House of Assembly of Lower Canada, 1826, 7 Geo. 4, 158.

introduced a Copyright Bill into the Assembly.[118] On 6 February 1827, he was given leave to bring in a Bill for the Encouragement of Learning by securing the Copies of Maps, Charts and Books, to the Authors and Proprietors of such Copies during the Times therein mentioned / *Bill pour encourager les Sciences, en Assurant les Copies des Cartes, Plans et Livres aux Auteurs et Propriétaires, durant le tems y mentionné*.[119] The erudite lawyer, who was first elected to the Assembly in 1808, served on a number of committees on education, including Blanchet's 1815 Committee to Enquire into the State and Progress of Education. Viger's involvement in the copyright file demonstrates yet again the extent to which this network of allies viewed the intrinsic connection between copyright and literacy and learning. However, Viger was unable to shepherd the Bill through the legislative process before Governor Dalhousie prorogued parliament on 7 March.[120] Copyright did not reappear on the legislative docket when Parliament resumed in 1828 for its last full session of that decade.

## The Early Copyright Bills and Their Provenance

The bilingual texts of the unsuccessful 1824 and 1826 Bills (the "Blanchet Bills") have survived the ages as a result of the efforts of a parliamentary librarian, who gathered and bound a miscellany of unenacted Bills.[121] As a result, one can establish the statutory provenance of these earliest attempts at legislating on copyright. The Blanchet Bills were copied from the American Copyright Act 1790 rather than from the Statute of Anne or

---

118   Journals of the House of Assembly of Lower-Canada, 1827, 7 & 8 Geo. 4, 77. On Viger (1774–1861), see entry in DCB. See also, Parizeau, *La vie studieuse et obstinée*.

119   Journals of the House of Assembly of Lower Canada.

120   The Bill was reported in *La Minerve* as having been introduced but not passed – among the orders of the day at the time of prorogation. *La Minerve*, 26 March 1826, 2.

121   The 1827 Bill is not available, but it is reasonable to presume that the text would have been the same as its predecessors. The 1824 and 1826 Bills were substantively identical, but the textual language of the 1826 version is more fluid than its predecessor, indicating that some stylistic editing had occurred. The French version offers some clues as to how the earliest legislative drafters conceived of the law. The Preamble refers to copyright as "privilège exclusif de faire imprimer" (exclusive printing privilege) – as opposed to *droit d'auteur*. Paratextual clues about the mutable nature of the terminology used by early legislators, legislative drafters, and official translators can be found in the indices to the Journals of the Assembly as well as in the marginalia of the journals as the Bill made its way through the process. The Bills were referred to in the following terms: Copy-rights to Authors and Proprietors / *Droit de publier* / *Droit de copie* (5 & 6 Geo. 4, 1823–24); Encouragement of Learning / *Encouragement des sciences* (6 & 7 Geo. 4, 1826). See Tawfik, "Copyright as *droit d'auteur*."

the more contemporaneous 1814 UK Act.[122] The Assembly had already relied on the American model for its Patent Act, so it was not surprising that it would seek the same legislative inspiration for its copyright law.

Under these Bills, Lower Canada's copyright law would have conferred on authors and proprietors of maps, charts, books, and other literary productions the exclusive right to, *inter alia*, print, reprint, publish, and import their works for a period of fourteen years with the possibility of renewal for another fourteen years by the author, if still living and resident in the province, descendible to the heirs or assigns. These authors or proprietors had to be British subjects resident in the province. Registration formalities included the entry of title at the office of the prothonotary or clerk of the court, a notice in one or more newspapers, and a deposit of one copy with the provincial secretary, a senior ranking official who, among other responsibilities, acted as a registrar of official documents. Copyright was also extended to works already in print at the time of the passage of the Act, as long as the authors were British subjects resident in the province and the work had been printed in the province. Other than in the specific case of books already in print, the statute did not require that the works be printed or published locally. This is an important indicator that, at least in North American constructions of the law, copyright was not intended to actively promote or protect the interests of the printing and publishing industry. This is to be contrasted with British copyright law, which required first publication in the United Kingdom, although the actual printing of the book could occur elsewhere.

Because of the vagaries of the political situation in Lower Canada, especially the frequent prorogations of Parliament, the repeated failure to enact a copyright law during this period can be ascribed to poor timing rather than opposition to the law itself. Copyright resurfaced on the legislative docket as the new decade began. This time the circumstances were more auspicious. In 1829, Joseph Lancaster arrived in Montreal and began his agitations for exclusive rights over his publications.

---

122  The Bills did not incorporate the 1802 amendments to the United States Copyright Act, which had extended copyright protection to engravings and etchings and established a notice requirement to be inserted after the title page of the published work itself. See *An Act supplementary to an act, entitled "An act for the encouragement of learning, by securing the copies of maps, charts, and books to the authors and proprietors of such copies during the times therein mentioned" and extending the benefits thereof to the arts of designing, engraving, and etching historical and other prints"* (Amendment of 1790 Act), 2 Stat. 171, 1802. The Blanchet Bills remained faithful to the 1790 text – whether this was by design or an oversight is impossible to know.

# Chapter Four

# Copyright, Education, and Schoolbooks: Joseph Lancaster in Montreal[1]

In September 1829, Joseph Lancaster and his family made their way to Montreal from Albany, New York. Disheartened by financial and personal setbacks, their intention had been to set sail from Quebec City to return to England, but Lancaster soon found that "the season was then too far advanced to think of a passage from Quebec, with a wife and family in tender health."[2] So instead, the family settled in Montreal for the winter and, in Lancaster's words, "decided that we would be useful."[3]

Lancaster had been in North America since 1818. The reasons for this bear some mention, since otherwise he would never have become involved in Lower Canadian copyright law. His monitorial system of education was highly regarded in the United Kingdom, Europe, and the Americas, yet the man himself did not enjoy similar esteem. Prone to self-aggrandizement and arrogance, he was also hopeless at managing his finances and was forever in debt.[4] His biographer David Salmon noted: "Lancaster had one enemy more powerful than priests or professors, deacons or archdeacons, deans or doctors, reviewers or pamphleteers, and that was Lancaster himself."[5]

---

1   This is the third examination of the impact that Joseph Lancaster made in Montreal. See George Spragge, "Joseph Lancaster in Montreal"; and Curtis, "Joseph Lancaster in Montreal *bis.*"

2   Lancaster, *Epitome,* 12.

3   Lancaster, *Epitome,* 13.

4   His difficult personality and his precarious financial circumstances are well documented by his biographers. See David Salmon, *Joseph Lancaster;* and Vaughan, *Joseph Lancaster en Caracas (1824–1827).* See also Taylor, who in *Joseph Lancaster* speculates that he suffered from bipolar disorder.

5   Salmon, *Joseph Lancaster,* 15.

It is not difficult to imagine how his success went to his head when he received letters from admirers who considered his "system of Education, the abolition of the Slave trade and the vaccine inoculation as the three events of our times most likely to add to the happiness and improvement of the human race."[6] His temperament and profligacy overshadowed the success of his pedagogical project to the extent that by 1808, he and his London school, which included a slate factory and a printing establishment, were on the verge of financial collapse. The project was rescued through the generosity of some of his supporters, who established the Society for Promoting the Royal British or Lancasterian System of Educating the Poor in order to keep Lancaster's good works alive under the supervision of trustees who would manage the school's finances.[7] The society was later renamed the British and Foreign School Society (BFSS) in an effort to further distance itself from its founder. The BFSS supported Lancasterian schools abroad, including the schools established in Lower Canada by the British and Canadian School Society (BCSS), which included Joseph-François Perrault's school in Quebec City.

Lancaster was offered the position of superintendent of the BFSS, but he took offence at this and resigned in the belief that the trustees wanted to "chain him to the oar of a sinecure in the almost stagnant Lethe of their usurpation."[8] In 1818, with money donated for his passage, he, along with his wife Elizabeth and their young daughter Betsy, left England for the United States.[9] Settling first in Philadelphia and then Baltimore, the peripatetic Lancaster devoted himself to advancing his pedagogical methods, touring and giving lectures. Unfortunately, his stay in the United States was fraught with professional and financial difficulties similar to those he had experienced in the United Kingdom – a pattern that would continue throughout his time in Lower Canada.

In 1824, upon learning that the Bolívar regime in Gran Colombia was looking to establish state-led public primary schools along Lancasterian lines, the now widowed Lancaster offered his services. He arrived in Caracas in May of that year.[10] Soon after, he married Mary Robinson,

---

6  William Maltby to Lancaster, Fishmongers Hall, 31 December 1808, box 1, folder 1, 1806–Oct 14, 1814, JLP.

7  See Vaughan, *Joseph Lancaster en Caracas (1824–1827)*. See also Wall, "Joseph Lancaster."

8  Salmon, *Joseph Lancaster*, 56.

9  See McCadden, "Joseph Lancaster in America."

10  See Vaughan, *Joseph Lancaster en Caracas (1824–1827)*. Colombia (Gran Colombia) consisted of what is now Venezuela, Colombia, Panama, and Ecuador.

the widow of a friend, who had three young children and a healthy inheritance. Unfortunately, what had started out at as a salutary opportunity for Lancaster ended in an acrimonious financial dispute with President Simón Bolívar. In his letter of invitation to Lancaster, Bolívar had promised 20,000 pesos to advance the education of children in Caracas, payable by bill of exchange in London. However, this undertaking was not honoured by the Colombian government, and in the interim, Lancaster had incurred debts on the strength of the bill.[11] Lancaster fled the country, leaving Mary Robinson behind to sell a large portion of her inheritance to pay her husband's creditors and permit the family to leave Colombia. Destitute, the Lancasters returned to the United States in 1827. They settled in Trenton, New Jersey, where Lancaster had secured a teaching position, but the struggles continued. He intimated some "ill-usage" of his wife and children by individuals "who do little to honour their country."[12] It was to escape these travails that the family settled in Montreal in 1829.

This was not Lancaster's first visit to Lower Canada. He had travelled to Montreal and Quebec City in 1828 to promote his educational projects and had been warmly received at the highest levels of the British colonial administration.[13] Governor Dalhousie responded effusively to Lancaster's request for a meeting in August 1828: "As all the world knows Mr. Lancaster by name and by the benevolence of his nature – As all have tried to follow his plans to give them the fullest effect – So have we in Canada honoured the one and adopted the other. I trust therefore you will not leave Quebec before I have the pleasure to assure you of my personal respects."[14]

This time, however, Lancaster was in Lower Canada for an extended stay. Ludger Duvernay's *La Minerve* announced his arrival and

---

11   Roldán Vera, *The British Book Trade*, 127. See also Salmon, *Joseph Lancaster*; and Vaughan, *Joseph Lancaster en Caracas (1824–1827)*.

12   See Lancaster, *Epitome*. McCadden refers to it as a serious dispute; see "Joseph Lancaster and Philadelphia."

13   Joseph Lancaster, in a letter to his daughter Betsy alludes to a visit to Lower Canada around 28 January 1828; see box 2, folder 4, JLP. He was in Quebec City on a lecture tour in August 1828, at which time he met with Governor Dalhousie: The *National Gazette and Literary Register*, 6 September 1828, 2, refers to a *Quebec Star* report that Joseph Lancaster was in the city in August to give a series of public lectures; see "Quebec Announces Arrival Joseph Lancaster Public Lectures." *The Baltimore Patriot*, 9 September 1828, reported that Lancaster was lecturing in Montreal at that time; "Joseph Lancaster, Montreal," 2.

14   Dalhousie to Lancaster, 28 August 1828, box 3, folder 3, 185, JLP. Lancaster, in *Epitome*, says that he was well-received by Dalhousie.

expressed the hope that since "le système Lancasterien a produit des avantages immenses dans toutes les parties du globe; espérons que son auteur n'aura pas à se plaindre d'être négligé."[15] Lancaster wasted no time in establishing himself in the province. On 15 September 1829, he delivered a public lecture and took up a collection in aid of his projects, which included opening a small school. Shortly thereafter, he travelled from Montreal to Quebec, where he met with Governor James Kempt, who provided him with some financial backing for his educational experiments.[16] In October, he taught eight young boys to read and documented his success in a two-page broadside titled *New method of Lancasterian education: Brief outline of the result of an experiment, to ascertain in how short a time, it was possible to teach eight ignorant boys, to read the first chapter of John; by a new and simple process in education, invented by Joseph Lancaster.*[17] By January 1830, Lancaster was petitioning the Assembly for financial aid for his pedagogical endeavours. John Neilson introduced the petition, which was referred to a Special Committee on Education chaired by François Blanchet, with Neilson and Denis-Benjamin Viger among its members. The special committee recommended that Lancaster be awarded £100. The Assembly doubled the grant to £200.[18]

The Assembly's enthusiasm over Lancaster's projects may have reflected their awe at his celebrity rather than a dearth of monitorial schools in the province. Lancasterian schools were already flourishing in Montreal and Quebec City, and the success of legislative initiatives like the 1829 Trustees School Act meant that the public school system was on surer footing. Indeed, education scholars have questioned whether Lancaster's presence in Lower Canada actually furthered the province's education agenda. Education historian George Spragge concluded, "It can hardly be suggested that Lancaster's residence in

---

15  *La Minerve*, 14 September 1829, 3. [The Lancasterian system has produced immense advantages in all parts of the world. Let us hope that its author will not have any complaints about being neglected.]

16  Governor Kempt pledged £10. See Lancaster, *New method of Lancasterian education*, broadside dated 23rd of 11th month (November), 1829, American Broadsides and Ephemera, series 1, no. 3682. Reference to the bank draft received from Kempt can be found in box 3, folder 3, #145, 190, JLP.

17  Lancaster, *New method of Lancasterian education*. Lancaster later elaborated on this experiment in *Report of the Singular Results*.

18  Journals of the House of Assembly of Lower Canada, 10 & 11 Geo. 4 (1830), 345. See too Appendix to the XXXIXth volume of the Journals of the House of Assembly of the Province of Lower Canada, 10 & 11 Geo. 4 (1830), Appendix R.

Montreal had any special significance."[19] Sociologist Bruce Curtis is somewhat more sanguine, arguing that "Joseph Lancaster was a catalyst for educational debate and discussion," although he determined that "his political choices and personal instability ensured that his direct influence on colonial educational policies would remain slight."[20] Even if Lancaster's presence in Lower Canada was not momentous from the vantage point of education history, his influence on Canada's copyright history was profound. As we will see, Lancaster was as concerned about protecting his copyright interests as he was in advancing his educational projects. In 1831 he began a self-interested campaign for copyright protection. His timing was opportune.

**Joseph Lancaster: Author and Publisher**

Lancaster was as much an author, printer, and publisher as he was a teacher. His involvement in the book trade began at an early age, when, for a brief period, he started a business as a bookseller by reselling his own books.[21] At some point, he learned how to operate a printing press, and the printing office became a permanent feature of his educational enterprise. The press produced Lancaster's advertisements, broadsides, and subscription and other notices, as well as his school lessons and some of his pamphlets and books.[22] He even toyed with the idea of giving up teaching in favour of becoming a printer, but he was dissuaded by a friend, who advised him that "a man cannot conduct that which he has never been brought up in, so well as one who has."[23] His printing press was so essential that when his creditors came to seize his property in his absence, he instructed his father to save his papers, his writings, and his press above all else.[24] Later, as his life took an itinerant turn, he ensured that he always had a printing press with him wherever his travels took him.[25]

---

19  Spragge, "Joseph Lancaster in Montreal," 41.

20  Curtis, "Joseph Lancaster in Montreal *bis*," 2, 57.

21  Miscellaneous notes by Lancaster, Burlingham, and others, chapter 7 of Lancaster's autobiography, box 5, folder 1, JLP. See also Wall, "Joseph Lancaster and the Origins." Although Lancaster had only a very rudimentary education, he loved to read and he purchased books from money earned working at his father's shop.

22  See Wall, "Joseph Lancaster and the Origins," 101–2.

23  Bennett Cross to Lancaster, 13 August 1814, box 2, folder 2, no. 140, 5, JLP.

24  Joseph Lancaster to Richard Lancaster, 28 September 1814, box 2, folder 6, no. 142, 23, JLP: "The Printing Office is the utmost consequence to be preserved ... it is a mine of comfort and profit if well-managed."

25  M. Foster La Guayra to Lancaster, Caracas, 17 January 1826, box 3, folder 2, no. 145, 147, JLP: "The whole of the Printing Establishment should have been sent to

As Lancaster's fame as an educator grew, so did his need to capitalize on his reputation and his writings. He was a zealous self-promoter who sought to leverage his name, his method of instruction, and his publications to advance his campaign for universal education and to maximize his personal and financial returns. As entrepreneurial as he was, however, his business acumen left much to be desired, as his life-long poverty attests.

His first pamphlet, *Improvements in Education*, first published in 1803, was the catalyst for his later high profile and strong influence.[26] The work was reprinted around the world, including in the form of extracts, which the Lower Canadian Assembly had circulated in 1815. The rapid spread of his pedagogical method fostered his global celebrity. In reference to the first American edition, printed in 1804 and sold by Isaac Collins & Son in New York, Lancaster proudly reported that "1000 copies of my Tract have been reprinted at New York and afford much satisfaction there, as I am informed by Letters from America."[27] In 1807, Lancaster was sent a copy of the second American edition by its printer, Benjamin Perkins, who suggested that "the preface will shew how useful thy labors are likely to become on this side of the Atlantic."[28] The lengthy Preface consisted of a variety of material relating to the New York Free School and extolling the virtues of Lancaster's system.

In his early years as a teacher and author in England, Lancaster did not register any of his books with the Stationers' Company. The only mention of a British copyright was a letter he sent to his daughter Betsy not long before he and his family left London for the United States,

---

you today; but I have found it impossible to procure mules (?), without paying an exorbitant freight." According to Edgar Vaughan, when Lancaster returned to the United States from Caracas, he rejoiced "to find that his printing press and types and school lessons, including a new method for teaching arithmetic, had arrived intact." Vaughan, *Joseph Lancaster in Caracas*, 262, JLP (unpublished print manuscript that was revised from the published Spanish text).

26  Lancaster, *Improvements in Education*. The book was revised and enhanced in at least four subsequent editions. Lancaster printed and sold an abridged edition (1808) himself. Joseph Lancaster, *Improvements in Education; Abridged*. Lancaster proposed a new edition while he was in Montreal. See Lancaster, *Epitome*, 53 et seq.

27  Joseph Lancaster to Duke of Bedford, 1804, box 1, folder 3, JLP. Lancaster had received a letter from Thomas Eddy in New York advising him that Patrick Calquhoun had sent him a copy of *Improvements in Education* and that Eddy was having 1,000 copies printed.

28  Benjamin D. Perkins to Lancaster, New York, 20 November 1807, box 1, folder 1, no. 21, JLP. Perkins was also the secretary of the Society for the Establishment of a Free School in the City of New York.

wherein he advised her that: "I requested [Richard] Jones to <u>enter my Book</u> at Stationers Hall and <u>give the certificate to Grandfather.</u>"[29] It is not clear to which book Lancaster was referring. Perhaps he was alluding to *Oppression and Persecution, or a Narrative of a Variety of Singular Facts That Have Occurred in the Rise Progress and Promulgation of Royal Lancasterian System of Education* – a venomous diatribe against his perceived enemies at the BFSS, printed and published in 1816. This was the only work of any length that he composed prior to his departure from England.[30] Regardless, the Stationers' Records are silent in relation to any registrations by Joseph Lancaster or any of his publishers for the relevant period.[31]

However, the fact that Lancaster had not registered any of his British publications with the Stationers' Company should not be taken to signal indifference on his part. We know that under the law in the United Kingdom, the absence of registration was not a bar to a copyright claim for damages, and there are enough examples in the Lancaster Papers to demonstrate that he was vigilant in safeguarding his reputational and economic interests in other ways. For example, a hallmark of Lancaster's system was the use of large lesson sheets, which he printed in-house and which were displayed at the front of the class to instruct the entire group at once. Lancaster wanted to be the sole provider of these teaching tools for all Lancasterian schools. Maintaining a monopoly over their reproduction ensured that Lancaster profited from their sale and controlled their content.[32] According to one of his critics, English poet and essayist Robert Southey:

> A sheet thus printed … will not contain more matter than half a page of the closely printed duodecimo tracts … Every sheet therefore upon the most moderate calculation must cost twenty times as much as the same matter

---

29  Joseph Lancaster to Betsy Lancaster, 5 March 1818 [emphasis Lancaster], box 2, folder 2, no. 141, p. 6, JLP. Richard Maddox Jones was one of Lancaster's first students and, later, his son-in-law. Jones travelled to the United States with the Lancasters in 1818.

30  Lancaster, *Oppression and Persecution*.

31  A search through the index of registrations of the Stationers' Company from 22 September 1813 to 6 February 1819, and each entry from 1 January 1816 to 31 December 1818, elicited no results.

32  Lancaster economized on the printing costs by exploiting his student boarders, who were required to work in the print shop without pay. Joseph Lancaster Autobiography, box 6, folder 2, ch. 18, 61, JLP. The JLP has a draft of twenty-six chapters of Lancaster's autobiography, spanning his early life up to 1805–6.

printed in the customary form, and the saving must consist in this, that a whole school ... would consume only a very small number of copies. The publisher therefore must run a great risk, unless he is sure of the custom of very many schools ... All managers of schools must apply to this conductor, for if they print for themselves, there is an end to the promised economy. He will therefore have the power of withholding whatever he disapproves, and of propagating whatever he thinks fit.[33]

In 1809 an inquiry had been made on Lancaster's behalf on the question of whether he could hold copyright in his lesson sheets. The question turned on whether the collection of individual lessons constituted a "book" for copyright purposes. In all probability, there had been some incidents of unauthorized reprinting that had caused him concern:

We have inquired about Copy Rights and hear that it is not the <u>form</u> of the book which entitles to Copyright but the <u>Originality</u>. Now it does not appear that you can retain any Copy right as to your publications – you can only publish them as Lancaster's Editions. The Arithmetic is certainly original – but another person may publish an edition with different figures etc(?) in his sums – the only thing that I think you ought to do is to sell your publications so cheap as to destroy the covetous disposition of pirates.[34]

The advice about the definition of a "book" for copyright purposes was sound. At the time of this opinion, a British court had already decided that "there was nothing in the word *book* to require that it shall consist of several sheets bound in leather, or stitched in a marble cover."[35] In other words, it was not the format that was determinative. Instead, copyright was predicated on the work being original in sense of it being the result of the author's effort, skill, and ingenuity and not a colourable imitation of the work of others.[36] By Lancaster's own description, his spelling sheets were merely reproductions of the alphabet and of words consisting of two, three, or more syllables. These were not sufficiently original to meet the threshold for legal protection. The arithmetic lessons were different. Reading between the lines, it must

33  Southey, *The Origin, Nature and Object*, 67–8.
34  Joseph Fox to Lancaster, 20 March 1809, [emphasis Fox], box 1, folder 1, 19, JLP. It is not clear from Fox's letter to whom the inquiry was made.
35  *Hime (or Hine) v. Dale*, 1803, 2 Camp. 27, ctd in Godson, *A Practical Treatise*, 219.
36  See for example, Maugham, *A Treatise on the Laws*, 126 et seq ("Of Pirating Copyright").

have been the case that Lancaster had constructed the particular sums or mathematical tables himself and had expended a minimal degree of skill and judgment in their creation. The opinion he received was to the effect that he could claim copyright in the specific sums but that his legal entitlement was weak. He could not prevent someone else from preparing similar lessons using different sums. Lancaster was counselled that to overcome these copyright challenges, he should sell the lessons so cheaply that there would be no incentive for anyone else to reprint them, a common strategy for deterring competitors. He was also advised to print his lessons as "Lancaster's Editions" so as to distinguish his works from those of others and to maintain control over this method of teaching by dint of his name and reputation.

Lancaster was nothing if not shrewd about his brand. Even before he received this advice, he had begun identifying his teaching material as "Lancaster's New Spelling Book," "Lancaster's Series of Reading Lessons," and "Lancaster's New System of Arithmetic" in his publications and promotional notices.[37] He eventually printed and sold a "Lancaster's Edition" of another author's work, namely John Freame's *Scripture Instruction: digested into several sections, by way of question and answer ...,* first published in 1713.[38] Lancaster had been routinely reprinting and using Freame's publication in his schools, but in 1813, he began to identify himself with the work by producing an edition "as taught in the Royal Lancasterian Schools," substituting his own preface for Freame's and using the opportunity to accuse Andrew Bell, his main competitor in monitorial pedagogy, of stealing some of his ideas.[39]

Another of Lancaster's strategies was to issue "certificates of competence" to the teachers he trained. No one would be permitted to teach using the Lancasterian method without a certificate.[40] The censure wrought on those who falsely claimed to have obtained a certificate was severe, as James Edwards discovered. The former schoolmaster of the first Lancasterian school in Montreal, Edwards had moved to Philadelphia and opened a school claiming to have been certified to teach by Lancaster himself when, in fact, he had learned Lancaster's method

---

37   See Joseph Lancaster, *Improvements in Education, abridged,* iv–v.

38   Freame, *Scripture Instruction.*

39   Lancaster, *Scripture Instruction.* See also McGarry, "Joseph Lancaster," 349. Andrew Bell had developed his own monitorial system, which incorporated Anglican religious instruction under the aegis of the National School system. Lower Canadian English schools that were established by the Royal Institution were National Schools. See Kominek, "The Royal Institution."

40   See McGarry, "Joseph Lancaster," 349.

from one of Lancaster's former pupils, William Scott.[41] A public controversy ensued. Although Edwards defended himself by arguing that he was entitled to claim certification because of Lancaster's letters of support, the damage was done. The disgraced schoolmaster left Philadelphia sometime in the summer of 1818.[42] Lancaster followed the dispute closely and exchanged correspondence on the matter with his friend Robert Ould. Ould wrote, "Yes, I had before heard of Edwards' forgery, a very neat trick to be sure and well calculated in his own private language to 'gull the public.'"[43] Clearly, Lancaster was incensed by the apparent misrepresentation and the tarnishment of his "brand," even though he and Edwards had been correspondents of long standing and Lancaster had supported him in his teaching endeavours.[44]

As narcissistic as he was impecunious, Lancaster remained watchful of any untoward activity, and his vast network of correspondents kept him apprised of possible wrongdoings. In one instance, a concerned supporter expressed his fears that "the Bellites" – in other words, those who adhered to Andrew Bell's monitorial system – would appropriate Lancaster's writings if he did not protect himself: "Some of them will (without thy method of instruction of the Classicks be ensured to thee by Patent) endeavour to rob thee of the advantage for their meanness may be seen by their printing thy method of teaching and calling it their own – they are liable to an <u>action</u> for printing and publishing thy new mode of spelling."[45] In another example, Nicolas Gouïn Dufief, who had developed a system of French-language instruction, had to defend himself publicly against a charge that "the new mode of tuition lately announced by N.G Dufief … as his own discovery, is the original invention of Joseph Lancaster."[46] Dufief alluded to a report circulating in the United States accusing him of plagiarism. Lancaster may have had something to do with that accusation, but the source of the claim against Dufief remains unknown.

---

41   William Scott wrote to Lancaster in January 1813 to the effect: "A young man whose name is James Edwards who was Monitor General in my school has … settled in a school at Montreal and conducting it on the Lancaster System as far as circumstances will permit." Scott to Lancaster, 1 January 1813, box 12, folder 1, JLP.

42   Ellis, "Lancasterian Schools in Philadelphia."

43   Robert Ould to Lancaster, Georgetown, 17 December 1818, box 3, folder 1, no. 145, JLP.

44   See Ellis, "Lancasterian Schools in Philadelphia."

45   George Hartford to Lancaster, Bristol, 3 September 1812, box 2, folder 1, no. 155a, JLP. The reference to a patent here was likely intended as exclusive privilege, although Lancaster had often mused about securing a patent for the teaching method he had invented.

46   "Systems of Tuition," *Daily National Intelligencer* (Washington, DC), 14 December 1816, vol. 4, no. 1228, 2. Dufief was a French language teacher living in the United States.

Lancaster was quick to react if there was any hint that Lancasterian schools were considering reprinting his lesson sheets themselves. Yet because of Lancaster's inability to keep up with demand, those who requested copies from him often waited months if not years for the prints to arrive. In the case of the Edinburgh School Society, for example, an exasperated Mr Muir had written to Lancaster about the long delays and appears to have suggested that if the society did not receive the lessons in a timely way, it would consider printing its own copies. Muir's letter has not survived, nor has Lancaster's angry response. However, the letters from the society's treasurer, William Braidwood Jr, and its Secretary, the Rev. Dr Fleming, attempting to mollify a clearly outraged Lancaster offer some indication of what must have transpired. Braidwood assured Lancaster: "We would not hurt your feelings or deprive you of the funds which are necessary for your support and that of your family. We are unanimously of the opinion that Mr. Muir acted very improperly – in future all correspondence will be carried on by the Secretary or Treasurer, both of whom being your sincere friends and well wishers."[47] Fleming wrote: "We have certainly meditated for nearly 12 months to have portions of Scripture and lessons printed, but no intention of interfering with you ... so that the idea of <u>piracy</u> is out of the question. I conceived it as a matter of favor that you supplied us. Mr Muir had no authority to say a word on the subject."[48]

These letters may have gone a long way toward reassuring Lancaster that the Edinburgh School Society's intentions were honourable, but they did nothing to resolve the problem that had given rise to the angry exchange in the first place. The society was still requesting the lessons a year later. In June 1813, Lancaster received a reproachful note from a Mr Cruickshank, another director of the society: "Respecting the lessons divers times written for by the Directors – we ought to be punctual in fulfilling our engagement. I cannot make an apology to the Directors who are quite dissatisfied, with such long delay – beg thou wilt lose no more time in forwarding them."[49]

---

47   William Braidwood Jr. to Lancaster, 2 June 1812, box 1, folder 6, JLP. Alluding to a letter from Lancaster of 22 May.

48   Rev. Dr Fleming to Lancaster, 3 June 1812, box 1, folder 6, JLP.

49   A. Cruikshank to Lancaster, 25 June 1813, box 1, folder 6, JLP. The Lancaster papers are rife with these kinds of exchanges of correspondence, especially from Lancaster's supporters wanting copies of his materials to spread the Lancasterian system around the world. Their letters demonstrate increasing frustration at their orders remaining unfulfilled.

It is not clear whether the society ever received the material. Some schools must have been reprinting the lesson sheets without Lancaster's acquiescence; otherwise the vast network of Lancasterian schools would have ceased operating. Lancaster was certainly aware that these practices were occurring, despite his rebuke of the Edinburgh School Society. An 1812 letter from Robert Ould to Lancaster attests to the fact that American Lancasterian school societies were reproducing the lessons for use in their schools. Ould advised: "The Committee has nobly determined to print the whole of your lessons and to incorporate grammatical lessons with them."[50]

In many cases, the BFSS supplied the lessons without Lancaster's knowledge. A case in point can be found in the correspondence of Walter Bromley, who was on his way to Nova Scotia to establish the Royal Acadian School under the auspices of the BFSS. He wrote to Lancaster not long before his departure, asking for one copy of each lesson to take with him "as there are several Printers in Halifax who will readily furnish me with more."[51] It appears that Bromley did not receive any word from Lancaster, for he followed up by letter dated 19 March 1813 advising that he was to leave town that evening and still hoped that Lancaster would send him the requisite lessons: "My dear Friend – I wrote to you sometime ago respecting the information necessary for the Establishment of your system in Nova Scotia … [M]y son has a very good idea of the practical part, but I could wish to know a little more of the theory. Now … as I shall leave town this evening … it will be impossible for me to see you, and therefore if you wish to communicate with me on the subject, and think proper to send me a form of each lesson before I embark, I shall be happy to act agreeably to your instructions."[52]

Lancaster appears to have ignored this appeal as well. Instead, the British and Foreign School Society supplied Bromley with the lessons.[53] Indeed, Lancaster's railings against the BFSS for the way the society had treated him extended to accusations that his publications had been pirated.[54] It was, however, entirely unrealistic for him to believe that his printing operation could satisfy the demand, especially given the

---

50   Robert Ould to Lancaster, Georgetown, 5 February 1812, box 1, folder 1, JLP. The British-born Ould had opened the first Lancasterian School in Georgetown. See British and Foreign School Society, *Report [1815]*, 13.
51   Walter Bromley to Lancaster, 9 March 1813, box 2, folder 1, no. 125, 2, JLP.
52   Walter Bromley to Joseph Lancaster, 19 March 1813, box 2, folder 1, no. 125, 14, JLP.
53   British and Foreign School Society, *Report [1815]*.
54   Legal document, 29 April 1814, box 2, folder 2, no. 139, 36, JLP.

timing. Lancaster was headed toward bankruptcy and the final acrimonious break with the BFSS would exile him to North America.

Although Lancaster's lesson sheets may not have been sufficiently original to secure copyright, his books and pamphlets on education certainly were. In 1812, the Committee of the Society for the Promotion of Education of the Poor of Ireland (the "Dublin Committee") approached him asking that he grant them "the privilege of their having a right of using and publishing the whole or such parts of thy publications on the subject of education and the books used by thee in thy Schools as the Society shall from time to time judge expedient."[55] They were especially interested in his *Hints and Directions for building fitting-up and arranging schoolrooms on the British system.*[56] A licence agreement was entered into, and Lancaster received a royalty payment of £105.[57] As a further measure to safeguard Lancaster's interests, the Dublin Committee expressly acknowledged his copyright in their annual meeting to make it clear that they were reprinting with permission and that the author retained all rights.[58] This appears to be the only example of Lancaster licensing his copyright. Perhaps opportunities like the one presented to him by the Dublin Committee were rare. Certainly, his frequent upheavals were not conducive to deriving full benefit from his writings. He went bankrupt not long afterwards, and the rest of his life was characterized by displacements from one country to the next, which made it difficult for him to maintain the type of oversight necessary to manage his intellectual property effectively.

One thing is demonstrably clear, however. By the time Lancaster left the UK in 1818 for a friendlier reception in North America, he was

---

55   Richard B. Warren to Lancaster, Dublin, 23 June 1812, box 1, folder 1, JLP. They offered 100 guineas; Lancaster negotiated for 105 guineas (roughly £110).

56   Lancaster, *Hints and Directions.*

57   The society also wanted to reserve the right to reprint "the 8 vo. Volume," without specifying the title. McGarry, citing the Kildare Place Society Archives, says they were referring to *The British System of Education*; see McGarry, "Joseph Lancaster," 146. Lancaster appears to have refused. The final agreement included an undertaking to exclude the book. Samuel Bewley to Lancaster, 8 March 1812, box 1, folder 1, JLP.

58   Samuel Bewley to Lancaster, 5 November 1813, box 1, folder 1, no. 11, JLP: "We acknowledge thy <u>Copyright</u>, which so far as its circulation may extend – will have a tendency to prevent thy Right from being invaded" [emphasis Bewley]. It is to be remembered that copyright was recognized under British law even if the work was not registered with the Stationers' Company. The copyright could still be enforced before the courts, but the remedies would be more limited and the copyright would still be tied to the statutory term of protection.

familiar with the benefits of copyright; he was also someone who aggressively worked to protect his reputational and commercial interests. Upon his arrival in the United States, he busied himself with building his connections and seeking patronage and support. He set up schools, embarked on ambitious lecture tours, petitioned prominent citizens for subscriptions, and promoted his pedagogical successes in broadsides and pamphlets, which he often printed himself at his printing office. He also began paying more assiduous attention to copyright. On 5 May 1820, he registered his copyright in *Letters on National Subjects Auxiliary to Universal Education and Scientific Knowledge* in the District of Columbia.[59] A year later, he produced a new version of his seminal treatise on education. *The Lancasterian System of Education with Improvements* was printed by W.O. Niles and sold at Lancaster's school in Baltimore. Lancaster registered his copyright on 24 January 1821 in the District of Maryland.[60]

As he had in the past, Lancaster sought copyright advice, this time from American inventor and patentee William Shotwell on the question of whether he should secure his rights in the UK as well as in the United States. He received the following counsel:

> Unless the work is published in England before it is at any other place there can be no exclusive privilege. It will therefore be necessary to furnish [Longmans] with a Copy and give them time to get out the Press before it is published here [in the United States]. Thou can take this into view and use thy discretion. Whether it will not militate against thy claim to a privilege here I cannot say but if it does it would be right to consider which is likely to be of the most value. I am inclined to think America under existing Circumstances would be likely to produce most.[61]

The letter, dated 1819, doesn't specify the work in question. Lancaster may have been making an inquiry of a general nature or he may have been seeking advice about the new *Lancasterian System of Education*, which was intended for a cross-Atlantic audience. Shotwell was correct to suggest that Lancaster had to give his London publisher time to "get out the Press" before publishing in the United States, since first

---

59  Joseph Lancaster, *Letters on National Subjects*. The full text of the official copyright registration was reproduced after the title page of the book.

60  Joseph Lancaster, *The Lancasterian System of Education with Improvements*. The full text of the official copyright registration was reproduced after the title page of the book.

61  William Shotwell to Lancaster, New York, 1819, box 3, folder 1, no. 145, p. 26, JLP.

publication in the UK was required for a British copyright. He was, however, unsure about Lancaster's ability to secure his copyright in both countries, and he suggested that an American copyright would be more advantageous. Lancaster followed this advice: he published both works exclusively in the United States and secured his copyright there.

When Lancaster left for Caracas in 1824, he was undoubtedly dismayed to learn that Colombia had no copyright laws. It is not surprising then that he interceded on behalf of his friend, the printer, publisher, and bookseller Rudolf Ackermann, who had previously petitioned the Colombian government for copyright. The London-based Ackermann was Colombia's major supplier of books, especially schoolbooks, in the Spanish language.[62] On 15 August 1825, Lancaster wrote to Colombian vice president Paul Satander to add his voice to Ackermann's request:

> My friend ... has written for some exclusive priviledge [*sic*] as to copy right. I know not of what nature or terms of years, but this I think that an encouragement of the sort is really what he merits and that with this encouragement I may induce him to invest much larger sums in supplying the superior class in all Elementary Schools with valuable I may say invaluable additions to the Stock of such books already sent to me.[63]

It is not clear whether Lancaster received any official response, but in December, Ackermann again sought Lancaster's help. He was under the impression that his petition had been granted; a newspaper had reported as much.[64] He asked Lancaster to intervene with customs officials to prevent unauthorized reprints of Spanish books from entering the country:

> I am informed from Paris that some ill-principled Frenchmen are reprinting my Spanish Books and they having no Authorship to pay, could much undersell me. I anticipated such Piratical Rogueries not only from France but also from the United States. I addressed nearly Twelve Months ago a Petition to your Congress, praying for Protection of Copyright, for Fourteen Years, Similar to the Laws of England and many other States

---

62 Vaughan, *Joseph Lancaster in Caracas*, 160. Vaughan says that Ackermann (1764–1834) and Lancaster were friends. On Ackermann and the Spanish book trade, see Roldán Vera, *The British Book Trade*, 127.

63 Vaughan, *Joseph Lancaster in Caracas*, 148.

64 *El Colombiano* had incorrectly reported that Ackermann's petition was successful. See Cadavid, *De los privilegios a la propriedad intelectual*, 110. See also Vaughan, *Joseph Lancaster in Caracas*, 168.

of Europe. I hope orders have before now reached your Custom House on that Subject, if not, please communicate(?) it to the comptroller ... The annexed printed Catalogues will serve to inform you what Spanish Books are my Property, and I most honestly request your Friendship in preventing Spurious Imitations to enter your Territory. In my next Shipment I will forward a Collection of all my books in the Spanish Language for the Head Gentlemen of the Customs House ... to enable them the better to know the Spurious from the Genuine editions, in the interim I rely on your kindness to have an Eye on the protection of my Property.[65]

Ackermann was mistaken. The Colombian legislature rejected his claim for copyright in January 1826, in what appears to have been a misunderstanding about his intent. The belief was that Ackermann was asking that he be granted the exclusive monopoly over the importation of Spanish books into the country, rather than a copyright to prevent the circulation of unauthorized reprints. As he related to Lancaster a few months later: "The Government at Bogota have not granted my request respecting the protection of Copy Right; they suppose I want an exclusive privilege for importing Spanish Books into the Republic; which is far from my meaning. What I ask is a protection of property to every Bookseller and Speculator who is at the expense of employing authors and paying high prices for manuscripts."[66]

Lancaster left the country not long after this exchange. Had he stayed, he would undoubtedly have continued to lobby for copyright. He had a number of writing projects that he wanted to complete, and copyright was increasingly becoming an essential feature of his overall financial strategy, especially in terms of providing for his new family, whose assets he had squandered. The most ambitious of these plans was to publish his autobiography, which he believed would vindicate him in the eyes of his detractors and whose copyright would be of great value. Not long before his death in 1838, he wrote to his spouse Mary: "[C]ertain I am that I cannot be better employed, in any way, for my family interests than in writing this life; which will become a precious property for you."[67]

Lancaster had begun to write his memoirs shortly after his arrival in the United States in 1818, opining to his daughter Betsy that his papers

___

65   Rudolf Ackermann to Lancaster, 7 December 1825, box 3, folder 145, 140, JLP.
66   Rudolf Ackermann to Lancaster, 4 October 1826, box 3, folder 2, no. 145, 163, JLP.
67   Lancaster to Mary Lancaster, Miscellaneous Material on Lancaster, box 3, folder 5, JLP.

would prove to be of great importance. He urged her to "preserve them, with all I write to thee, as documents. These, and many other old letters, will be valuable one day, in case it should please Providence to remove me without finishing the manuscripts of my life. These papers, and my other papers, would be worth something considerable to thee ... a Painter's pictures fetch more after his death than during his life, because he can paint no more; and so it is with authors when they can write no more."[68]

Lancaster's intent was to print the book himself. As he explained to his son-in-law, Richard Maddox Jones: "My printing office is likely one day to produce the history of my life and travels."[69] Of course, in order to bring such an elaborate project to fruition, he needed a stable lifestyle. At least at the outset, Lower Canada appeared to provide him with an auspicious environment where he could complete his autobiography and chronicle his teaching successes in publications from which he hoped to earn a living. He expressed to one of his former students, John E. Lovell, that he did not recollect a period in his life when he was as happy.[70] Of course, things eventually soured and he returned to the United States in 1833, but in these early halcyon days, his prospects seemed promising save in one important respect. Once again, he found himself in a jurisdiction that offered no domestic copyright protection. This being a deficiency to be remedied, Lancaster began his interventions to bring copyright to the British colony he now considered home. It all began with a remarkable petition to the Assembly from Joseph-François Perrault, submitted not long after Lancaster's arrival in the province.

### "… But Here Is No Copy Right or Present Security": Joseph Lancaster, Joseph- François Perrault, and Copyright in Lower Canada

Hailed as the "father of education in Lower Canada," Joseph-François Perrault played a critical role in the growth and development of public education in the province. At great personal and financial cost, he took

---

68   Lancaster to Betsy Lancaster, Boston, 19 July 1819 [emphasis Lancaster], box 2 folder 3, no. 141, 29–31, JLP.

69   Lancaster to Richard Maddox Jones, 28 January 1828, box 2, folder 4, no. 141, JLP.

70   John E. Lovell to Lancaster, New Haven, 1 April 1831, box 2, folder 7, 53, JLP. "You say you do not recollect a period in your life when you were so happy as at present. I am justified I presume in inferring from this remark that your pecuniary circumstances have improved" [emphasis Lovell].

a principled stance for the cause of non-confessional, universal public education through his philanthropy, his writings, and his leadership in the establishment of school societies, elementary schools, and teacher training. Born in Quebec City in 1753 to a prosperous merchant family, his early years read like a fictional tale of high adventure.[71] In an attempt to join his father in the United States, the nineteen-year-old Perrault was shipwrecked and suffered deprivations and misery. Once reunited with his father in St. Louis, his life took a more fortunate turn as he spent a period as interpreter and then French secretary to the Governor of Illinois. He was captured by the British in 1779 and released into the care of his maternal uncle, Jacques Baby dit Duperont, in Detroit, a British possession at that time. Perrault returned to Lower Canada in 1780, engaging in a number of business ventures before training as a lawyer. He was appointed Clerk of the Peace in 1795 and as prothonotary to the Court of King's Bench at Quebec in 1802. A prolific writer, he compiled, wrote or translated legal treatises and manuals of practice and procedure at a time when this kind of material was scarce.[72]

In the 1820s, Perrault directed his considerable energies to the cause of public schooling. Noticing the want of appropriate teaching materials, he began to write and compile a variety of schoolbooks for use in his schools. As Bruce Curtis explained: "Perrault's production of nine schoolbooks in French, including primers, tables of words divided into syllables with demonstrative uses, grammars, and a history of Canada, facilitated the use of the Lancasterian pedagogy for French-speaking students, but also provided a home-grown elementary school curriculum that could have been used in rural schools if legislators had been sympathetic to his larger plans for school boards."[73]

Perrault was a steadfast admirer of Lancaster's monitorial system of instruction. His first educational treatise, *Cours d'éducation élémentaire à l'usage de l'école gratuite établie dans la cité de Québec en 1821*, was a summary, with modifications, of Lancaster's pedagogical method.[74] In

---

71  Perrault (1753–1844) described his early life in his autobiography, published in 1834: Perrault, *Biographie*. See also "Quatre lettres inédites" and entry for Perrault in DCB.

72  Lawrence Hart described Perrault as "the first Canadian to instruct and combine, in one workable system, the laws of two great countries … He belongs to the rarefied atmosphere of pioneer professional thinkers and doers." Hart, "Joseph-François Perrault," 281.

73  See Curtis, *Ruling by Schooling*, 175.

74  Perrault, *Cours d'éducation élémentaire*. See also Magnan, "Le centenaire du premier traité."

it, Perrault extolled monitorial education: "L'adoption du mode d'enseignement mutuel, par les peuples les plus civilisés de l'Europe, est une preuve non équivoque de sa supériorité sur les anciennes méthodes d'enseigner."[75] In 1831 he won a prize for his essay *Plan raisonné d'éducation générale et permanente le plus propre à faire la prospérité du Bas-Canada, en égard à ses circonstances actuelles*, in which he expressed his views on the essential features of an effective educational system, which included the adoption of monitorial teaching, which he claimed was universally recognized as the best method of instruction.[76]

One important feature of Lancaster's educational approach was its non-denominational nature. Lancaster was a Quaker and had suffered from discrimination because of his religious beliefs. His curriculum adhered to Christian principles without favouring a particular group: "This School," he once wrote, "is not established to promote the Religious Principles of any particular Sect; but setting aside all party distinctions, its object is to instruct Youth in useful Learning, in the leading and uncontroverted principles of Christianity, and to train them in the practice of moral habits conducive to their future welfare as virtuous men and useful members of society."[77]

Perrault's educational philosophy was similarly non-denominational – which did not win him friends among the Lower Canadian Catholic clergy. He was scorned for operating impious schools by the Bishop of Montreal Monseigneur Jean-Jacques Lartigue, who refused to support his school: "cet établissement se tourne évidemment en école biblique, c'est-à-dire en école de protestantisme ou d'impiété."[78] The religious hierarchy perceived Lancasterianism as a manifestation of the insidious liberal and anti-religious sentiments prevalent among certain segments of Lower Canadian society. Lartigue also objected to an 1825 education

---

75   Perrault, *Cours d'éducation élémentaire*, 7. [The adoption of the system of mutual education by the most civilized peoples in Europe is unequivocal proof of its superiority over the old methods of teaching.]

76   Perreault, "Plan raisonné d'éducation."

77   Lancaster, *Improvements in Education* (1805), 25. For scholarship critical of the "civilizing" mission of these schools, see, for example, Kharem, "The African Free Schools"; and Rayman, "Joseph Lancaster's Monitorial System." The Lancasterian Jews' Free School was opened in London in 1817, but the BFSS refused to grant a dispensation from lessons on the New Testament. See Levin, "The Origins of the Jews' Free School."

78   Letter from Msgr Lartigue, Bishop of Montreal, to Msgr Plessis, Bishop of Quebec, cited by Jolois, *Joseph-François Perrault*, 111. [This establishment is obviously turning into a biblical school, that is to say a school of Protestantism or of impiety.]

bill, drafted by Perrault, that sought to introduce monitorial pedagogy in public schools throughout the province:

> Ceci est une affaire majeure où tous les vrais Canadiens et les catholiques doivent se réunir pour faire tomber à plat un projet aussi désastreux pour ce pays. C'en est fait de l'éducation chrétienne dans notre patrie et par conséquent de la religion des générations futures, si on laisse introduire ce système biblique gazé sous le nom de Lancastre. Malheureusement, il paraît que votre protonotaire Perrault, qui en est engoué, fait tous ses efforts pour le faire prévaloir … j'espère que vous ferez tous vos efforts pour faire avorter ce nouveau plan d'impiété.[79]

Perrault's activism mirrored Lancaster's, although their circumstances were quite different. Perrault's family were merchants with fairly significant connections. Also, Perrault had the benefit of a classical education at the Séminaire de Québec. In contrast, Lancaster came from poverty and was poorly educated. However, both men were zealous champions of universal education and genuinely concerned about the need to educate the poor. Operating independently of religious establishments, they also had to combat virulent critics who undermined their attempts to provide universal, non-sectarian public schooling. Perrault suffered additionally because of his pro-British sympathies: "Perrault offended both the majority in the Assembly by his support for the Crown, and the Catholic hierarchy by his insistence on admitting students of all religious denominations to his school."[80]

It is hard to imagine that someone who had so dedicated himself to Lancasterian education, and who had withstood censure and criticism because of it, would not have corresponded or otherwise communicated with Lancaster. There is no direct evidence that the two men knew each other, but it seems implausible that they would not have had

---

79 Letter from Msgr Lartigue, Bishop of Montreal, to Msgr Plessis, Bishop of Quebec, cited in Jolois, *Joseph-François Perrault*, 112. [This is a major affair where all true *Canadiens* and Catholics must come together to reject a project that would be disastrous for this country. It would be the end of Christian education in our homeland and consequently the end of the religion for future generations, if this biblical system is allowed to be introduced under the name of Lancaster. Unfortunately, it seems that your prothonotary Perrault, who is infatuated with it, is making every effort to make this system prevail ... I hope you will do your utmost to defeat this new impious plan.] The Bill failed to become law. See Curtis, *Ruling by Schooling*, 97–9.

80 Curtis, "Joseph Lancaster in Montreal *bis*," 7. See also Jolois, *Joseph-François Perrault*.

some contact, especially during Lancaster's visits to Quebec prior to his settling in Lower Canada. Lancaster was certainly acquainted with William Morris, the schoolmaster at the British and Canadian School at Quebec. In a letter from Quebec dated 25 August 1828, Lancaster wrote to his "Respected friend Morris," noting that "though our acquaintance has been short ... my happiness has been greatly increased on this visit by a sight of thy school."[81] It is reasonable to speculate that Perrault, who was the president of the British and Canadian School Society at that time, might also have met with Lancaster during this visit to the school. More compelling still, the events surrounding the enactment of Lower Canada's first copyright statute offer evidence from which to surmise that the two men were in close touch.[82] In fact, I suggest that Lancaster directly influenced Perrault and his actions during the parliamentary session that began the year of Lancaster's arrival.

On 15 January 1830, mere months after Lancaster had settled in Lower Canada, Perrault submitted a petition to Governor James Kempt, who referred it to the Assembly. The petition, introduced by Denis-Benjamin Viger on 27 January 1830, followed immediately on John Neilson's introduction of Joseph Lancaster's first petition for financial aid for his school. Perrault contended that "there being a deficiency in this Country of books, for giving instruction methodically in the French Language, the Petitioner has compiled a few, which in his opinion are adapted to the use of Elementary Schools."[83] Perrault described these books as ranging from an *abécédaire* (spelling book) to a *Manuel pratique* (book of practical exercises). He further related that his "means are not ample enough to enable him to have a sufficient number of copies printed of these works so as to reduce them to the moderate price of one shilling each, which would place them within the reach of every individual." He asked the Assembly to undertake the expense of printing one edition – not at all an unusual request at that time. However,

---

81  J. Stewart, "To the Editor of the Times," *The Times* (London), 27 August 1833, 7.

82  Curtis draws a similar conclusion: "Perrault and Lancaster were almost certainly acquainted personally, for not only was Lancaster frequently in Quebec, but also the two agitated before the Executive Council at the same period for the passage of a colonial copyright law to protect their educational publications." Curtis, "Tocqueville," 120; Jolois, *Joseph-François Perrault*, 126, also speculated that they must have met.

83  Journals of the House of Assembly of Lower Canada 10 & 11 Geo. 4, 31. Perrault's original handwritten petitions in both French and English can be found at LAC, Civil Secretary's Correspondence, Quebec, Lower Canada, and Canada East (1760–1863), vol. 307, no. 128 (15 January 1830).

Perrault concluded the petition with the following: "that the exclusive property in these works shall be declared to be vested in the Petitioner, his heirs and assigns and that all others shall be prohibited from printing or selling them for the future, subject to the usual penalties in such cases *à peine* without his or their approbation."[84]

This was the first time in Canadian copyright history that an author expressly sought an "exclusive property" over the printing and sale of his writings for himself and his heirs or assigns. Perrault's petition was unprecedented. As will be recalled, Hamilton Leslie had requested only a premium or reward for his new pedagogical method. Joseph Bouchette had routinely requested financial aid in general terms, asking for "whatever the Assembly deemed fit," including during the same parliamentary session as Perrault. A contemporaneous petition from Samuel Hull Wilcocke, in respect of his *History of the Session of the Provincial Parliament of Lower Canada for 1828–29*, requested only "relief, by a grant of money, or in any other way that the House in its wisdom may seem fit."[85] None of these authors sought rights over the publication itself. Something, or *someone*, had prompted Perrault to think in copyright terms.

Of course, Perrault may well have been acting without Lancaster's guidance. However, I suggest the contrary. Cast in clear copyright language, Perrault's request represented a significant departure from the tenor of his previous petitions to the Assembly, which had all been directed toward securing funding for his schools. As we have seen, Perrault was a prolific author and compiler of law books, but he had funded those publications through private subscriptions.[86] In 1823 he had launched a subscription for printing and publishing his schoolbooks, but this effort failed because influential members of the Catholic clergy refused to subscribe.[87] Indeed, by 1829 Perrault was trying to

---

84  Journals of the House of Assembly of Lower Canada 10 & 11 Geo. 4, 31.

85  Journals of the House of Assembly of Lower Canada 10 & 11 Geo. 4, 121. Wilcocke, *History of the Session*. On Wilcocke (1766–1833), see his entry in DCB.

86  LAC, Neilson Collection, Business, Legal, and Political Records 1794–1845, vol. 16, 41a, reel C-15772. Contract between Perrault and Neilson dated 25 January 1806 for subscription printing of Perrault's *Dictionnaire portatif et abrégé*.

87  In November 1823, Mgr Lartigue wrote to Mgr Plessis to let him know that he had refused to subscribe for the printing of Perrault's books. Moreover, he found it surprising that Plessis didn't disapprove of the subscription. Cited in Jolois, *Joseph-François Perrault*, 111. In his autobiography, Perrault alluded to having borne most of the financial burdens of his schools as well as the publishing costs of his books.

support two schools on meagre government grants, and the bulk of his educational oeuvre had been written in anticipation of the needs of these schools. Finding a way to have his schoolbooks printed must have been a top priority, yet he had never sought a printing privilege or any other form of governmental aid, grant, or concession for his manuscripts until Lancaster arrived on the scene.

Perrault's copyright petition was referred to the Special Committee on that part of His Excellency's Speech relating to Education, which was chaired by Blanchet and whose members included Neilson and Viger. The special committee ignored Perrault's request for exclusive rights, which is surprising given its composition. The final recommendation was that Perrault be awarded £500 to print his spelling books, syllabaries, vocabulary tables, and treatise on arithmetic. Inexplicably, the Assembly reduced the amount of the grant to £100 to print "Elementary School Books," without specifying which ones.[88]

Significantly, during this last parliamentary session before his death, François Blanchet not only chaired the Special Committee on Education that addressed Perrault's request but also presented Wilcocke's petition and chaired the committee that reviewed it. Wilcocke had asked for a grant to cover publication cost overruns, and the committee recommended that the Assembly subscribe for 100 copies.[89] Given his interest in encouraging parliamentary reporting, Blanchet's involvement in this file is not surprising: Wilcocke's work has been described as "the first approach in Canada to Hansard."[90] However, it does seem curious that Blanchet did not use the Wilcocke and Perrault petitions as a vehicle to revive his previous attempts to introduce a copyright Bill. This omission is all the more mystifying when one remembers that Perrault clearly requested "copyright" – an unprecedented step. Whatever Blanchet's reasons for not taking up this opportunity, the fact remains that Perrault's request for an exclusive property in his writings was unusual for its time and suggests that he had some assistance or at least drew some inspiration, if not prompting, from someone like Lancaster. As we know,

---

88   Journals of the House of Assembly of Lower Canada, 18 March 1830, 10 & 11 Geo. 4, 346. Perrault used the Assembly's £100 along with his own funds to print 1,000 copies of his speller, two syllabaries, and two hundred copies of his *Manuel Pratique*. See Journals of the House of Assembly of Lower Canada, 31 January 1831, 1 Will. 4, 40–1.

89   Journals of the House of Assembly of Lower Canada, 10 & 11 Geo. 4 (1830), 173. It doesn't appear that the House of Assembly acted on the recommendation.

90   Wilcocke's handwritten petition is available at LAC, Civil Secretary Correspondence Quebec, Lower Canada, and Canada East, 1760– 863, vol. 311, no. 85.

Lancaster had first-hand experience with copyright, both in jurisdictions with mature copyright laws and in those that offered no protection all.

Two months after his copyright claim was rejected, Perrault tried a different tack. On 6 May he wrote to Governor Kempt once again, this time seeking the issuance of a patent to provide him, his heirs, or his assigns the exclusive right to print ten of his elementary schoolbooks, which he enumerated in the petition. Perrault argued that his claim fell within the purview of the existing Lower Canadian Patent Act.[91] The matter was referred to Attorney General James Stuart, who did not deliberate for long. On 12 May, Stuart denied Perrault's request on the grounds that "the Provincial Statutes to which Mr. Perrault grounds his application do not extend or relate to literary property, or copy right in Books or Writings."[92] Stuart declared that patent laws related "exclusively to inventions, and the publication and introduction of inventions of a new and useful art, machine, manufacture of composition of matter. Literary Property and copy right are things altogether distinct from these subjects of exclusive priviledge [*sic*] and as yet no Legislative Provision has been made in this Province for conferring on, or securing to, authors or compilers, a copy right in their respective Productions."[93]

Perrault's request under the Patent Act had been a long shot, and it is not at all clear what prompted this approach. One might see in this attempt another example of Lancaster's involvement with Perrault, since Lancaster had long held the view that he could patent his teaching method as well as his writings. One of Lancaster's last inquiries before his death was whether he could patent a proposed new edition of his book, *Improvements in Education*. The reply he received from the Attorney General of the United States, Benjamin F. Butler, was very similar to Stuart's reply to Perrault: "I fear you would be obliged, for your pecuniary security, to rely exclusively on the Copy Right; but I will confer with Mr. Ellsworth, the Commissioner of Patents and inform you whether the improvement can be made the subject of a Patent."[94]

---

91  LAC, Civil Secretary's Correspondence, Quebec, Lower Canada, and Canada East (1760–1863), 6 May 1830, vol. 322, 91.

92  LAC, Civil Secretary's Correspondence, Quebec, Lower Canada, and Canada East (1760–1863), file May 1830, Opinions of the Law Officers, 12 May 1830, 28.

93  LAC, Civil Secretary's Correspondence, Quebec, Lower Canada, and Canada East (1760–1863), file May 1830, Opinions of the Law Officers, 12 May 1830, 28. See discussion of this legal opinion in chapter 1 in relation to common law copyright.

94  Benjamin F. Butler to Lancaster, Washington, 31 March 1838, box 3, folder 3, no. 145, 248, JLP. It is not clear whether Lancaster was asking about a patent on the book itself or, rather, on his teaching method.

The strategy of looking to the Patent Act to protect one's publications was an interesting, albeit short-lived, approach to filling the legislative gap. It is reminiscent of the Assembly's own muddled approach to Hamilton Leslie's petition as well as to the ambiguity surrounding the nature of copyright and patent at the time – perceptions of their interchangeability were still present. This latest rejection proved to be the final one for Perrault. He never again asked the legislature for exclusive rights over his books. It was Joseph Lancaster who would now take matters in hand. He must have known of Perrault's failed attempts at copyright, because he began his own interventions not long afterwards.

On 9 September 1830, Lancaster composed an early draft of a letter that he would later amend in the final version he sent to "Administrator in Chief" Sir James Kempt on 23 September 1830. It is quite illuminating to compare them.[95]

In both drafts, which are reproduced in full on the next page, Lancaster claimed to have made inquiries about the state of copyright law in the province. Perhaps these inquiries had been made of Perrault? Both letters described the state of affairs for a British author in colonial Lower Canada. His reference to the fact that the "mother country" recognized copyright, while the colonies did not, lent a sense of urgency to his claim. Of course, Lancaster could have continued to enjoy the benefits of British copyright protection for any work first published in the United Kingdom. He was certainly aware of this, given his previous inquiries on the matter while still in the United States, but Lancaster was not interested in publishing in the United Kingdom. Rather, his focus was on ensuring that he could protect and derive economic benefits from his future Lower Canadian publications. He sought the establishment of a copyright registration process similar to the American system to which he was accustomed. However, his recommendation for the deposit of a copy of the work in the Parliamentary Library was more consistent with British copyright requirements, although, under British law, the deposits were to be made to university libraries. The copyright law of the United States only required a deposit with the Secretary of State.

Of more interest, however, is the striking difference between the two missives. In his initial letter he justified his request for copyright on the

---

95   The draft handwritten letter can be found at JLP, Lancaster to Sir James Kempt, 9 September 1830, box 3, folder 3, no. 145, 197, JLP. The final handwritten letter can be found at LAC, Lancaster to Sir James Kempt, Montreal, 23 September 1830, LAC, Civil Secretary's Correspondence Quebec, Lower Canada, and Canada East, 1760–1863, vol. 336, 81.

| Letter #1: Lancaster's draft, 9 September 1830 | Letter #2: Lancaster's final letter, 23 September 1830 |
| --- | --- |
| Honoured Friend<br><br>The following statement is respectfully submitted to thy consideration –<br><br>I cannot find on enquiry that there is any law of security for copy right in Lower Canada.<br><br>Consequently – If one man writes a book and invests in its publication Time talent and money – another man may reprint the work – and infringe his right with impunity.<br><br>When an Englishman settles in this Province – If he is an author, he may have his copy-rights secured in England and lose them by coming here.<br><br>How desirable it is, then a suitable Legislative act should pass securing all rights to British emigrants which the law may have given them when in England and that a proposition be submitted to Parliament to establish the Law of copy right by depositing [?] the title page of the book – and when complete a copy of every book published with the <u>clerk of the County</u> in Montreal or Quebec or with some official character and on paying a small fee – the author or proprietor, to be furnished with an official copy of the record which shall be documentary evidence in any Court of Justice.<br><br>If I feel at leisure I may publish in perhaps 12 months an account of my Life and travels – Here I can correct the proofs under my own eyes and send the impression or part of it to England – but here is no copy right nor present security.<br><br>This case is most respectfully considered worthy of thy notice and a remedy hoped for by thy obliged friend. | Honoured Friend<br><br>The following statement concerning security of property, in copyrights is respectfully submitted to thy consideration. – On enquiry I do not find that there is any law of security for copy right in Lower Canada. – Consequently if one man writes a book and invests in its publication Time talent and money; another man may reprint the work and infringe the said right with impunity.<br><br>–   If an Englishman has a copy right in England, the law protects his copy right, but on coming to this province he loses his right, for it seems that he has no local – legal – protection.<br><br>The remedy may be found in a law which shall enact<br><br>1.   That there be a record office – and a recording officer appointed in the cities of Quebec and Montreal, where all persons having copy rights to secure may have the same registered on depositing the copy of the title of the work of which they claim copy right<br><br>–   That whenever any work is published after being so registered a copy be deposited with the recording officer<br><br>–   for the parliamentary Library and another copy for the Governor for the time being.<br><br>That the copy of the register of the claim of copyright, be granted on paying a small fee (say $1) and be allowed as evidence in courts of justice as far as concerns the legal Register of prior claims of copy right<br><br>The above considerations may have an extensive future bearing on British literary property hereafter seeing Canada is and may long continue to be a great outlet, in part, for the surplus population of England the book market and manufactory for whom will one day be of no small importance.<br><br>I have the happiness to remain thy obliged and respectful friend. |

basis that he was intending to finish his autobiography within twelve months: "If I feel at leisure I may publish in perhaps 12 months an account of my Life and travels – Here I can correct the proofs under my own eyes and send the impression or part of it to England – but here is no copy right nor present security." Here again one gets a sense of just how important completing his autobiography had become to him – it was Lancaster's defining project, and he intended to finish it within a year. One sees, as well, the extent to which his initial impulses regarding copyright were entirely self-serving. However, by the time he sent his official letter he had, presumably, obtained some sober second opinion, because the last substantive paragraph is entirely transformed.

In the revised text, Lancaster omitted any reference to his autobiography, arguing instead that a copyright law would be an important public benefit for it would encourage the literary pursuits of British immigrants and foster a Lower Canadian book trade to support their endeavours. He argued that "Canada is and may long continue to be a great outlet, in part, for the surplus population of England the book market and manufactory for whom will one day be of no small importance." He would, of course, be among those British immigrants to benefit, but his request is clearly directed away from himself. It is ironic that Lancaster, the champion of education for the poor, argued for copyright exclusively in relation to its benefits for authors and the book trade. He never referred to the impact of copyright on the advancement of learning and literacy, even though this was an issue of particular concern for the politicians and pedagogues in his inner circle. Lancaster's views of copyright were clearly informed by his own self-interest.

We can only speculate as to why he made the changes in the final version, or who might have advised him to moderate his message. He was certainly sufficiently self-absorbed that the first iteration was likely closer to his true intent. There may, however, be a small indication of what might have prompted him to produce the more public-minded official letter. After his initial success in securing public funding for his educational endeavours, Lancaster's subsequent petitions to the Assembly were not unanimously approved but were, instead, taken to a vote. This suggests that not everyone in the Assembly felt that he deserved public patronage. His fortunes were waning. In the fall of 1831, the *Montréal Courant* took the position that "on two previous occasions Mr. Lancaster had obtained liberal grants, and we do, with all due deference to our 'collective wisdom,' think that unless the public are shown what improvements, or at least on what progress on improvement

Mr. L has made, no more of the monies of the Province should be granted him."[96]

If ambivalence had been growing when it came to allocating public funds for Lancaster's educational projects, a petition for the enactment of a copyright law drafted exclusively around his own interests would perhaps have met greater resistance than one framed in terms of supporting authors and the Lower Canadian book trade. He may even have been reminded of the misunderstanding regarding Ackermann's petition to the legislature of Colombia and sought to make it clear that he was asking for something of general benefit rather than a monopoly for himself alone.

In October 1830, James Kempt acknowledged receipt of "Mr Lancaster's communication respecting the Security of Copy Right Property" and referred the matter to the incoming Governor, Lord Aylmer, who was to assume his position the following month. In his letter, Kempt told Lancaster that his copyright request was a subject "to which His Excellency would have given every attention had he continued in the Administration of the Government" but that he was confident that Lord Aylmer would give it equal attention.[97]

The Journal of the Assembly for Aylmer's first parliamentary session is silent in relation to Lancaster's copyright claim. The delay was likely due to the transition from one governor to the next. However, one does find a petition from Lancaster for aid for his school in Montreal, as well as another from Perrault for aid to print his books, without, however, any claims for copyright protection.[98] Perrault asked only for "such pecuniary assistance as [the Assembly] in its wisdom it may deem expedient" and was awarded £50 to print his *Abrégé de l'histoire du Canada*.[99] His remaining manuscripts were not given Assembly support.

Lancaster's copyright petition was finally presented in the fall of 1831 by John Neilson. The language of the petition was framed much more succinctly than Lancaster's letter to the governor had been, but it was equally clear and unequivocal in its objective. Before the Assembly,

---

96   As cited in the *Columbian Register* (New Haven), 17 December 1831, 3. See also Curtis, *Ruling by Schooling*, 183–4, on similar criticisms of Lancaster in the press.

97   Sir James Kempt to Lancaster, Castle of St Lewis, 16 October 1830, box 3, folder 3, no. 145, 195, JLP.

98   Journals of the House of Assembly of Lower Canada, 1 Will. 4 (1831), 41.

99   Journals of the House of Assembly of Lower Canada, 1 Will. 4 (1831), 41. See also an *Act to make further provision for the Encouragement of Education in this Province*, 1831, 1 Will. 4, c. 7.

Lancaster sought "an Act to secure the Copyright of any of his Publications respecting Education, or for the use of Schools in this Province."[100] The petition was referred to the Standing Committee on Education and Schools ("The Education Committee"), which was chaired by Neilson. It was indeed fortuitous that Joseph Lancaster arrived on the scene when he did, as he proved to be the stimulus for renewed legislative attention to the question of copyright. However, as will be discussed in the next chapter, the final push for the successful enactment of the Copyright Act was not Lancaster's alone. Instead, it emerged out of the collective efforts of a close network of like-minded Lower Canadian politicians and reformers who cared deeply about the cause of education and who were especially concerned about the state of schoolbook production in the province.

---

100   Journals of the House of Assembly of Lower Canada, 2 Will. 4 (1831–1832), 49.

# Chapter Five

# The Making of the 1832 Copyright Act

**The Standing Committee on Education and Schools: Copyright
Policy and the Politics of Education, Literacy, and Learning**

The Standing Committee on Education and Schools (the "Education
Committee") that served during the second session of the fourteenth
provincial Parliament (1832–3) consisted of eleven members, including
veteran politicians like John Neilson and Louis Lagueux, both of whom
had both in the Assembly at the time of the Blanchet Bills. There were
also some newly minted parliamentarians noted for their involvement
in educational causes, Augustin-Norbert Morin among them. Elected to
fill the vacant seat of the late François Blanchet, Morin was, like his predecessor, an advocate for universal public education and a supporter of
Lancasterian teaching methods.[1] He believed that "il faut que le pauvre
ait comme le riche l'occasion de s'instruire."[2] It was Morin who introduced the copyright Bill that ultimately became law in the province.

The Education Committee was first established as a standing committee in 1831. Its status as a permanent body attests to the significance

---

1  In an undated manuscript Morin developed his ideas for a provincial system of
   education, and he recommended Lancaster's system for elementary schools. See
   "'Écoles élémentaires, d'après la manière de Lancaster': Plan de la société d'encouragement : partie qui regarde l'éducation," documents divers, Fonds Augustin-
   Norbet Morin, Centre d'Archives Saint-Hyacinthe, CH006/000/000/039.034. The
   work was likely written sometime after 1841, when he was elected to the Société
   d'éducation du district de Québec. Some of the ideas contained in this document
   appear to have formed the basis of his address to the Institut canadien in 1845. See
   Augustin-Norbert Morin, *Lecture prononcée par L'Hon. A.-N. Morin.*
2  Paradis, *Augustin-Norbert Morin*, 75. Reported in *Le Canadien*, 1 March 1841. [The
   poor must have the same opportunity to be educated as the rich.].

of the education portfolio, since committees of this kind were tasked with matters of ongoing legislative importance.[3] Indeed, the drive toward universal schooling that had begun in the first decades of the nineteenth century gained momentum in the 1830s. As concerns over the provision of schoolbooks and other teaching materials increased, copyright law, schoolbook production, and the development of public elementary education became even more intertwined in the minds of the education reformers in the Assembly. And no one would have understood the relationship between copyright, book production, and the encouragement of learning better than John Neilson himself, who, as chair of the Education Committee, exercised considerable influence over its deliberations.

John Neilson was the most important printer, publisher, and bookseller of his day. His business was the largest and most significant printing establishment in British North America during the late eighteenth century and the first half of the nineteenth. Its most important publication was the *Quebec Gazette*, a newspaper issued weekly in both French and English. The Neilson firm was also a substantial importer and vendor of schoolbooks, supplying both the Lower Canadian and Upper Canadian markets. When he entered politics, the circumspect Neilson divested himself of the business so that he could dedicate himself to the affairs of the province and avoid any conflict of interest. His son Samuel took over the firm in partnership with William Cowan; the elder Neilson nevertheless remained the *éminence grise* of the enterprise.[4]

Neilson had a great sympathy for and affinity with the *Canadiens*. A Presbyterian who married into a prominent francophone Roman Catholic family, he was in a unique position to mediate the linguistic, religious, and political conflicts of nineteenth-century Lower Canadian society.[5] Alexis de Tocqueville described him as "un homme d'un esprit

---

3   The Lower Canadian Assembly began to establish more standing committees in 1831, instead of its previous practice of appointing special committees on a case-by-case basis. The Education Committee was among the first to be designated as permanent.

4   According to Bateson, the perception remained that John Neilson was still involved with the *Quebec Gazette* at least indirectly. See Bateson, "John Neilson of Lower Canada." In addition, the Neilson Collection at LAC contain numerous examples of business correspondence addressed to John Neilson, which he forwarded to Neilson & Cowan.

5   Neilson married Marie-Ursule Hubert, a niece of the Bishop of Quebec. Religiously tolerant, Neilson supported initiatives for equality for religious minorities, including Jews, Methodists, and Baptists. See Neilson, "Constitutionalism and Nationalism."

vif et original. Sa naissance et sa position sociale en opposition l'une à l'autre forment quelquefois dans ses idées et dans sa conversation de singuliers contrastes."[6] In his day, he was referred to as Canada's Benjamin Franklin.[7]

In 1818, at the age of forty-two, Neilson was elected to the Assembly for the riding of Quebec County, serving until 1834. It speaks volumes about his character that a Scottish Presbyterian was elected and re-elected to serve a predominantly French Catholic constituency. Broad-minded and tolerant, he distinguished himself as an able parliamentarian and one of the Assembly's most active and highly regarded politicians. Respected for his integrity, he embodied the perfect mix of business acumen and selfless dedication to public service. Neilson was twice sent to London by the Assembly to speak on its behalf and was one of the most trusted advisers of Louis-Joseph Papineau, nationalist politician and Speaker of the House, until their political views diverged in the mid-1830s.[8]

At the time he took the helm of the Education Committee, Neilson was the senior statesman of the Assembly and a long-standing proponent of universal public education. We have already seen that he was a key figure among education reformers and policy-makers and a strong supporter of Lancaster's monitorial system of instruction. His commitment to public education informed his political life. In 1828, speaking before the Select Committee on the Civil Government of Canada, Neilson stated that "the Canadian party will do every thing that is possible to promote education, no matter by what party; they are persuaded that the country cannot get on without a general education."[9] Augustin-Norbert Morin spoke of him as "l'homme du Canada dont l'avis et

6  De Tocqueville, *Regards sur le Bas-Canada*, 168. [A man with a lively and original mind. His birth and his social position are in opposition to each other and sometimes create singular contrasts in his ideas and in his conversation.]

7  Chauveau, in *François-Xavier Garneau*, clxxvi: "M. Neilson, lors de sa seconde mission en Europe fut appelé le Franklin Canadien. Imprimeur comme lui, M. Neilson avait beaucoup des dispositions et des idées de l'auteur de la *Science du bonhomme Richard*." [During his second mission to Europe, Mr Neilson was called the Canadian Franklin. Being a printer himself, Mr Neilson had many of the ideas and inclinations of the author of *Science du Bonhomme Richard*.]

8  Neilson's final rupture with Louis-Joseph Papineau occurred in 1834, when he disagreed over the appropriate approach to resolving the impasse with the British regarding Lower Canadian political and financial autonomy.

9  Lower Canada, *Report from the Select Committee*, 121. Quote from John Neilson recorded in the Minutes of Evidence on 5 June 1828.

l'appui sont indispensables pour tout ce qui se rattache à l'instruction publique."[10]

Neilson's views on education were tied to enterprise, industry, and economic productivity:

> A new country cannot support many professional men, and still less, would-be mere gentlemen, idlers and scholars. By persons of education applying themselves to farming and business pursuits, these occupations will gradually become more respected; and the most independent classes of society, will at the same time, when successful in the industrious pursuits, be better qualified to give a share of their attention to public concerns and advance the general prosperity.[11]

Fiona Black suggests that Neilson's "philanthropic work in relation to schools may have been a combination of astute business practice and a Scottish tendency to promote education in general."[12] True to this vocational philosophy, Neilson served as president of the Agricultural Society and of the Quebec Mechanics Institute.[13] His earlier involvement with Lower Canadian patent legislation was a direct consequence of this utilitarian orientation. This same belief system informed his views on copyright, which became a defining issue for him once the question of copyright intersected with the cause of education.

It was fortunate that the chair of the Education Committee had an intimate knowledge of the book trade and the difficulties surrounding the availability of schoolbooks. In addition to his various engagements with Blanchet and Perrault on the education front, Neilson authored the 1831 Education Act, which included the first systematic attempt to map the use of schoolbooks in the province. Under the statutory scheme, appointed school visitors were required to report on "whether proper books are used" in each of the schools they visited.[14] Through his professional and political experiences, Neilson possessed a unique appreciation of the connection between the cost of printing, the dearth of schoolbooks, and the law designed to encourage domestic book production.

---

10   L.J. Lamoult to Augustin-Norbert Morin, LAC, Fonds Denis-Benjamin Viger, vol. 3, 1308. [The man from Canada whose advice and support are essential for all matters pertaining to public instruction.]

11   *The Quebec Gazette*, 26 August 1840, as cited by Neilson, "Constitutionalism and Nationalism," 90.

12   Black, "Horrid Republican Notions."

13   See DCB. See also Neilson, "Constitutionalism and Nationalism," 88.

14   *An Act to make further provision for the Encouragement of Education in this Province*, 1831, 1 Will. 4, c. 7, s. 9.

## The Report of the Education Committee

During the 1831–2 Parliamentary session, the Education Committee received a record number of requests from individuals and groups seeking financial assistance for schools and other educational projects.[15] Among the tasks assigned to the committee by the Assembly was the determination of "whether it would not be expedient to appropriate a certain sum of money for the purchase of School Books for pauper Children."[16] The committee never reported back to the Assembly on this question, perhaps because it believed that its recommendation in support of Lancaster's petition for a copyright law would provide a more lasting solution.

Joseph Lancaster's petition placed the issue of copyright back on the legislative agenda. However, his was not the only request of its kind during that session. The legislature also heard from Lancaster's acquaintance William Morris and from Swiss immigrant Amury Girod. William Morris's petition was introduced four days before Lancaster's by Thomas Lee, John Neilson's son-in-law and the member from Quebec (Lower Town). In his petition, he advised "that he has prepared a small Volume comprising Arithmetic in a simple form, Geometry, Measuration and Bookkeeping, and [prayed] the House to grant an aid towards the publication thereof."[17] Morris, who was the schoolmaster at the British and Canadian School at Quebec, belonged to the same network of educators as Joseph Lancaster and Joseph-François Perrault.[18] He was definitely well-acquainted with Perrault, who was the school's founder and president. We also know that he met Joseph Lancaster when the latter paid the school a visit in 1828. The timing of Morris's

---

15  First Report of the Standing Committee on Education and Schools, 1832, Appendix to the XLIst volume of the Journals of the House of Assembly of the Province of Lower Canada (1831–1832), 2 Will. 4, Appendix I.i., preamble, 1–2; *Report of the Standing Committee of the House of Assembly of Lower Canada on Education*, Appendix to the XLth volume of the Journals of the House of Assembly of the Province of Lower Canada, (1831), 1 Will. IV, Appendix B.B, preamble, 1: referred to "twenty-eight Petitions for aids for Schools and the diffusion of Useful Knowledge."

16  Journals of the House of Assembly of Lower Canada, 20 December 1831, 2 Will. 4, 198.

17  Journals of the House of Assembly of Lower Canada, 29 November 1831, 2 Will. 4 (1831–1832), 100. This was Morris's first and only petition to the Assembly on his own behalf. Previously, he had appeared as a witness on behalf of the Trustees of the British and Canadian School at Quebec in respect of petitions for financial aid for the school.

18  See Spragge, "Monitorial Schools," 77.

petition suggests that he knew the two men well enough to be aware of their interest in copyright. The same can be said for Amury Girod.[19]

Girod was a newcomer to Lower Canada, having arrived in Quebec City in the summer of 1831. He was keenly interested in agricultural education, and he soon developed connections in influential literary and educational circles. He found a platform for his pedagogical proposals in the newspaper *Le Canadien*, whose editor, Étienne Parent, had become a close friend. Parent introduced Girod to Joseph-François Perrault in the fall of that year.[20] The two men found a common interest in agricultural education and developed a plan for an agricultural school for boys in Quebec. To that end, Girod petitioned the legislature for financial aid to establish the school.[21] The petition was referred to a special committee instead of the Education Committee; however, four out of five of its members served on both, including Neilson and Morin.[22]

Amury Girod's petition, especially his witness testimony, must be read in light of his close association with Perrault.[23] Their discussions about agricultural schooling must also have touched on questions of copyright, given the nature of his remarks to the special committee:

> I offer to submit in a fortnight a little work, upon the Linnean plan; according to the system of Lancaster, or that of mutual instruction; as likewise, at the end of six or eight months the first part of a Universal History, such as I have described in my system of education for Canada … That I never mean to think of asking for any aid towards the printing of any elementary works which I may write or cause to be written; but only that, after having submitted the work to a Committee of five persons, two of whom to be chosen by myself, I may obtain the approval of the Honorable House,

---

19   On Girod (1800–1837), see his entry in DCB; Bernard, *Amury Girod*; Jolois, *Joseph-François Perrault*.

20   See Perrault's testimony, Appendix to the XLIst Volume of the Journals of the House of Assembly of the Province of Lower Canada, 3 December 1831, 2 Will. 4 (1831–1832), Minutes of Evidence, 19.

21   Journals of the House of Assembly of Lower Canada, 28 November 1831, 2 Will 4 (1831–1832), 80.

22   Journals of the House of Assembly of Lower Canada, 28 November 1831, 2 Will. 4 (1831–1832), 79–80. The report of the Special Committee was ultimately referred to the Standing Committee on Education and Schools (15 December 1831, 2 Will. 4, p. 180). Louis Lagueux and Valère Guillet were the other two members of both committees.

23   Phillippe Bernard speculates on whether Girod might have also met with Lancaster. See Bernard, *Amury Girod*.

in fixing the sale prices of such works, *guaranteeing to me the copy-right thereof*, and directing their introduction into the Schools maintained at the public expense. [emphasis added][24]

Girod asked specifically for copyright in respect of two proposed schoolbooks: a book on line drawing, to be taught using the Lancasterian system of mutual instruction; and a history of the world.[25] He was not looking for a printing subsidy from the Assembly. Instead, he sought a grant of copyright, a fixed sale price for his books, and a guarantee that they would be used in "schools maintained at the public expense." This was an unusual stipulation, for there were no schools entirely maintained at the public expense and mandatory curricula would not be adopted until much later, but it does demonstrate that, for authors of schoolbooks, both copyright and a captive market were essential for financial viability.

Although the special committee's report did not refer to the copyright request and the petition itself was later withdrawn, Girod's testimony lends support to the idea that Lancaster and Perrault had communicated their interest in copyright to their close associates.[26] And while William Morris asked only for financial assistance and not exclusive rights, his request must be viewed in conjunction with the others. Taken as a whole, the efforts of Lancaster, Perrault, Morris, and Girod seem aligned and strategic.

The Education Committee issued its report on 23 January 1832 with the following recommendations:

Your Committee have recommended an allowance of Fifty pounds as an aid for publishing a Book of Arithmetic, Geometry, and Bookkeeping,

---

24  *Minutes of Evidence taken before the Special Committee to whom was referred the Petition of Amury Girod, for an aid towards the establishment of a Normal School*, Appendix to the XLIst volume of the Journals of the House of Assembly of Lower Canada, 2 Will. 4 (1831–1832), 19–20.

25  In the French text of the Assembly Journal, "Linnean plan" is referred to as "dessin linéaire." In France, Louis-Benjamin Francoeur published *Le dessin linéaire d'après la méthode de l'enseignement mutuel* (1819), which was introduced in French Lancasterian schools. Francoeur, Louis-Benjamin. *Le dessin linéaire d'après la méthode de l'enseignement mutuel* (Paris: L. Colas, 1819). Girod may have been writing something similar or adapting from Francoeur's book. The reference to Linneaus in the English text may have been referring to drawing scientifically accurate representations of nature. Girod never published the work.

26  Girod's petition was withdrawn by Joseph-François Perrault in his capacity as president of the society formed to establish the agricultural school.

adapted to the Country, by Mr. Morris, the Teacher of the British and Canadian School at Quebec, provided that an edition of at least one thousand Copies is published and sold, substantially bound, for not more than two shillings each, and they trust that this very valuable Book may be improved and translated in French for the use of the Elementary Schools throughout the Province. *The necessity of such Books, and the little encouragement existing at present for time, talents and capital employed in this way, as well as the special application of Mr. Lancaster for a Copyright induced your Committee to recommend the introduction of a Bill securing Copyright generally nearly upon the plan which has so much contributed to the success of the publication of School Books and other Books in the adjoining States.* [emphasis added][27]

This is the only passage in the lengthy text that addressed the question of copyright. Despite its brevity, one can nevertheless discern three considerations that informed the committee's decision to recommend a copyright law for the province: (1) the necessity of schoolbooks, (2) the lack of incentive to produce them, and (3) the special application of Joseph Lancaster for a copyright. Lancaster proved to be an effective catalyst for the enactment of the law. However, William Morris's plight clearly resonated as well.

### The Necessity of Schoolbooks and the Little Time, Talents, and Capital to Produce Them

In the 1830s, provincial education initiatives increased the demand for schoolbooks.[28] However, the cost of producing domestically authored books remained an intractable challenge. Lower Canadian printers and publishers preferred to act as agents for foreign publishing interests or as reprinters of popular works rather than as full-fledged publishers

---

27   First Report of the Standing Committee on Education and Schools, 1832, Appendix to XLIst volume of the Journals of the House of Assembly of the province of Lower Canada (1831–1832), 2 Will. 4, Appendix I.i., 3. See also *Act to Appropriate Certain Sums of Money therein Mentioned to the Encouragement of Education in this Province*,1832, 2 Will. 4, c. 30, 500.

28   According to Paul Aubin, "between 1778 and 1839, forty-four printers in Quebec and Lower Canada produced 119 textbook titles for a total of 169 publications including reprints. The output increased steadily from decade to decade, peaking in the 1830s with 70 books marketed, or 58.8% of all production." See Aubin, "Books of Instruction in New France," 257. The 1829 Trustees School Act increased the number of schools and therefore the demand for schoolbooks.

who would assume the financial risks of bringing a book to market.[29] It was generally expected that authors would assume the costs by canvassing the public for subscriptions or orders to purchase in advance of publication. However, this form of financing could not guarantee publication if unexpected delays resulted in cost overruns or if subscriptions were insufficient to cover the expenses.[30] For example, Joseph Bouchette had to return to the Assembly to request an increase in financial support for his *British Dominions in North America* because the sum he had been granted turned out to be inadequate. The costs had escalated, and he was forced to raise the subscription price in the United Kingdom. He sought a similar adjustment from the Lower Canadian Assembly.[31] In 1830, journalist Samuel Hull Wilcocke turned to the legislature for financial help because delays caused by a serious illness had prevented him from obtaining sufficient subscriptions to cover the costs of printing and publishing his book on the history of the legislative session of 1828–9.[32] Similar problems with subscription publishing arose throughout British North America. Upper Canadian schoolteacher Alexander Davidson sought 1,500 subscribers to print and publish a proposed music book but had to abandon the project when only 500 placed advance orders.[33]

Even when there were sufficient subscribers, authors would not always recover their printing and publishing costs. Subscribers were frequently offered a preferential rate as an inducement to commit to the purchase of a future publication. An advertisement seeking subscribers for John Richardson's *The Canadian Brothers* announced: "As the infant state of literature in the CANADAS, has necessarily, compelled the pub lication to be one of subscription, it will be but justice to those who have assisted the work with their names, that there should be a difference in the subscribing and selling prices."[34] As Amédée Papineau explained

---

29   See, for example, Parker, *The Beginnings of the Book Trade*, 116.

30   On book publishing in Lower Canada up to the mid-nineteenth century, see generally, HBC, vol. 1, including John Hare and Jean-Pierre Wallot, "The Business of Printing and Publishing," 71–8; and Mary Lu Macdonald, "Subscription Publishing," 78–80. See also Hare and Wallot, "Les entreprises d'imprimerie."

31   Journals of the House of Assembly of Lower Canada, 5 February 1830, 2 Geo. 4, 117. The Assembly had allocated the sum of five guineas per copy, but Bouchette asked that they increase the contribution to eight guineas.

32   Journals of the House of Assembly of Lower Canada, 5 February 1830, 2 Geo. 4, 121.

33   See Riddell, "The First Copyrighted Book."

34   Richardson, *The Canadian Brothers*, ed. Donald Stephens, xlvii (editor's preface citing announcement in *Montreal Gazette*, 2 January 1840).

in a letter to his father Louis-Joseph: "Il est préférable de souscrire, je crois, que d'acheter l'ouvrage après impression, car les souscripteurs l'ont toujours à meilleur marché."[35] An author could not necessarily rely on these discounted subscriptions to fully cover expenses, let alone allow for a modest profit.

In addition, North American subscribers were not required to disburse the funds at the time of the subscription, and it was not uncommon for them to renege on their promise to purchase the work once it was published. In Richardson's case, one third of his subscribers

> had been kind enough merely to lend me the encouragement of their names, and nothing, therefore, was more natural when called upon, to decline their copies – some under the pleas that the volumes, the price of which had been made known to them on subscribing – were too dear; some, that they had been too long delayed in the publication; and not a few, that they did not feel inclined to take them at the moment.[36]

Joseph Lancaster had a similar experience in the United States. He had been accustomed to the practice in the United Kingdom where subscribers would provide payment in advance of publication. Lancaster expected the same from American subscribers but was advised that "the practice of the Country is not to ask the money at the time of subscribing, but to put on a percentage that might cover a little failure, but which with us is mostly usually made up by the sale to non-subscribers."[37] He was also warned that "the people are unaccustomed to pay before they get the work (and between us, it is counted lucky if it is got then)."[38]

For impecunious authors, subscription publishing was a risky proposition. In the case of schoolbooks, the prohibitive printing costs and the risks associated with subscription financing were especially harmful as they stymied efforts to advance the province's public education objectives. In his testimony before the Education Committee, William Morris was clear and unequivocal about the deleterious effect of high printing

---

35   Amédée and Lactance Papineau to Louis-Joseph Papineau, 15 February 1836. As cited by Lamonde "La lecture et 'le livre de l'histoire' chez Amédée Papineau (1835–1845)," 86. [I believe it is better to subscribe than to buy the book after publication because the subscribers always have it cheaper.]

36   Richardson, *Eight Years in Canada*, 108.

37   Burwell Bassett to Lancaster, Washington, 27 February 1819, box 3, folder 1, 21, JLP.

38   Robert Ould to Lancaster, 28 February 1819, box 3, folder 1, 22, JLP.

costs on elementary education. The concerns he raised would play an instrumental role in the Education Committee's final deliberations.

> I lay before the Committee a Manuscript Book containing a treatise on Arithmetic and practical Geometry. I have adopted in my School, as much as I could, the system contained in my Book; the want of printed Copies has prevented me from making use of it altogether. I am of opinion that if my work was printed and put into practice, children could learn all the rules that it contains in one year. I have not dared to get it printed. Mr Cary would not print it, but at a price I feared to give. From a note of the prices which Mr. Cowan has given to me, I believe the work would cost about 81 pounds for 1000 which would make about 2 shillings per Copy, for the printing solely, which added to the binding, would make it too dear to expect an extensive sale.[39]

To appreciate the gravity of the situation, William Cowan's cost estimate to print 1,000 copies of the book was £21 more than Morris's £60 annual salary at the British and Canadian School at Quebec.[40] Morris's inability to finance the printing of his book echoed Perrault's earlier entreaties to the Assembly regarding the scarcity of appropriate teaching materials, which impeded the advancement of elementary education in the province. It is also reminiscent of Hamilton Leslie's frustration in having only one manuscript copy of his book to teach from. To compound the problem, Lower Canadian printers were disinclined to print certain kinds of schoolbooks. Mathematics books like Morris's included numbers, tables, and columns that required greater skill, time, and effort at typesetting. As Morris related to the Civil Secretary of Lower Canada, printers considered these books "the least profitable kind of printing."[41] In fact, one printing estimate expressly excluded the "mathematical figuring."[42] And Morris had testified that Thomas Cary would only print the book "at a price [he] feared to give." These circumstances meant that Morris would be unable to sell the bound

---

39  *First Report of the Standing Committee on Education and Schools*, Appendix to the XLIst volume of the Journals of the House of Assembly of Lower Canada, 2 Will. 4, Appendix I.i (7 January 1832) – Examination of William Morris.

40  Morris's annual salary was reported in Curtis, *Ruling by Schooling*, 169.

41  William Morris to Col. Craig, 18 March 1833, LAC, Civil Secretary's Correspondence Quebec, Lower Canada, and Canada East, 1760–1863, vols. 404–7, no. 90.

42  An unsigned handwritten estimate, presumably from Neilson & Cowan, can be found at BAnQ (Quebec District), Fonds Famille Neilson, P192–26, Papiers John

books for less than two shillings. In contrast, at around the same time, Cary provided a printing estimate to Joseph-François Perrault for his *Abrégé de l'histoire du Canada* that would allow a sale price per book of 1s 6d halfbound.[43]

The Assembly was sympathetic to the plight of these teachers. Indeed, the legislature treated these petitions differently from other book printing petitions by agreeing to subsidize the up-front costs instead of committing to the purchase of copies of the book once published. From the first parliamentary session of 1793 up to and including the 1831–2 session, eight petitioners, all authors or compilers of useful books, had sought some form of financial aid or other incentives to print their works. Five of the petitions were in respect of schoolbooks or teaching manuals, beginning with Hamilton Leslie's in 1826 and followed by those of Joseph-François Perrault in 1830 and 1831. The other two petitioners in this group were Joseph Lancaster and William Morris, who made their requests during the fateful 1831–2 legislative session.

The remaining three petitions were for didactic works not specifically intended for use in schools. As previously mentioned, in 1830 Samuel Hull Wilcocke came before the legislature in respect of *The History of the Session of the Provincial Parliament of Lower Canada for 1828–29*. Between 1814 and 1833, Joseph Bouchette made frequent requests for financial support for his *Topographical Description of the Province of Lower Canada* (1815) and *The British Dominions in North America* (1832). In 1831, Marie-Marguerite Gagnier, the widow of Jacques Labrie, petitioned for aid to enable the posthumous publication of his *Histoire du Canada*.[44] Because these claims didn't involve schoolbooks, the three cases were referred to special committees rather than to the Education Committee, and the results were consistent. The Assembly was instructed to subscribe for copies of the books once published either by setting aside a fixed sum toward their purchase or, alternatively, by procuring a certain

---

Neilson 1791–1845 MSS. The estimate stated that printing 700 copies of 100 pages would cost £55 and 150 pages at £82 10, excluding "mathematical figuring." A handwritten note in red ink at the top of the page stated: "Gave a Copy of This to Mr. Morris – 28th December 1831." The back of the letter reads: "May 1832, Price for Printing Mr Morris' Arithmetic." This appears to be a different estimate from the one that Morris described in his testimony.

43   Handwritten note dated 3 May 1831 and signed by Thomas Cary, attached to Perrault's petition to James Kempt, LAC, Civil Secretary's Correspondence Quebec, Lower Canada and Canada East, 1760–1863, vol. 307, no. 208.

44   Journals of the House of Assembly of Lower Canada, 1831, 2 Will 4, 34. See also "Dossier Jacques Labrie," .

number of copies. In Wilcocke's case, the decision was to subscribe for 100 copies of his book, which was already in press at the time of his petition.[45] In 1828, Bouchette received a commitment toward the purchase of copies of *The British Dominions in North America* upon the completion and publication of the work:

> As Lieutenant Colonel Bouchette has not as yet completed his work ... your Committee have not sufficiently been able to form their opinion on the merits, and do not feel authorized to make a pecuniary aid for the said publications. Nevertheless, should Mr. Bouchette determine to publish his work, Your Committee think it would be expedient to encourage him in his undertaking by authorizing the Executive Government to subscribe for a certain number of Copies.[46]

Jacques Labrie's case was somewhat different. Labrie was a physician and a member of the House of Assembly from 1827 until his death in 1831. At the time of his death, he had been working on a history of Lower Canada; in his will, he had delegated to Augustin-Norbert Morin the task of completing the work. Through the intermediary of Labrie's widow, Morin asked the legislature to commit £500 toward the purchase of copies to ensure that the work could be completed and published.[47] The members of the Assembly debated whether such an up-front expenditure was the desirable approach, since they were not in a position to evaluate the worth of the book before committing public funds. Solicitor General Charles Ogden was concerned about setting a precedent and opening the floodgates to many more applications of this kind.[48] Others, like John Neilson, argued that Lower Canada was not yet sufficiently developed to guarantee the publication of such an important work without public assistance.[49] In the end, the Assembly

---

45  Journals of the House of Assembly of Lower Canada, 1830, 11 Geo. 4, 121, 173.

46  Journals of the House of Assembly of Lower Canada, 9 Geo. 4, 10 January 1829, 323.

47  See "Dossier Jacques Labrie," 413.

48  "Dossier Jacques Labrie," 414; *Le Canadien*, 3 December 1831, reported on Ogden's remarks: "[I]l est question de prendre £500 du trésor public et excepté les membres qui en ont fait l'éloge, personne ne connait suffisamment l'ouvrage en question ... Si l'on voulait introduire cette manière d'agir, bientôt tout le monde ferait de semblables applications." [It is a question of taking £500 from the public treasury and, except for the members who have praised it, no one knows enough about the work in question ... If we wanted to introduce this course of action, soon everyone would be making similar applications.]

49  "Dossier Jacques Labrie," 416.

voted forty-five to nine in favour of the request, although ultimately, the Legislative Council rejected the claim and the matter ended there.[50]

This debate provides insights into the considerations attendant to the allocation of public funds toward publishing ventures. Whether to provide aid at the outset or only after the work had been published was a perennial concern in the Lower Canadian legislature. The Labrie case was the exception that proved the rule. The debate in the Assembly affirms that the legislature took a deliberate approach to supporting printing petitions. Its preference was to purchase copies of a book once published on the basis that the public should not have to bear the risks of advancing funds to support a work that might never see the light of day or that might not be sufficiently useful or meritorious. The legislature's commitment to purchase copies upon publication provided sufficient incentive for authors to complete and publish their manuscripts, since they and their publishers were assured a certain amount of sales revenue.

In cases involving schoolbooks, the Education Committees and, ultimately, the Assembly adopted the opposite approach, for they were unwilling to risk the possibility that these kinds of books would remain unpublished. However, the legislature frequently imposed conditions on the grant to ensure that these publicly subsidized materials would be widely disseminated at affordable prices. For example, in granting the award to Joseph-François Perrault to assist with the printing of his *Abrégé de l'histoire du Canada*, the Education Committee stipulated that the sale price per copy could not be greater than eighteen pence.[51] In Morris's case, he was awarded £50 so long as he published 1,000 copies of the book to be sold for not more than two shillings each.[52] Stipulations as to maximum sale price, which were made only in relation to schoolbooks, underscore the legislature's concerns about both availability and affordability. Finally, policy-makers were mindful of Lower

---

50   See Journals of the Legislative Council of the Province of Lower Canada, 1831, 2 Will. 4, 201–2: The only copy of Morin's completed manuscript was lost to fire in 1837, and the book was never published.

51   Appendix to the XLth volume of the Journals of the House of Assembly of the Province of Lower Canada, 1 Will. 4 (1831), App. B.B, March 15, 1831. Eighteen pence was roughly a shilling and a half. This was consistent with Thomas Cary's printing estimate to Perrault of a shilling and six pence.

52   As Augustin-Norbert Morin noted in his review of the work: "I think that, in order that the work to be of general use, it ought not to be sold for more than 2s. per copy." Appendix to the XLIst volume of the Journals of the House of Assembly of the Province of Lower Canada, 2 Will. 4, App. I.i, 1832, Ii-18.

Canada's linguistic needs and sought to ensure that publicly funded books in English would also be available in French. In his assessment of Morris's manuscript, Morin noted: "It is to be regretted that there does not exist in the French language, that is for the greater part of the Schools in the Country, any elementary work that can fulfil the same object as this."[53] The Education Committee drew on Morin's observation and suggested to the Assembly that Morris's "valuable book be improved and translated in French for the use of Elementary Schools throughout the Province."[54]

The only exception to the Assembly's approach to schoolbook petitions involved Hamilton Leslie. The committee reviewing his claim awarded him an exclusive printing privilege instead of a grant to cover his printing costs. As will be recalled, Leslie had asked for a "reward" (i.e., a sum of money), not an exclusive privilege (i.e., a legally enforceable monopoly). While the committee's recommendation was never considered by the Assembly (instead, the Assembly moved on the second recommendation to introduce a copyright bill), this singular occurrence represents the most far-reaching response to any request by an author whether in respect of teaching materials or otherwise. The legislature never again considered granting an exclusive printing privilege to a petitioner, not even to Perrault, who had specifically requested one.

The timing of the Lancaster and Morris petitions in 1831 was therefore auspicious. These were initiated at a time when momentum was building on the education front and copyright had recently been on the legislative agenda. Read in tandem, the two petitions highlighted both a serious problem that needed to be addressed and the promise of a meaningful and permanent solution. Morris outlined for the Education Committee the financial barriers attendant to providing children with locally produced schoolbooks. Lancaster suggested a pragmatic remedy, one that would spur book production and relieve the Assembly of further requests for printing subsidies. However, it was John Neilson and his committee who pulled these elements together to articulate the legislative policy underlying Canada's first copyright law. It was they who established the connection between copyright, schoolbooks, and the promotion of public education.

---

53  Appendix to the XLIst volume of the Journals of the House of Assembly of the Province of Lower Canada, 2 Will. 4, App. I.i, 1832, Ii-18.

54  Appendix to the XLIst volume of the Journals of the House of Assembly of the Province of Lower Canada, 2 Will. 4, App. I.i, 1832, Ii-18.

These parliamentary records provide the rationale for Lower Canada's adoption of a copyright law in 1832; they also call into question the assertion, in 1833, made by French social commentator Isidore Lebrun that the legislation was enacted to curb plagiarism and piracy. In his treatise *Tableau statistique et politique des deux Canadas*, Lebrun claimed that schoolbooks were being reprinted without permission and that this had caused the legislature to intervene: "c'est sans doute à cause de ces plagiats que la législature vient d'adopter en faveur de la propriété littéraire, un bill qui, autrement, semblerait être une anomalie avec l'état présent du Bas-Canada."[55] He further suggested that, given its early stage of development, Lower Canada had no other reason to provide for copyright except to prohibit these infringing activities. Lebrun was clearly mistaken.

Lebrun never visited British North America to conduct the research for his book on Lower Canada and Upper Canada.[56] Instead, he relied on information solicited from a number of influential Lower Canadians, including Denis-Benjamin Viger, Augustin-Norbert Morin, and Ludger Duvernay. Although Viger and, most especially, Morin were the ones closest to the copyright file, it is doubtful that they were the sources for Lebrun's opinion on Lower Canada's circumstances. Neither they nor Duvernay were reliable correspondents. Lebrun expressed frustration with the three men for failing to provide him with information and material in a timely way and complained that their neglect had led to inaccuracies in his book.[57] There are also indications that Lebrun's egotism may have contributed to errors in his treatise. Lebrun's friend

55   Lebrun, *Tableau statistique et politique des deux Canadas*, 201–2. [It is undoubtedly because of this plagiarism that the legislature has just adopted a bill in support of literary property, a bill that would otherwise appear to be an anomaly given the present state of Lower Canada.]

56   Lebrun's correspondence makes it clear that he never travelled to Lower Canada. See LAC, Fonds Denis-Benjamin Viger. The scholarly consensus is to the same effect. See, for example, Fontaine-Bernard "Le Bas-Canada dans la presse française." Only Marcel Trudel suggested that he visited the province, but he cited no sources. See Trudel, *L'influence de Voltaire*, 195.

57   LAC, Fonds Denis-Benjamin Viger. Lebrun, or Lemoult writing on his behalf, frequently complained that he did not hear from Viger or Morin for long periods of time. On 20 March 1832, Lemoult wrote to Morin that "votre inexactitude…me paraît nuire au succès de la brochure de M. Lebrun qui m'a paru fâché de n'avoir pas été secondé comme il s'attendait à l'être dans une entreprise beaucoup plus utile à votre pays qu'au nôtre" (N. Lemoult to A.-N. Morin, 20 March 1832, vol. 3, no. 1306, LAC, Fonds Denis-Benjamin. [Your tardiness … seems to me to be detrimental to the success of M. Lebrun's pamphlet, who seemed upset that he was not

N. Lemoult, who did visit Lower Canada in 1831 and who acted as Lebrun's intermediary in procuring source material for the book, described Lebrun's stubborn refusal to follow the guidance of those with more direct knowledge: "M. Lebrun est un singulier corps qui a voulu faire à sa tête dans une affaire à laquelle il ne connait rien, et qui par cela même la gâtera en partie, je crains. Mes conseils, mes observations n'ayant rien pu sur son *amour-propre d'auteur*, je l'ai abandonné à son étoile."[58]

To Lebrun's way of thinking there could be no other explanation for the legislation other than to protect against plagiarism and piracy, despite the absence of supporting evidence from his Lower Canadian sources. But he was merely speculating. The truth lay elsewhere. John Neilson and his colleagues in the Assembly were looking for ways to stimulate elementary education in the province. Providing Lower Canadian children with appropriate and affordable schoolbooks in two languages was a significant and ongoing challenge. Copyright offered a promising way out of the impasse.

### The Influence of the Copyright Law of the United States

The Education Committee's report did not end with the recommendation that the province enact a copyright law. The committee went further by suggesting that the law follow "generally nearly upon the plan which has so much contributed to the success of the publication of School Books and other Books in the adjoining States." In other words, Lower Canada should emulate the law in the United States.

It is not surprising that Lower Canadian politicians followed the American lead. John Neilson greatly admired the American public school system. He marvelled that in New York State, half a million children from the ages of six to sixteen were being provided with schooling and schoolbooks at a cost of $2 per child. In Lower Canada the cost of schooling would reach an unsustainable £100,000 per year by the mid-1830s even

---

being assisted as he had expected to be in an enterprise much more useful to your country than to ours.] In addition, Viger's exchanges with Lebrun on the substantive aspects of his book are silent on the subject of copyright. Similar reproaches about long periods of silence were made by Lemoult to Ludger Duvernay as well. See Québec, *Rapport de l'archiviste.*

58  Lemoult to Duvernay, Angoulême, 27 February 1832, no. 112, 156, *Rapport de l'archiviste.* [Mr Lebrun is a singular individual determined to do things his own way in matters about which he knows nothing, and which will, as a result, spoil it in part, I fear. My advice and my observations could not compete with his self-esteem as an author, so I left him to his fate.]

without factoring in the cost of schoolbooks.[59] Adopting the American approach to copyright was borne of the conviction that the success of public education in the United States, especially in the eastern states, was at least partly due to the widespread availability of schoolbooks. Indeed, the introduction of copyright law in the United States followed a similar pattern to Lower Canada in that it arose in large measure as a response to printing petitions from schoolteachers.[60] Educator and lexicographer Noah Webster was instrumental in securing the first state laws in the late 1780s.[61] The first Federal Copyright Act of 1790 was enacted in part at the behest of geographer Jedidiah Morse, who appealed to the US Congress for a copyright law, alleging that two maps contained in his textbook had been reprinted without his permission.[62]

Yet even in the United States, the law did not achieve results on its own, nor were its beneficial effects immediately felt. Without going into a comprehensive exploration of the history of American publishing, one can distil from the scholarly literature a number of critical developments during the first half of the nineteenth century that significantly advanced schoolbook publishing in that country.[63] Historians have documented the role of parents and communities in promoting literacy and learning.[64] The importance that early Americans placed on education and reading, coupled with a dramatic rise in population (which trebled between 1790 and 1841), had led to an increasing demand for schooling and schoolbooks and created a market for locally produced material.[65] The public school movement in the United States provided

---

59   Report of the Education Committee, Appendix to the XLth volume of the Journals of the Assembly of Lower Canada, 1 Will. 4 (1831), Appendix B.B.

60   This pattern was repeated throughout British North America as well, as will be explored in chapter 7. Farther afield, the first New Zealand copyright statute of 1842 was initiated to protect a local schoolbook (a grammar by Rev. Mr Maunsell). See Weatherall, "The Emergence and Development."

61   Webster, *A Collection of Papers*, esp. ch. 5: "Origin of the Copy-Right Laws in the United States." Some dispute the importance of Webster's role in the emergence of copyright in the United States. See Micklethwait, *Noah Webster*.

62   House of Representatives, 1790, January 25 (J.H 20), reproduced in "Proceedings in Congress," 258.

63   On early American publishing, see generally Amory and Hall, *A History of the Book in America*, vol. 1; Gross and Kelley, *A History of the Book in America*, vol. 2. See, especially Green, "The Rise of Book Publishing."

64   See for example, Davidson, *Revolution and the Word*; Vinovskis, *Education, Society, and Economic Opportunity*; and Beadie, *Education and the Creation of Capital*.

65   See for example, Gross and Kelley, *History of the Book in America*, 301: "The expansion of schooling contributed to the growth in literacy in the new republic ... As the

a strong impetus for schoolbook publishing, but other factors contributed as well. An important priority for post-revolutionary America was to shed the vestiges of its British colonial past and develop a distinct national identity. Schoolbooks provided a means of advancing this nationalist cause.[66] Noah Webster explained: "[E]very child in America should be acquainted with his own country. He could read books that furnish him with ideas that will be useful to him in life and practice. As soon as he opens his lips, he should rehearse the history of his own country; he should lisp the praise of liberty, and of those illustrious heroes and statesmen, who have wrought a revolution in her favor."[67]

The growing demand for American schoolbooks enabled some of the more enterprising members of the book trade to embark on ambitious publishing projects. Because American law offered no protection to foreign authors, many American printers and publishers took advantage of the lucrative British reprint market and applied some of the profits to support domestic publishing initiatives. According to historian Robert Gross, these individuals "built American publishing on the recycling of British and European books."[68] Massachusetts printer and publisher Isaiah Thomas shrewdly built his printing business into one of the most successful schoolbook publishers of this era:

> Thomas was first to recognize the potential of a captive "mass market" in education after the Revolution, and he began producing textbooks for schools throughout New England. Thomas recognized the superiority of Noah Webster's speller and grammar, Nicholas Pike's arithmetic and works of literature appropriate for school children. Thomas launched what became a golden age of early publishing, with education at its core. Of 2.5 million books published in 1820, 750,000 were schoolbooks. The

---

market for texts expanded and printing technology improved, the quality of printed schoolbooks improved and became more attractive for students. By the second quarter of the nineteenth century publishers also became more organized and specialized in providing books for the growing school market. While reprinting British books continued, American schoolbooks slowly gained a larger market share."

66  See Goff, "The First Decade of the Federal Act"; Brian Lee Pelanda, "Declarations of Cultural Independence"; Bruckner, "Lessons in Geography"; and Nash, "Contested Identities." Nash says that other than virtue and piety, none of the early textbooks advanced any other common national goal.

67  Webster, *On the Education of Youth in America*. On Webster's nationalist agenda, see also Warfel, *Noah Webster*; Kendall, *The Forgotten Founding Father*.

68  Gross, "Building a National Literature," 321. See also McGill, *American Literature and the Culture of Reprinting*, 48.

industry total climbed to 3.5 million in 1830, with schoolbooks accounting for 1.1 million; to 5.5 million in 1840.[69]

As print technologies improved and transportation routes opened up, American printers and publishers were also able to expand their distribution networks to rural areas.[70] The resultant efficiencies permitted increased production, sales, and profits.

John Neilson and the Education Committee believed that the introduction of copyright could achieve similar results in Lower Canada even though the province did not enjoy the same confluence of sociopolitical, cultural, and economic conditions. If American success in schoolbook printing and publishing was attributable, at least in part, to a strong education system, then the deficiency in public schooling in Lower Canada made it that much more difficult for the domestic book trade to flourish there, as much as the Education Committee might have hoped otherwise. In addition, the market for books in Lower Canada was much smaller than the United States, given the province's size and its colonial status. The members of the Lower Canadian book trade were not similarly situated to their American counterparts, whose reprint businesses provided them with revenues they could reinvest in domestic publishing projects. Instead, Lower Canada's printers, publishers, and booksellers were dependent on the largesse of the British authorities, who were frequently their most important clients. Since British copyright law forbade colonists from reprinting British copyright works without permission, the kind of reprint culture that had developed in the United States was impossible in colonial Lower Canada.

Finally, Lower Canada was a linguistically and religiously polarized society. The nation-building patriotism that spurred the increase in domestic schoolbook publishing in the United States was impossible in Lower Canada. The *Canadiens* would not have promoted British nationalism or a Lower Canadian identity based on it, and they faced censure from the imperial authorities whenever they asserted their desire for self-determination and political autonomy. Lower Canadian journalists and newspaper publishers knew all too well that they risked imprisonment if they printed material deemed disloyal to the Crown. François

---

69   Unger and Williams, *Encyclopedia of American Education*, vol. 1, 906. On Thomas and his printing and publishing empire see Emblidge, "Isaiah Thomas Invents the Bookstore Chain," 53–64.

70   See Hackenberg, *Getting the Books Out*; Remer, "Preachers, Peddlers, and Publishers."

Blanchet and Denis-Benjamin Viger were among those who had been detained for publishing material considered libelous and seditious by the British authorities. Thus, while Lower Canadian teachers argued that schoolbooks with local content were preferable to imported books, prudence and politics made them stop short of arguing that they were essential for identity formation. We will see in later chapters that copyright and nationalist objectives eventually converged in the Province of Canada in the decades leading up to Canadian Confederation in 1867.

At the time the Lower Canadian Copyright Act was passed, the political tensions between the British authorities and the Assembly's Parti Patriote were moving inexorably toward a violent climax. We are here only five years away from the Lower Canadian rebellions, when frustration over the lack of democratic reforms spiralled into bloodshed. By 1840, Lower Canada would cease to exist. Of course, the Education Committee and the Assembly did not anticipate this when, in the winter of 1832, they considered the copyright question. The United States had undertaken a major revision of its law in 1831, and that statute was the basis of Lower Canada's legislation, enacted a little more than a year after its American counterpart. The legislative process that François Blanchet had initiated eight years before was finally brought to fruition.

### An Act for the Protection of Copy Rights, 2 Will. 4 c. 53 (1832)

The first "Canadian" Copyright Act entered the statute books with little fanfare; most of the major newspapers of the day merely noted its passage without further discussion.[71] Lower Canadians had other matters to think about besides securing exclusive rights over their publications. The summer of 1832 brought with it a devastating cholera epidemic that claimed thousands of lives. Political tensions between the Parti Patriote in the Assembly and the English administration were reaching their peak. Given the graver issues of the day, the new copyright law would not have been viewed by the public as of any great consequence.

---

71  For example, *Le Canadien*, 25 February 1832, 3, listed all Bills passed during that session, including "Le bill de la propriété littéraire." *Quebec Mercury*, 25 February 1832, 2–3, announced that the Legislative Council had agreed to the "Copy-rights Bill" and that Royal Assent had been given to the "Act for the Protection of Copyrights." *La Minerve*, 26 January 1832, 2, noted that "M. Morin introduit un bill pour assurer les droits d'auteur," and on 27 February 1832, 2, it announced that the statute had received Royal Assent.

Nevertheless, it seems somewhat odd that Augustin-Norbert Morin, who steered the Bill through the legislature, did not think to comment on its passage in his letters to Ludger Duvernay, to whom he frequently wrote about events at the Assembly. Although he described in some detail his contemporaneous interventions in respect of Jacques Labrie's manuscript, Morin never mentioned copyright to his friend, at least in writing, during the entire period the Bill was being debated.[72] Nevertheless, the Lower Canadian statute represents a pivotal moment in Canada's copyright history. This piece of legislation was the first of its kind in British North America; it was also, in substance and in spirit, rooted in the American copyright tradition, which privileged the advancement of knowledge as its principal objective. Indeed, the Lower Canadian Act of 1832 was a close copy of the American statutory revision of 1831.[73]

The 1832 Act provided authors of literary publications and engravers, as well as their executors, administrators, and legal assigns, the sole right to print, reprint, publish, and sell books, maps, charts, musical compositions, prints, cuts, or engravings for twenty-eight years with the possibility of renewal for an additional fourteen. Like the American statute, its scope was wider than the Statute of Anne, which was restricted to books and other writings. Engravings, prints, cuts, and musical compositions fell within the statute's purview. Eligibility for copyright was dependent on the author's residency in the province, but printing and publishing did not have to occur in the jurisdiction. As was not the case with the Blanchet Bills, resident authors did not have to be British subjects. The absence of domestic copyright protection for non-resident authors did not affect British copyright holders (be they citizens, subjects, or foreign authors), since they could enforce their rights in Lower Canada by virtue of the 1814 UK Act.

To claim the copyright, resident authors, engravers, or proprietors were required to deposit, prior to publication, a printed copy of the title page with the Clerk of the Superior Court in the district in which they resided.[74] The registration was to be recorded in an official registry as follows:

---

72  BAnQ (Vieux-Montréal), Fonds Ludger Duvernay (1815–1835), P680.

73  *An Act to amend the Several Acts Respecting Copy Rights*, 1831, c. 16, 21st Congress, 2nd Session. 4 Stat 436. In force February 3, 1831.

74  The statute provided for an initial processing fee of five shillings with another five shillings for each copy of the registration. The account ledgers of the Neilson & Cowan firm show an amount of ten shillings expended for various copyright registrations, suggesting that they routinely obtained a certified copy for their records.

DISTRICT Of

Be it remembered that on the … day of … in the year … A.B of the said District hath deposited in this office the title of a book (map, chart or otherwise as the case may be) the title of which is in the words following, that is to say – (insert the title) the right whereof he claims as author (or proprietor as the case may be)

In addition, a notice of the copyright registration was to be included on the book's title page or just after, in terms specified in the legislation: "Entered according to an Act of the Provincial Legislature in the year … by A.B in the Clerk's office of the Court of … (as the case may be)." Finally, a copy of the book was to be deposited with the Court Clerk within three months of publication. All of the deposited books were to be sent to the provincial secretary on an annual basis. For example, an entry in the provincial secretary's letter books for 12 November 1832 acknowledged receipt of the "Records of Copy Rights with the copies of Books therein named, for District of Three Rivers, in compliance with the Provincial Statute 12 Wm 4. Cap 53."[75] Copyright could be awarded retroactively to works that had been printed and published prior to the coming into force of the statute so long as the same statutory formalities were met. In addition, the legislation provided for an extension of the copyright for an additional fourteen years. The renewal formalities included a second recording of title, with a copy of the record published for four weeks in newspapers in Quebec and Montreal.

Although this was never tested at the time, it is probable that Lower Canadian courts would have followed the American example and found that the completion of the formalities was essential to obtaining legal protection. We have seen that in the United Kingdom, non-compliance with the statutory formalities did not defeat the ability to enforce a claim for damages at common law. In Lower Canada, a failure to abide by the statutory requirements would have left the author or proprietor without any copyright protection at all.[76]

---

Fonds Imprimerie Neilson, P193–2: Ledger 1824–1836, BAnQ (Québec). BAnQ Fonds Imprimerie Neilson and LAC, Neilson Collection, contain original official handwritten copies of the registrations of some of the Neilson & Cowan copyrights.

75  LAC, Canada East: Provincial Secretary Letterbooks, Quebec, Lower Canada, and Canada East, vol. 3, correspondence 1826–1832, 164, letter addressed to the prothonotary of the district of Trois-Rivières, W.H.C. Coffin Esq.

76  Samuel Dawson documented a case that arose in Canada in which a plaintiff with a strong case on its merits lost because of the failure to comply with the registration formalities under *An Act respecting Copyrights*, 1875, 38 Vict., c. 88 (The "Copyright

Without going into a detailed analysis of the legislation, some textual aspects of the 1832 Act are worth highlighting. The first thing to note in the 1832 Act was its title: *An Act for the Protection of Copy Rights* replaced the earlier *Act for the Encouragement of Learning* of the Blanchet Bills.[77] The use of the term "copyright" instead of "encouragement of learning" in the title of the Act followed similar shifts in the British and American legislation.[78] Also, the opening phrase of the preamble to the 1832 Act read: "Whereas it is expedient to secure to the authors of literary publications and to Engravers the property of their respective works and to make certain provisions on the said subjects." The Blanchet Bills began with the phrase: "Whereas for the encouragement of learning and of literature in this Province it is expedient to secure copy-rights ... to the Authors & Proprietors of same." The phrase "encouragement of learning and of literature" was removed from both the title and the preamble. Instead, the preamble referred to expediency and property. However, from what I have argued about the underlying policy that informed the Education Committee's deliberations on copyright, this change in terminology should not be interpreted as an ideological shift toward a more author- or industry-centric view of the law. As previously discussed, the idea of copyright as an author's property was compatible with overarching concerns about advancing learning because it was well-understood that copyright was as much defined by the limits it placed on the right-holder's monopoly as it was on the exclusive rights it conferred.

Section 2 of the 1832 Act reproduced verbatim the text of section 2 of the American Act. It provided for a right of renewal of fourteen years vesting either in the author, if alive at the expiry of the term, or in the widow and children, if the author was not then living. The way this provision was drafted bears mention. First, the gender bias is obvious. The statute presumed that only men could be authors since the

---

Act of 1875"). French title: *Acte concernant la propriété littéraire et artistique.* See Dawson, *Copyright in Books,* 32.

77  A similar change arose in the French text. The Blanchet Bills were titled Bill pour encourager les sciences en assurant les Copies des Cartes, Plans et Livres aux Auteurs et Propriétaires de ces Copies durant le tems y mentionné. The 1832 Act was titled *Acte pour protéger la propriété littéraire.*

78  The American statute of 1831 was titled: *An Act to amend the Several Acts Respecting Copy Rights.* The UK 1814 Act was the first to use the term copyright in the title of the legislation: *An Act to Amend the Several Acts for the Encouragement of Learning, by Securing the Copies and Copyright of Printed Books to the Authors of such Books or their Assigns.*

right of renewal was given to the author's widow.[79] Second, the right of renewal could only be exercised by the widow and children, not by an assignee of the author. If, after having assigned the copyright to a publisher, the author died during the first twenty-eight-year period, the publisher's legal entitlement would automatically be extinguished at the end of the initial term. Some scholars have argued that the inability of publishers or other assignees to exercise the right of renewal was a deliberate move by American lawmakers that reflected pervasive public distrust of the members of the book trade.[80] It will be recalled that the crafting of the Statute of Anne had been motivated by similar concerns about the monopolistic abuses of the Stationers. During the congressional debates on the legislation, William Ellsworth, Noah Webster's son-in-law, stated: "Your committee do not perceive any reason for denying to authors the protection of the law, to the extent proposed. There is no serious danger of a monopoly. The question is, whether the *author* or the *bookseller* shall reap the reward. It is for the interest of the author to supply the market upon such terms as will ensure the greatest sale; and he will always do this."[81]

That passage demonstrates a clear preference for the author over the bookseller or proprietor, the belief being that the author would be the one most likely to ensure that the book remained affordable and accessible to the reading public. It seems unlikely that the Lower Canadian legislators were cognizant of this particular nuance when they adopted the American statute. It seems more plausible that the provincial legislature merely reproduced the text without independent consideration. There was no similar antipathy to printers, publishers, and booksellers in Lower Canada, and it would have been surprising for John Neilson and his Education Committee colleagues to have recommended a provision that they knew to be motivated by anti-publisher sentiments. In fact, the same language was carried forward in the copyright statutes of the Province of Canada in 1841 and in the Dominion of Canada in 1868 and again in 1875.

---

79  Ross, "Copyright Corner." Ross suggests that the absence of reference to women as authors was deliberate.

80  See for example, Patry, *Copyright Law and Practice*. See too Everton, *The Grand Chorus of Complaint*; and Robert Spoo, *Without Copyrights*, on the perceived lack of ethics of American publishers, especially reprinters.

81  United States, *Judicial Committee Report*, 21st Congress, 2nd Session (1830) House of Representatives, Rep. No. 3 "Copy-Right" 1830, 2 (17 December 1830).

The third element of interest in the renewal provision is that there was a discrepancy between the English and French texts. In the English version, the provision stated that the process of renewal of copyright was to be exercised within six months *after* the expiration of the first term. Both the French version of the 1832 Act and the US Act stipulated a six-month deadline *before* the expiry of the first term. This iteration made the most practical sense. The renewal formalities would be fulfilled before the first term expired to ensure that legal protection was uninterrupted and that there would be no public uncertainty about the copyright status of the work. The earlier Blanchet Bills and the US 1790 Act also had renewal formalities that were to be exercised six months *before* the expiry of the first term. It is curious, then, that in the 1841 Act of the Province of Canada that repealed the 1832 Lower Canadian Act, the French version of section 3 was amended to render it consistent with the English text.[82] In other words, under the 1841 Act, the renewal was to be exercised within six months *after* (*après*) the expiration of the term. This would suggest that the English version was deemed to be the correct one. As drafted, this formulation seems counterintuitive and would have generated a period of legal uncertainty, since the official records would have provided no evidence of renewed protection during this interim period. Nevertheless, this same provision was reproduced in every subsequent Canadian copyright statute throughout the nineteenth century; indeed, the period for the exercise of the renewal was extended even further to within *one year* after the expiry of the first term.[83]

These drafting peculiarities aside, the 1832 Copyright Act of Lower Canada was enacted to support the legislature's education agenda. Copyright would provide sufficient incentive so that books – especially schoolbooks – that would not otherwise have been written, or printed and published, would now be produced and disseminated. This certainly was the conviction at the policy level. Whether the law actually achieved this result is another question entirely. The impact of the 1832 Act is the subject of the next chapter.

---

82   *An Act for the Protection of Copy Rights in this Province 4 & 5 Vict. c. 61* (1841) (Copyright Act 1841). French title: *Acte pour protéger les Droits d'Auteurs dans cette Province.*
83   The provision was abandoned with the repeal of mandatory formalities in the Copyright Act 1921.

# Chapter Six

# Authors and Publishers, Teachers and Schoolbooks: The Impact of the 1832 Copyright Act

This chapter explores the question of whether Lower Canada's new copyright law actually enhanced the creation, manufacture, and circulation of schoolbooks and other didactic works. It studies the way in which copyright was operationalized in practice by assessing its transformative impact on the actions of the legislature as well as on the relationships among authors, readers, and the book trade. The Assembly's treatment of book petitions after the advent of copyright indicates that the legislature no longer felt a responsibility to subsidize the costs of printing and publishing. However, copyright proved to be a flawed policy solution to the challenges associated with schoolbook and other book production in the province.

### Impact of the Act on Policy-Makers: The Education Committee and the Assembly

With the advent of the 1832 Copyright Act, the legislature's position on schoolbook printing and publishing shifted quite dramatically. Lower Canadian policy-makers believed that copyright would resolve the problems associated with book production, and the reports of the Education Committee no longer referred to the dearth and cost of schoolbooks as legislative preoccupations. The small number of printing petitions introduced after 1832 were either ignored or summarily dismissed by the Assembly.

Between 1832 and the repeal of the Lower Canadian statute in 1841, five individuals petitioned in respect of their books. Three of them initiated their requests during the legislative session of 1832–3, a few months after the Act became law. Nicolas Gauthier sought "an aid to enable him to publish a French Grammar which he had compiled."[1] Joseph-François Perrault returned to the Assembly requesting "an aid to enable him to print two Works compiled by him, one upon Veterinary Medicine ... and the other demonstrating the principles upon which are founded the Agricultural labours recommended by him in his Treatises upon gardening and farming, in order to afford the youth of the Country the first notions of two such useful sciences."[2] Finally, Montreal lawyer Henri Des Rivières Beaubien prayed "the House to grant him an aid towards publishing a Work entitled, 'A Treatise on the Civil Laws of Lower Canada' of which he is the author; and to take in return a stated number of Copies of the said Treatise as the House may be pleased to subscribe for."[3] All were referred to the Education Committee, which did not report back on any of the requests.[4] This silence is unusual when one considers that Perrault and Gauthier had petitioned in respect of their schoolbooks. Prior to this, the Education Committee had always responded to schoolbook petitions.

Despite the Assembly's inaction, Des Rivières Beaubien's three-volume *Traité sur les lois civils du Bas-Canada* was printed and published by Ludger Duvernay, as will be recounted in more detail later in this chapter. However, no trace remains of Gauthier's French grammar or Perrault's manuscript on veterinary medicine. Perrault's schoolbook on agricultural practices may have been *Éléments de l'agriculture à l'usage des collèges à établir dans le Bas-Canada pour l'enseignement de cette science*, which he had asked Amury Girod to review in October 1832. Girod provided a favourable opinion of the text and expressed the hope that the work could be produced cheaply for the benefit of Lower Canadians from all walks of life: "C'est en répandant de bons livres qu'on paroient à donner aux masses du peuple cet amour de l'instruction qu'est le principal ressort d'une grande civilisation."[5] In early 1833, Perrault

---

1   Journals of the House of Assembly of Lower Canada, 1832–1833, 3 Will. 4, 112 (27 November 1832).

2   Journals of the House of Assembly of Lower Canada, 1832–1833, 3 Will. 4, 81 (23 November 1832).

3   Journals of the House of Assembly of Lower Canada, 1832–1833, 3 Will. 4, 133 (30 November 1832). The petition was introduced by Augustin-Norbert Morin.

4   First Report of the Standing Committee of Education and Schools, Continuation of the Appendix to the XLIInd volume of the Journal of the House of Assembly of the Province of Lower Canada (1832–1833), Appendix I-I. John Neilson remained the Chair of the Education Committee until he lost his seat on the Assembly in 1834.

5   LAC, Collection Joseph-François Perrault, undated document MF 3133. [It is by spreading good books that one imparts to the masses a love of education that is

instructed printer Jean-Baptiste Fréchette to produce 360 bound copies as long as the printing costs did not exceed £50.[6] Unfortunately, the trail ends there. There is no record of Fréchette having printed this book.

The next printing petition occurred during the 1834 legislative session, when Montreal engraver James Turpin asked "the House to subscribe for a certain number of Copies of two Maps which he is about to publish of Upper and Lower Canada, including a portion of the United States adjoining thereto, and also the Provinces of Nova Scotia, New Brunswick and Prince Edward Island."[7] This petition was referred to the Education Committee, but it too was left unanswered. Instead, the Education Committee expressed its disapproval of petitioners expecting legislative "hand-outs":

> Another class of Petitioners are those who wish for aid to enable them to enter upon undertakings alleged to be highly conducive to the advancement of knowledge and general Education. Your Committee have in this respect been guided by the practice which has latterly prevailed in Your Honorable House in confining its liberality to cases where the Petitioners had effected something useful to the public, with their own capital and at their own risk, rather than depending on Legislative aid for the support or reward of useful exertions in speculative undertakings.[8]

Even though the committee did not specifically refer to the Turpin petition in this remark, this comment is broad enough to include petitioners for printing subsidies. Authors of useful books, including schoolbooks, were expected to turn to the new Copyright Act to support their publishing endeavours. The legislature was not inclined to reward speculative undertakings where the petitioners had not committed themselves in any material way. This private remedial model for book publishing was consistent with the overall philosophy of the legislature – rewarding individual industry and enterprise while discouraging

---

the mainstay of a great civilization.] LAC has the manuscript copy of *Éléments de l'agriculture à l'usage des collèges à établir dans le Bas-Canada pour l'enseignement de cette science* dated 1832. This is a different work from Perrault's *Traité d'agriculture, adapté au climat du Bas-Canada,* which Fréchette & Cie published in 1831 and reissued with copyright in 1839.

6  LAC, Collection Joseph-François Perrault, undated document MF 3133.

7  Journals of the House of Assembly of Lower Canada, 1834, 4 Will. 4, 33.

8  Second Report of the Standing Committee on Education and Schools, Appendix to the XLIIIrd volume of the Journals of the House of Assembly of the Province of Lower Canada, 14 February 1834, 4 Will. 4, App. D.d, D.d-1.

dependence on government backing. This position was also consonant with the Education Committee's views on public education more generally: that parents and communities should shoulder the burden of school financing instead of expecting the legislature to cover the costs: "Your Committee trust that the time is not far distant, when the whole Country will be persuaded that it is much better to trust to themselves for the discharge of the duty of affording useful instruction to their offspring, rather than depend upon Legislative appropriations."[9]

James Turpin petitioned again the following year, repeating his request for subscription copies, only this time he offered the Assembly a discounted price:

> A Petition of James Turpin, of the City of Montreal, Engraver; praying the House to encourage him in the compiling, engraving and publishing two Maps, one of Lower Canada, embracing also the Provinces of Nova Scotia, New Brunswick and Prince Edward Island, the other of Upper Canada, including a portion of the United States adjoining thereto, either by subscribing for a certain number of Copies for the use of the several Schools throughout the Province, subject to a deduction of 33 per cent, on the publishing price, or on such other conditions as the House may deem expedient.[10]

Would the legislature have been more inclined to provide assistance if it could subscribe at a wholesale or discounted rate? The answer remains unclear, for the petition fell with that parliamentary session.

Turpin reintroduced his petition in the next session (1835–6), reverting back to his original language by asking the Assembly to subscribe for "a certain number of copies of two Maps which he is about to publish."[11] At the same time, the legislature heard from geographer Zadock Thompson, who asked for "£75 currency towards publishing a Geography and History of the Province of Lower Canada and also a small Map of the Province, which he has compiled and adapted to the use of Schools."[12] It was in response to these two petitions that the Education Committee clarified its position on printing petitions. In refusing to grant financial support to either man, the committee, now chaired by Hector-Simon Huot, stated:

---

9　Second Report of the Standing Committee on Education and Schools, Appendix to the XLIIIrd volume of the Journals of the House of Assembly of the Province of Lower Canada, 14 February 1834, 4 Will. 4, App. D.d, D.d-2.
10　Journals of the House of Assembly of Lower Canada, 1835, 5 Will. 4, 67.
11　Journals of the House of Assembly of Lower Canada, 1835–1836, 6 Will. 4, 66.
12　Journals of the House of Assembly of Lower Canada, 1835–1836, 6 Will. 4, 26.

With regard to the Petitions from Authors, praying to be indemnified for the cost of publishing Works which they consider well adapted to advance Education ... *Your Committee consider that the Legislature by the Act of the 2nd Will IV. Cap 53, intituled, "An Act for the protection of Copyrights", have granted sufficient advantage to the Authors of Works of this nature.* Besides which, if the Works are as valuable as they are represented to be, they must command a sufficient sale to indemnify their Authors. [emphasis added][13]

This passage confirms that the Copyright Act was understood to have freed the legislature from having to subsidize books, including schoolbooks and other educational materials. Nova Scotia's legislature adopted a similar stance after enacting that province's copyright law in 1839, advising that with the introduction of copyright, the legislature would no longer provide public funding to authors.[14] The availability of copyright meant that authors and their publishers were now expected to absorb the costs and the risks associated with book production. They would have to rely on the profits, if any, from book sales over the life of the copyright. The Education Committee did allow, however, that, in some circumstances, schoolbooks might still require legislative intervention. It therefore remained amenable to certain concessions in their favour:

Your Committee would, nevertheless, have thought they were justified in recommending that a certain number of Copies of Mr. Thompson's Geography should be subscribed for, if such subscription had met the views of the Petitioner, and had been sufficient to indemnify him for his labour.

Your Committee would in like manner have recommended that a certain number of copies of Mr. Turpin's Maps, should be subscribed for, if they had been published, and the Committee could have been assured of their utility for Elementary Schools; but as no Copies have yet been struck

---

13   Continuation of the Appendix to the XLVth volume of the Journals of the House of Assembly of the Province of Lower Canada, 6 Will. 4, O.o-7 (28 December 1835). See entry for Hector-Simon Huot (1803–1846) in DCB. Huot had been a member of the Education Committee at the time of the introduction of the 1832 Act. He took over as Chair after John Neilson lost his seat on the Assembly in 1834.

14   Journal and Proceedings of the House of Assembly of the Province of Nova Scotia, session 1848, 11 Vict., appendix 38. The legislature was responding to a petition by Abraham Gesner for an aid to publish his work on industrial resources in Nova Scotia. The petition was referred to a Select Committee and was declined (at 84).

off, Your Committee think that this subscription may be deferred until the Maps are published.[15]

What is of particular significance in this response is that if any legislative encouragement were to be sanctioned, it would now take the form of a commitment to purchase a fixed number of copies rather than to provide seed funding to help defray the up-front costs. We have seen that prior to 1832, the legislature provided financial support at the outset to assist with the costs of printing schoolbooks. This policy changed with the advent of the Copyright Act. With the availability of copyright, the legislature was unwilling to commit public funds to supporting a schoolbook that was not close to completion or already in print. Furthermore, any financial support that would be granted for eligible schoolbooks would now take the form of the purchase of copies. This new position regarding schoolbooks now matched the Assembly's approach to books more generally. A few years later, the legislature of the Province of Canada confirmed this rule "not to recommend appropriations on behalf of works which are not already in print, unless special reasons exist to the contrary."[16]

In Zadock Thompson's case, his book, *Geography and History of Lower Canada*, was in press at the time of his appeal to the legislature. The petition was dated 31 October 1835, and the Education Committee's report was delivered at the end of December.[17] The book's preface indicated that it was printed sometime that autumn. The copyright was registered by the printers and publishers Gaylord & Walton, likely while Thompson's petition was pending. The committee refused to indemnify the author for his printing costs but would have considered the purchase of copies of the book once published had Thompson specifically requested this form of relief.

James Turpin's circumstances were different. Even though he had asked for a subscription for the purchase of copies, the Education Committee would not commit on speculation since the work was not yet close to being finished. It seems that Turpin never managed to publish his book of maps, although there is ample evidence that he had been

---

15  Continuation of the Appendix to the XLVth volume of the Journals of the House of Assembly of the Province of Lower Canada, 6 Will. 4, p. O.o-7 (28 December 1835).

16  Journals of the Legislative Assembly of the Province of Canada, 1854, 18 Vict. 1, pt. 1, 473 (7 December 1854).

17  Journals of the House of Assembly of Lower Canada, 1835–1836, 6 Will. 4, 311.

working diligently to see his project through.[18] It is unclear whether his inability to publish the work was the result of financial considerations that might have been alleviated by a legislative grant, but if so, it offers yet another indication that copyright law was an inadequate response to the financial risks associated with book publishing. As in the cases of Perrault and Gauthier, whose schoolbook petitions were ignored and whose works were never published, copyright was not an effective substitute for a legislative grant where private means to finance publication were lacking.

The Assembly disregarded its rule regarding start-up costs in one exceptional situation that arose in the same session in which the Turpin and Thompson petitions were dismissed. Concerns over poor agricultural production and a decline in economic conditions during the 1830s led the legislature to inquire into the cost and desirability of having William Evans's *A treatise on the theory and practice of agriculture: adapted to the cultivation and economy of the animal and vegetable productions of agriculture in Canada* translated into French and published in an abridged form.[19] The treatise had been published in English, but the Assembly wanted the book accessible to rural *Canadiens*. The legislature provided Evans with £215 to commission a translation of his treatise and to print 1,000 copies to be distributed "throughout the whole of the province by the School Visitors."[20] This significant allocation highlights the dire circumstances that necessitated a response inconsistent with the Assembly's overall position on book subsidies. This example also underscores the limitations of copyright. Evans had registered his copyright in the original work in 1835, but neither he nor his printers or publishers could produce a much-needed French translation without public support.

---

18  *La Minerve* for 23 July 1833 and 31 October 1833 have notices from James Turpin referring to delays in completing the work. A broadside dated 4 June 1834 advised that he was removing himself to a quieter location to devote himself fully to his book of maps (see Canadian Pamphlets and Broadsides Digital Collection, Thomas Fisher Rare Book Library, University of Toronto). Turpin wrote to John Neilson in December 1835 asking Neilson for answers to a number of statistical and demographic questions. He said that "this information is sought to enable me to make the necessary corrections and addition to the Statistical Tables etc. that are to accompany my forthcoming work Maps of the Canadas, now shortly to be published." LAC, Neilson Collection, vol. 8, reel no. 15770, 530–1.

19  Journals of the House of Assembly for Lower Canada, 1835–1836, 6 Will. 4, 6 Will. 4 (9 November 1835), 91.

20  *An Act to grant an Aid towards printing in the French Language, the Treatise on Agriculture written by William Evans*, 6 Will. 4, c. 44.

Amury Girod was commissioned to prepare the translation, which was published in late 1836 or early 1837 under the title *Traité théorique et pratique de l'agriculture*.[21] As it turned out, however, the publication did not fulfil the Assembly's objectives. The work was intended to benefit the Lower Canadian farming community, but, as Superintendent of Education Pierre-Joseph-Olivier Chauveau related in 1857: "Malheureusement, peu d'entr'eux, à cette époque, savaient lire: et la législature, qui fit bien de reproduire ainsi l'ouvrage de M. Evans, n'aurait pas dû s'en tenir là."[22] The problems of illiteracy and the absence of a solid public education system continued to plague the province. The encouragement that copyright offered was predicated on an ample supply of readers and robust sales, and these conditions did not yet exist in nineteenth-century Lower Canada.

### Rates and Patterns of Copyright Registrations

Even after the passage of the Copyright Act, the majority of the works of Lower Canadian authors were not secured by copyright. This was not unusual: low take-up rates were also characteristic of early British and American practices. In relation to the Statute of Anne, book historian Michael Suarez determined that "after an initial rush in 1710, when 678 titles are registered, the average between 1711 and 1760 is a mere 65 works per year ... An analysis of the data from the English Short-Title Catalogue indicates that the *minimum* number of titles published annually in this period was about 1,600."[23] R.C. Barrington-Partridge, who reviewed the period from 1798–1814, noted a steady decline in the total number of works entered with the Stationers' Company, especially after

---

21   The original book was printed in 1835. Evans registered copyright on 9 July 1835. Evans, *A treatise on the Theory and Practice of Agriculture*. On 8 July 1836, Evans also registered his copyright in *Supplementary Volume to a Treatise on Agriculture*. Girod's translation was dated 1836–37 and printed by Louis Perrault, Montreal. Amury Girod was not identified as the translator. Evans, *Traité théorique et pratique de l'agriculture*.

22   See Chauveau, "Bibliographie Canadienne – William Evans L'Agronome," *Journal de l'instruction publique* 1, no. 2 (February 1857) 33–4 at 34. [Unfortunately, few of them at that time knew how to read: and the legislature, which did well by reproducing Mr Evans' work in this way, should not have stopped there.] Chauveau suggested that the establishment of a model farm accompanied by public lectures would have achieved better results in rural communities. Chauveau (1820–1890) was appointed Superintendent of Education in the Province of Canada in 1855. See his entry in DCB.

23   See Suarez, "To What Degree?," 57.

the decision in *Beckford v. Hood* in 1798 which held that copyright was not dependent on the completion of the statutory formalities. Failure to fulfil the registration requirements would deny the copyright holder the statutory remedies of a penalty and the forfeiture of the infringing works, but legal recourse could still be had before the courts for damages, injunctive relief, and accounting of profits. In this legal environment, publishers had less incentive to engage with statutory copyright. Barrington-Partridge counted 651 registrations in 1797, 366 in 1800, and 271 in 1812.[24]

In the United States, by contrast, the choice for domestic authors and their printers and publishers was either compliance with the statutory formalities or no legal protection at all. One would therefore expect to see increasing rates of registration once authors and their printers and publishers began to recognize the commercial value of copyright. Indeed, individuals like Noah Webster and Isaiah Thomas understood the benefits of copyright almost immediately.

> Webster and Morse were among the first writers to benefit from copyright in the early 1790s, and among the very few who made a living from what they thought of as their literary labor. From such books, publishers learned the value of copyright. They learned that it was not an unwelcome extra expense but a capital investment which could be depreciated over its fourteen-year term and which sometimes paid a gratifying dividend … Isaiah Thomas began reckoning his copyrights as assets and not as expenses as early as 1794.[25]

However, they were among the exceptions; registration rates were low overall in the decade after the passage of the Copyright Act of 1790. Estimates vary from 566 registrations relative to 13,000 publications between 1790 and 1799,[26] to 779 registrations relative to more than 15,000 published works up to 1800.[27] There was little incentive for American authors and publishers to submit to the statutory process if they had already priced their books cheaply: "The new law at first, however, had

---

24   Barrington-Partridge, *The History of the Legal Deposit of Books*, 43–4.
25   See Green, "The Rise of Book Publishing," 101.
26   Tebbel, *A History of Book Publishing in the United States*, 139.
27   Wills, and Gilreath, *Federal Copyright Records 1790–1800*. A study conducted by Zvi Rosen and Richard Schwinn demonstrates that registrations in the United States only began to spike after 1865. See Rosen and Schwinn, "An Empirical Study." See also Ross and Maher, "Copyright Term."

surprisingly little effect. Although authors could, after 1790, legally claim as their own their published work, a comparatively small number actually did ... Why go to the trouble if one knows one will make nothing from a volume?"[28]

Lower Canadian authors, printers, and publishers were in a similar predicament. We will see that registration take-up rates remained low relative to overall printing and publication. This was so, even though Lower Canadian courts would presumably have interpreted the statutory formalities as mandatory, similar to the position taken in the United States. The market for local books was very small. Lower Canadian authors, printers, and publishers would have seen little point in engaging with copyright for books that had only limited circulation and sales. A considered and deliberate decision had to be made in each case, based on the type of work in question, the expected return, and the risks associated with not securing legal protection at all. The fact that there was no great rush to copyright suggests that the legislation had a limited impact on authors and the book trade. This was true even for those authors who had more than a passing interest in copyright, namely the early petitioners for printing subsidies.

*Copyright and the Early Petitioners for Printing Subsidies (1824 to 1831)*

Of the eight petitioners who came before the Assembly between 1824 and 1831 asking for some form of financial assistance to print their books, seven did not or could not take advantage of the legislation. Hamilton Leslie was ineligible since he was no longer resident in Lower Canada. Augustin-Norbert Morin's ambitious project to finish and publish posthumously Jacques Labrie's historical treatise came to an end when the manuscript was destroyed by fire. Joseph Bouchette had published his books in the United Kingdom and secured his copyright there. That said, he did attempt, unsuccessfully, to exploit his British copyright in Lower Canada by offering to sell the copper plates of his topographical maps to the province so long as he, and his heirs and assigns, would, "as an indemnity for the Copy Right ... be hereafter entitled by Act of Parliament, to the net proceeds of one fourth of the annual revenue to the province, arising from the future and continued sale of the Maps struck off from the said Plates."[29]

---

28  Davidson, *Revolution and the Word*, 97.

29  "Minutes of Evidence taken before the Special Committee to whom was referred the Petition of Joseph Bouchette, Esquire, Surveyor General of Lower Canada, for

Samuel Hull Wilcocke's circumstances were somewhat different. Although his *History of the Session of the Provincial Parliament of Lower Canada 1828–29* had been published prior to the coming into force of the 1832 Act, he would have been able to secure his rights since the law allowed for copyright to be registered for works already in print. However, by 1832 Wilcocke was quite ill – he died a year later. It is likely that his poor health prevented him from following through, but it is possible that, as the recipient of a legislative grant to help defray his printing debt, he was precluded from simultaneously securing a private advantage. Amury Girod hinted at this understanding in his testimony before the committee reviewing his petition in 1831: "That I never mean to think of asking for any aid towards the printing of any elementary works which I may write or cause to be written; but only that ... I may obtain the approval of the Honorable House ... guaranteeing to me the copy-right thereof."[30] In fact, none of the petitioners who were granted some form of public financial support for printing their books simultaneously secured copyright in the same publication.

The experiences of the quartet of schoolbook petitioners who were more actively involved with the copyright file offer further insights into some of the factors that affected registration rates. William Morris published his book on arithmetic in 1833 but did not secure its copyright, presumably because he was a recipient of public funds to aid in publication. The cover page of *The Accountant's Guide for Elementary Schools in Canada* makes it clear that the book was published "By the authority of the Parliament of Lower Canada," in recognition of the legislature's financial support. In a notice after the title page, Morris acknowledged the £50 parliamentary grant "that the price might be so reduced, that all the children may be supplied with a copy." He concluded with the hope that "if the work should advance the cause of Education in our Elementary schools, the beneficence of the Parliament will be repaid, and the object of the Compiler will be fully attained."[31] In the end, Morris was compelled to have the work printed in the United States, for the Assembly's grant was insufficient to cover the costs of a Lower

---

renumeration for losses sustained by him in the publication of his various Maps, Statistical Tables, &c," 7 February 1833, Continuation of the Appendix to the XLIInd volume of the Journals of the House of Assembly of the Province of Lower Canada, 3 Will. 4, 1832–1833, 77.

30  Minutes of Evidence, Appendix to XLIst volume of the Journals of the House of Assembly of the Province of Lower Canada, 2 Will. 4, 10 December 1831.

31  Morris, *The Accountant's Guide*, notice by author after title page.

Canadian printer. In a letter to the civil secretary in March 1833, he reported that he was unable to find a local printer who could manage on the £50 allocated to him by the legislature: "I found that their Estimates far exceeded the sum appropriated by the Legislature."[32] A New York printer would print 1,000 copies for £50 (with contingencies, the total cost would be £60), which Morris could manage if the governor agreed to cover the imperial import duties. Governor Aylmer agreed to Morris's request.[33] Clearly, the authorities were of the view that facilitating the production and circulation of schoolbooks like Morris's took precedence over the commercial interests of Lower Canadian printers and publishers. *The Accountant's Guide* was Morris's only book. He does not appear to have written or published anything else. By September 1833, he had left the British and Canadian School at Quebec to join the National School, which offered a higher salary, greater job security, and an established curriculum with prescribed schoolbooks.[34]

Amury Girod published three books before he took his own life during the rebellions. Neither he nor his printer or publisher registered copyright in any of them, and none of these works appear to have been the Lancasterian schoolbook or the universal history, which had been the subjects of his request to the special committee of the Assembly in 1831.

In 1834, Girod wrote *Conversations sur l'agriculture par un habitans* [*sic*] *de Varennes*, which he dedicated to Joseph-François Perrault.[35] This work was first published as a series of newspaper articles and later as a pamphlet, to instruct farmers in basic agricultural practices. In 1835, he published seven lengthy essays under the title *Notes diverses sur le Bas-Canada*.[36] Girod's final work was his translation of William Evans's

---

32   William Morris to Col. Craig, 18 March 1833, LAC, Civil Secretary's Correspondence Quebec, Lower Canada, and Canada East, (1760 – 1863), vol. 404–407, no. 90. In his original petition to the Assembly, Morris advised that he had obtained a quote from William Cowan of £81 for 1,000 copies unbound.

33   LAC, Provincial Secretary Letterbooks, Quebec, Lower Canada, and Canada East, C-10464, vol. 12, no. 349 (22 March 1833).

34   A letter from Dunbar Jameson of the National School to Col. Craig, 21 September 1833, LAC, Civil Secretary's Correspondence Quebec, Lower Canada, and Canada East, (1760–1863), 415. Dunbar was acting on behalf of William Morris, whom he described as being "late of the British Canadian School," and requesting the payment of the £50 allocation from the legislature. See also Spragge, "Monitorial Schools," 307, who cited a Report on Schools in Quebec dated between 1836 and 1840, showing Morris at the National School.

35   Girod, *Conversations sur l'agriculture*.

36   Girod, *Notes diverses sur le Bas-Canada*.

agricultural treatise. At the time of his death in 1837, Girod owed £1,333 to Jean-Philippe de Boucher Belleville for the printing costs of his *Notes diverses*.[37] He also owed £1,086 to Joseph-François Perrault, as a result of the failure of the agricultural school.[38] Given the turbulent political climate, Girod's engagement in the rebellion, and his personal financial embarrassment, securing copyright would likely not have figured high among his priorities.

It is perhaps most surprising of all that Joseph Lancaster did not avail himself of the law he had so fervently pursued. He had most certainly intended to protect his Lower Canadian publications, but legal troubles compelled him to make a hasty retreat to the United States sometime after July 1833.[39] On 6 April 1833, Lancaster printed a broadside, *New and Singular Improvement in the Mode of Tuition for Youth*, in which he announced his intention to chronicle his successful educational experiments "in a publication, the copy rights of which will be secured to himself and his family."[40] The same year he released a pamphlet, *Report on the Singular Results of Joseph Lancaster's New Discoveries made in Montreal from the commencement in 1829 to complete developement [sic] of systematic principle in 1833*, in which he again referred to the need to secure his rights: "The interests of his family; and the education he intends to give his own children ... oblige him to secure his copyrights on behalf of his wife and family."[41] In both documents, he wrote of his plan to issue a new edition of his celebrated *Improvements in Education*, over which he would claim the copyright.

Another hint at Lancaster's Lower Canadian copyright intentions appears in an undated letter to John Neilson probably sent some time after May 1832, in which Lancaster alluded to a petition "for the copy right publication of my system Seminary for teachers."[42] There

---

37  See Bernard, *Amury Girod*, 219.

38  Bernard, *Amury Girod*, 219.

39  JLP suggests that he was still active in Lower Canada in June 1833 but had left by October. He had been charged with assault and battery in Lower Canada and had left the province to avoid the trial. In November 1833, he was at John Lovell's in New Haven, Connecticut, where he wrote the preface to *Epitome*.

40  One sheet broadside printed by Lancaster in Montreal. It was reprinted in *Epitome*.

41  Lancaster, *Report of the Singular Results*, 8.

42  LAC, Neilson Collection, vol. 8, 157–86. The letter is undated but the year 1833 was added by an unknown hand. I believe that it is more likely that Lancaster corresponded with Neilson in 1832. The petition itself is not in the file, and the Neilson Archives do not include Neilson's response.

is nothing in the records to suggest that this petition ever reached the Assembly. In fact, Lancaster did not petition at all during the 1832–3 session.[43] It also is difficult to ascertain the publication to which Lancaster was referring as there is no record of a Lower Canadian book or pamphlet titled *Seminary* or *Seminary for Teachers*. It is possible that he was referring to a draft of his *Epitome of Some of the Chief Events and Transactions in the Life of Joseph Lancaster*, which he eventually published and registered for copyright in the United States, and which contains a few paragraphs under the heading *Seminary for Teachers*. The final text of Lancaster's *Epitome* repeated much of the material contained in the broadside and pamphlet and, like these, was intended to herald a new edition of *Improvements on Education*, for which he was seeking 3,000 subscribers.[44] Lancaster did not complete the work. He never returned to Lower Canada after his abrupt departure in 1833 and died in New York City in 1838.

Only Joseph-François Perrault took advantage of the new copyright statute. This is not surprising, given his active – albeit unsuccessful – pursuit of exclusive rights before the legislature. By 1832, Perrault had already written a number of schoolbooks and legal treatises. He was also the prothonotary of the Court of King's Bench District of Quebec, and in that capacity, he acted as the copyright registrar. He was, therefore, especially well-placed to understand the new legislation and its intricate legal formalities.

The first of Perrault's works to benefit from copyright was his five-part treatise *Abrége de l'histoire du Canada*, published in instalments between 1831 and 1836. As will be recalled, Perrault had been awarded £50 to publish the first part of his book in 1831, which he did that same year with Quebec printer and publisher Thomas Cary & Co. In 1832, Cary & Co. produced a second edition that consisted of parts one and two of the work. In 1833, Perrault assigned his copyright to printers,

---

43 Lancaster had a falling out with Speaker of the Assembly Louis-Joseph Papineau over his support for a pro-British candidate during the 1832 elections. Lancaster explained in *Report of the Singular Results*, 8: "He made no application to the present session of parliament, because of the name in which threats had been used, implying that he should have no grant if he exercised his right of voting on the principles of British freedom." According to Curtis, in "Joseph Lancaster in Montreal *bis*," 26, Lancaster went directly to Governor Aylmer, complaining bitterly about his treatment by the Assembly.

44 Lancaster, *Epitome*, 28. The subscriber list included in *Epitome* reveals that Governors Kempt and Aylmer had subscribed for four copies each in 1830 and John Neilson for two copies in 1833.

publishers, and binders P & W Ruthven, which produced its own version of parts one and two, registering its copyright on 21 May 1833.[45] The Ruthven version was not a reprint of the Cary publication as the typography was entirely different. Perrault would therefore not have been acting in bad faith in obtaining financing from the Assembly for the original edition and securing his copyright in the new edition. Ruthven also registered separately each of parts three and four on 21 May 1833 and part five on 1 September 1836, as evidenced by the copyright notices contained in each volume.

Perrault printed and published two other works in 1832 but without securing their copyright. The *Rural Code for the Old and New Inhabitants of Lower Canada concerning their religious and civil duties* was published in English by Thomas Cary & Co. and in French by Imprimerie Fréchette & Cie under the title *Code rural à l'usage des habitants tant anciens que nouveaux du Bas-Canada: concernant leurs devoirs religieux et civils, d'après les lois en force dans le pays.*[46] The other work was *Moyens de conserver nos institutions, notre langue, nos lois*, also printed by Fréchette & Cie.[47] In 1834, Perrault published his autobiography, without registering copyright.[48] However, the 1839 reissue of his *Traité d'agriculture adapté au climat du Bas-Canada*, first published in 1831, was registered by Fréchette & Cie.[49] This demonstrates that even those as astute as Perrault and his publishers did not systematically secure copyright in every publication. Copyright was determined on a case-by-case basis, and whether printing and publishing occurred or failed to occur was dependent on factors that had little to do with the availability of legal protection.

*Rates and Patterns of Lower Canadian Copyright Registrations*

Although the findings are incomplete, of the hundreds of books, pamphlets, broadsides, and maps produced in Lower Canada between 1832 and 1841, eighty-two separate titles were registered

---

45   Perrault, *Abrégé de l'histoire du Canada.*

46   Joseph-François Perrault, *Rural Code*, and Joseph-François Perrault, *Code rural.*

47   Joseph-François Perrault, *Moyens de conserver nos institutions, notre langue, nos lois.* This short pamphlet, dated 1832, was published sometime after the 1832 Copyright Act was passed, since Perrault makes reference to events that succeeded the legislation.

48   Perrault, *Biographie de Joseph-François Perrault.*

49   The copyright notice (in English) after the title page is dated 29 November 1839.

for copyright.[50] There were ninety-three protected works in total, including eleven reissues or new editions of previously registered works that recorded the original copyright after the title page.[51] This figure also incorporates some material for which a copyright registration has been presumed.[52] In addition, extant copyright registration records where I could find no physical or bibliographical evidence of an associated publication have been counted.[53] Finally, some of the registrations for the year 1841 occurred after the repeal of the 1832 Act and its replacement with the Copyright Act of the Province of Canada. Given that these registrations fell within a short transition time between the two statutes, they are included in the Lower Canadian count. This tally of ninety-three protected works represents roughly 10 per cent of all the books and pamphlets produced in the province.[54] Not surprisingly, registrations dipped at the height of the Lower Canadian rebellions, in 1838, as did printing and publishing overall, as many members of the book trade closed their businesses.[55]

---

50  The only official copyright registry that survives is that of Trois-Rivières. The registry books of the two largest printing and publishing centres, Montreal and Québec, have not been located despite extensive searches. Thus, the registration data in this chapter are derived from my own reconstruction of the registries. See Appendix 1 for an elaboration of the method used to determine the copyright registrations for Lower Canada from 1832 to 1841 and Appendix 2 for the reconstructed list of those registrations.

51  I am using the term "edition" to include reissues of earlier publications rather than in bibliographic terms as a new setting of type. The books in question were referred to as new editions.

52  For example, the Calendrier de Montréal and the Calendrier de Québec were published and registered annually. I was able to look at many of them in digital format or in hard copy in order to confirm the copyright notices. In cases where I could not review the actual print material, I have assumed registrations based on likelihood.

53  LAC, Neilson Collection , contains two copyright certificates for works that do not appear in any of the bibliographical records I consulted. Similarly, the registry book of Trois-Rivières includes one copyright registration without an actual publication. Either this material was never printed and published – a multitude of intervening factors could have prevented their publication after the title was registered – or else no trace of them remains.

54  A statistical analysis conducted by Sandra Alston and Jessica Bowslaugh determined that between 1821 and 1840, Lower Canada produced 1,671 imprints. See HBC, vol. 1, 88. My unscientific count shows at least 1,090 publications between 1832 and 1841, including those protected by copyright.

55  For example, Ludger Duvernay fled the province because of his political activities. See Monière, *Ludger Duvernay et la révolution intellectuelle.* John Lovell of Montreal shut his business temporarily to join the Royal Montreal Cavalry. See entry for Lovell (1810–1893) in DCB.

## Protected Works in Lower Canada per Year, 1832–1841

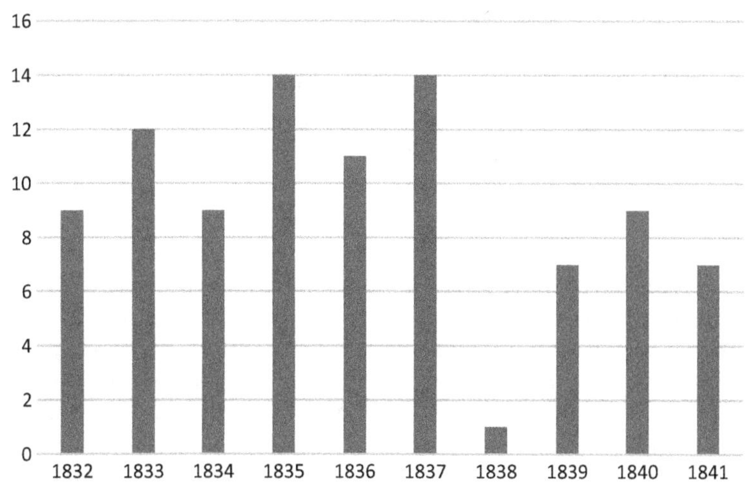

## Copyright Registrations in Lower Canada Relative to Estimated Total Publications

There was no demographic diversity in the records. Copyright was held by those belonging to the two dominant ethnic, linguistic, and religious groups in Lower Canada, namely *Canadiens* and English Lower Canadians. The first book to be registered for copyright under the new statute was David Chisholme's lengthy polemic *Observations on the rights of the British Colonies to representation in the Imperial Parliament*, printed in Trois-Rivières by George Stobbs. The Scottish-born Chisholme was a newspaper editor in Montreal before being appointed clerk of the peace for the district of Trois-Rivières in 1829. He was the first author to register a copyright in British North America. The copyright was secured on 22 March 1832, within a month of the legislation taking effect.[56] The copyright notice appeared after the title page of the publication in terms consistent with the requirements of the 1832 Act: "ENTERED according to the Act of the *Provincial Legislature*, in the year one thousand eight hundred and thirty two, by DAVID CHISHOLME in the Clerk or Prothonotary's office of the Court of King's Bench for the District of Three-Rivers." The entry in the official registry, made by prothonotary W.C.H. Coffin, was also consistent with the dictates of the statute:

> Be it remembered that on the twenty-second day of March in the year One Thousand Eight Hundred and Thirty Two, David Chisholme Esquire of the said District hath deposited in this office the title of a Book the title of which is in the words following that is to say "Observations on the Rights of the British Colonies to Representation in the Imperial Parliament by David Chisholme. Pulchrum est bene facere Reipublica. Three Rivers. Printed and Published by G. Stobbs 1832. The right whereof he claims as Author. Recorded at Three-Rivers this 22 March 1832. W.C.H. Coffin.

The printer and publisher George Stobbs was the editor of the bilingual *Three-Rivers Gazette*, founded in 1832.[57] Stobbs has the distinction of being the first printer and publisher to hold a British North American copyright. He registered his copyright in I. Pigott's *The Canadian*

---

56   The copyright registry for the district of Trois-Rivières can be found at BAnQ. Given the proximity in time to the coming into force of the legislation, Chisholme's book would appear to be the first to be registered, at least until the Montreal and Quebec copyright registries surface. See also Appendix 1.

57   Bourinot, *The Intellectual Development of the Canadian People*, 57, claimed that *Stobbs's Gazette* was the first newspaper in Trois-Rivières. This is incorrect. Ludger Duvernay started a bilingual paper by the same name in 1817 (French title *La Gazette des Trois-Rivières*), which he produced until he left for Montreal in 1827. See Tessier, "Ludger Duvernay et les débuts."

*Mechanic's Ready Reckoner or Tables for converting English Lineal, Square and Solid Measures into French, and the contrary,* the second book to be protected in Lower Canada.[58]

Further analysis of the registration records yields no discernible patterns. Consistent with the legislative requirements regarding resident authors, all the works that were registered were either authored or compiled by Lower Canadians, although some were closely derived from existing works first printed and published abroad. For example, Edouard Moreau's *Instructions sur l'art des accouchemens* [*sic*] *pour les sages-femmes de la campagne* was a very close approximation of *Catéchisme sur l'art des accouchemens* [*sic*] *pour les sages-femmes de la campagne* by French doctor Anne-Amable Augier du Fot, published in Paris in 1775. In the preface, Moreau acknowledged that he relied on the classic masterworks on the subject of childbirth and midwifery.[59]

The types of works for which copyright was sought varied greatly, ranging from one-page almanacs and maps to short pamphlets and multivolume treatises. As Perrault's case exemplifies, authors and publishers were not systematically registering their rights. The same author would register some works but not others. Similarly, printers and publishers sometimes troubled to obtain copyright in some of the works they themselves had compiled, such as almanacs and directories, and sometimes they did not bother. For example, the firm of Neilson & Cowan registered its one-page *Calendrier de Québec* every year but didn't protect the lengthier annual, the *Quebec Almanack and British American Royal Calendar.*

The categories of publications protected by copyright were diverse. There were twenty-six almanacs, calendars, and directories, thirteen religious works, thirteen mathematics and science books (including works on agriculture), eleven history books, seven geography books (including one book combining history and geography that has been counted once for each genre), six maps, three political tracts, three law books, three language books and grammars (one English, one French, one Greek), two works of fiction, two spellers, two literary anthologies (one French, one Greek), one treatise on philosophy, one memoir, and one book catalogue.

There are some indications that certain kinds of publications were commonly considered outside the scope of the Act. As previously

---

58  I. Piggott, *The Canadian Mechanic's Ready Reckoner.*
59  Moreau, *Instructions sur l'art des accouchemens* [*sic*]. Copyright registered by Moreau.

discussed, copyright was never secured in books whose printing costs had been subsidized by the legislature. Copyright protection was also never obtained for government publications, including commissioned reports and other materials printed by the official printer or under contract with private printers. The records are silent as to whether these works were considered to be in the public domain, whether they were protected outside of copyright through the Crown printing prerogative, or whether it was just not worth the effort because the risk of harm was low.[60]

Nor were newspapers ever registered during this period, for reasons that were likely consistent with the position taken under both American and British law, that facts were not protectable.[61] However, other kinds of periodical publications were registered, including those reporting facts, such as the *Calendrier de Québec*. In most of these cases a new copyright was taken out for each issue, but this was cumbersome and costly. The authors of the *Quebec Commercial List* managed to bypass this requirement. They were able to register their copyright once annually even though the periodical was produced monthly. The same copyright registration, in the names of John Bruce, Charles Secretan, and James Pendergast, was reproduced in each monthly issue.[62] We

---

60   British law protected certain kinds of Crown works against unauthorized reprinting under the Crown prerogative, regardless of the availability of copyright. See Monotti, "Nature and Basis of Crown Copyright," 305: "The sovereign has a duty, based on the grounds of public utility and necessity, to superintend and ensure authentic and accurate publication of matters of national and public concern relating to the government, state and the Church of England. That duty carries with it a corresponding prerogative which is not specifically defined in any of the cases, but clearly extends to publishing and printing that material." Vague in its scope and potentially perpetual in nature, the more modern iteration of the prerogative has been deemed to cover statutes and judicial decisions, at the very least, if not other legal material. In the Canadian context, see Torno, *Crown Copyright in Canada*; and Judge, "Crown Copyright and Copyright Reform in Canada."

61   See Slauter, *Who Owns the News*. The uncertainty about copyright in newspapers remained well into the century. As per the *Report of the Royal Commission on Copyright*, xvii, para. 88: "Much doubt appears to exist in consequence of several conflicting legal decisions whether there is any copyright in newspapers. We think it right to draw Your Majesty's attention to the defect, and to suggest that in any future legislation, it may be remedied by defining what parts of a newspaper may be considered copyright, by distinguishing between announcements of facts and communications of a literary nature."

62   The registrants were the clerks of the Customs Office at the Port of Quebec. *The Quebec Commercial List* for 1837 was not independently registered. The monthly issues for that year reproduced the date of registration for vol. 21 of 23 May 1836. See Bruce, Secretan, and Pendergast, *The Quebec Commercial List*.

will see in the next chapter that this practice was eliminated under the 1841 Copyright Act of the Province of Canada.

Religious works might also have been considered inappropriate for copyright, for reasons expressed by the Quebec Superior Court in the 1874 decision in *Langlois v. Vincent*, which involved *Le grand catéchisme de Québec*: "Considering the nature of the work and the source whence it emanated, it being a summary of religious doctrine compiled by the head of the church in this country obviously for the comfort and use of his flock, it is to be presumed that it was intended for the widest and most unfettered circulation, and with no eye to private advantage."[63]

However, of the large numbers of catechisms, canticles, prayer books, sermons, and other religious works printed and published between 1832 and 1841, thirteen were registered for copyright. A close review of these individual copyright works yields no great insights as to why these publications were deemed worthy of private advantage while the rest were not. François-Xavier Noiseux's *Liste chronologique des évêques et des prêtres, tant séculiers que réguliers employés au service de l'Église du Canada* is an easier case to explain than the others.[64] Published in 1833 with copyright registered by the printer and publisher Thomas Cary & Co., the pamphlet consisted of a compendium of biographies of members of the clergy in British North America, written by Noiseux. It is much harder to understand why copyright was sought for books like the *Petit manuel des cérémonies romaines; à l'usage du diocèse de Québec* (Quebec: Fréchette & Cie, 1832) – copyright in printers and publishers Fréchette & Parent) and the *Extrait du rituel du Québec contenant l'administration des sacrements de baptême* (1836 – copyright in printers and publishers Cary & Desbarats), or again, *Le grand catéchisme, à l'usage du diocèse de Québec* (1836 – copyright in Cary & Desbarats). Issued by the Church for liturgical purposes, these books were precisely the kinds of works that the *Langlois* court identified as intended "for the widest and most unfettered circulation."

*Schoolbook Registrations*

Copyright take-up rates were low throughout the Anglo-American world. Schoolbooks represented the largest proportion of books for which copyright was sought. In the United States, Frederick R. Goff found a "heavy incidence of textbooks in the early copyright registers

---

63  *Langlois v. Vincent*, 1874, 18 LCJ 160, p. 162.
64  Noiseux, *Liste chronologique des évêques et des prêtres*.

[indicating] ... that a healthy demand existed for primers, geographies and arithmetics."[65] In fact, the first book registered for copyright under the US Copyright Act of 1790 was a schoolbook: *The Philadelphia Spelling Book, Arranged upon a Plan Entirely New* by John Barry.[66]

In Lower Canada, thirty-three of the ninety-three protected works (35%) were schoolbooks, or they were books, like Evans's agricultural treatise, that were intended for more general educational purposes within the school system. Thirty of these were new schoolbooks; the remaining three were new editions of previously registered books. However, the fact that schoolbooks figured prominently in the registration records does not tell us anything about whether the copyright legislation itself increased schoolbook production. Although the publishing data do reveal a steady rise in Lower Canadian schoolbook publishing during the 1830s, this increase began prior to the advent of the Copyright Act. Paul Aubin noted that from 1765 to 1839, the average publication rate was two schoolbooks per year, with the rate doubling in the years after the coming into force of the Trustees School Act of 1829.[67] The number of schoolbooks authored and printed in Lower Canada jumped from nine schoolbooks in 1829 to twenty-three in 1831. The fact that most schoolbooks or educational materials were *not* registered after 1832 suggests that copyright was not the primary driver for local schoolbook production. Instead, the growth appears to have been tied more directly to education reforms that increased the demand for textbooks and other didactic materials. Even if copyright was not the direct cause of the increase in schoolbooks in Lower Canada, did its introduction accelerate the pace of production? If the law had made an appreciable difference in this regard, one would have expected a steady rise in schoolbook registrations over time. The findings are to the contrary. The percentage of copyright registrations relative to the overall publication of schoolbooks and other educational material did not rise over time. Instead, the registration pattern was erratic, confirming that copyright was not, at this early stage at least, a catalyst for sustained schoolbook production in the province.

Of the thirty-three schoolbooks protected by copyright, nine were history books and seven were geography books (including one book

---

65   Goff, "The First Decade of the Federal Act," 4. See also Bracha, "The Ideology of Authorship Revisited," 204: "Copyright was widely used to protect materials such as textbooks, dictionaries and a host of other 'useful' or didactic works. Throughout the nineteenth century, the largest relative share of the publishing market continued to be occupied by such works." See also Khan, *The Democratization of Invention*, 236.

66   Barry, *The Philadelphia Spelling Book*. Registered in Philadelphia by Barry on 9 June 1790.

67   Lebrun, *Le manuel scolaire*, 29–30.

Total number of schoolbooks (incl. educational treatises) published in Lower Canada relative to copyright registrations for schoolbooks, 1832–1841

|  | 1832 | 1833 | 1834 | 1835 | 1836 | 1837 | 1838 | 1839 | 1840 | 1841 |
|---|---|---|---|---|---|---|---|---|---|---|
| Total schoolbooks* | 19 | 24 | 17 | 14 | 11 | 16 | 9 | 8 | 16 | 19 |
| Copyright registrations – new schoolbooks | 1 | 6 | 0 | 7 | 4 | 6 | 0 | 1 | 1 | 4** |
| New "editions" with original registrations | 0 | 1 | 0 | 0 | 1 | 0 | 0 | 1 | 0 | 0 |
| Total protected schoolbooks | 1 | 7 | 0 | 7 | 5 | 6 | 0 | 2 | 1 | 4 |

* The entries in the ManScol database were the starting point, but I eliminated duplicate entries, and those printed and published outside of Lower Canada (even though the statute did not require domestic printing), as well as those listed as undated. The undated entries are accounted for in the overall numbers where I was able to determine an approximate date. These figures also include additional books that I compiled from multiple biographical sources and that are not found in ManScol. Finally, I have also counted one book (*Le livre* [sic] *des enfans, nouvel alphabet français, deuxième édition* [Quebec: Samuel Neilson, 1836]) where a copyright registration certificate can be found in LAC Neilson Collection but no record exists of it having been published. Furthermore, where copyright registration dates differ from publication dates, the date of registration has been used.

** Two of the schoolbooks were registered after the repeal of the 1832 Act but have been included here.

Registered schoolbooks relative to total number of schoolbooks published in Lower Canada, 1832–1841

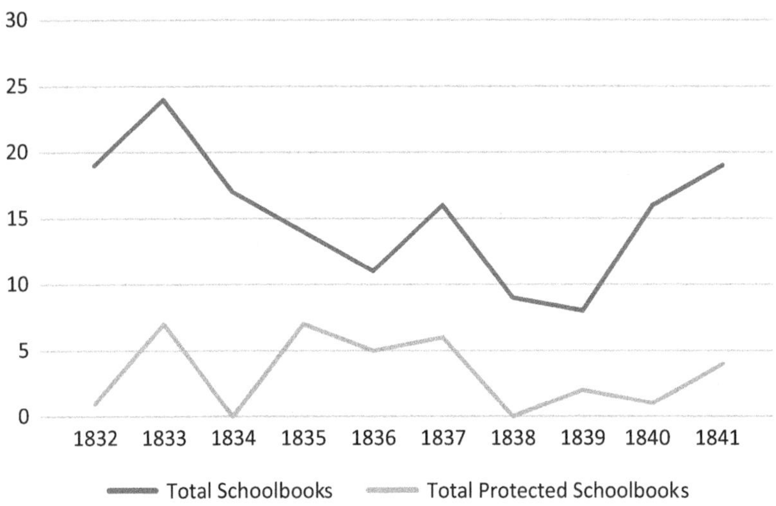

of history and geography, counted once for each genre). These were the most numerous categories, reflecting the fact that these subjects, more than any others, necessitated treatment of local conditions best addressed by Lower Canadians rather than by foreigners with little or no connection to the province. Indeed, the first schoolbook to be protected by copyright under the Lower Canadian statute was Jean Holmes's *Nouvel abrégé de géographie moderne, suivi d'un appendice, et un abrégé de géographie sacrée à l'usage de la jeunesse*. Copyright was registered on 23 May 1832 by Neilson & Cowan.[68] There were four science books (three agriculture, one physics), three books of mathematics and arithmetic, two French spellers, one book of French literature, one book of English grammar, one of Greek grammar, one of Greek literature, one of philosophy, and one on rhetoric and argumentation. Of the religious works, there were two catechisms and one hymnal, specifically prepared for use in schools. Twenty-five of these schoolbooks were printed in French, six in English, one in Latin, and one in Greek and French. The fact that most of the protected books were written in French is unsurprising given the language of the majority of the population. However, the large number of copyright registrations for French-language schoolbooks also suggests that these books were profitable.

## The Impact of Copyright on Authors, Printers, and Publishers in Lower Canada

*New Strategies and New Publishing Practices*

Nineteenth-century printing and publishing activities were often financed by subscriptions solicited in advance of publication. The Copyright Act did not disrupt this established method of book financing. What the statute did, rather, was empower authors by giving them control over the publication of their manuscripts. It provided them with negotiating leverage with printers and publishers, who now had to enter into agreements with them to secure exclusive rights. For printers, the security of copyright offered an incentive to transition from jobbers to entrepreneurs, either sharing the financial burden of publishing with the authors or bearing them entirely if they believed that a particular book would be popular. Copyright guaranteed to copyright holders a

---

68   Holmes, *Nouvel abrégé de géographie moderne*. In addition to the copyright notice after the title page of the book, an official handwritten copy of the registration can be found at LAC, Neilson Collection.

minimum of twenty-eight years to recover their investment and turn a profit on a bestseller. Members of the book trade were the largest copyright holders in Lower Canada, suggesting that copyright had a positive impact on the industry, at least to the extent that some recognized its value as a commercial asset.

Of the ninety-three protected works, sixty (64.5%) were held by the province's printers, publishers, and booksellers. However, this figure is somewhat misleading, since most of these registered works were compilations of information such as calendars, tables, and directories, which the printers and publishers authored or compiled themselves. Works for which printers and publishers held the copyright as assignees of authors were far fewer in number, and the books in question tended to be either schoolbooks or religious in nature, or both.[69] This confirms that Lower Canadian printers and publishers were not ready to assume the risks of more speculative undertakings. The books in which they held copyright were generally of low risk – for example, new editions of popular works, or schoolbooks destined for use in schools with secure funding, such as those run by the Catholic Church.

There was one series of registrations where copyright was held by someone other than the author or the printer and publisher. Joseph-Vincent Quiblier, Roman Catholic priest and director of the Petit Séminaire de Montréal, registered copyright in five schoolbooks intended for use at the school. Quiblier is not known to have written any schoolbooks himself. Indeed, three of the books in question were reprints of commonly used texts circulating at the time. In the two other cases, Quiblier registered his copyright as proprietor in books written or compiled by Jean Larkin, a priest and teacher at the Petit Séminaire. These were *Grammaire grecque, à l'usage du Collège de Montréal* and *Eklekta muthistorias*, both printed in 1837 by John Jones of Montreal.[70] It is not known whether Larkin assigned his rights or whether they assumed that, as director of the seminary, Quiblier was entitled to the copyright.

The Neilson family firm, including successively Neilson & Cowan, Samuel Neilson, and William Neilson, account for twenty-two of the sixty copyrights held by printers and publishers. This is unsurprising,

---

69  I have assumed that the copyright was held by the printers and publishers in certain cases in which the identity of the copyright holder is not indicated in the notice after the title page. See Appendix 2.

70  Larkin, *Eklekta muthistorias*; Larkin, *Grammaire grecque, à l'usage du Collège de Montréal*.

since the family ran the largest printing and publishing operation at the time. However, the records make it clear that the Neilsons understood the commercial value of copyright, especially the firm of Neilson & Cowan, which held the bulk of the Neilson copyrights. The firm of Neilson & Cowan was formed in 1822 when John Neilson divested himself of the business to pursue a life in politics. John Neilson's eldest son Samuel held two thirds of the business, and William Cowan held the remaining one third share. Between 1832 and the partnership's dissolution in 1836, Neilson & Cowan built a solid copyright portfolio by taking assignments of copyright from authors or by registering copyright in works they themselves produced, such as almanacs and calendars.[71] The firm took few risks in terms of the material they published, relying on safe bets like religious works and almanacs, which sold well. Of the publications they did not compile themselves, most were by authors who would not expect much by way of compensation for the copyright, such as schoolteachers or members of the clergy. Their most significant copyright expense was the administrative cost of registration, which was easily offset by the revenue from sales.

The Neilson & Cowan copyright portfolio was valuable. For the years 1832 to 1836, the firm held copyright in thirteen publications, including new editions of previously copyrighted works. The value of the firm's copyright interests is set out in a letter from William Cowan to John Neilson on 7 March 1837. Cowan wrote to the senior Neilson because the ailing Samuel was unavailable to respond to his concerns.[72] It appears that Cowan had agreed to transfer his share of the firm's copyright assets to Samuel for a stipulated sum, but the agreement the notary sent for his signature was silent on the issue.[73] As a result, Cowan complained that he was being deprived "of all compensation

---

71   Assignments of copyright from the Reverend John McDonald for the *Christian's Pocket Library in Four Parts*, and from Jean-Baptiste Boucher in respect of *Recueil de cantiques*, can be found in LAC, Neilson Collection. Boucher's publishing relationship with the Neilsons will be discussed in more detail later in this chapter.

72   On Samuel Neilson (1800–1837) see DCB. See also Claude Galarneau, "Samuel Neilson (1800–1837)." The partnership was dissolved on 30 April 1836, with Samuel retaining the business. The same year, Samuel passed the business to his brother William.

73   William Cowan to John Neilson, 16 March 1837, box 192–1, folder: W. Cowan, BAnQ, Fonds Imprimerie Neilson. Thomas Fisher Rare Book Library has a printed and unsigned form letter announcing the dissolution of the partnership effective 30 April 1836, with Samuel Neilson retaining the "business of The Quebec Gazette, and the Bookselling and Printing business" (broadsides: RBD00441, 1836).

for relinquishing for ever my interest in Copy Rights (although the amount of that compensation had been fixed by Mr. S. Neilson himself only three days before at £100 in Stock and £50 in his note)."[74] Since Cowan held a one third share in the partnership, the value of the firm's copyright holdings was £450, which was not an insubstantial amount. William Morris's annual salary of £60 can serve as a benchmark. The value of Neilson & Cowan's copyright portfolio was almost double Morris's earnings for that same four-year period.

Lower Canadian printers and publishers, including the Neilsons, were strategic in their management of their copyright assets. In 1849, William Neilson was winding down the business, having inherited it from his late brother Samuel in 1836. William Neilson sold the Neilson & Cowan copyright holdings to other Lower Canadian printers and publishers. In some instances, the term of the copyright was already more than half over, but these books were valuable – so much so that these assignees used a number of devices to prolong their exclusivity beyond the statutory period and outside of the statutory renewal process. It will be recalled that the 1832 Copyright Act provided for an initial term of protection of twenty-eight years from registration. The first registrations would have begun to lapse in 1860 unless renewed for an additional fourteen years by the author, if alive, or by the author's spouse and children. However, by 1860, the Lower Canadian statute had been repealed and the 1841 Copyright Act of the Province of Canada was the governing legislation. This statute failed to provide any clear direction as to the status of unexpired Lower Canadian registrations. In addition, the 1841 Act offered no guidance on whether Lower Canadian registrations could be renewed at the expiry of the initial term.[75] As will become more evident in the next chapter, the 1841 Act had been meant to extend, throughout the new province, the same copyright protection that Lower Canadians had enjoyed. This suggests that existing rights would continue to be recognized in the united province.

Contemporaneous practice corroborates this interpretation. After 1841, new issues and editions of works registered under the 1832 Act continued to include the original registration notices as if the earlier Act had not been repealed. For example, Neilson & Cowan's 1842 edition of

---

74 Cowan to Neilson, 16 March 1837, box 192–1, folder: W. Cowan, BAnQ, Fonds Imprimerie Neilson.

75 In contrast, later Canadian statutes specified that unexpired copyrights could be renewed "as if the Act had not been repealed." See section 20 of the Copyright Act of 1868.

Jean-Baptiste Boucher's *Recueil de cantiques à l'usage des missions, retraites et catéchismes* included the original 1833 registration notice. What is less clear is whether a Lower Canadian copyright could have been renewed under the terms of the 1841 Act. Although the registration records do not indicate any renewals of Lower Canadian copyrights after 1860, this fact alone is not determinative of the legal question. Most of the works registered between 1832 and 1841 were one-off titles without lasting appeal, so the initial term would have sufficed. In addition, the renewal provision was unavailable to authors who died without immediate heirs. It also excluded publishers and other assignees, who were unable to exercise the statutory renewal in their own names. This explains why some copyright holders, like the purchasers of the Neilson & Cowan copyrights, attempted to prolong their rights by repackaging existing copyright works as new, revised, and improved editions. They would then claim these editions as new books entitled to a fresh copyright registration, emulating a practice that was common in the United States.[76]

One such case involved Jean Holmes's *Nouvel abrégé de géographie moderne*, the first schoolbook registered under the statute. Neilson & Cowan registered the copyright in 1832. The book became such an educational staple that three more editions followed within the Neilson publishing family (the 4th edition was published by William Neilson in 1846). These later editions contained the original 1832 copyright notice after the title page, consistent with the legislative requirements. In 1854, the firm of J. & O. Crémazie purchased the Neilson & Cowan copyright and issued a revised edition of the book. After the title page of this 5th edition, "revue, corrigée et augmentée," they included the original 1832 copyright registration along with the notice of assignment of copyright.[77] The Crémazies only acquired the remaining six years of the copyright, given that the initial twenty-eight-year period would end in 1860. However, the assignees clearly did not consider this an impediment. In 1862, two years after the expiry of the copyright, the firm issued another edition – "6ᵉ édition, revue, corrigée et augmentée" – with the 1832 copyright registration and notice of the assignment prominently displayed after the title page. This edition could not have been a renewal of the existing copyright. The assignees were ineligible by law, and Holmes, a Catholic priest who died in 1852, did not have a spouse or children to exercise the right of renewal.

---

76   For example, Noah Webster routinely employed this strategy. See Micklethwait, *Noah Webster and the American Dictionary.*

77   Holmes, *Nouvel abrégé de géographie moderne.*

The chain of assignments did not end there. A notice in the *Journal de l'Instruction Publique*, dated 16 January 1863, advised that the firm of Desbarats & Derbishire had, by way of judicial sale, acquired various copyrights formerly held by J. & O. Crémazie, including in the *Nouvel abrégé de géographie moderne*.[78] In 1864, the firm of G. and G.E. Desbarats reissued the 6th edition of Holmes's work, claiming the copyright assignment from the Crémazie firm.[79] This edition included the original 1832 copyright registration and the assignments by William Neilson to J. & O. Crémazie and from Crémazie to G. & G.E. Desbarats. For good measure, Desbarats also included a notice of its own copyright registration under the 1841 Copyright Act of the Province of Canada.[80] In 1870 the Rolland firm purported to acquire Desbarats' rights and issued a 7th edition, this time with Louis Onésime Gauthier as co-author.[81] Gauthier, who taught history at the Quebec Seminary, had substantially revised, corrected, and enhanced Holmes's original text. The publisher registered its copyright under the Copyright Act of 1868 of the Dominion of Canada and was asserting this new "co-authored" version as a fresh copyright work, although, presumably, had this been litigated, the new copyright would only have covered the additional material provided by Gauthier and not the book in its entirety. The same formula was repeated under the Canadian Copyright Act of 1875 when J.B. Rolland & Co. registered its 9th co-authored edition and included the original Neilson & Cowan registration of May 1832 after the title page.[82] In this way, these publishers ostensibly kept a twenty-eight-year

---

78  Québec, *Journal de l'instruction publique*, vol. 8 (Montréal: Dept. de l'instruction publique, 1863), 4. A similar announcement appeared in *Le Canadien* on 23 January 1863. The firm also acquired the copyright in Jean-Antoine Bouthillier's *Traité d'arithmétique* and his *Élements de géographie moderne*. The Crémazies got into serious financial trouble in 1862. See entry for Jacques or Octave Crémazie, DCB.

79  George-Édouard Desbarats came from a long line of Quebec printers. His grandfather Pierre-Édouard and father George-Paschal were both official government printers. George-Édouard was appointed official printer for the Dominion of Canada in 1869. On G.E. Desbarats (1838–1893), see his entry in DCB. See also Galarneau, "The Desbarats Dynasty," in HBC, vol. 2, 87.

80  See also LAC, Index of Copyright Registrations for the Province of Canada, 1841–1865, RG 105, vol. 378, registration no. 312, 21 January 1863.

81  Holmes, L.O Gauthier, *Nouvel abrégé de géographie moderne* (Montréal: J.B. Rolland & fils, 1870). Gauthier is referred to as "professeur d'histoire au séminaire de Québec" in the *Journal de l'instruction publique*, which advertised the new edition and alluded to the various transfers of copyright from Neilson & Cowan onward. See *Journal de l'instruction publique* 14, no. 9 (1870): 127 (Québec (Province): Ministère de l'instruction publique).

82  Holmes, Gauthier, *Nouvel abrégé de géographie moderne* (Montréal: J.B. Rolland & fils, 1877).

copyright alive for more than fifty years as if the right could be passed down indefinitely.

A similar strategy was employed in the case of Jean-Antoine Bouthillier's *Traité d'arithmétique pour l'usage des écoles*, the third edition of which was published and registered by Neilson & Cowan in 1835. In 1855, J. & O. Crémazie issued a revised and corrected edition claiming an assignment of copyright from Neilson & Cowan and invoking the original 1835 copyright registration.[83] In 1863, the year of the expiry of the original copyright, G. & G.E. Desbarats published a new edition, claiming rights from Cremazie and "re-registering" the copyright under the 1841 Act of the Province of Canada.[84] It is extremely doubtful that this new copyright would have withstood judicial scrutiny. It could not have been claimed as a renewal of the original registration since the author Bouthillier was dead and his spouse and children had predeceased him.[85] Furthermore, unlike in Holmes's case, there was no attempt to add a co-author in order to claim rights over a "new book." This copyright would have expired in 1863 regardless of the publishers' machinations. In practice, however, the continued inclusion of the copyright notices and the new registration under the 1841 Act may have deterred prospective competitors from reprinting the original material, even though, legally speaking, they could not have been prevented from doing so.

A somewhat different example arose in relation to Joseph-François Perrault's *Traité d'agriculture adapté au climat du Bas-Canada*, first published and registered by Fréchette & Cie in 1839. In 1865, two years before the initial term was to expire, Perrault's grandson, the agronomist Joseph-Xavier Perrault, registered the work under a slightly different title (*Traité d'agriculture pratique*) under the copyright legislation of the Province of Canada, at least according to the copyright notice in the book.[86] The younger Perrault would not have been eligible to renew the original copyright since the right did not pass to the author's grandchildren. The title page of this new version identified Joseph-François

---

83   Holmes, Gauthier, *Nouvel abrégé de géographie moderne* (Quebec: J. & O. Crémazie, 1855).

84   See notice after title page. See also LAC, Index of Copyright Registrations for the Province of Canada 1841–1865, RG 105, vol. 378, registration no. 310, 21 January 1863.

85   On Jean-Antoine Bouthillier (1782–1835), see his entry at DCB.

86   Joseph-François Perrault, *Traité d'agriculture pratique*. The index of copyright registrations from 1841 to 1865 does not record this book.

Perrault as the author but added "J. Perrault" as a second author, presumably because a twelve-page section was added to the work on the subject of the cultivation of flowers. Otherwise, this book was a textual reproduction of the earlier work with only slight typographical changes and rearrangements. Nevertheless, Joseph-Xavier Perrault claimed a new copyright for what was, technically speaking, a different book, although it is likely that only the additional material would have been protected. In the end, Joseph-François Perrault's treatise enjoyed fifty-four years of copyright protection.

By dint of their public assertions of subsisting copyrights, these publishers professed to having exclusive control over the printing and reprinting of their books well past the statutory duration. Although legally suspect, these manoeuvres were never challenged before the courts. It is doubtful that this practice would have been upheld. The United Kingdom in *Donaldson v. Becket* (1774) and the United States in *Wheaton v. Peters* (1834) had already dismissed any claims to copyright outside of the statutory term, and there is every reason to expect that the courts in the Province of Canada and later, the Dominion of Canada would have decided the same way.

*The Changed Relationship between Authors and Their Publishers*

The three examples that follow offer compelling illustrations of author-publisher publishing practices on a continuum that began prior to the enactment of the 1832 Act. In the first example, we revisit the case of author J.H. Willis and Montreal publisher H.H. Cunningham, discussed in the first chapter in relation to the existence of common law copyright in Lower Canada. Their publishing relationship offers an intriguing example of a printer and publisher who purchased a "copy right" from an author without the promise of exclusive rights since the entire transaction occurred well before the 1832 Act came before the legislature. The second example involves a publishing relationship that spanned the pre- and post-copyright eras. A long-standing arrangement between Jean-Baptiste Boucher and John Neilson was altered with the coming of the Copyright Act, but the publisher engaged with the work and its readers in a manner unchanged. Here, the printer and publisher benefited from the new statutory monopoly but did not further the law's design of increasing the diversity of didactic publications. In contrast, the third example provides insight into the new arrangements and the new possibilities that were forged with the advent of the legislation. Publisher Ludger Duvernay embarked on an ambitious publishing venture, which he probably would never have undertaken but for the promise of copyright. This case stands as an exemplar of one of the intended consequences of the Copyright Act, namely to encourage printers and publishers to assume greater publishing risks. It proves, however, to be a cautionary tale.

COURTESY OF THE TRADE? J.H. WILLIS AND H.H. CUNNINGHAM (1831)
In the case of author John Howard Willis and his Montreal publisher Henry Hill Cunningham, the copyright relationship began and ended before the Act was introduced. In 1831, Cunningham published a compilation of essays by Willis under the title *Scraps and Sketches, or the Album of a Literary Lounger*. The essays had been previously printed and published in serial form. On 11 January 1831, the *Quebec Mercury* reported:

> We learn that the copy right of this volume was purchased from the author by the publisher, Mr. Cunningham of Montreal, and that it is the first instance in this province in which a bookseller has ventured upon such a speculation; the few books hitherto published having been printed by the authors at their own risk and expense. Mr. Cunningham deserves credit for setting the example which if followed by the trade will prove the best encouragement to literature.[87]

In the 1 February 1831 issue of *Halifax Monthly Magazine*, an editorial advised that

> the provinces seem about entering on a new era of literary respectability … a volume entitled "Scraps and Sketches" by J. H. Willis, published by Cunningham, Montreal. The publisher has purchased the copy right from the Author; it is the first instance of such a speculation in Lower Canada; may it succeed, the "trade" have long been the best patrons of old country literature.[88]

---

87   *Quebec Mercury*, 11 January 1831, vol. 27, no. 4, 1. See also ch. 1.
88   *Halifax Monthly Magazine*, 1 February 1831, vol. 1, no. 9, 368. See also Macdonald, "Three Early Canadian Poets," http://canadianpoetry.org/volumes/vol17/macdonald.html. According to Macdonald, "the Montreal printer and bookseller, H.H. Cunningham, purchased the copyrighted [*sic*] from Willis and produced the book for his own profits – an arrangement unique [in] the history of early Canadian publishing, and a tribute to Willis' popularity with the public. How much the author was paid we do not know."

Why would Cunningham have "purchased the copy right" from the author without any guarantee of exclusivity to prevent competitors from reprinting the book once it was published? His actions could not have been in anticipation of the new legislation, because he did not register the copyright once the Act came into force even though he would have been entitled to. Another possibility suggests itself. In the absence of copyright legislation, Cunningham, who was anxious to embark on a publishing career, may have been initiating a form of "courtesy of the trade" in Lower Canada to establish an ethical claim of priority over this work. Cunningham would have been familiar with the courtesy tradition given his close ties to the American book trade. He had arrived in Montreal from the United States in the early 1800s. His network included printer and publisher Isaiah Thomas, who, like many of his day, was well aware of the practice.[89] Before immigrating to Lower Canada, Cunningham had been a bookseller in Windsor, Vermont, where he worked closely with one of Thomas's apprentices, Nahum Mower, who operated a printing establishment there.[90] The two men moved to Montreal, where Mower served as the printer for many of Cunningham's Lower Canadian publications, including Cunningham's reprint of John Perrin's *The Elements of French Conversation: With Familiar and Easy Dialogues*.[91]

It is unclear whether Cunningham orchestrated the announcements in the Lower Canadian and Nova Scotian periodicals, but these venues made his actions publicly known. His competitors were given notice of his claim and were implicitly being asked to voluntarily refrain from reprinting the work. Cunningham was also signalling to authors that he would negotiate with them for a financial return for the right to print and publish, even though he was under no legal obligation to do so. In this context, the use of the term "copyright" signified the payment of royalties rather than the legal entitlement of exclusivity over the work.[92]

---

89   Cunningham visited Isaiah Thomas from Montreal in May 1811 and again in April 1815. See Thomas, *The Diary*.

90   See Colgate, *Nahum Mower*.

91   Perrin, *The Elements of French Conversation*.

92   For example, the American publishing firm of Ticknor and Fields commonly used the word copyright to mean royalty payments to authors. See Winship, *American Literary Publishing*.

The timing of Cunningham's actions may also suggest a more calculated strategy. He may have been asserting his priority over Willis's work in the face of possible copyright legislation in neighbouring Upper Canada. On 25 January 1831, Upper Canadian schoolteacher Alexander Davidson had petitioned the Upper Canadian Assembly for copyright legislation for that province.[93] Although nothing ultimately materialized from Davidson's actions, and no copyright Bill was introduced, the timing is interesting. Davidson submitted his petition at around the same time as the newspaper editorials about Cunningham's purchase of Willis's copyright appeared. Cunningham would likely have known about Lower Canada's failed attempts to pass copyright legislation. He may have been concerned that Upper Canadian printers and publishers would attempt to secure rights from Lower Canadian authors who might have been willing to relocate to that jurisdiction since copyright laws of the period generally imposed residency requirements. As an English-language publisher, Cunningham sought to reassure Lower Canadian authors that he would deal with them as though copyright legislation were in place in the province.

For all the laudatory publicity he received in the press, Cunningham's experiment with courtesy, if this was indeed his intent, would have been short-lived. The 1832 Copyright Act supplanted the need for voluntary arrangements between authors and the book trade. In addition, interprovincial reprinting within British North America was not of sufficient concern to prompt Lower Canadian printers and publishers to establish courtesy arrangements with their counterparts in the other British North American provinces. The political circumstances in Lower Canada were such that Cunningham declared bankruptcy sometime around the time of the rebellions.[94] He later resumed his publishing career in the Province of Canada, and his only involvement with copyright was as printer and publisher of John Richardson's *Eight Years in Canada* in 1847 and its sequel *The Guards in Canada, or the Point of Honor*.[95] In both cases, Richardson registered his copyright as author.[96]

---

93   The history of copyright in Upper Canada is discussed in more detail in chapter 7.
94   Appendix to the third volume of the Journals of the Legislative Assembly of the Province of Canada, 7 Vict. 1843: Appendix NN[-4].
95   Richardson, *The Guards in Canada*.
96   LAC, Index of Copyright Registrations for the Province of Canada 1841–1865, RG 105, vol. 378, registration nos. 49 (1 March 1847) and 54 (24 December 1847).

JEAN-BAPTISTE BOUCHER, JOHN NEILSON, AND NEILSON & COWAN
(1795–1842)

The lengthy commercial association between the Catholic priest Jean-Baptiste Boucher and John Neilson and Neilson & Cowan spanned more than fifty years. This case illustrates the changing nature of the relationship between author and printer/publisher brought about by the introduction of copyright. While the law provided printers and publishers with a new and valuable business asset, it also put them at a disadvantage if they failed to secure an assignment of the copyright from the author.

In 1795, Boucher compiled a collection of canticles, which John Neilson printed and sold under the title *Recueil de cantiques à l'usage des missions, des retraites et des catéchismes*. Neilson had begun his career in the book trade just two years before, so this was one of his first major undertakings. Boucher's *Recueil de cantiques* turned out to be a very profitable publication. The book was reissued multiple times between 1795 and 1842 by Neilson, then Neilson & Cowan, and, finally, by William Neilson.

Correspondence between Boucher and John Neilson began in 1796, after the first edition of the book had been printed and had quickly sold out. Boucher inquired of Neilson whether he was interested in producing a corrected and enhanced second edition and advised that "since the first edition had been so readily exhausted, you need not seek other means to give this work a greater vogue."[97] And so began a long, amicable and profitable relationship. The first five editions of the *Recueil de cantiques* (1796–1809) were printed from a manuscript submitted by Boucher, who financed the printing costs by subscribing for large quantities for use throughout the Catholic school system.[98] Neilson also sold copies at his shop and filled wholesale orders from booksellers like Fabre in Montreal.[99]

With the publication of the second edition, Boucher expressed concerns about mistakes and inaccuracies in the printed version of the

---

97  Jean-Baptiste Boucher to John Neilson, 7 June 1796, reel 15769–15770, 26, LAC, Neilson Collection. Original letter in English.

98  By letter dated 11 August 1797, Boucher asked Neilson to find a cheaper way of sending the books to him at LaPrairie because the cost of postage raised the price considerably. He suggested that Neilson ship them by boat: Jean-Baptiste Boucher to John Neilson, 11 August 1797, reel 15769–15770, 83, LAC, Neilson Collection.

99  E.R. Fabre to Neilson & Cowan, 19 April 1828, vol. 6, reel 15770, 100–1, LAC, Neilson Collection.

work. He assiduously documented the errors and requested their correction, to no avail. Presumably, Neilson was using the same plates to reprint the work, hence the recurring errors. This practice would have been to his financial advantage if he was charging Boucher the same amount for printing, as he would be saving the typesetting costs. A frustrated Boucher wrote to Neilson in anticipation of the fifth reissue of the book, advising him that "this edition will probably be the last of which I will be the publisher, and to you alone I give and transfer as author the right I have in the work."[100]

This passage clearly demonstrates Boucher's belief that he enjoyed some right to his work that could be defended in the absence of copyright legislation. His statement also makes it clear that he was divesting himself of responsibility for publication. This would not have been of great concern to Neilson. The *Recueil de cantiques* was a bestseller, and each new reprinting sold out. His publishing risk was negligible. In fact, the firm had been profiting from this book from the very beginning, and Neilson frequently expressed his gratitude to Boucher both in words and in deeds. For years, Neilson provided his friend with a free subscription to the *Quebec Gazette*, which the latter tried routinely and unsuccessfully to pay for.[101] Neilson also made Boucher a gift of beautifully bound editions of the *Recueil de cantiques*. Boucher mused that these gifts rendered him unable to claim "the *sic vos non vobis* of Virgil" – namely, that he couldn't complain about his work being appropriated without permission or reward.[102] This is the clearest statement of his belief that, as an author, he retained a certain moral, if not legal, claim to his work.

What did the advent of copyright change in respect of the printing and publishing of the *Recueil de cantiques*? We discussed the question of non-statutory copyright in the first chapter. In Lower Canada, authors enjoyed the sole right to permit the first publication of the manuscript copy of their works, but it was unclear whether they retained any rights over their works once published. With copyright law in place, there

---

100  Jean-Baptiste Boucher to John Neilson, 18 March 1809, vol. 2, reel 15769, 113–14, LAC, Neilson Collection.

101  Jean-Baptiste Boucher to John Neilson, 15 May 1818, vol. 3, reel 15769, 220–1, LAC, Neilson Collection: For example, by letter dated 15 May 1818 Boucher, wrote to Neilson "to pray you again to send me your charges against me for your Gazette for which I must certainly be indebted to you."

102  Jean-Baptiste Boucher to John Neilson, 18 June 1819, vol. 3, reel 15769, 339–40, LAC, Neilson Collection: The phrase "thus we labour but not for ourselves" was used by the ancient Roman poet Virgil to decry an act of plagiarism against him.

was no longer any ambiguity or uncertainty. Authors were afforded rights after first publication. Printers and publishers were now legally obliged to obtain permission to deal with a published work. Correspondence between Samuel Neilson and his father after 1832 illustrates this changed circumstance. In 1829, Neilson & Cowan had produced a ninth edition of the book without having communicated with Boucher at all, let alone having obtained his prior permission to print. However, with the passage of the Copyright Act, they were now required to deal with the author. As a result, on 28 September 1832, Neilson & Cowan wrote to John Neilson seeking his advice as to "the propriety of applying to the Rev. Mr. Boucher in order to obtain a copy right." The printers explained that they wanted to issue another edition since the work was "favourably known to the country and is likely to continue profiting ... for a long time." They continued: "We believe it has not been printed by any other House – but if a copy is not secured it will probably become decommissioned stock after this printing ... If we could obtain the copy right we could be able without risk to print."[103]

What is interesting about this exchange is that, prior to the introduction of copyright law in Lower Canada, printers and publishers had always been at "risk to print," yet Neilson & Cowan had still been printing and publishing this book. Why did they think this work would now become decommissioned stock if Boucher did not assign his copyright to the firm? Neilson & Cowan admitted that they were not aware of any other firm currently publishing the *Recueil de cantiques*, so why were they concerned? The risk they now faced, which they had not before, related to the possibility of being excluded by a competitor who successfully obtained Boucher's assignment of copyright before they did. The legislative scheme was designed around the principle of one copyright holder enjoying exclusive control over the printing and publishing of a particular work for the statutory duration. In this new legal order, Neilson & Cowan would have had to entirely renounce a ready seller if they could not secure the copyright from Boucher. With the copyright, their position as the book's sole source of supply was assured.

John Neilson replied to this missive by advising that "I have to inform you that I have always considered that Mr. Boucher gave the work to me to dispose of as I thought proper ... However delicacy requires that your intention of securing copy right should be submitted to

---

103   Neilson & Cowan to John Neilson, 28 September 1832, reel 15771, vol. 12, 400, LAC, Neilson Collection.

Mr. Boucher requiring his approbation."[104] The earlier correspondence between the two men would seem to confirm Neilson's view that Boucher had left the printing and sale of the book entirely to his discretion and that the author expected nothing in return. However, Neilson's opinion that Boucher's permission be sought merely as a polite courtesy was incorrect. The statute vested the copyright with the author, so in order for Neilson & Cowan to print and publish Boucher's book it now needed his consent. This was the case even where the work in question was a reissue or a new edition of a book printed and published prior to 1832.

Following from Neilson's reply, Neilson & Cowan wrote to Boucher:

> As we are desirous of publishing a new Edition of the Recueil de Cantiques a l'usage des missions, the copy of which was formerly furnished by you to our predecessor Mr. John Neilson – we wrote to this gentleman with a view to secure a copy right under the law passed last year. We beg … to enclose herewith Mr. Neilson's answer to our request and also to solicit your kind acquiescence respecting the said Copy right. Should our [request?] meet your approbation we shall publish the work at a very reduced price which will probably increase its circulation.[105]

Neilson & Cowan certainly understood some of the implications of the new law. They indicated to Boucher that, with the copyright, they could sell the book at a reduced price. At least in theory, the law provided printers and publishers with an incentive to spread the costs of printing and publishing over the life of the copyright, leading to a reduction in book prices that, in turn, would make books more accessible to a broader Lower Canadian readership. We will see later in this chapter that this assumption was erroneous, as copyright does not appear to have had the desired effect on book prices.

On 3 November 1832, Boucher assigned his copyright to Neilson & Cowan on the following terms: "Ayant depuis plusieurs années remis et livré mon Recueil de cantiques … entre les mains de John Neilson … qui en a fait plusieurs impressions, s'il vous plait de vous … transmettre ses droits à l'impression dudit Recueil sous le titre même de Copy right, je me joins à lui et je donne volontiers mon consentement à ce que vous jouissiez du dit droit."[106]

___

104   John Neilson to Neilson & Cowan, 25 October 1832, reel 15771, vol. 12, 403, LAC, Neilson Collection.

105   Neilson & Cowan to Jean-Baptiste Boucher, 29 October 1832, reel 15771, vol. 12, 404, LAC, Neilson Collection.

106   Boucher to Neilson & Cowan, 3 November 1832, reel 15770, vol. 7, 498, LAC, Neilson Collection. [Having for several years remitted and delivered my *Recueil*

Neilson & Cowan registered its copyright in the tenth edition of the *Recueil de cantiques* on 7 May 1833. The firm's accounting ledger shows a payment of ten shillings to prothonotary Edward Burroughs for "recording Copyright of Cantique – copy of record of" dated 20 May 1833.[107] The eleventh and final edition, published by William Neilson in 1842, included a notice of the 1833 copyright registration after the title page.

Whatever time and expenses were attendant to this new copyright system – in terms of exchanges with the author, registration fees, and other administrative costs – it was worth the effort for the Neilsons since this was such a profitable book. However, circumstances were not always as auspicious for some of their peers. The final example demonstrates that the risks inherent in publishing ventures remained acute despite the advent of copyright.

HENRI DES RIVIÈRES BEAUBIEN AND LUDGER DUVERNAY (1831–1834)

The publishing arrangement between author Henri Des Rivières Beaubien and his Montreal publisher Ludger Duvernay demonstrates that the law could not provide a complete solution to the risks inherent in book publishing in nineteenth-century Lower Canada. In this instance, the copyright relationship between the author and his publisher began in step with the introduction of the copyright bill to the Assembly in 1831. Ludger Duvernay had more than a passing interest in the new legislation, although this was not evident from his correspondence with Augustin-Norbert Morin while the statute was before the legislature, as described in the previous chapter. His newspaper *La Minerve* provided a brief summary of each section of the new Copyright Act, unlike the other Lower Canadian papers, which only reported the passage of the legislation without further details.[108]

In October 1831, as the Copyright Bill was making its way through Parliament, Duvernay entered into a publishing agreement with author Henri Des Rivières Beaubien in respect to his *Traité sur les lois civiles du*

---

de cantiques ... to John Neilson, Esquire, who printed it several times, if it please you to transmit to yourselves his rights to the printing of the said *Recueil* under the same title of Copy right, I join him and voluntarily give my consent for you to enjoy the said right.]

107  BAnQ, Fonds Imprimerie Neilson, P193–02: Ledger 1824–1836, 34. The statute required payment of 5 shillings to the prothonotary and 5 shillings for every copy provided to the registrant. On Neilson's account books generally, see Kennedy, "What Marie Tremaine did not Find."

108  *La Minerve*, 24 May 1832, 3.

*Bas-Canada.*[109] This was an ambitious undertaking – the work would consist of three volumes of about 900 pages in total and would sell for thirty shillings. The agreement provided for 1,000 sets to be published by subscription. The copyright was assigned to Duvernay, who would be the sole proprietor of the work. Author and publisher were to share equally in the profits and the losses, an arrangement that was common where the publishing project was risky and the value of the copyright was tenuous.

Commencing with the 3 November 1831 edition of Duvernay's newspaper, *La Minerve* regularly announced that the printer and publisher had acquired the author's rights to the manuscript and to its publication:

Le Soussigné prévient les souscripteurs à cet ouvrage et ceux qui pourront le devenir, que par suite des arrangemens pris avec l'auteur, H. Des Rivières Beaubien, Écuyer, il en est devenu propriétaire, et est le seul autorisé à recevoir le montant des souscriptions, tous reçus qui seront donnés par d'autre devant être nuls.

Le nombre des souscripteurs permet de commencer immédiatement l'impression de cet ouvrage (que plusieurs personnes instruites ont regardé comme devant être d'une grande utilité) et il sera publié dans le cours de l'hiver ...

L'ouvrage sera publié en trois volumes in 8o. sur bon papier et avec de beaux caractères. La souscription est de trente chelins, brochés.[110]

For good measure, Duvernay included Des Rivières Beaubien's signed statement to the effect that "Le Soussigné annonce aux nombreux souscripteurs à son 'Traité sur les lois civiles' qu'il a disposé de son manuscript en faveur de M. Ludger Duvernay, imprimeur, qui de cette date est seul autorisé à recevoir le montant des souscriptions et à en donner reçu."[111]

---

109   BAnQ (Vieux Montréal), Fonds Ludger-Duvernay, 31 October 1831, P680, box 1, no. 101. See also Monière, *Ludger Duvernay.*

110   [The undersigned informs those subscribed to this work and those who may subscribe, that as a result of arrangements made with the author, H. Des Rivières Beaubien, Esquire, he has become the owner and is the only one authorized to receive the amount of subscriptions, and all receipts given by others will be void. The number of subscribers allows us to begin printing this work (which many learned people have regarded as being of great use) immediately and it will be published throughout the winter ...The work will be published in three volumes in 8°. on good paper and with beautiful characters. The subscription is thirty shillings, stapled.]

111   *La Minerve,* 3 November 1831, 3. [The undersigned announces to the many subscribers of his *Traité* ... that he has disposed of his manuscript in favor of Mr. Ludger Duvernay, printer, who from this date forward is the only one authorized to receive the amount of the subscriptions and to issue receipts.]

Apparently, subscriptions were brisk, but Duvernay was unable to produce all three volumes in a timely way. [112] On 2 July 1832, he announced that the first volume was available for delivery, but he also advised his subscribers of delays in printing the entire three-volume set. He suggested that they pay for the full set in advance, along with a delivery charge of six shillings, adding that "ils faciliteront beaucoup par ce moyen l'éditeur qui a été obligé de faire des débourses considérables pour une si grande entreprise."[113] The second volume was completed in February 1833,[114] and on 19 August 1833 he announced that volume three was available to subscribers.[115] It took two years to produce the entire collection from the time the first prospectus was issued to subscribers.

Duvernay registered his copyright on 6 July 1832, after volume one was released.[116] On 30 November 1832, Des Rivières Beaubien petitioned the Assembly for financial assistance to defray the printing and publishing debts. The Assembly ignored the request, perhaps because copyright had already been secured. The legislature would not have been inclined to provide any more support under the circumstances. The author and publisher had already assumed the publishing risks and had exercised their rights under the statute. Unfortunately, the project proved too ambitious and was a financial failure.[117] To add insult to injury, in 1834 a fire destroyed some of Duvernay's inventory.[118]

Des Rivières Beaubien's case is a good example of the new relationship between authors and publishers that was initiated by the legislation. Both author and publisher could benefit financially if the project succeeded. It also evidences the risks associated with ambitious publishing ventures, especially when printers and publishers did not have a large copyright portfolio of popular, cost-effective books to offset

---

112  *La Minerve*, 9 July 1832: An announcement appeared to the effect that there weren't many copies of volume 1 left that were not already subscribed for.

113  *La Minerve*, 9 July 1832, 3: [By these means, [the subscribers] will greatly assist the publisher who has been forced to make considerable disbursements for such a large enterprise]. This notice appeared in the paper until 19 November 1832.

114  *La Minerve*, 14 February 1833.

115  *La Minerve*, 19 August 1833.

116  BAnQ, Fonds Ludger-Duvernay, contains the handwritten copyright registration. The notice in the book appears at the end of volume 1 rather than after the title page.

117  Denis Monière suggests that the publisher's losses were considerable. See Monière, *Ludger Duvernay*, 87.

118  BAnQ, Fonds Ludger-Duvernay, 31 October 1831, P680, box 1, no. 206. Duvernay referred to the loss of nine sets of the books printed on Royal paper valued at £21 2.

more speculative endeavours. Although Duvernay routinely secured copyright in some of the almanacs and calendars he compiled and printed, he never amassed the same portfolio as Neilson & Cowan. Des Rivières Beaubien's treatise was his only large publishing undertaking. Duvernay was active in the rebellions of 1837–8 and fled to Vermont after the rebels were defeated. He returned to Montreal in 1842 and re-established himself as a newspaper publisher. He never resumed his book publishing activities.

These three cases reflect the overall haphazardness of the situation at the time. Duvernay's case suggests that copyright encouraged some printers and publishers to take greater publishing risks. However, his unfortunate experience would have had a chilling effect on other ventures of this kind. In the other two cases, the introduction of copyright did not have a transformative impact on established practices. The law did not factor into Cunningham's actions at all, since the statute had not yet been enacted. In the case of Boucher, one can assume that, had the legislation not intervened, Neilson & Cowan would have continued to produce new editions for as long as there was demand for the book. The only change brought about by the law was the obligation to secure the author's prior permission to print and publish. Copyright did not encourage Neilson & Cowan to commit to books that did not already enjoy a solid market share. The historical evidence indicates that the Lower Canadian market for books was not sufficiently robust for authors or printers and publishers to take full advantage of the law. While readership was growing, it was still not at levels sufficient to encourage investment in speculative publishing ventures bolstered by copyright and subsidized by high-volume sales of ready sellers. Copyright offered no guarantee of publication regardless of how the Assembly may have viewed the matter.

### Readers and Books: Access and Affordability

Neilson & Cowan's assertion to Boucher that copyright in the *Recueil de cantiques* would reduce the book's sale price is indicative of a belief that the law would have a positive influence on book prices.[119] No evidence survives on which to determine whether Neilson & Cowan did lower

---

119   Similar arguments about the relationship between exclusive rights and low book prices were made by stationers in the United Kingdom. See Plant, "The Economic Aspects." This also occurred in pre-revolutionary France, where printers, seeking printing privileges, argued for the need to keep book prices down. See McLeod, *Licensing Loyalty.*

the price of Boucher's book after securing the copyright. Indeed, there is nothing to suggest that, in general, Lower Canadian printers and publishers offered their copyrighted books at reduced rates. It is likely that their margins were such that, even if willing, they were unable to lower their prices.

The relationship between copyright and book prices was an important issue for policy-makers. Although the Lower Canadian Education Committee did not raise this aspect as a factor in its recommendations to introduce a copyright law, its members were certainly mindful that book prices, especially schoolbook prices, needed to be kept low to ensure broad accessibility. We know that the legislature often set the sale prices for publicly funded schoolbooks, as was the case with William Morris, for example. Empirical studies of book prices in the United Kingdom after the enactment of the Statute of Anne show that prices actually *increased*. Historian William St Clair's analysis of the book market after the passage of the Statute of Anne demonstrates that prices increased immediately after the legislation. Publishers segmented the market to ensure maximum returns over the life of the copyright and only lowered their prices when the copyright neared its expiry. The cheapest books were those in which copyright had expired: "During the romantic period, the minimum price of out-of-copyright books halved, halved again, and went on falling, and the print runs and sales soared and went on soaring. Over the same period, the price of newly published copyright books rose and went on rising, most vividly seen in the price of new novels whose prices doubled and then trebled."[120] Similar empirical work conducted in relation to the 1814 UK Act confirms this same trend, namely that prices did not decline until the copyright was about to lapse.[121]

In the United States, book prices remained roughly the same in the first half of the nineteenth century. Their real cost to readers, however, increased: "It is generally assumed that technology made books cheaper, but that does not seem to have been the case before 1840. Considering the fact that consumer prices were halved between 1814 and 1840 while book prices remained relatively stable, the real cost of books may have actually gone up."[122] American printers and publishers preferred to profit from volume sales of cheaper books instead of smaller

---

120  St Clair, *The Reading Nation*, 120.
121  Li, MacGarvie, and Moser, "Dead Poets' Property." The authors also concluded
     that book prices declined by 15 per cent once the works entered the public domain.
122  Green, "The Rise of Book Publishing," 112. Gross and Kelley, *History of the Book in
     America*, vol. 2.

runs of more expensive editions, and this strategy worked for them. For example, Joseph Lancaster was advised that "costly books do not sell in this Country; elegant and costly plates will not remunerate you: – the lower the price the more profit."[123]

What of Lower Canada? The state of the archival and bibliographical record makes it very difficult to accurately determine Lower Canadian book prices, including schoolbook prices, both prior to and after the introduction of copyright.[124] What *can* be said is that the prevailing socio-economic circumstances did not permit the same kind of pricing strategies that had occurred in the United Kingdom. The situation in Lower Canada was more closely aligned with practices in the United States. From the scant records available, book prices would not have increased in Lower Canada after 1832 for reasons of affordability. It is unlikely, however, that they declined. From William Morris's example, we know that Lower Canadian printing costs remained higher than in the United States. Given the small size of the market, economies of scale would not have been as easy to realize. Regardless of Neilson & Cowan's representations to Boucher, there is no evidence to suggest that copyright resulted in cheaper books.

When all was said and done, copyright law was not the panacea the Assembly had envisaged. The policy objectives underlying the law were one thing, but the practical reality was another. Copyright could not, on its own, correct the difficult market conditions under which the Lower Canadian book trade operated. Book publishing, including schoolbook publishing, remained a financially risky business. The low rates of registration suggest that copyright was not perceived to be an effective stimulus for book production, including schoolbook production, at least in the short term. The law encouraged neither a reduction in printing costs nor a decrease in book prices; nor did it systematically encourage authors to write more or printers and publishers to take greater publishing risks. Other policy initiatives, especially those tied more directly to public education, had a more immediate impact

---

123   Burwell Bassett to Lancaster, Washington, 27 February 1819, box 3, folder 1, 21, JLP.

124   Fiona Black has noted that evidence of book prices in British North America is virtually non-existent. See Black, "Importation and Book Availability," 115. In her dissertation, "Book Availability in Canada," Black provided some limited book pricing data but only up to the 1820s and mostly in the context of the Maritimes. Kominek, in her dissertation "The Royal Institution," offered some Lower Canadian data on book prices at the National Schools, but her research was also limited to the 1820s. A comparative study of British North American book prices prior to and after various copyright laws were enacted would be revealing.

on the increased availability of a greater variety of books, even though copyright law itself must be understood within the broader education policy framework.

The most palpable consequence of the introduction of copyright can be found in the Assembly's resistance to new printing petitions rather than in the law's implementation in practice. Ironically, legislative grants proved to be more effective inducements for publication than copyright. In all cases where the Assembly provided financial support, the books in question were published. In contrast, the availability of copyright offered no guarantee of publication, and political instability in Lower Canada in the latter half of the 1830s would have interrupted whatever incremental benefits copyright might have produced over time. However, even without the same political unrest, the history of copyright in the other British North American provinces was similarly sluggish, as the next chapter will illustrate.

# Chapter Seven

# Copyright Law in British North America Leading Up to the UK Copyright Act of 1842

Lower Canada's path to copyright did not arise in isolation. The policy that informed the legislature's actions was rooted in the American copyright tradition and can be situated within the larger contextual framework of nineteenth-century North America. Books and other print materials supported the sociopolitical, cultural, and economic objectives of these developing societies. A learned electorate would establish the social structures and institutions under which they chose to live. An educated public would advance themselves intellectually and economically through their effort and industry.

The genesis of copyright law in the other British North American provinces follows a similar path to that in Lower Canada, although the connection between education and copyright was most acutely drawn in that province. Lower Canada had to accommodate the interests of two distinct communities. The sociopolitical tensions heightened the importance of public education. However, the patterns of parliamentary activity were comparable in the other British North American provinces that either considered or enacted copyright legislation within a decade of Lower Canada, namely, Nova Scotia, New Brunswick, Upper Canada and the Province of Canada.[1]

---

1 *An Act to Amend the Copyright Act*, 5 & 6 Vict., c. 45 (UK) ("The UK Copyright Act 1842"). This chapter does not discuss Prince Edward Island or Newfoundland since they enacted their first copyright laws much later in the century (1861 and 1888 respectively) and after the enactment of the UK Copyright Act 1842, whose impact is discussed in detail in the next chapter. The fact that they only considered copyright laws after 1842 meant that they were operating within a more highly charged geopolitical environment. Nevertheless, similar patterns of printing petitions occurred in those provinces as well. For example, the first printing petition put before the legislature of Prince Edward Island was that of teacher Thomas Irwin, who in 1840 requested financial aid in support of his elementary schoolbook in the Mi'kmaq language. See Journal of the House of Assembly of Prince Edward Island 3 Vict., (1840) at 91.

This chapter will explore the emergence of copyright in these other provinces leading up to 1842, the year the imperial authorities intervened for the first time in colonial copyright affairs. The eighteen-year span that began with Lower Canada's first copyright Bill in 1824 and ended with the UK Copyright Act of 1842 represents a distinct moment in Canadian copyright history. This early stage offers insights into copyright as it evolved organically, unburdened by external interference. During this period, despite their colonial status, the British North American provinces were left free to craft their domestic copyright laws in line with their own policy interests and aspirations.

Lower Canada followed the American model very closely, in terms of both statutory language and conceptual principles. The other provinces that considered copyright during this period built on existing examples but also introduced innovative concepts that would become standard features of Canadian copyright law. Nova Scotia introduced the first library deposit provisions. New Brunswick was the first to consider questions of copyright in relation to materials emanating from the judicial branch of government. Upper Canada brought nationalist objectives into the realm of copyright, which intensified in the Province of Canada. The collective experience of these provinces represents the strongest evidence of a British North American consensus on the intrinsic value of copyright for the advancement of knowledge and the encouragement of learning, in terms of both individual edification and the common good.

## Copyright in Nova Scotia

Although the first printing shop in British North America was established in Halifax in 1752, it took nearly a century before a copyright law was enacted in Nova Scotia.[2] Just as in Lower Canada, the law did not emerge to advance the printing and publishing industry. Instead, it was more closely tied to the prevailing preoccupation with establishing systems of public education and the desire to encourage learning. The scarcity of affordable schoolbooks and other didactic works, especially with content that reflected the lived realities of local communities, was as much a concern in that province as it was throughout British North America.[3]

---

2  On the first printing establishment of John Bushell of Halifax, see, for example, Fauteux, *The Introduction of Printing in Canada*.

3  The National School in Halifax was supplying free books to poor students. See Journal and Proceedings of the House of Assembly for the Province of Nova Scotia, 1826, 613.

Nova Scotia's *Act for Securing Copy Rights* was brought into force on 30 March 1839, seven years after Lower Canada's legislation.[4] The copyright Bill was introduced by educator and entrepreneur Hugh Bell, the member of the House of Assembly from Halifax Township.[5] Bell was involved in a variety of school-related initiatives. He helped secure funding to establish a school at the Wesleyan Methodist Church in Halifax.[6] He also served as a member of the Royal Acadian School Society and later as the school's vice president.[7] The Royal Acadian School was a Lancasterian monitorial school founded in 1814 by Walter Bromley.[8] Printing petitions to the legislature likely also played their part in influencing the course of events, but Bell's copyright Bill does not seem to have been directly connected to a specific request the way the petitions of Joseph Lancaster and William Morris had been in Lower Canada.

Four petitioners came before the Assembly requesting financial assistance for their books in the period leading up to Bell's introduction of the copyright Bill in February of 1839. The legislature was parsimonious in directing public funds toward book production.[9] The only petition that was successful prior to the enactment of the copyright statute was that of lawyer John George Marshall, who in 1837 offered his manuscript on provincial judicial officers to the public if the legislature would cover the printing and publishing costs.[10] The Assembly agreed to have 500 copies of *The Justice of the Peace, and County and Township Officer in the Province of Nova Scotia* printed at the public's expense.[11]

---

4   *An Act for Securing Copy Rights*, 1839, 2 Vict. c. 36.

5   Journal and Proceedings of the House of Assembly of the Province of Nova Scotia, 1839, 501 (5 February 1839).

6   See *An Act for applying certain Monies therein mentioned for the service of the year of our Lord One Thousand Eight Hundred and Forty, and for other purposes therein specified*, Acts of the General Assembly of the Province of Nova Scotia ,1840, c. 1. On Hugh Bell (1780–1860), see entry in DCB.

7   See Royal Acadian School, *Report*, listing Bell as vice-president in 1851. Bell was also on the board of governors for Dalhousie College. See *To Appoint a New Board of Governors of Dalhousie College*, Statutes of Nova Scotia, 1840, c. 7.

8   As discussed in chapter 4, Bromley had corresponded with Joseph Lancaster about the Royal Acadian School. See entry for Bromley (1774–1838) in DCB; see also Fingard, "English Humanitarianism."

9   Laurence, "'Never Been a Very Promising Speculation,'" chronicles the experiences of nine petitioners for financial aid for their books from 1833 to 1848.

10   Journal and Proceedings of the House of Assembly of the Province of Nova Scotia, 1837, 124 and appendix 45.

11   Journal and Proceedings of the House of Assembly of the Province of Nova Scotia, 1838, 97 (Appendix no. 34). The committee reviewing his petition recommended an additional £125 as compensation for his time and effort in supervising the publication process (Appendix no. 34), but he was only granted £50 from the Assembly.

Joseph Bouchette was the only other petitioner favourably considered, but his request was never fully acted on by the legislature. As will be recalled, Bouchette had made numerous requests to the Lower Canadian Assembly for financial assistance to cover his large printing debt in respect of *The British Dominions in North America*. He also appealed to the assemblies of Upper Canada and the Maritime provinces. Nova Scotia's Assembly agreed to purchase five copies, but the Committee of Supply, to whom the recommendation was referred, did not report back, and the matter appears to have ended there.[12]

The Assembly's sparing treatment of individual printing petitions may have induced Hugh Bell to turn to copyright law as a more sustainable alternative to support authors of useful books. Bell had unsuccessfully sponsored two book petitions prior to 1839. In 1837, he presented the request of land surveyor William MacKay, and, the following year, that of illustrator and engraver William Eagar. MacKay asked for help in financing the publication of his land surveyor's guide for instruction in geometry and mathematics. The committee reviewing the petition considered the work to be something that "may be useful to the youth of the Country" and recommended £100 toward its publication.[13] The Assembly ultimately rejected the recommendation. In Eagar's case, he asked for "support and patronage of the House towards an extensive Provincial Work in which Petitioner is engaged, entitled *Landscape Illustrations of Nova Scotia*." The petition was withdrawn before it could be considered.[14] In 1839, lawyer Daniel Dickson came before the legislature requesting financial aid to help defray some of the printing debt in respect of *A Guide to Town Officers, Shewing their Appointments, Duties, Liabilities and Privileges: According to the Laws of the Province*.[15] He too was unsuccessful.[16] Although there is no evidence to tie the two men together, Hugh Bell introduced his copyright Bill three weeks after Dickson's petition was read.

---

12  Journal and Proceedings of the House of Assembly of the Province of Nova Scotia, 1834, 643.

13  Journal and Proceedings of the House of Assembly of the Province of Nova Scotia, 7 Will. 4, 1837, 214.

14  Journal and Proceedings of the House of Assembly of the Province of Nova Scotia, 1838, 323. On Eagar, see O'Neill, "William Eagar." O'Neill speculates that the petition was withdrawn "because it was suggested to Eagar privately that more Nova Scotian views produced closer to home, would serve a better purpose" (77).

15  Daniel Dickson, *A Guide to Town Officers*. See also Laurence, "'Never Been a Promising Speculation.'"

16  See Journal and Proceedings of the House of Assembly of the Province of Nova Scotia, 1839, 465 (18 January 1839). See also Appendix 42 for the decision on the petition (19 February 1839).

Hugh Bell was not the first member of the legislature to champion copyright legislation. His predecessor in Halifax Township, Charles R. Fairbanks, had launched an unsuccessful bid to enact copyright legislation a decade before Bell. In 1829, the Haligonian lawyer introduced a Bill for Securing Copyrights, which was passed by the Assembly but which failed at the Legislative Council.[17] Like Bell, Fairbanks placed a high premium on education. In 1825, he chaired the joint parliamentary committee on education that recommended compulsory schooling "in order that none, even in the remotest and poorest settlement, may be without some provision for the instruction of their Youth."[18] Fairbanks was also a proponent of monitorial schools and a supporter of the Royal Acadian School.[19] This shared interest in public schooling likely played a part in their respective efforts to bring about copyright law, but Fairbanks's motivation for introducing a copyright bill was as opaque as Bell's. Indeed, there were no printing petitions during the 1829 parliamentary session. There was, however, one book-related item on the Assembly's agenda, to which Fairbanks was closely connected. A resolution was passed lauding Thomas Chandler Haliburton for his book *An Historical and Statistical Account of Nova Scotia*.[20] Haliburton served with Fairbanks on the Assembly until 1829, and they were part of the same social network. In the book's preface, Haliburton expressed his gratitude to Fairbanks for his "goodness" in helping him with his research. An editorial in *The Novascotian* newspaper reported that Fairbanks had "cordially approved of the resolution: he had seen parts of the work, and was convinced it would be found extremely useful to that house and to the country." The same editorial expressed the view that

> we do want men to illustrate and preserve the early Histories of the Colonies – to develop their commercial, agricultural and mineralogical resources – to unite them in a closer union, by making them better acquainted with each other, and to excite and keep alive a fondness for intellectual improvement; and we therefore hope to see those who devote their

---

17   Journal and Proceedings of the House of Assembly of the Province of Nova Scotia, 1829, 468 (20 March 1829). The Bill was passed by the Assembly and sent to the Legislative Council (see Journal at 497, 28 March 1829), but it stalled there. On Fairbanks (1790–1841), see his entry in DCB.

18   Cited in Goulson, *A Source Book of Royal Commissions*, doc. no. 17.

19   See Fingard, "Attitudes," quoting Fairbanks at Assembly debate, 12 February 1828.

20   Haliburton, *An Historical and Statistical Account of Nova Scotia*. Volume 2 reproduced the Assembly's congratulatory remarks. Haliburton is best remembered for his internationally renowned Sam Slick series. On Haliburton (1796–1865), see his entry in DCB. See also Davies, *Inventing Sam Slick*.

time and attention to such pursuits meet encouragement commensurate with the advantages which the public must derive from their labours.[21]

Fairbanks likely saw in his copyright Bill the legislative means of encouraging individuals to "illustrate and preserve the early Histories of the Colonies" and "keep alive a fondness for intellectual improvement."

The Nova Scotian Assembly received only a smattering of printing petitions after the 1839 Copyright Act was enacted, and, like the Lower Canadian legislature, it adopted the position that copyright relieved it of its responsibility to subsidize the printing of books. In 1848, when Abraham Gesner petitioned for financial aid for his proposed publication, *The Industrial Resources of Nova Scotia*, the select committee to which the petition was referred denied the request on the basis that "since the law of copyright has been introduced into this Province, the Legislature have declined to recompence authors by any contribution from the Treasury."[22]

The textual provenance of Nova Scotia's Copyright Act is difficult to ascertain. Nova Scotian lawmakers did not reflexively transplant the law from another jurisdiction. The statute was not drawn directly from Lower Canada's and was not a verbatim reproduction of the existing British or American legislation. The Nova Scotian Act conferred copyright on authors and their assigns in respect of maps, charts, books, engravings, and prints and protected them against unauthorized printing, reprinting, publishing, selling, or importing.[23] As with all of the copyright laws of the day, registration formalities included the deposit of the title page at the time of registration and a notice of copyright displayed on the work itself. However, the legislation also introduced some distinctive features. The duration of copyright was fixed at an initial term of twenty-one years with the possibility of a fourteen-year renewal period. The statutes in Lower Canada and the United States provided for a term of twenty-eight years with a possible fourteen-year renewal. The Statute of Anne 1710 provided for an initial twenty-one-year term for works already published, but the general term was fourteen years with the possibility of a fourteen-year renewal. Under the 1814 UK Act, the term was fixed at twenty-eight years with residue for life if the author was still living at the expiry of that term.

---

21  *The Novascotian*, 2 April 1829, 4.

22  Journal and Proceedings of the House of Assembly of the Province of Nova Scotia, 1848, 145 (Appendix No. 38).

23  Unlike the Lower Canadian statute, the legislation did not expressly extend to musical compositions.

Two library-related provisions confirm that Nova Scotia acted independently in devising its copyright law. First, by virtue of section 2, half of the statutory penalty for all copyright infringements was to be applied "to the use of the Public Libraries in Halifax," likely a reference to the Halifax Library and the Mechanics' Library, which were the two most important subscription libraries at the time.[24] This provision is remarkable in its solicitous concern for sustaining public libraries and reinforces the connection between copyright and the other social institutions and agencies, like libraries, entrusted with the broad diffusion of knowledge. Nothing similar appeared in any of the contemporaneous statutes in Lower Canada, the United Kingdom, or the United States. Second, Nova Scotia's copyright law was the first in British North America to require the deposit of a copy of the published work with each of the two parliamentary libraries. A mandatory deposit of copyright works to a library helped build a national collection of books and other print materials, which in turn fostered a collective sense of identity. The question of copyright and library deposits will be discussed in more detail later in this chapter.

### Copyright in New Brunswick

New Brunswick failed in its one attempt to enact a copyright law prior to Canadian Confederation. In 1838, William End, the member from Gloucester County, "moved for leave to bring in a Bill, for the protection of Copy Rights of original publications."[25] The *Halifax Pearl* reported that the copyright Bill was introduced in support of a schoolbook, Leggett's *English Grammar*:

> The House resolved itself into a Committee, to consider a Bill introduced for the purpose of protecting the copy-right of publications to authors. Mr. End explained the nature of the Bill, which was copied from the English statutes; and during the course of his observations, which went to meet any objections that might exist, on the ground of inexpediency, he stated that he had seen the manuscript of an English Grammar, which has been written by the Rev. Mr. Leggett, and was well calculated for the instruction

---

24   See in this respect Smith, "Early Libraries in Halifax." See also Harvey, "Early Public Libraries in Nova Scotia." This provision for the benefit of public libraries was repealed in the 1851 statutory revision. Title XXXI, *Of the Law of Copyright*, R.S, 1851, c. 119.

25   Journal of the House of Assembly of the Province of New Brunswick, 1838, 104. About End (1827–1871), see his entry in DCB.

of youth; whose author would require the protection which the proposed Bill would afford.[26]

A few printing petitions had been presented to the legislature leading up to 1838. In 1833, Joseph Bouchette tried without success to have the Assembly purchase copies of his *British Dominions in North America*.[27] In the 1836–7 parliamentary session, Saint John native Alexander Wedderburn was awarded £100 for the time, money and effort he had expended to produce *Statistical and Practical Observations relative to the province of New Brunswick*.[28] However, none of the petitions encouraged legislative consideration of copyright until William End took up the cause of Leggett's schoolbook.

After its introduction, the copyright Bill was retitled; the phrase "for the protection of Copy Rights" was replaced with "for the encouragement of Literature." The *Bill for the Encouragement of Literature by Vesting Copies of Printed Books in the Authors and Purchasers during the Times therein mentioned* passed the Assembly but stalled at the Legislative Council and was never revived.[29] The legislature did not revisit the question of copyright.[30] Canadian Confederation brought copyright to New Brunswick by virtue of the Copyright Act of 1868 of the Dominion of Canada.

Although New Brunswick did not enact a copyright law of general application, it did confer copyright on the official reporter of the decisions of the New Brunswick Supreme Court. This approach to the printing and publishing of judicial decisions was unique in British North America.

---

26  *The Halifax Pearl*, 30 March 1838, 102, citing from the Parliamentary Reports of New Brunswick. The Leggett in question may have been William Martin Leggett, a Methodist minister and schoolteacher, but there is no specific reference to him or his book in the Assembly journals. McFarlane, *New Brunswick Bibliography*, provides a biography of William Leggett, but no mention is made of a schoolbook.
27  Journal of the House of Assembly of the Province of New Brunswick, 1833, 22. The petition never proceeded past its introduction.
28  Journal of the House of Assembly of the Province of New Brunswick, 1836–37, 364. Wedderburn, *Statistical and Practical Observations*.
29  The full title was identical to the Statute of Anne save for the substitution of "encouragement of learning" with "encouragement of literature." New Brunswick also referred to school legislation in the same terms, as in *An Act for encouraging and extending Literature in this Province*, 1805, 45 Geo. 3, c. 12. The term literature seems to have been used to mean "literacy" or "to become literate" (i.e., educated).
30  See Journal of the House of Assembly of the Province of New Brunswick, 1838, 138–9. See also Journal of the Legislative Council of the Province of New Brunswick, 1838, 336.

*Copyright in Reports of Judicial Decisions*

The question of whether government publications should benefit from copyright is one of long standing and remains a live issue to this day. For democracies to thrive, the public must be fully informed of the actions of their elected representatives. François Blanchet's early attempts to establish a system of parliamentary reporting were in furtherance of this principle of government accountability. Individuals must also have unfettered access to the laws that govern them so that they are aware of their rights and responsibilities and can defend themselves against imputed transgressions. The fulfilment of this objective necessitates the accurate and timely reporting and publication of the laws of the jurisdiction, especially statutes and the decisions of the courts. Countries diverge, however, on whether works like these should benefit from copyright or whether they should belong to the public and be entirely excluded from proprietary capture.

The United States takes the position that government documents, especially the laws of the land, are in the public domain and can never be the subject of exclusive rights. In 1834 the Supreme Court of the United States established that there could be no copyright in judicial decisions, at least those emanating from the federal courts, and this remains the law today.[31] Anyone can reproduce, print, and publish or distribute court judgments and statutes without restriction. Nevertheless, this rule was not uniformly adopted by individual states, and some state laws provided (and still do provide) for copyright in reported judgments.[32] In contrast, in Canada, government publications are not outside the bounds of copyright. Canada's current statute confers copyright in the Crown in respect of all works "prepared or published by or under the direction or control of Her Majesty or any government department."[33] This includes statutes and judicial decisions. The main

---

31   See *Wheaton v. Peters*. See generally, United States, *Copyright Law Revision, Studies prepared for the Subcommittee on Patents, Trademarks, and Copyrights of the Committee of the Judiciary United States Senate, eighty-sixth Congress, second session*, Study 33. Copyright in Government Publications.

32   See United States, *Copyright Law Revision*, Study 33. See also, Dmitrieva, "State Ownership of Copyright." However, a recent US Supreme Court decision in *Georgia v. Public.Resource.org Inc.* 140 S.Ct. 1498 (2020) declared that annotated state legal codes were not copyrightable.

33   See section 12, *Copyright Act*, R.S.C 1985, c. C-42. Crown copyright was first introduced in the Copyright Act 1921.

argument for recognizing copyright in this kind of material is to guard against inaccuracy and the misuse of official documents.

Pre-Confederation New Brunswick had grappled with the question of whether copyright could vest in the published reports of the judicial decisions of its courts. The *Act to Provide for Reporting and Publishing the Decisions of the Supreme Court* of 1836 introduced the position of official court reporter, who was entrusted with the task of systematically and accurately reporting and publishing the judgments of the Supreme Court of the province.[34] In addition to remuneration for services rendered, the court reporter was given copyright in the publications. By virtue of section 2:

> The sole liberty of printing and reprinting and publishing such reports shall be, and the same is hereby vested in and secured to the author and compiler thereof, his heirs and assigns, and if any person shall print, reprint or publish any such reports without the consent of the author and compiler or proprietor thereof, he shall be liable to an action on the case at the suit of such proprietor, in which action such proprietor shall recover double the damages he may have sustained by any such infringement of the copyright hereby secured to him.

The purpose of the legislation was clear from its preamble: "Whereas it is an object of great importance to obtain correct reports of the decisions of the Supreme Court." The first section of the statute set out the mandate of the official reporter and affirmed the policy imperative relating to the accuracy and availability of reports of judicial decisions: "[I]t shall be the duty of such reporter by his personal attendance or by any other means in his power, to obtain true and authentic reports of such opinions, decisions and judgments; and such reporter shall publish not less than two hundred copies of the same in pamphlets after each term of the said Court." There was no stipulated duration of the copyright. The statute had a sunset clause providing for its expiry after three years if not renewed, but there is no indication that the intention was for the copyright to lapse with the legislation. Whatever the intention, the statute has never expired and, astonishingly, remains in force nearly two hundred years later.[35]

---

34  *Act to Provide for Reporting and Publishing the Decisions of the Supreme Court*, 1836, 6 Will. 4, c. 14.

35  See sections 63–64, *Judicature Act*, RSNB 1973, c. J-2 (as amended). This raises some interesting constitutional questions that are beyond the scope of this book. On the history of the statute, see Migneault, "La pratique du droit en français." See also Sadler, "Maritime Entrepreneurism," 106.

In effect, this piece of legislation established a public/private partnership that satisfied the policy objective of ensuring trustworthy reports. Under section 1, the official reporter had to be a "suitable person learned in the law." In addition, the long-term financial sustainability of the enterprise was assured. The official reporters were not only paid for their services but also enjoyed an exclusive market through the exercise of the copyright and were entitled to all the profits from sales. Conferring copyright on the court reporters ensured that they would remain personally invested in the publication and actively enforce their rights. The fact that the statute allowed a claim of double the amount of actual damages bolstered their incentive to pursue infringers. The accuracy of reported judgments was thereby guaranteed without the province itself having to police the market for unofficial copies.

New Brunswick's approach to the reporting of judicial decisions is to be contrasted with the position taken by the Upper Canadian legislature. In 1823, Upper Canada passed *An Act Providing for the publication of reports of the decisions of His Majesty's Court of King's Bench in this Province.*[36] Here, the court reporters were paid for their services and were entitled to the profits from sales, but the legislation stopped short of providing them with a copyright in their publications. Upper Canada took a similar position in respect of the reporting of parliamentary debates. In 1826 the Upper Canadian Assembly established an inquiry to determine an effective means of providing consistent, accurate, and unbiased reporting of its activities, on the basis that "in every free country, the public have given every encouragement for the reporting of legislative proceedings."[37] During the course of its investigations, the Assembly heard from five journalists and printers, among them Francis Collins, who testified that there was no incentive for him to publish Assembly debates unless he had "a copy right for his reports." Collins claimed that "at present when he reports, other editors copy from him and avail themselves of his labours."[38] However, Collins was the only one to have raised this concern. The other witnesses suggested instead that

---

36  *An Act providing for the publication of reports of the decisions of His Majesty's Court of King's Bench in this Province*, 4 Geo. 4, c. 3 (1823).

37  Journal of the House of Assembly of Upper Canada, 1826–1827, 7 Geo. 4, 18–19. Issues of facilitating the dissemination of parliamentary debates had been of concern in Lower Canada as well. As will be recalled, François Blanchet championed the cause as early as 1819.

38  Journal of the House of Assembly of Upper Canada, 1826–1827, 7 Geo. 4, 18–19.

parliamentary reporting was too problematic either because it did not increase their subscribers, or that the price paid by the Assembly was too low and that it took too long to get paid. Ultimately, the committee rejected copyright as a solution, concluding that "[i]t is not desirable to give to any one person a copy right of the proceedings of the house, because he has been at the labour and expense of reporting them."[39] One cannot necessarily interpret this response as an affirmation that, as a matter of principle, copyright in parliamentary reports was inappropriate. The reticence to provide a copyright might have resulted from the highly partisan nature of newspaper publishing in Upper Canada. Elizabeth Nish explained that "in Upper Canada, the reporting, printing and newspaper businesses were inextricably entwined, and all were politically-oriented. The political commitments of specific reporters took their toll of [*sic*] objective parliamentary reporting."[40] The Assembly was looking specifically for "consistent, accurate and unbiased reporting." It wouldn't have helped that Collins was an outspoken critic of the government and had been imprisoned for libel the year before the inquiry.[41] Under these circumstances, it would have been difficult for the legislature to provide any newspaper publisher, let alone Collins, with exclusive rights over the reporting of the debates.

Lower Canada's position on the question of copyright in government materials is equally ambiguous. Lower Canada's Copyright Act did not specifically address this issue. We do know, however, that copyright was never registered for publications that were publicly funded or were produced by or on behalf of the legislative or executive branches. However, in 1834, Quebec City lawyer George Okill Stuart compiled the judgments of the Lower Canadian Court of King's Bench and the Court of Appeal and registered his copyright in the volume.[42] He had received no public funding and had not been commissioned by the government to produce the work. One could surmise from this example that published judicial decisions were not automatically excluded from copyright in that province.

---

39  Journal of the House of Assembly of Upper Canada, 1826–1827, 7 Geo. 4, 18–19.

40  See Nish, *Debates*, vol. 1, p. xxx.

41  See entry for Francis Collins (1799–1834) in DCB. See as well Hulse, *A Dictionary of Toronto Printers*, 67.

42  George Okill Stuart, *Reports of cases argued and determined*. The initial printing in 1834 does not have a copyright notice, but a second printing in 1835 contains a copyright notice dated 1835 at the back of the volume.

## Copyright in Upper Canada Prior to the Union: Proper Schoolbooks Suited to the Scenery

The vexing issue of schoolbook supply was as much a part of Upper Canada's copyright history as it was for its closest neighbour. In 1824, Upper Canada made some provision for schoolbooks, but it was limited in its scope. *An Act to make Permanent and Extend the Provisions of the Laws now in force for the Establishment and Regulation of Common Schools throughout this Province and for granting to His Majesty a Further Sum of Money to Promote and Encourage Education within the Same* had allocated £150 to purchase schoolbooks of "moral and religious instruction" to be distributed to all schools.[43] The legislation did not enable the purchase of schoolbooks that were not moral or religious in nature, nor did it seek to encourage the production of local schoolbooks. A few years later, in 1829, William Buell Jr, Chair of the Select Committee on Education of the Upper Canadian legislature, argued: "The difficulties of procuring proper school books … operate against the advancement of education in this province. The encouragement not being sufficient to induce men of capital to embark in the printing and publishing of elementary books at reasonable terms. The country is therefore, necessarily, in a great measure dependent on the parent state, or the United States, for a supply."[44]

The Committee therefore recommended: "That encouragement be given to the publishing and circulating of elementary books in the Province and in all the branches of manufacture connected therewith."[45] This recommendation, which strongly hints at copyright law as a remedy, was not pursued further by the legislature. Two years later, the petition of schoolteacher Alexander Davidson provided the impetus for the introduction of the first Upper Canadian copyright Bill.

In 1831, Alexander Davidson turned to the legislature to request "an Act whereby the Copyright of 'the Upper Canada Spelling Book' be vested in him."[46] He had previously expressed his concerns to the

---

43  *An Act to make Permanent and Extend the Provisions of the Laws now in force for the Establishment and Regulation of Common Schools throughout this Province and for granting to His Majesty a Further Sum of Money to Promote and Encourage Education within the Same* 4 Geo. 4, c. 8 (1824).

44  Appendix to Journal of the House of Assembly of Upper Canada, 1829, App no. 43, A-99.

45  Appendix to Journal of the House of Assembly of Upper Canada, 1829, App no. 43, A-99.

46  As described in the Journal of the Legislative Council of Upper Canada, 1831, Index "Petitions." The petition was first introduced in the House of Assembly as "The petition of Alexander Davidson of Port Hope praying for the protection in

authorities that "unless some proper elementary books be got into general circulation, common school education will continue to be little better than a mere farce, and a useless expenditure of public money."[47] Davidson deemed those in use unsuitable, especially American ones.[48] He explained that spellers "of the United States origin are the most numerous. While spelling books from England are to *us* necessarily defective, not being suited to our scenery and other localities, those of a foreign origin are liable to more serious objections."[49] Many in Upper Canadian education circles anticipated that Davidson's Canadian speller would supplant the popularity of Noah Webster's *The American Spelling Book*, which was controversial because of its anti-British content. Anglican minister Alexander Neil Bethune expressed his "strong hope that [Davidson's speller] will entirely supersede the use in any of our Common Schools of that very questionable American Work: 'Webster's Spelling Book.'"[50] Indeed, Upper Canadian disquiet over the suitability of American schoolbooks was not limited to this vocal cadre of educators and clergy. Reflecting on his travels to Upper Canada in the early 1830s, author and emigrant agent Thomas Rolph observed:

It is really melancholy to traverse the Province, and go into many of the common schools; you find a herd of children, instructed by some anti-British adventurer, instilling into the young and tender mind sentiments hostile to the parent state: false accounts of the late war in which Great Britain was engaged with the United States; geography setting forth New-York Philadelphia, Boston, &c., as the largest and finest cities in the world; historical reading books, describing the American population as the most free and enlightened under Heaven; insisting on the superiority of their laws and institutions ... and American spelling-books, dictionaries, and grammar[s], teaching them an anti-British dialect, and idiom; although living in a Province, and being subjects, of the British Crown.[51]

---

the publication of a provincial spelling book in such way, and for such period, as to the house may appear reasonable." As cited in Riddell, "The First Copyrighted Book," 3. The petition was referred to a committee but did not proceed any further. See Journal of the House of Assembly of Upper Canada, 1831, 1 Will. 4, 21 and 25. More on Alexander Davidson (1794 – 1856) at DCB.

47  Letter to Civil Secretary Hillier, June 1828, cited in DCB entry for Davidson.
48  On schoolbooks in use in Upper Canada, including American books, see Wilson, "Common School Texts."
49  Davidson, *The Canada Spelling Book*, Preface.
50  Cited by Riddell, "The First Copyrighted Book," 5, as reported in *Niagara Chronicle*, 13 May 1841. See too Love, "Cultural Survival and Social Control."
51  Rolph, *A Brief Account*, 262.

The Imperial and provincial governments also took note. In a communiqué issued in 1822 from Sir Peregrine Maitland, Lieutenant-Governor of Upper Canada, to the Colonial Secretary Lord Bathurst, Maitland referred to the "mischiefs that may result from the introduction of School Masters and School Books from the United States."[52] In 1839 the Upper Canadian Assembly's Education Committee, tasked with inquiring into the state of education in the province, urged that "those Republican productions that tend to poison the minds of the youth of the country, should be driven out of the Province."[53]

Although similar questions about the pernicious effect of American schoolbooks had been raised within the English-speaking community in Lower Canada, this issue was not a priority for copyright champions like Joseph Lancaster or John Neilson. Concerns about American schoolbooks, especially spellers and grammars, were more prevalent in Upper Canada and had some traction with policy-makers and educational reformers, even if their proliferation in Upper Canadian schools may not have been as significant as claimed.[54] The anti-American, anti-Webster rhetoric served as a useful device for advancing English Canadian cultural nationalism.[55] In his study of the first decade of the American copyright statute, Frederick R. Goff found a "heavy incidence of textbooks in the early copyright registers [indicating] ... that a healthy demand existed for primers, geographies and arithmetics ... The former colonists having achieved independence did not wish their progeny to be corrupted by British texts."[56] In similar fashion, Upper Canada promoted copyright and local schoolbook production so that provincial children would not be corrupted by American texts.

It is interesting that spellers were the flashpoint for this cultural awakening. Spelling books were as ideological as they were practical. In writing *The American Spelling Book*, Noah Webster sought to "diffuse an uniformity and purity of language in America ... [and] to promote

---

52   Cited in Hodgins, *Documentary History of Education*, 3.

53   Hodgins, *Documentary History of Education*, 215 (Reports of Grammar and Common Schools in the Various Districts of Upper Canada, for the year 1838).

54   See for example, Houston and Prentice, *Schooling and Scholars*; Love, "Anti-American Ideology"; Curtis, "Schoolbooks and the Myth"; McLaren, "Anti-British in Every Sense"; and Black, "Horrid Republican Notions." See also more generally, Brouillette, "Books of Instruction," 259.

55   Writing about his travels to British North America between 1839–1842, British author and traveller James S. Buckingham observed a prevalence of what he felt were gratuitous and unbecoming anti-American opinions expressed by those he met in Toronto and Montreal. See Buckingham, *Canada*.

56   Goff, "The First Decade," 4.

the interest of literature and the harmony of the United States."[57] Webster lamented: "We have a multitude of books which gives us the state of *other countries*, but scarcely one which affords us any account of our own."[58] Alexander Davidson and those in his Upper Canadian educational network expressed similar concerns in advocating for locally produced schoolbooks. Schoolbooks needed to reflect the history, geography, languages, culture, and values of the individual societies for which they were intended. In addition to being educational tools, they served as cultural markers of a national narrative. Alexander Davidson was as tenacious in promoting the introduction of copyright in Upper Canada as Noah Webster had been in the United States. Both men saw in copyright a policy vehicle for achieving the complementary objectives of advancing education and imprinting a national consciousness.

Nothing came of Davidson's petition during the 1831 session, and a similar fate befell another schoolteacher in the next parliamentary sitting. William Phillips of Upper Canada, a "teacher of writing, arithmetic, geography etc. in Ladies' Schools, and in private families," had requested "that a law may be passed granting him a Patent to secure the Copyright of a system of Arithmetic, of which Petitioner is Author; and that a place may be by law appointed for the registering of literary works for the benefit of Authors."[59] Although the legislature never acted on his petition, Phillips nevertheless published, by subscription, *A New and Concise System of Arithmetic* in 1833.[60]

The language of Phillips's petition is interesting. The author claimed a "patent to secure the copyright" in a manner reminiscent of Joseph-François Perrault's request for a patent for his writings under Lower Canada's Patent Act. Although Upper Canada had enacted a patent law in 1826, Phillips was clearly not applying under that statute. Instead, he was seeking the enactment of a copyright law for himself and, more generally, for all Upper Canadian authors. The term "patent" in the petition was used to signify a government grant. Davidson and Phillips were the only two teachers to petition the legislature in this pre-copyright period. Both sought the enactment of a copyright law, and both were unsuccessful. A review of the various book-related petitions in this period indicates that the Upper Canadian Assembly preferred to

---

57   Webster, *The American Spelling Book*, preface (emphasis Webster).

58   Webster, *The American Spelling Book*, preface.

59   Journal of the House of Assembly of Upper Canada, 1832, 3 Will. 4, 47. The petition did not proceed any further.

60   Phillips, *A New and Concise System*. The book was written for Upper Canadian schoolgirls.

subscribe for copies of works on a case-by-case basis rather than enact a law of general application. For example, Cobourg surgeon Dr William Rees asked the legislature to subscribe for copies of his book on medical topography, which was still in progress.[61] The Assembly agreed to purchase 500 copies once the book was published.[62]

It is difficult to understand why the Upper Canadian legislature hesitated when it came to copyright, especially since Davidson and Phillips made their requests on the heels of Lower Canada's statute. It is true that by 1832 it had become possible for Upper Canadian authors to secure copyright in the neighbouring province, but this circumstance should have had no bearing on Upper Canada's consideration of the law. To avail themselves of a Lower Canadian copyright, Upper Canadian authors had to pull up stakes and move to that province, since early copyright laws had stringent residency requirements. Some authors, like John Richardson, did make the effort. Richardson moved temporarily from Sandwich (near Windsor) to Montreal in 1839 or 1840 to secure his Lower Canadian copyright in *Canadian Brothers or the Prophecy Fulfilled*.[63] The copyright notice on the book confirmed that Richardson was "now resident in the City of Montreal." However, the benefits of this manner of proceeding were limited. In addition to the inconvenience of establishing a residence in Lower Canada, copyright could only be enforced in that province and was therefore of negligible value to Upper Canadians, who would be without recourse if their books were reprinted in their home province.

In 1833, the legislature made another abortive attempt at enacting a copyright law. The journal of the Assembly reported that on 10 December 1833, "Mr Boulton gives notice that he will, on Friday next, move for leave to bring in a bill to afford to the publishers of books, prints, maps, engravings and magazines, in this Province, the benefit of the copyright of such works."[64] George Strange Boulton was the representative from Durham, and, like Alexander Davidson, he was concerned about the use of American schoolbooks in the province.[65] It was Boulton who

---

61   Journal of the House of Assembly of Upper Canada, 3 Will. 4, 112 (1833).

62   Appendix to Journal of the House of Assembly of Upper Canada, 1835, App. 103. There is no evidence, however, that Rees ever published the book.

63   Richardson, *The Canadian Brothers*. Copyright dated 2 January 1840.

64   Journal of the House of Assembly of Upper Canada, 1833, 4 Will. 4, 37 (10 December 1833).

65   Reply of George Strange Boulton, MPP Cobourg, to House of Assembly Education Committee, 10 December 1839. See Report of a Commission on Education in Upper Canada 1839, in Hodgins, *Documentary History*, 268. On Boulton (1797–1869), see his entry in DCB.

had introduced Davidson's first petition for copyright to the Assembly in 1831. This time, however, Boulton's actions were not preceded by a petition. Perhaps he was merely intending to revive the issue that had fallen from view two years before. Whatever the case, Boulton never actually introduced the Bill. A month later, Allan MacNab from Wentworth County introduced the petition of Levi Davis and eleven unnamed individuals "praying that an Act may be passed for securing to authors the copy right of their publications."[66] Nothing came of this petition, and the circumstances surrounding it remain shrouded in mystery. The fact that there were a dozen petitioners specifically requesting the enactment of a copyright law for Upper Canadian authors seems significant, but there is nothing more in the legislative records. It has proven difficult to locate the petition itself and to determine who Levi Davis was and why he may have had an interest in copyright.[67] No insights can be gleaned from his eleven compatriots, since their names are unknown. After this extraordinary session, the legislature resumed its conventional practices with respect to individual printing petitions and made no further mention of copyright. Four subsequent book petitions were presented, but the requests were limited to financial aid to support printing and publishing.[68] It was as though the proponents of copyright, who began their legislative interventions in 1831, had simply given up after Levi Davis's petition.

Matters surrounding copyright in Upper Canada would likely have continued to advance in fits and starts had the union with Lower Canada in 1840 not brought the matter to a head. The Act of Union of 1840, which took effect in February 1841, created the Province of Canada, which was divided into two sections, Canada East (formerly

---

66  Journal of the House of Assembly of Upper Canada, 1833–1834, 4 Will. 4, 74 (introduced 13 January 1834).

67  The Civil Secretary's correspondence and other official materials do not contain a petition by Davis et al., and most of the parliamentary records of the province of Upper Canada were destroyed by fires in 1849 and 1854.

68  In the 1839 session, Toronto printers and publishers, Charles Fothergill and his son, Charles Forbes Fothergill, were successful in their bid to have the Assembly purchase copies of their Royal Calendar of Canada. That same session, Parliamentary Librarian Alpheus Todd was granted £25 for his time and effort in compiling an Index to the Statutes of the Imperial Parliament. However, Deputy Land Surveyor Publius V. Elmore was unsuccessful in his petition for the purchase of copies of his published map of the Midland and Prince Edward districts in 1836 and again in 1838. A similar fate befell Toronto lawyer John Hillyard Cameron in 1839. His request for financial aid to publish a revised edition of the provincial statutes was never considered by the Assembly.

Lower Canada) and Canada West (formerly Upper Canada).[69] The new jurisdictional configuration resulted in the anomalous situation of copyright protection in Canada East pursuant to the Lower Canadian Copyright Act but not in Canada West.[70] This untenable circumstance, coupled with a fresh petition from Alexander Davidson, forced the issue. The 1832 Copyright Act of Lower Canada was repealed and replaced by the 1841 Copyright Act of the Province of Canada.

### *An Act for the Protection of Copy Rights in This Province* 4 & 5 Vict. c. 61 (1841)

The Province of Canada was the most populous and economically developed jurisdiction in British North America. It was created following a recommendation by the Governor General of British North America, Lord Durham, who had been commissioned to report on the rebellions that had taken place in both Lower Canada and Upper Canada in 1837 and 1838.[71] The insurrections in both provinces had been, at least in part, a response to the lack of political autonomy and the absence of accountability for the appointed members of the executive and legislative branches of government. These individuals were answerable to the imperial authorities and not the local electorate. In his report, Durham had recommended a fully responsible form of government for the Province of Canada, but the British authorities disagreed. The provincial governance structure therefore remained similar to that of its predecessors, at least until the late 1840s, when

---

69  *An Act to reunite the Provinces of Upper and Lower Canada, and for the Government of Canada*, 1840, 3 & 4 Vict., c. 35 (UK). (Passed in July 1840, proclaimed in force on 10 February 1841) ("Act of Union").

70  The 1832 Act had been limited by a sunset clause that set its expiry date at 1 May 1840. Because of the rebellions, the Lower Canadian Parliament was dissolved before this clause could take effect and the business of the province was entrusted to the governor and an appointed special council. See *An Act to Make Temporary Provision for the Government of Lower Canada* (The Constitutional Act Suspension Act, 1838), 10 February 1838, 1 Vict., c. 9. The governor and special council issued an ordinance that the statute would remain in force until 1 November 1845. See *Ordinance further to continue, for a limited time, certain Acts therein mentioned* 1840, 3 Vict., c. 15.

71  Her Majesty's High Commissioner, *Report on the Affairs of British North America*. See also Craig, Ajzenstat, and Laforest, afterword to *An Abridgment of Report*. On John George Lambton, Lord Durham (1792–1840), see DCB.

responsible government was finally achieved.[72] The executive branch of government was represented by a governor who was appointed by the British Crown and not answerable to the legislature. The legislative branch remained bicameral, but only the members of the Legislative Assembly were elected. The members of the Legislative Council were political appointees.

Lower Canadian copyright advocates John Neilson, Denis-Benjamin Viger, and Augustin-Norbert Morin were elected to the first Assembly of the new Province of Canada, but only Morin remained active on the copyright file.[73] On 14 July 1841, Alexander Davidson appealed to the new Assembly "praying for an exclusive right to publish the Canada Spelling Book, for a number of years."[74] That same sitting, Edward Clarke Campbell, the member from Niagara, introduced a "Bill for the protection of Copy Rights in that part of the Province formerly constituting Upper Canada."[75] Campbell's Bill was intended as a temporary measure to provide residents of Canada West with copyright protection pending the enactment of a copyright law for the entire province. Instead, the Bill was referred to a select committee consisting of veteran politicians from Canada East, including Augustin-Norbert Morin, with the instruction "to extend the provisions of the said Bill to the Province of Canada."[76] The 1841 Copyright Act of the united province became

---

72  On responsible government, see, for example, Girard, Phillips and Brown, *A History of Law in Canada*, vol. 1.

73  John Neilson served on the Assembly of the Province of Canada from 1841 to 1844, after which he was appointed to the Legislative Council. He died in 1848. Denis-Benjamin Viger served from 1841 to 1844 and again from 1845 to 1846. He was appointed to the Legislative Council in 1848 and served there for a decade. He died in 1861. Morin, the youngest of the three, served from 1841 to January 1842 and then again from November 1842 to 1855, at which point he was appointed to the Bench. During his parliamentary career he served as Speaker of the House and joint premier of the province for Canada (East). In 1859 he was appointed to serve on the commission to codify the civil law of Canada East. He died in 1865.

74  Journal of the Legislative Assembly of the Province of Canada, 1841–1842, 4 & 5 Vict., 175.

75  Journal of the Legislative Assembly of the Province of Canada, 1841–1842, 4 & 5 Vict., 182 (14 July 1841). Each section of the province could enact laws that applied only within their territory, but they could also, collectively, pass laws for the entire province.

76  Journal of the Legislative Assembly of the Province of Canada, 1841–1842, 4 & 5 Vict., 322. The members were Solicitor General Charles Dewey Day, Henry Black, Benjamin Holmes, and Augustin-Norbert Morin.

law on 18 September 1841.[77] Alexander Davidson's *The Canada Spelling Book* was the first book to be registered under the new statute.[78]

The 1841 Act of the Province of Canada was a replica of its Lower Canadian predecessor. The statute provided resident authors with protection for their books, maps, charts, musical compositions, prints, cuts, or engravings for twenty-eight years with the possibility of an additional fourteen to be exercised by the living author or the widow or children. As was the case in the 1832 Act of Lower Canada, the work did not have to be printed or published in the province. Writing about this statute many years later, Toronto publisher J. Ross Robertson explained that the absence of manufacturing requirements was due to the fact that "the publishing trade in Canada was at that time in its infancy."[79] Robertson's remark confirms that copyright policy during this period was motivated primarily by the need to encourage local authors to write local books for the edification of local readers. Fostering the growth of the domestic printing and publishing industry was not a priority.

The 1841 Act diverged from the Lower Canadian Act in certain respects. The French title was changed from *Acte pour protéger la propriété littéraire* to *Acte pour protéger les droits d'auteurs dans cette province*. The change in terminology was consistent with international developments, in that the phrase "encouragement of learning" gave way to "copyright" and the term "propriété littéraire" gave way to "droit d'auteur." The legislation was also organized differently from its predecessor, and some typographical corrections were made to the text. The sunset clause was eliminated so that the legislation would not automatically lapse. Also, the new statute required that copies of the published work be deposited in a central repository. These legislative amendments suggest a maturation in copyright policy and signal the beginning of

---

77   Journal of the Legislative Assembly of the Province of Canada, 1841–1842, 4 & 5 Vict., 639, 643 (Royal Assent). According to Riddell, "The First Copyrighted Book," Solicitor General Day drafted the legislation. Interestingly, the legislature did not proceed in a similar fashion in respect of provincial patent law, presumably because patent protection was available in both sections of the province. Not until 1849 was a new patent law enacted for the entire province: *An Act to Consolidate and Amend the Laws of Patents for Inventions in this Province*, 1849, 12 Vict., c. 24.

78   LAC, Copyright Registries, Province of Canada, RG 105, vol. 378. The registration date was 14 December 1841, and the copyright was held by the author. However, an 1859 report to the Assembly recorded Christie's *A History of the Late Province* as the first registration. For reasons I explain in more detail in Appendix 3, I consider Davidson to be the first registrant.

79   Robertson, *Copyright in Canada*, 8. On Robertson (1841–1918), see DCB.

a more purposeful approach to the law that recognized its potential to achieve both educational and nation-building objectives.

*Legal Deposit under the 1841 Act*

Copyright laws of that era often provided for two different types of legal deposit, an administrative deposit and a library deposit. The first was of the kind contemplated in the Lower Canadian statute, which required an initial deposit, with the Court Clerk, of the title page of the book, followed by a deposit of a copy of the entire work within three months of publication. This kind of mandatory deposit was intended to serve as evidence of the existence of the work and as a guarantee of protection, similar to disclosures of inventions for patents or the filing of copies of words or designs for trademark protection. The second type of legal deposit, the library deposit, was of an entirely different nature. It obliged authors or publishers to deposit copies of the published work in a national or university library. Mandatory library deposits served a nation-building function: "It was understood that the books were to serve as a permanent and tangible record of the literary output of the nation."[80] The copyright statute of the Province of Canada included both types of legal deposit. It substantially modified the earlier Lower Canadian administrative deposit process and introduced a library deposit provision.

ADMINISTRATIVE DEPOSIT

Many copyright laws of the period required a deposit of the title page of the work at the time of registration and a subsequent deposit of a copy of the entire book or other work after registration. This was the procedure under the Lower Canadian and Nova Scotian statutes. The Province of Canada adopted a different rule entirely, requiring that a copy of the entire published work be furnished at the outset. Section 5 stipulated that "no person shall be entitled to the benefit of this Act unless he shall, before publication, deposit a printed copy of such book or books, map, chart, musical composition, print, cut, or engraving, in the Office of the Registrar of the Province." The realities of printing and publishing were such that a printed title page did not necessarily mean that the entire book would soon follow. Copyright policy was now more firmly directed toward encouraging tangible outcomes by rewarding only those with completed works in hand.

---

80  Barrington-Partridge, *The History of the Legal Deposit*, 2. See also Gilchrist, "Copyright Deposit," 177.

This new deposit procedure had interpretive consequences in relation to periodical publications. Under the 1832 Lower Canadian Act, serial publications were eligible for copyright, but there had been some uncertainty as to how to fulfil the registration formalities, especially where such publications were issued in weekly or monthly instalments. In the case of the *Quebec Commercial List*, which was produced monthly with different content, the authors eschewed monthly registrations in favour of a single annual registration. They used that registration to claim copyright over the subsequent issues. This manner of proceeding was no longer possible under the 1841 Act. When the application to register the *Quebec Commercial List* was rejected, Charles Secretan, one of the earlier Lower Canadian registrants, appealed to the Provincial Registrar R.A. Tucker, who replied: "It seems ... to be perfectly clear ... that no periodical Publication the contents of which will vary in every successive number can be entitled to the protection of the Copy right conferred by that Statute, because, as respects such "Periodical Publication," the previous deposit of a Copy, which is made a condition precedent upon which the protection afforded by the Act must entirely depend, is obviously impracticable."[81]

When Secretan remonstrated that he had previously secured copyright under the Lower Canadian statute, Tucker countered: "I will ... only remind you that the 'Act for the protection of Copy Right in Lower Canada' under which 'the Quebec Commercial List' was deemed entitled to protection has now been repealed; and that no argument founded upon the construction of it can be extended to the 4th and 5th Victoria C. 61, unless in some instance in which the provisions of the two Statutes should happen to be similar."[82]

Because the language of the 1841 Act now required the deposit of a copy of the entire work, rather than its title page alone, it was no longer possible to claim rights over an issue or volume of a periodical that was not yet in print. The only legitimate way of securing copyright in serial publications was to fulfil the registration process for each completed issue. Deputy Registrar William Kent confirmed this requirement to Samuel McLaughlin when he sought unsuccessfully to register a single copyright in the periodical publication *The Photographic Portfolio: A Monthly View of Canadian Scenery*: "If you intend to Copy Right the respective monthly issues, then the objection ... vanishes."[83]

---

81 LAC, Provincial Secretary Letter Books, Quebec, Lower Canada, and Canada East, RG 4 C 2, vol. 2, 1843–1856, 6, 14 January 1844.

82 LAC, Provincial Secretary Letter Books, Quebec, Lower Canada, and Canada East, RG 4 C 2, vol. 2, 1843–1856, 8.

83 LAC Provincial Secretary Letterbooks, Quebec, Lower Canada and Canada East, RG 4 C2, vol. 3, 1857–1864, 59, 4 January 1859.

LIBRARY DEPOSIT

The 1841 Copyright Act introduced a mandatory library deposit for the benefit of the library of the Legislative Assembly.[84] In this respect, the statute was a departure from the earlier Lower Canadian legislation and the American precedent from which it had been derived. In the United States, library deposits of copyright works were not introduced until 1846 by virtue of *An Act to Establish the Smithsonian Institution for the Increase and Diffusion of Knowledge among Men*.[85] The province's deposit provision is reminiscent of the Nova Scotian statute, which required a deposit to each of the libraries of the House of Assembly and the Legislative Council. Making parliamentary libraries the repositories of copyright deposits made sense in British North America, whether it be to the Assembly's library alone, as in the Province of Canada, or to the libraries of each legislative house.[86] The legislative libraries of the provinces maintained the most significant collections of books and other print materials. A central repository of provincial copyright works served the ends of education and learning. It would also inculcate in the minds of provincial readers a distinct cultural identity beyond their British colonial roots and distinct from that of their American neighbours.

In the Province of Canada, the parliamentary libraries were open to some members of the public; they effectively acted as national libraries, albeit in a limited way. Lower Canada was the first to allow designated groups to use the Assembly's library. By 1825, access was permitted as long as the visits took place between parliamentary sessions and were limited to "the Members and Officers of the Legislative Council and Assembly, to the Members of the Executive Council, to the Judges of the King's Bench, and to all persons who shall have obtained permission in writing from any one of the Members of this House, which permission shall be valid during one month only, and may be renewed."[87] This

---

84   Section 5 provided that "the author shall also deposit a copy of the work, for which a Copy Right is obtained in the Library of the Legislative Assembly of this Province."

85   *An Act to Establish the Smithsonian Institution for the Increase and Diffusion of Knowledge among Men*, 29th Congress, Session 1, chapter 178 (1846), section 10, required a deposit of copies of copyright works at the Smithsonian and the Library of Congress. See also United States, *Copyright Law Revision*, Studies 20.

86   The Copyright Act of Prince Edward Island of 1861 had a similar deposit provision in favour of the "Legislative library of this Island," as did the Copyright Act of Newfoundland (1888) in favour of the "Legislative Library of this Colony."

87   Journals of the House of Assembly of Lower Canada, 1825, 6 Geo. 4, 361 (17 March 1825).

was a significant initiative in its day, one that historian Gilles Gallichan attributes to the prevailing desire to enhance the political awareness of Lower Canadians and to improve their educational and cultural sophistication.[88] Amable Berthelot, the member from Trois-Rivières, was instrumental in steering this library proposal through the Assembly during the same period that François Blanchet and John Neilson were engaged in the question of public education. A close parliamentary ally of theirs, Berthelot shared their belief in universal education and the broad diffusion of knowledge that was so central to the copyright agenda as well.[89]

Upper Canada took notice. In a piece written in 1827 for his newspaper the *Colonial Advocate*, printer and publisher William Lyon Mackenzie urged the province to emulate its Lower Canadian neighbours so that the library of the Assembly of Upper Canada "may be enlarged and kept open at all seasons of the year, not only to the members, but also to those whom they may introduce to the librarian. This is the practice of Lower Canada, and it is worthy of our initiation. For until our studious men can have access to proper books, we will never boast of profound scholars."[90]

Mackenzie was elected to the Assembly of Upper Canada the following year and continued his advocacy for wider access to the library. By the late 1830s, the idea that the Upper Canadian Assembly's library should serve a broader public purpose was firmly entrenched among parliamentarians.[91] It is not surprising then that, in the wake of the union, the Assembly of the Province of Canada had a similar vision for its library.[92] In April 1849, the Assembly adopted a resolution to permit library access, during the legislative recess, "to persons introduced by a Member of the House, or admitted at the discretion of the Clerk or one of the Librarians."[93]

---

88   Gallichan, *Livre et politique*.

89   As discussed in chapter 3, Berthelot was involved in parliamentary initiatives on education and was a member of the committee that reviewed Hamilton Leslie's petition in 1826.

90   As cited by Gallichan, *Livre et politique*, 262. See also Watson, *A Credit to this Province*.

91   See Watson, *A Credit to this Province*; Gallichan, *Livre et politique*.

92   See Journal of the Legislative Assembly of the Province of Canada, 1844–1845, 8 Vict. See also Watson, *A Credit to this Province*, 32. The Assembly wanted the library to be "capable of affording means of information upon every important branch of Literature and Science" (Journal of the Legislative Assembly, 1844–1845, 378)

93   Journal of the Legislative Assembly of the Province of Canada, 1849, 12 Vict., 228 (12 April 1849).

The question of library collections and public access took a poignant turn only two weeks later, when rioters in Montreal set fire to the Parliament Building in protest over the indemnification of Lower Canadian rebels for the property losses they had incurred during the rebellions.[94] The library collections of both houses of the legislature were destroyed in that conflagration. Tens of thousands of volumes were lost, including irreplaceable manuscripts and historical documents.[95] The effects of this devastating set-back were keenly felt. Augustin-Norbert Morin, then Speaker of the Assembly, lamented:

> Of the many deplorable consequences [of the fire] … the entire destruction of the valuable Libraries attached to the two Houses of the Legislature, and which contained in all about 25,000 volumes, may be reckoned as among the greatest. In this instance, especially, the loss has fallen not merely upon the Parliament itself, but generally upon the people of the Province, who, by the liberality of the Members of both Houses, were permitted access to the Books, in default of other opportunities for literary gratification and research, there being no other Libraries of Canada, of any magnitude, to which the Public were admitted.[96]

The process of rebuilding the collection began almost immediately. While it never fully recovered from the loss, the Parliamentary Library in the Province of Canada continued the tradition of allowing the public access to its holdings.[97]

Copyright deposits to university libraries, as opposed to parliamentary libraries, were never contemplated in British North America,

---

94  *An Act to Provide for the Indemnification of Parties in Lower Canada whose Property was Destroyed during the Rebellion in the years 1837 and 1838*, 1849, 12 Vict., c. 58 (the Rebellion Losses Bill). This was similar to what had already been afforded to Upper Canadian rebels.

95  Journal of the Legislative Assembly of the Province of Canada, 1849, 12 Vict. The Bill was introduced on 3 April 1849 (205) and was given Royal Assent on 30 May (365). The fire occurred on 25 April.

96  Journal of the Legislative Assembly of the Province of Canada, 1850, 13 Vict., 6.

97  See Journal of the Legislative Assembly of the Province of Canada, 1852–1853, 16 Vict., 983; Journal of the Legislative Assembly of the Province of Canada, 1860, 23 Vict., 404. In 1850, the libraries of both legislative houses were joined under the administration of two librarians, one for each house; Journal of the Legislative Assembly of the Province of Canada, 1850, 14 Vict., 6, 50 228–9. From the Speaker: "it is in contemplation to establish one Joint Library for both Houses of the Legislature, to which there is no doubt the Public will be as freely admitted as heretofore." (at 6).

presumably because colonial institutions of higher learning were still in their infancy. This is to be contrasted with the British precedent, whereby deposits were to be made to enumerated university libraries and the British Museum, which served as an unofficial national library at the time. With the 1841 Copyright Act, the legislature reinforced the centrality of the Parliamentary Library in preserving the province's book and print heritage. The provincial legislature did, however, give some consideration to the question of university library collections outside of its copyright legislation.

In 1847 the University of McGill College made a plea to the Assembly that "duplicates of Works in the Library of the House as are superfluous, may be bestowed upon the said University."[98] The Assembly never acted on the petition, but even if it had, the measure would have been a far cry from establishing a mandatory library deposit for the benefit of McGill University. The University of Toronto was more successful. In 1849, by virtue of *An Act to amend the Charter of the University established at Toronto*, provincial printers and publishers were obliged to deposit any books, pamphlets, letter-press sheets, music sheets, maps, charts, or plans at the library of the University of Toronto within six months of publication.[99] The deposited volumes were to be bound and printed on the best paper. Failure to comply would result in a penalty of up to £5 in addition to the value of the copy, which the defaulting publisher was to remit to the university librarian to apply toward "the augmentation of the library."[100]

The section was much broader in scope than the library deposit provision contained in the 1841 Copyright Act because it applied to

---

98   Journal of the Legislative Assembly of the Province of Canada, 1847, 11 Vict., 96 (2 July 1847).

99   *An Act to amend the Charter of the University established at Toronto by His late Majesty King George the Fourth, to provide for the more satisfactory government of the said University, and for other purposes connected with the same, and with the College and Royal Grammar School forming an appendage thereof*, 1849, 12 Vict., c. 82.

100   Section 31 read in part:

> And be it enacted That a printed copy of the whole of any book which shall be published in this Province after the passing of this Act ... and of every pamphlet, sheet of letter-press, sheet of music, map, chart or plan separately published ... bound, sewed, or stitched together ... and upon the best paper ... shall, within six calendar months after the same shall first be sold, published, or offered for sale, be delivered on the part of the publisher at the Library of the said University ...; and on default of such delivery within the time aforesaid, the publisher ... shall forfeit, besides the value of such copy ... a sum not exceeding five pounds to be recovered by the Librarian ... for the use of the said University, to be applied for the augmentation of the said library.

every work published in the province, not merely to those registered for copyright. It appears to have been copied verbatim from the UK Copyright Act of 1842, which obliged publishers, including those in the British colonies, to deposit any books, maps, prints, or other engravings "bound, sewed, or stitched together, and upon the best Paper" with the British Museum.[101] There is no conclusive evidence regarding why the provincial Parliament introduced this measure in favour of the University of Toronto, although the timing of the University Charter Bill is interesting. The devastating fire at the Parliamentary Library in Montreal had occurred at the time the Bill was making its way through the legislature.[102] The legislature may have considered it advisable to establish a second repository to safeguard the province's print heritage. Whatever the motivation, there is no indication that provincial printers and publishers complied with the deposit requirement or that the library ever enforced this statutory obligation. The library deposit provision was repealed in 1853.[103]

Indeed, deposit obligations were often disregarded. The reports of the Parliamentary Librarian of the Province of Canada demonstrate that far fewer copyrighted books were deposited than were registered under the 1841 Act. For example, the report of the Assembly's librarian for 1847 listed four books registered in 1846 and deposited by the printer and publisher H. Rowsell of Toronto. However, the index to the copyright registry for 1846 identifies thirteen registrations for that year. A decade later, the librarian's report for 1856–7 listed only one copyright deposit. The index to the copyright registry for that same period recorded thirty-seven registrations. The British Museum suffered a worse fate with respect to colonial deposits of books pursuant to the UK Copyright Act 1842. In 1850, the Keeper of Printed Books at the British Museum acknowledged that "of the works published in the colonies we get none at all."[104] This is not surprising. Library deposit

---

101   The UK Copyright Act 1842, ss. 6 and 10. The deposit provision in the University of Toronto Act is the only example of British copyright law being reproduced in a British North American statute, albeit not into the province's copyright legislation.

102   The parliamentary debates surrounding the legislation do not discuss the reasons for inserting this deposit provision. See Nish, *Debates*, vol. 8, pt. 3.

103   *An Act to amend the Laws relating to the University of Toronto, by separating its functions as a University from those assigned to it as a College, and by making better provision for the management of the property thereof and that of Upper Canada College*, 1853, 16 Vict., c. 89, repealed the earlier legislation and did not reintroduce the library deposit provision (April 1853).

104   Barrington-Partridge, *The History of the Legal Deposit of Books*, 147. See also Gilchrist, "Copyright Deposit"; and Sternberg, "The British Museum Library."

obligations were extremely difficult to enforce. Furthermore, it must have been galling for the small and struggling colonial printing and publishing trade to be forced to send a bound copy on the finest paper across the sea, assuming they could bear the costs to begin with. To make matters worse, these provincially produced books would not have been protected by copyright in the United Kingdom, since they were not first published there. However laudable as a matter of policy, library deposits fell short in practice as a means of preserving a record of a nation's printed works. Nevertheless, their inclusion in copyright statutes remained an essential feature of provincial and, later, federal legislation.[105]

**British North American Copyright up to 1842**

It is worth reflecting on the key themes that animated domestic copyright law prior to the transformative impact of the UK Copyright Act of 1842 that charted the next stage in British North American copyright history. Up to this point, the British North American provinces enjoyed considerable independence over their copyright laws. This changed after 1842 as domestic and British copyright interests increasingly collided.

Events between 1824 and 1841 demonstrate conclusively that provincial copyright laws were motivated by the need to encourage education and learning within the population. The focus was on supporting resident authors who would write suitable books to edify and enlighten provincial readers, as well as to inculcate in them a sense of belonging and community. The new library deposit formalities introduced in the copyright statutes of Nova Scotia and the Province of Canada reinforced the cultural policy dimension that was already implicit in the law. The desire to capture and make available a society's intellectual production was an early indication that the provinces viewed themselves as distinct North American societies rather than solely as British colonies. After 1842, the themes of autonomy, education, and national identity became intertwined within domestic copyright law and policy. These aspirations grew

---

105  Library deposits to the parliamentary library continued well into Confederation under the Copyright Acts of 1868 and 1875 and 1886. Today, the deposit requirement is no longer contained in the copyright statute. Instead, deposits are to be made to Library and Archives Canada pursuant to the *Library and Archives Canada Act* S.C. 2004, c-11.

in importance precisely because of increased imperial interference in colonial copyright affairs, especially in the Province of Canada. In its desire for legislative autonomy and cultural self-determination beyond its colonial circumstances, the Province of Canada shaped Canada's copyright trajectory well into the twentieth century. The UK Copyright Act 1842 and its considerable ripple effects are addressed in the next chapter.

# Chapter Eight

# Imperial Interposition and Colonial Defiance: The Circulation of British Books in British North America, 1842–1850

The period from 1842 onward marked a turning point in imperial–colonial copyright relations. The UK Copyright Act 1842 and its aftermath charted the next, more tumultuous, stage in the history of Canadian copyright law. It was at this point that the trajectory of British North American law (and, after Confederation, of federal law) shifted to meet a new environment, characterized by more direct British interference in domestic copyright affairs and in the North American cross-border book trade. The coexistence of domestic and imperial copyright laws that had characterized the earliest period gave way to a hierarchical structure that subordinated British North American sociocultural and economic interests to those of British authors and the powerful lobby of printers and publishers who plied their trade on London's Paternoster Row.

It is intriguing to speculate about what the history of copyright in Canada might have looked like if British North Americans had been able to continue to develop the law independently. After all, provincial copyright laws did not interfere with British copyright interests since their objective was to facilitate the availability of didactic material for local consumption, a market that had little appeal to the British book trade. However, Canada's copyright story cannot be divorced from the broader geopolitical and imperial contexts. Domestic schoolbooks and other print materials satisfied only a small part of the reading needs of British North Americans. Colonial readers also enjoyed liberal access to the most popular British books because cheap unauthorized American reprints of those works flowed easily across the border. This was a circumstance that *did* interfere with British copyright interests. Travel writer James Silk Buckingham's contemporaneous account of the inventory in Montreal bookstores underscores the gravity of the problem:

The books chiefly met with in the book-stores of Montreal, are American reprints of English works, which, though imported at a duty of 30 per cent., when passed through the Custom House here, can be sold at about half the price of the English editions; and when smuggled across, as is often the case, and the duty of 30 per cent evaded, they can of course be sold at so much less. The consequence is, that few English editions are sold of any work, of which the Americans make a reprint; as these having nothing to pay the authors for copyright, can furnish them so much cheaper than any English publisher could do.[1]

An economic depression in the United States in the late 1830s led to a massive expansion of the reprint business.[2] Unauthorized American editions of British copyright works were circulating liberally in the British colonies and were making their way back into the United Kingdom, undercutting the market there. The British Parliament could do nothing to stop the Americans from reprinting British books, but it could legislate to prohibit those reprints from crossing its borders and those of its colonies. The UK Copyright Act of 1842 was enacted in part to address this scourge of American reprinting. With its passage, British North America's domestic copyright interests became mired in the protracted dispute between the British and the Americans over the circulation of unauthorized reprints.[3] Issues surrounding copyright, education, and schoolbooks still resounded within British North America after 1842, but copyright also became a rallying point for questions of self-determination and national cultural identity, especially in the province of Canada, foreshadowing more vociferous agitations on these fronts by the government of the Dominion of Canada after Confederation. As this chapter will show, events between 1842 and 1850 would define Canadian copyright policy from that point forward.

## The UK Copyright Act 1842 and Its Impact in British North America

The UK Copyright Act 1842 was the first imperial copyright statute in that it expressly protected British copyright works throughout the

---

1  Buckingham, *Canada*, 141. Buckingham toured British North America between 1839 and 1842.

2  In this regard, see McGill, *American Literature.*

3  On Anglo-American copyright relations, see, for example, Barnes, *Authors, Publishers and Politicians*; Nowell-Smith, *International Copyright Law*; and Seville, *The Internationalisation of Copyright Law.*

empire, although it was not the first British copyright statute to apply in the colonies.[4] The 1814 UK Act had extended the reach of British copyright in books and other print matter by making it unlawful for colonial printers and publishers to print or reprint British copyright works without the permission of the copyright holder. The legislation also banned unauthorized importations into the United Kingdom of British copyright works and of unauthorized prints or reprints of those works. However, the statute was silent on whether the prohibition included unauthorized importations into the colonies. In addition, it was not clear whether border seizures of infringing imports, be they at ports of entry in the United Kingdom or in the colonies, were allowed, since the Act made no provision for this remedy. Eventually, aggrieved British copyright holders could block the entry of infringing works into the United Kingdom through customs legislation, but the law did not apply to seizures at colonial borders.[5]

The UK Copyright Act 1842 resolved these uncertainties. The Act retained the existing prohibition on colonial printing, reprinting, and importing of British copyright works but now also expressly forbade the importation of unauthorized foreign reprints for sale or hire anywhere within the British Empire.[6] The statute also provided that unauthorized reprints could be seized and destroyed at any colonial border or port of entry.[7] The British government's intention was to deny entry

---

4   On the 1842 Act specifically, see Seville, *Literary Copyright Reform*. In relation to British North America, see Bannerman, *The Struggle for Canadian Copyright*; MacLaren, *Dominion and Agency*; and Parker, *The Beginnings of the Book Trade*. See also Nair, "The Copyright Act of 1889"; and Moyse, "Canadian Colonial Copyright." In relation to other British colonies see, for example, Ailwood and Sainsbury, "The Imperial Effect."

5   *An Act for the General Regulation of the Customs*, 1833, 3 & 4 Will. 4, c. 52, forbade unauthorized foreign reprints from entering the UK. The Table of Prohibitions and Restrictions Inwards absolutely prohibited "Books first composed or written or printed in the United Kingdom, and printed or reprinted in any other Country, imported for Sale." This Act repealed the previous statute (6 Geo. IV c. 107, 1825), which did not have a similar prohibition. See too Barnes, *Authors, Publishers, and Politicians*. On the history of the importation provisions under British law, see Australia, Copyright Law Review Committee, *The Importation Provisions*.

6   Section 15 read in part: "If any Person shall, in any Part of the British Dominions … import for Sale or Hire any [copyright protected] Book so having been unlawfully printed from Parts beyond the Sea … shall be liable."

7   Section 17 read in part: "every such Book shall be forfeited, and shall be seized by any Officer of Customs or Excise, and the same shall be destroyed by such Officer, and every Person so offending, being duly convicted thereof … shall also for every such Offence, forfeit the Sum of Ten Pounds and Double the Value of every Copy of such Book."

to all unauthorized reprints. However, the language of the relevant copyright provision limited the ban to works imported for "sale or hire" and left open the question of whether reprints could be imported by individuals for their personal use. In 1845, the importation of individual copies for personal use was prohibited by virtue of customs and trade regulation legislation.[8] The British government made some allowance for travellers bringing their personal copies of books into the colonies as long as they had written permission from the copyright holder and paid the imperial import duty on books, but these prerequisites would have been impracticable in most cases. The upshot was that by 1845, virtually all unauthorized reprints of British copyright works, whether in book form or in serial or periodical publications, were barred from entering British North America and would be confiscated and destroyed at the border.

The procedure for initiating border seizures required that British copyright holders provide details of their protected print material to colonial customs officials, who would post lists of these protected works at every port of entry. The time it took for updated lists to be received and publicly announced provided a window of opportunity for some colonial importers and booksellers to continue to procure American reprints with impunity.[9] Those who complied with the law, like Toronto importers and booksellers Lesslie Brothers, complained of wasted time and effort in perusing lengthy catalogues when only a small proportion of the works listed were being reprinted without permission.

> It may be remarked that all British Reprints are not excluded … but only such as are included in certain Schedules, and which are not and cannot be at all times accessible to the Trade. This arrangement renders it necessary for the importer, before transmitting any order for American Reprints, to call at the Custom House to examine first the original Schedule; then the Appendix and every subsequent Supplement that may be transmitted officially from England to the Collectors in the Province, and all this for every separate work he designs to import; when, as it has not unfrequently happened, not one work in twenty is found in the list of prohibitions. Besides, in examining those Schedules, we think that we may say with safety, that not one-half of the works therein enumerated are such as would, in all

---

8  *An Act to Amend the Laws Relating to Customs*, 1842, 5 & 6 Vict., c. 47 (9 July 1842), at s. 23, prohibited importations into the United Kingdom for personal use. Section 9 of *The Act to Regulate the Trade of British Possessions Abroad*, 1845, 8 & 9 Vict., c. 93 (4 August 1845), extended the prohibition to books imported into the colonies.

9  Barnes, *Authors, Publishers, and Politicians*.

probability, ever be reprinted, since works of a local character, or of whose popularity there is any reasonable doubt, will not, particularly if they be in many volumes or of an expensive size.[10]

The logistical burdens of complying with the imperial legislation were difficult enough, but the way in which the customs controls were implemented was especially harsh. Imperial customs officers were sent to British North America to police the borders for print contraband. Armed with lists of British copyright works, they seized and destroyed infringing works. The Province of Canada was particularly affected by the severity of the actions of these customs officials. One officer, stationed in Montreal, was particularly officious in the discharge of his statutory duties.

Henry Pratt began his career as a clerk at the Montreal customs house on St Paul Street in 1844. Three years later, he was promoted to customs officer and began his assiduous enforcement of the law until he was removed from his position in 1850.[11] Mary Lu Macdonald provides a detailed account of the border enforcement practices in Montreal from January 1849 to September 1850; by her count, Pratt single-handedly seized 1,448 copies of 166 different books and periodicals in addition to one steamboat. Writing in 1882, Montreal publisher Samuel Dawson described those trying years:

> In those days ... Imperial officers responsible only to England watched over, in our customs-houses, the execution of Imperial laws. They examined the baggage of travellers and the packages of booksellers, and seized all United States reprints of English books, and all magazines containing matter derived from English sources. In Montreal especially they were very active. Every case or parcel for a bookseller was opened, and the title-page of each book was carefully compared with a voluminous printed

---

10   Appendix to the Journals of the Legislative Assembly of the Province of Canada, 1843, 7 Vict., Appendix P.P. In some colonial jurisdictions, the lists of British books became imbued with symbolic meaning. Isabel Hofmeyer argues that in South Africa, the lists of British copyright works were treated as marks of origin "denoting the book as British and hence as implicitly 'white' turning copyright itself into a racial trademark." See Hofmeyer, "Colonial Copyright, Customs and Port Cities."

11   Henry Pratt's exploits are recounted in Macdonald, "The Montreal Non-Tea Party"; and in Fraser, "John Murray's Colonial and Home Library." Fraser suggests that Pratt's final tally of seizures was close to 1,500 copies before he returned to England in October 1850.

list of many hundred folio pages. If the title was found in the list, the book was seized and burned ... The Canadian government in one or two cases issued permission to return some books that had been seized to the United States; but the English officer refused to give them up and destroyed them.[12]

The English officer contemplated in this passage was undoubtedly Pratt.[13] It was also Pratt to whom Dawson was referring when, in the same piece, he wrote of an official who seized books from "the shelves of the booksellers' shops, and threatened domiciliary visits to private houses."[14] Dawson must have been writing from personal knowledge. His father, Benjamin Dawson, owned a bookstore in Montreal and imported books, including unauthorized reprints, from the United States. His 1849 book catalogue advertised: "All the New and Popular Works in cheap form are received, by Express, from New York immediately after publication and sold at Publishers' Prices."[15] Of all the Montreal booksellers whose businesses fell under Pratt's scrutiny between 1849 and 1850, Benjamin Dawson endured the largest number of seized shipments. Nineteen consignments of books were confiscated, either as they entered the city or on the premises of his bookstore.[16] As Macdonald recounted: "On the information of a competitor, Pratt entered Benjamin Dawson's shop and seized copies of the popular *Rockingham*, which it appears Dawson had brought in his own luggage when returning from the States."[17] Samuel Dawson would have been around sixteen years old at the time of these events and would certainly have been privy to this incident. It is also likely that the younger Dawson's reference to threats of domiciliary visits was also drawn from his father's personal experience as Pratt went to great lengths in his search for American reprints. The customs officer went so far as to seize a ship, owned by beer and steamship magnate John Molson, that was transporting infringing

---

12  Dawson, *Copyright in Books*, 16–17.
13  James J. Barnes claimed that Pratt was ordered to compensate the provincial importer whose shipment he had seized and destroyed. Barnes expressed some sympathy for Pratt, who was caught between his interpretation of his orders from Her Majesty's Customs Office and the policies of the province's chief customs officer, J.W. Dunscombe. See Barnes, *Authors, Publishers, and Politicians*, 150.
14  Dawson, *Copyright in Books*, 16.
15  Dawson, *A Catalogue of Books*, 75.
16  Macdonald, "The Montreal Non-Tea Party."
17  Macdonald, "The Montreal Non-Tea Party," 9. The book in question was a novel by Philippe-Ferdinand-Auguste de Rohan-Chabot titled *Rockingham, or the Younger Brother*, which had been published in London in 1849.

books and print material into the city.[18] As Dawson described it: "On one occasion, vexed at his inability to stop the import of American reprints, [Pratt] seized the Laprairie steamboat instead for bringing them over the river with the other imports into the city."[19]

Samuel Dawson was not alone in his criticism. Other nineteenth- and early twentieth-century commentators provided their own pointed assessments of the law. In 1879, Toronto publisher and founder of the Canadian Copyright Association John Ross Robertson asserted that "the operation of the Imperial Copyright Act of 1842 was extremely distasteful to the people of Canada."[20] A few years later, Canadian novelist William Kirby, whose literary career had begun shortly after the passage of the UK Copyright Act 1842, wrote that "had it not been for that great stumbling block placed in the way of our rising literature – the passage of the Imperial Copyright Act of 1842 – Canadian letters and book-publishing, with all the prestige and power a good literature gives, would have been flourishing to-day among us in a degree worthy of the material progress of our country."[21]

In 1910, newspaper editor, historian, and President of the Royal Society of Canada Joseph-Edmond Roy offered his view of that period:

> [C]'était une loi bien peu sage que celle qui allait priver de jouissances intellectuelles la population de tout un pays.
>
> Les fonctionnaires impériaux au Canada mirent d'autant plus de vigueur à faire observer la nouvelle loi qu'elle était acceptée avec plus de répugnance par tout le public lettré... On fit saisir et brûler tous les livres importés en contravention. Jamais on ne vit un pareil autodafé.[22]

Equating these book burnings to the atrocities that had taken place during the Spanish Inquisition reveals the extent of the bitter feelings that lingered in the collective consciousness decades after the events in question.

---

18   Macdonald, "The Montreal Non-Tea Party," 14.

19   Dawson, *Copyright in Books*, 16.

20   Robertson, *Copyright in Canada*, 8.

21   Kirby, "Mr. Kirby on Copyright." On Kirby (1817–1906), see DCB.

22   Roy, "Discours présidentiel de la propriété litteraire," 93. [It was a very unwise law that sought to deprive the people of an entire country of intellectual enjoyment. The imperial officials in Canada were all the more vigorous in enforcing the new law because it was so strongly disliked by the literate public. All the books imported in contravention were seized and burned. Never before had we seen a similar auto-da-fé.]

## The Provinces Fight Back: "A Law So Repugnant to Public Opinion Cannot and Will Not Be Enforced"

The intent behind the UK Copyright Act 1842, which came into force on 1 July 1842, was to compel British North Americans to buy British copyright works directly from the British copyright holder.[23] However, because British imports were largely unaffordable to most colonists, the practical effect of the law was to deny them all access. This consequence proved catastrophic for British North American readers, who had become accustomed to the ready availability of inexpensive American reprints of British books. The new law also disrupted the businesses of British North American booksellers and importers like Benjamin Dawson, whose livelihoods depended on the reprint trade. In a letter to the Colonial Secretary Lord Stanley, Lieutenant-Governor Colebrooke of New Brunswick advised of "a sensation having been produced in the Province by the recent enforcement of the provisions of the Acts of Parliament ... for the protection of the Copy right on Books."[24]

Adverse reaction to the new law was swift. The provincial governments wasted little time in expressing their concern. In August 1842, Colebrooke's private secretary Alfred Reade wrote a lengthy letter to British diplomat Lord Ashburton highlighting the disadvantages of British North American geography and climate that affected the ability of the colonies to procure reading material directly from the United Kingdom: "For five months of the year the British Provinces may be said to be almost excluded from ship communication with England, so for that period the only mode of obtaining access to the new Works is through the United States."[25] Reade also wrote to the legislature of

---

23  Seville, in *The Internationalization of Copyright Law*, suggested that the UK Copyright Act 1842 took effect in the colonies a year after it was proclaimed into force in the United Kingdom, but I can find no corroborating evidence for this assertion, and Seville did not cite a primary source for the claim. Parker, *The Beginnings of the Book Trade*, cited an official directive dated 1 October 1842 instructing the Colonial Post Office to prohibit the entry of infringing print material into the colonies, suggesting that the law took effect in British North America at the date it was proclaimed into force on 1 July 1842, rather than 1 July 1843.

24  Colebrooke to the Colonial Secretary Lord Stanley, 20 July 1843, Fredericton, in Journal of the Legislative Assembly of the Province of Canada, 9 Vict., 4 May 1846, 194. Sir William McBean George Colbrooke (1787–1870) was Lieutenant-Governor of New Brunswick from 1841 to 1848. George Parker details the early confusion surrounding the implementation of the Act that prompted Colebrook's comment. Parker, *The Beginnings of the Book Trade*, 108–9.

25  A.S. Reade to Lord Ashburton, August 1842, Washington, in Journal and Proceedings of the House of Assembly of the Province of Nova Scotia, 1845, Appendix no. 42, 135.

the Province of Canada, urging a collective British North American response:

> The subject I feel to be of vital interest to our Colonies, and, in a natural point of view, of the greatest moment. It really seems to involve nothing less than the question of keeping our people in comparative ignorance or embuing [*sic*] the rising generation with Republican feelings, and, what is even worse, by inducing a laxity of feeling in reference to the observance of laws, for it is needless to say that the smuggling of these Works, in their cheapest form, will be carried on in defiance of all the Customs' Establishments in the world … I have frequently suggested an united effort on the part of Canada, Nova Scotia and New Brunswick.[26]

From the outset, officials from Nova Scotia, New Brunswick, and the Province of Canada were in close communication over this galvanizing issue. United in their concern, the provincial officials made their grievances known to the British government. They urged the imperial authorities to lift the prohibition on unauthorized reprints. Lieutenant-Governor Colbrooke expressed the hope "that the measure may be abandoned, of enforcing by Parliamentary authority, a prohibition which, if not evaded through the facilities every where presented, would have the effect of excluding English Literature from the Provinces."[27] Alfred Reade referred to the "extreme hardship" the ban caused to the colonists and "its extreme impolicy from a national point of view." Readmitting American reprints of British copyright books, he concluded, would be "proof of the real desire of the British Government to foster and encourage attachment to the parent country, and to place them [the British North American provinces] in a position in which … they shall have nothing in which to envy their neighbours."[28] The Assembly of the Province of Canada described the

---

26   Letter dated 3 November 1843 from New Brunswick. Although the correspondent was not named, the author attached his letter to Lord Ashburton, thereby permitting the identification of Reade. See Journals of the Legislative Assembly of the Province of Canada, 1843, 7 Vict., Appendix P.P. Excerpts of Reade's letter to Ashburton were also appended to the Committee inquiring into copyright in Nova Scotia. See Journal and Proceedings of the House of Assembly of the Province of Nova Scotia, 1845, Appendix no. 42, 131.

27   Colebrooke to Lord Stanley, 20 July 1843, reproduced in Journal of the House of Assembly of the Province of New Brunswick, 1847, 57, and in Journals of the Legislative Assembly of the Province of Canada, 1846, 9 Vict., 194–5.

28   Reade to Ashburton, reproduced in Journal and Proceedings of the House of Assembly of the Province of Nova Scotia, Appendix no. 42, 137.

British actions as "an evil" and urged the governor to "take such steps as he may deem necessary, to remove an evil ... of lasting importance to the internal happiness of this Province, and the connection with the Mother Country."[29]

The provinces explained that British books were costly to begin with and that the additional import duties as well as transportation and other ancillary costs made them prohibitively expensive. Libraries or book societies, which might have purchased these books for the public's benefit, were few and far between. In colonial British North America, individuals who wanted to read a book had to buy it themselves. The Nova Scotian Assembly described the situation thus:

> The high price of English Books, and the monopoly of the London Publishers, are felt as a serious grievance even in the United Kingdom. That these evils are there partially alleviated by ... the wide establishment of Circulating Libraries, Clubs and Reading Societies, by which a command of the fresh Literature is obtained on cheap and easy terms; but these facilities do not exist here; and hence the importation of the English editions of new Books is confined to a few copies for the use of libraries and of wealthy individuals who, although the American reprints were admitted free of duty, would still prefer the clearer type and more elegant binding of an English copy.[30]

The Assembly of the Province of Canada advised that "the circumstances of the population generally are so limited in their means, that they are unable to enjoy English Literature at English prices."[31]

The provinces also argued that the importation restrictions had no beneficial effect on British authors and publishers because British North Americans would continue to avail themselves of cheap American editions surreptitiously. They would disobey a law they perceived to be unjust. The Assembly of the Province of Canada asserted that "a law so repugnant to public opinion cannot and will not be enforced."[32] The Nova Scotian Assembly cautioned that "the public feeling is against

29 Appendix to the third volume of the Journals of the Legislative Assembly of the Province of Canada, 1843, Appendix P.P.

30 Journal and Proceedings of the House of Assembly of the Province of Nova Scotia, 1845, Appendix no. 42, 132.

31 Appendix to the third volume of the Journals of the Legislative Assembly of the Province of Canada, 1843, Appendix P.P, 1.

32 Appendix to the third volume of the Journals of the Legislative Assembly of the Province of Canada, 1843, Appendix P.P, 1.

it [the law]; that it is regarded as oppressive and impracticable in its provisions; and they are satisfied, that, under present circumstances no Statute however binding and no regulations however stringent could enforce it."[33] New Brunswick's Reade maintained that "[there] is scarcely an individual who thinks it either wrong to possess them [American reprints] himself, or to be the means of enabling their possession by others; they are felt to be a want almost equal to a necessary of life, and being ready and cheerful to pay any reasonable demand for them, they can see only injustice in being called on to suffer a privation which is a source of benefit to none."[34]

Finally, the provincial governments suggested that the effect of a prohibition on American reprints would be to weaken colonial attachment to the British Empire. According to the Assembly of Nova Scotia, "the practical operation of the present Law has a tendency to encourage ... the wide circulation of the Literary Periodicals, Newspapers and other light literature issuing from the American Press; and thus places in the hands of our population, Works often spurious in their morality, and propagating political opinions not favourable to British Institutions."[35] The legislature of the Province of Canada issued a particularly dire warning. Confining readers to American books would have the effect of inculcating in young minds "a hatred deep rooted and lasting of all we have been taught to venerate, whether British, Constitutional or Monarchical."[36]

These various representations conveyed a profound awareness of the particularity of British North America's book and print culture, which was being shaped by geography and the colonial status of the provinces. However, the arguments raised by the provincial governments were also very much about Old World and New World class structures, and about the changing nature of the Anglo-British North American relationship, matters to which the imperial authorities were decidedly insensitive. Nova Scotia's legislature argued that British actions interfered with its ability to provide public education. The legislature had a duty

---

33  *Journal and Proceedings of the House of Assembly of the Province of Nova Scotia*, Appendix no. 42, 132.

34  *Journal and Proceedings of the House of Assembly of the Province of Nova Scotia*, Appendix no. 42, 137.

35  *Journal and Proceedings of the House of Assembly of the Province of Nova Scotia*, Appendix no. 42, 133.

36  *Appendix to the third volume of the Journals of the Legislative Assembly of the Province of Canada*, 1843, Appendix PP.

to exercise the same vigilance and care in protecting and encouraging the Literature of the Province, as in founding and improving a general system of Education. That in some of the best systems of Education introduced into the older countries of Europe and the States of the neighbouring Republic, provision has been made for the establishment of School and Parish Libraries; and your Committee are satisfied from the peculiar circumstances of this Province – from the want and defects of the Educational Establishments in former years, that much benefit would result to our adult population from a wide dissemination of the cheap and popular Literature of the Age.[37]

The provinces believed they should have agency to act in their own best interests and should be free from imperial actions that could negatively affect their goals and aspirations, especially in matters of education and learning. The provincial legislatures were sympathetic to the British position that American reprints harmed the interests of British authors and the book trade, but they were equally if not more concerned about the harms that British interests caused to the colonies. The tone of the various entreaties reveals an incensed group of parliamentarians and colonial leaders, who peppered their statements about the British legislation with words like "evil," "impolitic," "oppressive," and "repugnant." British North America's reaction to British condescension and ignorance of provincial circumstances was captured by late nineteenth-century librarian Richard Lancefield, who wrote that "it was a stupid proceeding for the British publishers and the Imperial Government of 1842 to suppose that the colonists would for a moment submit to their supply of reading being confined to books published three thousand miles away, when far cheaper editions could be purchased at the border line."[38]

The controversy over the British copyright measures would have ended if British publishers had been willing to produce affordable editions for colonial consumption. Indeed, the British Colonial Office had hoped that British printers and publishers would step in to fill the gap in supply once the statutory ban on American reprints took effect. The Colonial Office had inquired of the British Board of Trade whether London publishers had been contacted "with the view of ascertaining whether some of the inconveniences alleged to be experienced [by the

---

37  Journal and Proceedings of the House of Assembly of the Province of Nova Scotia, Appendix 42, 131.
38  Lancefield, *Notes on Copyright*, para. 74.

British North American colonies] in consequence of the present state of this law might be remedied."[39] However, most British copyright holders were reluctant to agree to cheaper colonial editions for fear that these would be imported into the United Kingdom for sale. The concern over parallel importation – the practice of introducing into the country of origin cheaper editions intended for a foreign audience – and its damaging effect on British authors, printers, and publishers, was a decisive factor in the restrictive approach to colonial book supply.

Despite these concerns, some London publishers did attempt to provide affordable options. John Murray's ambitious Home and Colonial Library series, launched in 1843, was intended as a "substitute to the Canadas and other Colonies for the Yankee publications hitherto poured into them and which besides damaging the copyrights of British Authors by the piracy of their Works, are sapping the principles and loyalty of the Subjects of the Queen by the democratic tendency of the native American publications."[40] However, Murray's experiment failed. British North Americans condemned the effort almost immediately, complaining that the series was too costly and that the content was outdated. Montreal printer and bookseller William Greig carped:

> Murray, the great London Publisher, has put forth the prospectus of what he calls his cheap Colonial editions, – and what are the great advantages which he offers? Why, instead of issuing cheap editions of his latest works, he re-issues those that the "run" is chiefly over for, and which have been reprinted and extensively circulated on this side of the Atlantic long ago; and then he offers for 2s. Sterling, equal to 3s. in Canada, what is sold in the United States for 25 cents, equal to 1s 10 ½ d. currency in Canada.[41]

---

39   Colonial Office to Board of Trade, 26 August 1846, in *Colonial Copyright, Return to an Address of the Honourable House of Commons* (Ordered by the House of Commons to be printed, 29 July 1872), 11. From B. Hawes on behalf of Earl Grey.

40   John Murray III to F.B. Head, 20 November 1843, in John Murray Ltd., letter book, cited in Barnes, *Authors, Publishers, and Politicians*.

41   Greig's testimony, Appendix to the third volume of the Journals of the Legislative Assembly of the Province of Canada, 1843, Appendix P.P. Nova Scotia's committee also suggested that Murray's prices were too high. See Journal and Proceedings of the House of Assembly for the Province of Nova Scotia, 1845, Appendix 42, 132. Samuel Dawson referred to Murray's series as consisting of "old books only. It contained none of the new and fresh books which the colonists wanted." Dawson, *Copyright in Books*, 15. However, it is not clear that Murray's attempts to supply cheap reading material to the colonies were an abject failure elsewhere in the empire. Unlike other colonial readers, British North Americans were accustomed to an immediate supply of a wide variety of the most current British works through

The unwillingness or inability of the British book trade to provide colonists with affordable options left the British authorities with little choice but to relax the statutory prohibition on foreign reprints. Colonial arguments prevailed. On 5 November 1846 the Colonial Secretary Henry Grey advised the North American colonies that the British government would propose legislative measures in the next parliamentary session that would "place the literature of this Country within the reach of the Colonies on easier terms than it is at present."[42] The imperial government was going to leave it to the colonies to determine how best to balance the interests of British authors with the needs of provincial readers:

> Relying upon the disposition of the Colonies to protect the authors of this Country from the fraudulent appropriation of the fruits of labours upon which they are often entirely dependent, Her Majesty's Government propose to leave to the Local Legislatures the duty and responsibility of passing such enactment as they deem proper, for securing both the rights of authors and the interests of the public. Her Majesty's Government will accordingly submit to Parliament, a Bill authorizing the Queen in Council to confirm and finally enact any Colonial Law or Ordinance respecting Copyright, notwithstanding any repugnancy of any such Law or Ordinance to the Copyright Law of this Country.[43]

Simon Nowell-Smith recounted that Grey's circular to the colonies "had encouraged the belief that the imperial government would endorse any local legislation on copyright."[44] This would certainly seem to be the thrust of the message: the provinces would be trusted partners to look after British interests. In the end, however, the British Parliament did not go that far. In 1847, it enacted *An Act to amend the Law relating to the Protection in the Colonies of Works entitled to Copyright in*

---

the American reprint trade. They were impatient at having to wait for cross-Atlantic shipments of books when they could procure them quickly and cheaply from the United States. The disparaging judgment of British North Americans may have masked success elsewhere, in colonies that were not as privileged by their geography. See Fraser, "John Murray's Colonial and Home Library." Keighren, Withers, and Bell, in *Travels into Print*, make a similar point.

42　As reproduced in the Journals of the Legislative Council of the Province of Canada, 1847, 10 & 11 Vict., Appendix A8–172. Henry George Grey (1802–1894), the 3rd Earl Grey, was Colonial Secretary from 1846 to 1852.

43　Journals of the Legislative Council of the Province of Canada, 1847, 10 & 11 Vict., Appendix A8–172.

44　Nowell-Smith, *International Copyright Law*, 86.

*the United Kingdom*, commonly known as the Foreign Reprints Act.[45] Although the statute left it to the provinces to decide how best to secure the rights of British authors, the legitimacy of any provincial initiative remained subject to British oversight. Only an Order-in-Council issued by the Crown would lift the foreign reprints import ban, and only once the British authorities were satisfied that the province had arrived at an acceptable solution.

The British government had specific ideas about what kinds of measures would be sufficient, and they were confident that the colonies would fall in line.[46] The preferred option was the imposition of an import duty on foreign reprints, to be collected at colonial borders and ports of entry for distribution to British copyright holders. Nova Scotia had offered this solution in its plea for relief from the UK Copyright Act 1842, when it requested "that the Imperial Act may be so modified as to permit the Importation here of American Reprints of All English Works, on the payment of a protecting duty, say to the extent of 25 to 30 per cent, if in pamphlet shape and 15 to 20 per cent if in volumes bound."[47] In quick succession, Nova Scotia, New Brunswick, Prince Edward Island, and Newfoundland passed legislation to impose a 20 per cent *ad valorem* import duty on American reprints. The necessary Orders-in-Council were issued, and the cross-border book trade resumed. The lone hold-out was the Province of Canada. The legislature of the largest province in British North America acknowledged that "the subject was a difficult one; but the words of the despatch [Grey's circular] did not seem ... to point to one mode of protection more than another."[48] Buoyed by the belief that the provincial legislature had wide discretion to determine how best to protect the interests of British authors, the

---

45   *An Act to amend the Law relating to the Protection in the Colonies of Works entitled to Copyright in the United Kingdom* ("The Foreign Reprints Act"), 1847, 10 & 11 Vict., c. 95 (in force 22 July 1847).

46   See Bently, "The 'Extraordinary Multiplicity,'" who claims that the British government believed that instead of amending Imperial law, the reprints solution should devolve to the colonies as a matter of local policy. The British were confident that the colonies would respond in an acceptable way because colonial officials were English appointees or else they saw themselves as English and would conform.

47   Journal and Proceedings of the House of Assembly of the Province of Nova Scotia, Appendix 42, 132–3 (dated Halifax, 11 March 1845). New Brunswick's lieutenant-governor had made a similar suggestion in July 1843. See Parker, *The Beginnings of the Book Trade*, 109.

48   As per William Cayley, as reported in Nish, *Debates*, vol. 6, 1006. All references to the parliamentary debates on the issue of the Province of Canada's compliance with the Foreign Reprints Act are from Nish, *Debates*, vol. 6 (1847).

Province of Canada rejected the idea of a levy and proposed an altogether different solution.

### The Province of Canada: "Great Anxiety Prevails in Canada to Know the Decision of Her Majesty's Government"

Acting in anticipation of the Foreign Reprints Act and relying on Earl Grey's undertaking, the Province of Canada passed *An Act to extend the Provincial Copy-right Act to persons resident in the United Kingdom, on certain conditions*.[49] The statute, which amended the 1841 Copyright Act, was given Royal Assent and came into force six days after the Foreign Reprints Act. As its title suggests, the legislation enabled British subjects who were resident in the United Kingdom to obtain a provincial copyright. British subjects living in other British colonies or in foreign countries, like the United States, were excluded from its scope. To obtain the benefit of the provincial measure, the work had to be printed and published in the jurisdiction.[50] This is the first instance in North America of a copyright statute conferring rights on non-resident authors, by imposing a requirement for domestic printing and publishing. Domestic manufacturing requirements for foreign authors would become a staple of Canadian and American copyright legislation toward the end of the century, discussed in chapter 10.

The provincial Bill was introduced by William Cayley, the member from Huron, in Canada West. It is clear from the records that the province envisaged this amendment to the 1841 Copyright Act as its response to the Foreign Reprints Act. *The British Whig*, a Kingston newspaper, informed the public that the 1847 provincial amendment was "intended to obviate the evil which at present exists under the English Copyright Acts and the prohibition of the American reprints of English Works in

---

49   *An Act to extend the Provincial Copy-right Act to persons resident in the United Kingdom, on certain conditions* 1847, 10 & 11 Vict., c. 28 (28 July 1847) ("the 1847 provincial copyright amendment"). French title: *Acte pour étendre l'Acte Provincial des Droits d'Auteur aux personnes résidant dans le Royaume Uni, à certaines conditions*. The Act was passed by the legislature on 23 July 1847, one day after the Foreign Reprints Act came into force. The 1847 provincial copyright amendment was incorporated into the Copyright Act in the 1859 revised statutes of the Province of Canada: *An Act Respecting Copyright*, 1859, 22 Vict., c. 31. French title: *Acte concernant les droits d'auteurs*.

50   The fact that the books did not also have to be typeset in the province enabled local printers and publishers to borrow or purchase the original plates to reduce the production costs.

the Province."[51] Upon the issuance of an Order-in-Council lifting the importation ban on foreign reprints, British authors would be obliged to secure a provincial copyright to prevent the entry into the province of American reprints of their copyright works. Of course, the proposal was also contingent on British authors being willing to enter into agreements with provincial printers and publishers, a circumstance that was not at all assured. If these authors failed to register their copyright under the provincial Act, their works were fair game. The importation of American reprints of their works could resume unimpeded, subject only to the general 7 per cent *ad valorem* import duty on foreign books. At least one member of the Assembly recognized the implications for British authors who failed to secure a provincial copyright. William Hamilton Merritt observed that "the British author would never find it advantageous to republish books in the Province, and thus the old law would practically come into force, and the Canadian buyer get the reprints at a low price."[52] Another member of the legislature, lawyer Thomas Cushing Aylwin, questioned the constitutionality of the measure. He reasoned that since the 1847 amendment was designed to displace the existing rights of British copyright holders under the 1842 UK Act, "no Court would decide against the author, if the Provincial Statute clashed with rights conferred by Imperial Statutes or Common Law rights."[53]

James J. Barnes referred to the provincial measure as a "marvel of subterfuge," but it is not at all clear that any deception was intended.[54] The proposal was solicitous of the interests of British authors in a manner that was also aligned with the province's own educational, cultural, and economic interests. The province was acting in keeping with Earl Grey's message that it could approach the question of foreign reprints in a manner of its choosing. Cayley, who introduced the legislation, believed it would be more advantageous to encourage the local printing of British works than to impose a duty on American reprints, "for a duty could hardly give a great advantage, whereas, in a few years the Province might be sufficiently populous to make reprints within it pay the author."[55] The Assembly's measure was imbued with optimism and devised with an eye to the future. British authors were given

---

51   As reprinted in "Copyright," *The British Whig*, 4 August 1847, 2. The editorial questioned whether it would have been a better strategy to reduce the postage costs instead of trying to force British authors to print and publish in the province.

52   Nish, *Debates*, vol. 6 (1847), 1006.

53   Nish, *Debates*, vol. 6 (1847), 1006.

54   See Barnes, *Authors, Publishers, and Politicians*.

55   Nish, *Debates*, vol. 6 (1847), 1006.

an incentive to deal directly with provincial printers and publishers to secure the provincial market, which would only expand as the population increased. Colonial readers would be supplied with cheaper editions of British books without having to resort to American reprints. The domestic book trade would grow as a result of its enhanced repertoire. On surer financial footing, provincial printers and publishers would be positioned to take greater risks in publishing the works of local authors. The legislature was looking to the economic and cultural development of the province by crafting a copyright policy that was domestically driven and forward-looking and that, for the first time, expressly recognized the role printers and publishers played in the copyright paradigm.

However, the anticipated Order-in-Council never arrived. Booksellers pressed the local customs authorities for some word on when they could resume importing American reprints, and official inquiries were made to the governor's secretary from Francis Hincks, the Inspector General of Public Accounts:[56]

> To secure the rights of British Authors, the Canadian Legislature passed an Act ... which it was hoped would be satisfactory to Her Majesty's Government. That Act it appears has been by Her Majesty in Council, left to its operation, but it does not appear that any Order in Council has yet issued, so that the provisions of the [Imperial] Copyright Act cannot be considered as suspended. Great anxiety prevails in Canada to know the decision of Her Majesty's Government on this subject...[57]

The matter was referred to the British Board of Trade, known as the Lords of the Committee of Privy Council for Trade, which provided a lengthy explanation as to why the Order-in-Council would not be granted. The Board confirmed that the British authorities had been oblivious to the true intent of the 1847 provincial copyright amendment.

---

56  *The Globe*, 15 April 1848, reproduced a letter, dated 1 April 1848 by Customs Collector J.W. Dunscomb to printers and publishers Armour & Ramsey advising them that the provincial statute "had not yet been confirmed as required by law of the Imperial Parliament" and that until confirmation was received, the importation of foreign reprints was prohibited (J.W. Dunscomb Customs JGO, "Copyright Act," *The Globe (1844–1936)*, 15 April 1848, 3.

57  Francis Hincks, Memorandum to Governor General (30 May 1848). Hincks first brought the matter to the attention of the governor on 6 April 1848. See Journals of the Legislative of Assembly of the Province of Canada, 1850, 14 Vict., 147.

This explains why Royal Assent to the provincial statute had so easily been granted.

> When that Act was under consideration of this Department, My Lords abstained from entering into the question whether an Order in Council ought thereupon to be issued ... because it did not appear upon the face of the Act, not in any communication brought under the notice of this Department, that the Act was passed with a view to such a step being taken on the part of the Home Government. It now appears, however, that the Act was passed with that view.[58]

Once the intended purpose of the provincial legislation was made clear, the Lords remonstrated:

> Looking at the circumstances under which that Act [Foreign Reprints Act] was passed, they are of opinion that the arrangement effected by it was in the hands of a compromise between the claims of the Colonists on the one hand, and the rights of British Authors on the other; the intention being that the Colonists should be allowed to supply themselves with the cheap editions of British works which are re-produced in the United States, on the condition of making to the Author some compensation for the injury inflicted on him, by the gratuitous appropriation of his property; and it was on this understanding that the Act received the assent of Parliament ... The Acts which have been passed by the Legislatures of Nova Scotia and New Brunswick are strictly in accordance with this understanding, but the Canadian Act now under discussion is framed upon a totally different principle. Its effects, were it followed up by an Order in Council, would simply be to take away from British Authors, unless they republish in the Colony, the protection which they now enjoy, without making them any compensation for the injury. My Lords are, therefore, of opinion that to issue such an Order might expose the Government to a charge of breaking faith with the Authors.
>
> They are the more reluctant to recommend such a step being taken, because they do not perceive the justice of the distinction which the Canadian Legislature make between Works printed and published in England only, and Works re-printed and re-published in Canada. So far as they have the means of judging, they are of opinion that an edition

---

58   Letter from the Office of Committee of Privy Council for Trade, Whitehall, 30 June 1848, reproduced in Journals of the Legislative Assembly of the Province of Canada, 1850, 14 Vict., 147–8. All references to the response of the Lords of the Committee of Privy Council for Trade are from this source.

for the Colonial market could be printed here more cheaply than in Canada. To protect Works re-printed there and to leave all others unprotected would therefore fail to secure the advantages which are desired on all hands, namely, cheap publications of a legitimate character for the Colonists, and the repression of the illicit importation of pirated editions.[59]

The response from the British Board of Trade demonstrated a lack of genuine understanding of North American circumstances. The Lords underestimated the depth of the resentment felt by the North American colonies at having to accept British books at steep prices. They also failed to take into account the province's increasingly rivalrous relationship with the United States over book supply. Indeed, the Lords' assumption that the province could not produce books as cheaply as England must have caused some consternation. As Toronto publisher J. Ross Robertson commented many years later: "The paternal tone of 'My Lords' grates strangely on Canadian ears to-day."[60] The failure of English publishers like Murray to supply the provinces would have made the remarks even more objectionable. The provinces were certainly able to print and publish books at prices that were more affordable than expensive British editions. Additionally, printers and publishers in the Province of Canada could compete favourably with their counterparts to the South. As James S. Buckingham observed, printers and publishers in Montreal produced "school-books, local histories, and works for which the demand is likely to be large in the Province; and these are quite as well executed as they would be in any part of the United States."[61]

Although ultimately unsuccessful, the novelty of the Province of Canada's approach to the foreign reprints problem was its domestic printing and publishing requirement for non-resident British authors. However, the idea of imposing printing and publishing obligations as part of the province's copyright policy did not arise in isolation in 1847. Events that had transpired during the 1843 parliamentary session help explain why the Province of Canada diverged from the other British North American provinces when it addressed the question of foreign reprints four years later.

---

59  Journals of the Legislative Assembly of the Province of Canada, 1850, 14 Vict., 147–8.
60  Robertson, *Copyright in Canada*, 9.
61  Buckingham, *Canada*, 142.

## The Parliament of the Province of Canada (1843): Of Tariffs and Trade in Books

The legislature of the new Province of Canada sat from 28 September to 9 December 1843, during which two book-related matters were brought forward for consideration. Both resulted from imperial actions outside of provincial control. One was, of course, the passage of the UK Copyright Act 1842. The other related to the impact on French Canadian readers of imperial duties on foreign books.

The Assembly established committees to study the two issues. The first was the "Select Committee appointed to Inquire into the Effect of the *English* Copy Right Act, the consequent exclusion of *American* reprints, and the policy of that exclusion, as connected with the probable influence on the minds of the rising generation of the Province."[62] Its report provided the substance on which the legislature, acting in concert with its counterparts in New Brunswick and Nova Scotia, made its grievances known to the imperial authorities regarding the detrimental consequences of the new British copyright law.[63] The second was a "Committee of the Whole House, established to inquire into Imperial duties on foreign books," which sought the elimination of duties on imported French-language books for the benefit of the province's francophone population. The way in which the legislature addressed these two agenda items would inform the province's solution to the foreign reprints problem in 1847.

*Copyright and the Provincial Book Trade: "The Select Committee to Inquire into the Effect of the English Copy Right Act"*

The select committee was established almost as soon as the 1843 parliamentary session opened. To fulfil its mandate, the committee sent a survey to "every Importer and Publisher or seller of Books in the Province" to solicit feedback about the impact of the UK Copyright Act 1842 on the provincial book trade. This was a significant development. Prior to this moment, provincial printers and publishers had been largely invisible at the domestic and imperial copyright policy levels. However, the book trade had grown with the union of Lower Canada and Upper Canada in 1840. In 1843, there were thirteen printers and sixteen stationers,

---

62   Journals of the Legislative Assembly of the Province of Canada, 1843, 52 (17 October 1843).

63   Appendix to the third volume of the Journals of the Legislative Assembly of the Province of Canada, Appendix P.P. Report dated 9 December 1843.

booksellers, and bookbinders in Montreal alone.[64] In Canada West, the Toronto Directory for 1844 shows at least eleven printers in that city.[65] The *Quebec Mercury* newspaper lauded the committee for recognizing the importance of canvassing the "trade, and persons associated with literary pursuits, as might afford them assistance in framing their Report, and obtain for them a sure basis whereon to found it."[66] Printers, publishers, importers, and booksellers in the new Province of Canada had become an important constituency and had the expertise to assist the select committee in formulating its response to the British government's copyright policy. In fact, the select committee relied exclusively on the survey results in crafting its position on the UK Copyright Act 1842.

The select committee's report reproduced in full the survey responses of ten members of the provincial book trade.[67] The respondents were evenly divided between Canada East and Canada West. There were three each from Montreal and Toronto, two from Quebec City, one from Kingston, and one from Belleville.[68] All of the respondents from Canada East were members of the anglophone book trade. The two representatives from Quebec City, Thomas Cary & Company and William Cowan, were among the oldest and most established members of the industry. Notably absent was the once-dominant Neilson firm, even though William Neilson, who had taken over the family business from his older brother Samuel, was still active as a printer, publisher, and bookseller in Quebec. John Neilson was a member of the Assembly during that parliamentary session, but he too did not participate in the work of the select committee. The elder statesman responsible for Lower Canada's copyright legislation kept a low profile in his final few years of public life.

---

64   See McKay, *The Montreal Directory for 1842–1843*. Claude Galarneau counted sixty-two members of the book trade in Quebec City between 1840 and 1849. Of that number, forty-six were printers. Galarneau, "Le métier du livre à Québec," 145.

65   See Lewis, *The Toronto Directory and Street Guide for 1843–44*. According to Éric Leroux, by 1851 there were 195 printers in Canada East and 436 in Canada West. A decade later, the numbers had grown to 531 in Canada East and 895 in Canada West. Leroux, "Printers," 75–6.

66   *Quebec Mercury*, 19 December 1843, 2.

67   The report does not provide details about how many surveys were sent and to whom. It is assumed that the select committee reproduced all of the responses it had received.

68   The respondents from Canada East were: Armour & Ramsay, William Greig, and J. H Tebbets from Montreal and Thomas Cary & Company and William Cowan from Quebec City. Those from Canada West were James Harrison (Belleville), James MacFarlane (Kingston), Hugh Scobie, H. & W. Rowsell, and Lesslie Bros. (Toronto).

The questionnaire solicited responses to four questions. The first three related specifically to the provincial market for British books. The respondents were asked whether they had already been importing and selling books from the United Kingdom and, if so, whether the UK Copyright Act 1842 resulted in their increasing this trade. Their views were then sought on the question of whether allowing American reprints to continue to circulate would reduce the profits of British authors and publishers. Not surprisingly, provincial importers, booksellers, printers, and publishers painstakingly explained to the legislature that the UK Copyright Act 1842 was ill-advised. They argued that prohibiting American reprints would only harm colonial readers without any commensurate benefit to British copyright holders. British books were simply too expensive. Montreal bookseller William Greig advised that "the very high price at which British Copyrights are published is the chief bar to their importation."[69] Thomas Cary & Company confirmed that the "demand for English works has never been great owing to their heavy prices, and the difficulty and delay in obtaining them." Prohibiting American reprints would do nothing to alter this state of affairs, although some did allow that they would likely import more if British publishers provided cheaper colonial versions. Many suggested that colonists would smuggle American reprints across the border in defiance of the law. Thomas Cary & Company astutely pointed out that had it not been for cheap American reprints of British works, the population would never have acquired an appreciation for British literature in the first place: "piracy ... has done more to create a literary taste in Canada than English Legislation has done since the country became an appendage of the British Crown."

In his response, Montreal bookseller J.H. Tebbetts submitted a petition signed by an unspecified number of provincial inhabitants and addressed to the Governor General Sir Charles Metcalfe. The petition illustrated the scale of the unauthorized reprint trade in the province and the financial impact of the imperial interdiction. The petitioners claimed that the annual provincial rate of subscriptions for American reprints amounted to at least £14,000. Assuming an average price of two shillings per book, the subscriptions represented roughly 84,000 reprinted books and periodicals. This underscored the magnitude of the

---

69   Appendix to the third volume of the Journals of the Legislative Assembly of the Province of Canada, 1843, 7 Vict., Appendix P.P. ("Answers of Mr. William Greig, Bookseller, Montreal" – 9 December 1843). All references to and quotations from the survey responses are reproduced from Appendix P.P.

problem for British copyright holders. The abrupt closure of the border now meant that booksellers and the book-buying public, who had paid in advance for their reading material, could not recover their disbursements: "That these subscriptions are all payable in advance, and have in fact been paid for the current year. That for this large sum of money expended, no return of any kind will, if the enforcement of the said law be continued, ever be received."

There is no question but that provincial importers and booksellers had valuable insights to offer on these aspects of their trade. The prohibition on foreign reprints would not lead to an appreciable increase in imports of books from the United Kingdom. To make matters worse, they were suffering direct and immediate pecuniary harm because of imperial copyright actions. However, the nature of the final survey question demonstrates just how influential the book trade had become on larger questions of public policy. The respondents were asked to opine on "the effect on the minds and morals of the rising generation of the exclusion of cheap English Literature, and the free admission of American Literature, religious and political." The select committee was clearly exercised by the impact of the British measure on the education of colonial children, who would be deprived of British books and would inevitably become more reliant on American material. This last question spoke to the province's educational and cultural preoccupations. What content should be imprinted on the minds of colonial children? What should they read? What should they learn? Were English Canadian children to be British or American or something more distinctly "Canadian"? What did it mean to be "Canadian" – or, in this context, "English Canadian"? Instead of soliciting the advice of pedagogues on this important question of education and cultural policy, the legislature looked to the book trade for answers.

Hugh Scobie thought that depriving readers of British books would be "most pernicious" and would weaken their attachment to British institutions. James Macfarlane thought that American books were of good quality in matters of morality and religion but that their anti-British sentiments were problematic. Others were much more pointed in their criticism of the influence of American books. Thomas Cary & Company echoed the sentiments of Alexander Davidson and his cadre of Upper Canadian teachers regarding American schoolbooks. They reported: "In Canada West, we have painful experience of the effect produced by the all but universal adoption of American school-books ... and we cannot but anticipate still more dangerous results from minds so trained from early infancy ... American literature is unelevating in its character and uninstructive." Still others took the broader view that all books and print material, wherever they came from, should be freely available in the province. Lesslie Brothers spoke of the "universal evil arising to the Province by a heavy tax or restrictions upon knowledge." They argued that "the intelligence, morality and religion of the Parent State should be allowed, on equal grounds at least, to exercise upon its Colonies, through its Literature, an influence which may counteract the errors, moral, religious or political, of foreigners." William Greig was even more emphatic. Depriving colonists of affordable books was "the worst possible policy." He viewed the prohibition of cheap books as "the offspring of selfishness, narrow-mindedness, feudalism and the dark ages ... All restrictions ... on the spread of useful knowledge are powerful means of keeping the people in ignorance."

It is somewhat surprising that none of the respondents suggested that they be permitted to reprint British books themselves, especially given that only a few years later the province proposed domestic printing and publishing as its solution to the foreign reprints problem. Only Thomas Cary & Company seem to have alluded to this possibility, although their statement is ambiguous:

> Until some plan can be devised whereby cheap editions of every branch of English literature, and of the latest (as we heretofore obtained from the United States), can be supplied to Colonial readers, we are of opinion that the American Reprints should not be prohibited a circulation here. A strong disposition exists to prefer and encourage British enterprize as opposed to foreign, and it rests with our own countrymen, aided by generous concessions from our Government, to secure for themselves that preference and encouragement.

These remarks could be interpreted as suggesting that the provincial book trade would be encouraged to supply its own market if generous concessions were made in their favour. This seems to foreshadow the developments in 1847, when the province did devise an alternative plan that extended copyright protection to non-resident British authors. Indeed, the 1847 provincial copyright initiative became possible in large part because of the consultative process undertaken by the select committee. Policy-makers now realized that the advancement of knowledge and learning was tied as much to the success of the provincial book trade – whether importers and booksellers or printers and publishers – as it was to local authors and an engaged readership. This recognition was strengthened when, during that same session, the legislature debated the question of imperial duties on imported French books for the benefit of the French Canadian reading public.

The UK Copyright Act 1842 had little practical effect on French Canadian readers, since their grievances were not about the American reprint trade. Assuming they were even canvassed, no French Canadian bookseller or importer responded to the select committee's survey. Only Thomas Cary & Company alluded to the reading needs of French Canadians, but only to argue that the market for British books in Canada East was limited because

> a large proportion of the population of the late Province of Lower Canada were, and still are, debarred from the enjoyment of any literature but that of the French; and even of this, they partook but slightly, owing to their inability to purchase, want of education, secluded habits of life, and laborious employments, and remoteness from the only depots where reading matter can be had – in the Cities of Quebec and Montreal.

Imperial law did not prohibit the importation of books from France. However, foreign books were subject to imperial importation duties that rendered them unaffordable to most. To address this problem, a committee of the whole house was established to review the "Imperial Duties payable upon the importation into this Province of Works promoting useful information, and not issuing from the British Press."[70]

*The Reading Needs of French Canadians: The Three Great Departments of Religion, Literature, and Law*

The impact of the union of Lower Canada and Upper Canada in 1840 was felt most profoundly by the *Canadiens*, now French Canadians, who found themselves a minority in a predominantly English Protestant province, itself situated within a larger British colonial environment. Indeed, one of Lord Durham's objectives in recommending the union had been to create the conditions for the eventual assimilation of the French Canadian population to what he considered to be superior British values and culture: "The language, the laws and the character of the North American continent are English; and every other race than the English race is in a state of inferiority. It is to elevate them from that inferiority that I desire to give to the Canadians our English character."[71]

---

70  Journals of the Legislative Assembly of the Province of Canada, 1843, 7 Vict., 104–5 (7 November 1843).

71  Journals of the Legislative Assembly of the Province of Canada, 1843, 7 Vict., 104–5, 148.

Durham described French Canadians as "a people with no history, and no literature" because "the only literature which their language renders familiar to them, is that of a nation from which they have been separated by eighty years of foreign rule ... Yet it is on a people whom recent history, manners and modes of thought, so entirely separate from them, that the French Canadians are wholly dependent for almost all the instruction and amusement derived from books."[72]

The Act of Union weakened the political influence of French Canadians. The statute gave an equal number of parliamentary seats to both sections of the province, even though the population in Canada East, with its French Canadian majority, was larger than in Canada West. This meant that French Canadian parliamentarians could easily be outvoted by their English Canadian counterparts from both Canada East and Canada West. The Act of Union also established English as the only official language of the legislature, although it allowed for French translations.[73]

For the purposes of the copyright story, the most important consequence of the failure of the Lower Canadian rebellions and the subsequent project of assimilation, is what political scientist Guy Laforest has described as the birth of an "ideology or doctrine of national survival in French Canada."[74] This unifying concept of *la survivance* had as its principal aim "the conservation of the cultural, linguistic, religious, and other traditional institutions of the community."[75] Francophone politicians, including Augustin-Norbert Morin, and their allies worked within the existing system to advance francophone interests and committed themselves to preserving French Canadian institutions, language, and laws.[76] One of the first actions of the newly constituted Assembly was to provide for the French translation of all provincial statutes by virtue of *An Act to provide for the translation into the French Language of the Laws of this Province, and for other purposes connected therewith.*[77] In this

---

72   Her Majesty's High Commissioner, *Report on the Affairs of British North America from the Earl of Durham*, 149 (The "Durham Report").

73   *An Act to Reunite the Provinces of Upper and Lower Canada, and for the Government of Canada*, 1840, 3 & 4 Vict., c. 35 (UK Act of Union), s. 41.

74   Craig, Ajzenstat, and Laforest, *An Abridgment of Report*, 183.

75   Craig, Ajzenstat, and Laforest, *An Abridgment of Report*.

76   See for example, Bédard, *Les Réformistes* ; Bédard, *Survivance*; Lamonde, *Histoire sociale*; Paradis, *Augustin-Norbert Morin*. See also Matte and Gagné, "'Nos institutions, notre langue, nos lois.'" See also Mahé, "La Survivance."

77   *An Act to provide for the translation into the French Language of the Laws of this Province, and for other purposes connected therewith* 4 & 5 Vict., c. 11 (18 September 1841). The statutes were printed in both languages from 1841 onward, as were the

way, provincial laws remained accessible to French Canadians in their own language, even if the translated texts did not have the authority of law. The statute also provided that a competent translator would be someone with legal knowledge and classically trained in French. In other words, the preferred candidate would be a francophone; the legislation specified that only a sufficient knowledge of English was required.[78] Of course, the reading needs of French Canadians extended well beyond translated statutes and legislative journals. A wide variety of French-language material had to be procured directly from France or imported via the United States, and the costs were burdensome. As a result, in 1843 the provincial Assembly sought the elimination of all import duties on French books.

The question of imperial duties on books had long been a source of frustration in British North America, even though the Province of Canada imposed its own tariffs on books and other print material.[79] Individual requests to the governor for exemptions from the payment of imperial duties for all manner of books were customary. We saw earlier that while religious books were often granted dispensation, other books, including imported French books, were not. By the early 1840s, British

---

journals of the Legislative Assembly and the Legislative Council. It seems that the Assembly also ordered official material to be printed in both languages for use by members.

78  In 1845, the provincial Parliament sent an Address to the Crown asking for the repeal of section 41 of the Act of Union that established English as the only official language of the legislature. The official Address referred to the need to provide equal justice to all residents and that French should not be considered a foreign language in the province. (See Journals of the Legislative Assembly of the Province of Canada, 1845, 8 Vict., 289). There was no response during that session, but Queen Victoria agreed to the request in 1846. See Journals of the Legislative Assembly of the Province of Canada, 1846, 9 Vict., 13. The provision was finally repealed in August 1848 by virtue of *The Act to repeal so much of an Act of the Third and Fourth Years of Her present Majesty, to re-unite the Provinces of Upper and Lower Canada, and for the Government of Canada, as relates to the Use of the English Language in Instruments relating to the Legislative Council and Legislative Assembly of the Province of Canada*, 11–12 Vict., c. 56 (1847–1848 UK).

79  The Province of Canada imposed a 5 per cent provincial duty on books (falling within goods, wares, and merchandise not otherwise charged with duty, and not exempt under *An Act for granting Provincial Duties of Customs*, 1845, 8 Vict., c. 3 (7 March 1845)). These duties were eliminated in 1849 (*An Act to amend the Law relative to Duties of Customs*, 1849, 12 Vict., c. 1). In the 1847 legislative session, the duties on imports of books for public libraries were eliminated (*An Act for repealing and consolidating the present Duties of Customs in this Province*, 1847, 10 & 11 Vict., c. 31). Other provinces, like Nova Scotia, did not impose any provincial duties on books.

free trade policies had led to the progressive elimination or reduction of imperial tariffs.[80] This new era of liberalized trade provided an opportune moment to seek the removal of the duties on books throughout British North America. In 1841 the Nova Scotian Assembly petitioned for the elimination of all duties and other restrictions on books because "an unrestricted importation … would tend to the more rapid diffusion of intelligence, and would improve the capacity and elevate the character of our population."[81] In 1842 the imperial Parliament removed all duties and tariffs on British books imported into the colonies from the United Kingdom. Duties on foreign books were reduced from 30 per cent to 7 per cent *ad valorem*.[82] This was still insufficient for politicians in the Province of Canada. In a show of unity between English Canadian and French Canadian parliamentarians, the Assembly adopted a series of resolutions, which were presented to the Governor General:

> That the advancement of Useful Knowledge is of such primary importance as to merit the attention of every Government, but more especially of any Government conducted on the principles of the British Constitution.
>
> That to promote this invaluable object, one of the most efficacious means is to facilitate the introduction of the best Work of useful information, at the least possible expense.
>
> That without now calling in Question the wisdom of those regulations, by which the importation of reprints of Copyright Works published in the United Kingdom is prohibited, it cannot in our opinion, be wise or consistent with sound policy to discourage the importation of Works promoting useful information originally written and published in Foreign Countries.
>
> That in consequence of the peculiar situation and peculiar circumstances of this Country, a very large portion of the Inhabitants speak the French language; and that for this reason, the Standard Works required by them in the three great Departments of Religion, Literature, and Law, are French, and must be obtained from France.
>
> We therefore humbly pray that your Majesty will be pleased to adopt such measures as may in Your Wisdom be deemed expedient, to remove the discouragement arising from the Duties imposed by the Imperial Act

---

80   See for example, Hart, *A Trading Nation*.

81   See *Timber Duties &*. On Nova Scotia's position on tariffs see, for example, Gerriets and Gwyn, "Tariffs, Trade and Reciprocity."

82   *An Act to Amend the Laws for the Regulation of the Trade of the British Possessions Abroad*, 1842, 5 & 6 Vict., c. 49. Tariffs on British books had been previously fixed at 2.5 per cent. See Appendix to Journal of the House of Assembly of Upper Canada, 1835, 4 Will. 4, AXI-17.

on Works of the class above mentioned and calculated to promote the dissemination of important knowledge, and we beg to assure Your Majesty of our conviction that, in complying with this prayer, Your Majesty will increase the happiness and prosperity of Your Majesty's Subjects in this Province.[83]

The Assembly began its address with a polite but firm censure of British actions to protect its domestic publishers and its economic interests. While not "calling into question the wisdom" of the UK Copyright Act of 1842, surely, it was argued, it would not be "sound policy to discourage the importation of Works promoting useful information originally written and published in foreign countries." The advancement of useful knowledge required access to affordable books. English Canadians were being thwarted by imperial prohibitions on imports of cheap American reprints. French Canadians were disadvantaged by imperial duties in their procurement of books in French. As the Assembly saw it, the questions of American reprints and the tariffs on foreign books were intertwined. Indeed, John Simpson in Canada East, a former customs collector, led both committees reviewing these book-related questions.[84]

The Assembly debates on the question of the imperial duty on French books are illuminating. The fact that *any* imperial duties were imposed on imported French-language books was a critical political and cultural question for the province. The survival of French Canadians as a people was dependent on affordable access to books from France, especially works of religion, literature, and law. However, the Committee of the Whole House had initially debated requesting the removal of import duties on all foreign books regardless of language or country of origin. It was only once the question of American books surfaced that the legislature limited its discussion to imported French-language books. These were the same elected representatives who had introduced the province's Copyright Act in 1841 and who had debated Alexander Davidson's petition for *The Canada Spelling Book*. The prevalence of American schoolbooks in provincial schools remained a sensitive issue. Francis Hincks, who represented Oxford County in Canada West, explained:

---

83  Journals of the Legislative Assembly of the Province of Canada, 1843, 7 Vict., 112 (9 November 1843). The Address to the Governor General appears at 113–14 (10 November 1843).

84  This address on imperial duties was transmitted to the British Crown before the Select Committee had completed its review of the UK Copyright Act 1842. See entry for John Simpson (1788–1873) in DCB.

> American School Books were principally in use in the Province, although there were some printed and published in it, adapted more particularly for the youth of Canada, which were got up at considerable expense. At the time, however, that this enterprise was embarked on, the duty on American Books was thirty per cent., whereas now, the only protection for the Canadian publisher against the introduction of American books was twelve per cent. Should the resolutions be Acted upon, the only school books that would be used in Canada would be from the United States. If it was desirable to confer a benefit, the proposition should be limited to Books published in the French language.[85]

When Hincks was challenged by his colleagues on the basis that there should be no distinction between French-language and English-language books, he replied that his "anxiety was directed to prevent Canadian school books from being driven out of the province." Without the imperial import duty in place, the only buffer between Noah Webster's and Alexander Davidson's spellers would be the 5 per cent provincial duty, an insufficient deterrent given that production costs were greater in the province than they were across the border, and resulted in higher book prices. The combined imperial and provincial duties on American books of 12 per cent levelled the playing field for domestic printers and publishers, at least insofar as schoolbooks were concerned.

Henry John Boulton, brother of George Strange Boulton, who had been involved in the Upper Canadian copyright file in the 1830s, reportedly said that he "had no wish to keep out literary works in a foreign language, but was decidedly averse to taking off the duty on American books, which we did not want, and putting a bounty on our own. Canada was fully competent to furnish her own school books, without having recourse to the United States for them." Marcus Child, the representative from Stanstead, Canada East, suggested that "some consideration was due to native enterprise and genius. We had authors, paper mills and presses, and could produce books of this kind ourselves – encouragement should therefore be given to enterprises of this nature." Protectionist tariffs ensured that the cost of producing English-language schoolbooks domestically remained competitive and provided the opportunity for the industry to expand. The facts suggest otherwise, however. A schoolbook protected by copyright in the Province of Canada still cost more than an unprotected foreign

---

85  All quotations from the parliamentary debates on the question of duties on foreign books are from Nish, *Debates*, vol. 3, 709, 739–41, 748–9.

equivalent even with the import tariff. Alexander Davidson's speller continued to face stiff competition from its main American rival. In the period between 1846 and 1850, Toronto booksellers Scobie & Balfour sold Davidson's *Canada Spelling Book* for a modest one shilling. However, they sold Noah Webster's *American Spelling Book* and William Mavor's *English Spelling Book* for less than a shilling, at a price of 7½ pence each.[86] Cost differentials and pedagogical preferences meant that provincial booksellers continued to stock foreign schoolbooks at more competitive prices.

Whatever the reality on the ground, the concerns about harming the local production of schoolbooks by and for English Canadians led to the Assembly confining its resolutions to books in French. Even though, at the outset, the Assembly may not have been looking out for the interests of French Canadians *per se*, it is significant that its final address to the British authorities referred to the province's francophone community as an important segment of the population ("a very large portion of the Inhabitants speak the French language"). Its official request for relief from imperial duties was directed exclusively at supporting the ability of French Canadians to read essential books in French ("the Standard Works required by them … are French, and must be obtained from France"). British policy, as expressed in Lord Durham's report, would have discouraged *any* books in French, let alone French books on religion, literature, and law – the types of works that, by their very nature, would bolster French Canada's attachment to French institutions, culture, and values. Clearly, the provincial legislature felt differently about its responsibility toward the French Canadian population.

Unmoved, the British government refused the request. The duty had already been sufficiently reduced. If, however, evidence could be proffered to show that "this low rate of duty materially impedes the introduction into the Province of original French Works from France, the Queen, on being placed in possession of that evidence, will lose no time in considering how the evil may be best corrected."[87] The Crown indicated that it would revise its decision upon receiving proof of hardship; meanwhile, the status quo would be maintained. British books could be imported into the province duty free, but French-language books, including essential works on religion, literature, and law, could not.

---

86  Scobie & Balfour, *A Catalogue of books*, 44.

87  Journals of the Legislative Assembly of the Province of Canada, 1844–1845, 8 Vict., 65. Response dated 21 December 1843 from Lord Stanley to Governor Metcalfe.

Imperial actions aside, the Assembly debates on the question of tariffs underscore the province's perspective on the circulation of books. The provincial legislature balked at any restrictions on access to British or French books, arguing that these should be available as cheaply and as liberally as possible, even if this meant reintroducing American reprints of British copyright works. When it came to American schoolbooks, however, the Assembly advocated for barriers to entry through the use of tariffs. American schoolbooks competed directly with domestic ones, and their contents were inconsistent with the province's educational and cultural aspirations. The legislature's treatment of tariffs on American schoolbooks carved out space for provincial schoolbook publishing.

The events of the 1843 parliamentary session highlight the increased visibility of the province's book trade with regard to copyright and other book-related decisions. It also signalled a maturation of provincial policy in relation to domestic printing and publishing. These circumstances shaped the Province of Canada's solution to the foreign reprints problem in 1847. However, other factors contributed as well. In 1846, the year before the passage of the Foreign Reprints Act, the United Kingdom repealed the laws that had granted preferential treatment to colonial imports of corn, wheat, and other agricultural products. The elimination of trading privileges with the mother country marked a turning point in British and colonial relations as the British loosened commercial ties with the colonies. Without the benefit of imperial trade protections, the British North American provinces had to become more self-reliant.[88] This confluence of factors meant that when the issues surrounding foreign reprints came to the fore in 1847, the Assembly was already primed to advance the interests of the printing and publishing industry. The legislature chose a solution that it thought would satisfy British copyright interests while at the same time enabling the domestic industry to thrive. The province's efforts were in vain, however: the Crown refused to issue the Order-in-Council that would have suspended the prohibition on the importation of foreign reprints.

**The Politics of Colonial Copyright: "We Were Required at the Dictation of Downing Street to Put a Tax on Knowledge"**

With the failure of the 1847 amendment to lift the ban on American reprints, the legislature of the Province of Canada had no other option

---

88   See Barnes, *A History of English Corn Laws*; Schonhardt-Bailey, *From the Corn Laws to Free Trade*. See also Burn, "Canada and the Repeal of the Corn Laws."

but to toe the line. In 1850 the Assembly passed *An Act to impose a duty on Foreign re-prints of British Copyright Works.*[89] That Parliamentary session took place in the wake of significant democratic reforms in provincial governance. A system of responsible government had been won the previous year. The British-appointed colonial governor could no longer act independently of the will of the provincial Parliament. However, this new provincial self-determination did not seem to apply in matters of copyright. The debates surrounding the legislature's second attempt to comply with the Foreign Reprints Act reveal a disgruntled group of parliamentarians, affronted by continued imperial control over the province's copyright affairs. The members of the Assembly were frustrated at being forced to impose a levy on foreign reprints instead of their preferred alternative. William Cayley, who had spearheaded the 1847 provincial amendment, remarked that during a visit to England the previous year he had been informed that "we were quite at liberty to deal with the matter as we pleased."[90] Malcolm Cameron "saw no reason why there should not exist the same facility here, for reprinting the works of British authors as prevailed in the United States." Henry John Boulton protested that "[it] had been understood that this country was left to legislate for itself, but the introduction of the present bill was intended to deprive the country of any power whatever to legislate for the benefit of its own people, and placed them on a much worse footing in relation to the Mother Country than foreigners."

Boulton was especially incensed at the imposition of what he considered to be a tax on knowledge solely to protect British publishing interests. He questioned whether

> Great Britain had any right to ask us to pass such a bill. We were either a part of the British empire or we were not ... Why should we submit to the dictation of that dispatch which required us to protect English publishers. In what respect did they protect us? ... Yet we were required at the dictation of Downing Street to put a tax on knowledge ... If the British government cared anything about the colonies, it would encourage cheap colonial editions, instead of exercising Downing Street dictation to the detriment of the Canadian people.

---

89   *An Act to impose a duty on Foreign re-prints of British Copyright Works*, 1850, 13 & 14 Vict., c. 6 ("Duty on Foreign Reprints Act 1850"). French title: *Acte pour imposer un droit sur les impressions étrangères des ouvrages britanniques soumis au droit de propriété littéraire.*

90   All quotes relating to the parliamentary debates on the issue of the 1850 legislation are taken from Nish, *Debates*, vol. 9, 939–40, 1225–6, 1255–61. The debates also evidence a fair share of criticism lodged against the American reprinters, who were labelled "dishonest" and "scoundrels" for having created the problems in the first place.

However, Francis Hincks, who introduced the new Bill to impose an import duty, felt it advisable to proceed despite the misgivings: "It would be better to pass this bill … in the meantime. Nothing … could be worse than the present state of the law by which reprints are excluded." He concluded by saying that he did not believe that the Province of Canada would be "permitted to admit these works except on the same terms as the other Colonies." In other words, the Province of Canada could not adopt its own solution to the dilemma of foreign reprints. Instead, the course of provincial legislative action was dictated by the imperial authorities. Despite a final attempt by Boulton to postpone the Bill, the Duty on Foreign Reprints Act 1850 was passed. Unlike the statutes of the other British North American provinces, which had fixed the duty on foreign reprints at 20 per cent *ad valorem*, the Province of Canada's legislation stated only that the duty would not exceed 20 per cent. The tariff was ultimately fixed at 12.5 per cent.[91] This was the legislature's last act of defiance in relation to the Foreign Reprints Act. The Crown's Order-in-Council was issued on 12 December 1850.[92]

The 1847 provincial amendment that extended copyright to non-resident British authors remained in force in the province, subsisting alongside the Duty on Foreign Reprints Act 1850.[93] It had little impact, however, since British authors had little incentive to engage with provincial printers and publishers. Nevertheless, at least one colonial commentator remained hopeful that some British authors might avail themselves of a provincial copyright in preference to the foreign reprints duty. In 1861, the Assembly's law clerk G.W. Wicksteed wrote that the 1847 amendment

> remains in force for those British authors who choose to avail themselves of it, by printing their works in Canada, and so getting the benefit of our Copyright law, instead of the protection of the duty on Foreign reprints … This latter may be generally preferred on account of the obligation to reprint in Canada in order to obtain the former; but it is easy to conceive that cases might arise where the right given by [provincial Copyright law] … would be more valuable and effective.[94]

---

91   Barnes in *Authors, Publishers, and Politicians*, said that the British Board of Trade approved a 12.5 per cent duty in 1851.

92   Order-in-Council, 12 December 1850, Colonial Office 42–567/40.

93   Both statutes were later incorporated into the Copyright Act revision in 1859.

94   Letter by G.W. Wicksteed, 27 December 1861, Quebec, in *Upper Canada Law Journal*, vol. 8, ed. W.D. Ardagh and Robert A. Harrison (Toronto: W.C. Chewett & Co., 1862), 27.

This optimism proved misplaced. The indexes of copyright registrations for the period 1847–68 contain no record of any registrations by British authors or their publishers in accordance with provincial copyright law.[95]

The discontent that marked the provincial legislative session of 1850 can be traced back to the chain of events that began with the passage of the UK Copyright Act 1842 and that culminated in the debacle surrounding the Foreign Reprints Act. The United Kingdom's resolution of the problem of American reprints legitimated the practice of unauthorized reprinting and provided American printers and publishers with financial stability by re-establishing their control over the entire North American reprint market. This same economic sustainability was denied to colonial printers and publishers in British North America. In addition, the American government had little incentive to enter into a bilateral agreement with the United Kingdom to resolve the problem of unauthorized reprints, since American printers and publishers were now lawfully able to supply the British North American market and remained free from any legal obligation to compensate the British copyright holder. The Canadian importer and bookseller paid the duty, and the colonial reader ultimately bore the financial burden. Throughout this period, it was made clear to the colonies that British copyright interests would always carry the day. The subordinate status of the colonies was exacerbated by the fact that in 1844, the United Kingdom had conferred empire-wide copyright protection to foreign authors from countries that offered reciprocal protection to British authors and publishers.[96] There was no similar reciprocity for British North American authors, who would only be protected within the colonial jurisdiction in which they had obtained their copyright. The tipping point for politicians in the Province of Canada, however, was the British refusal to endorse the 1847 provincial copyright amendment. Imperial objections to the Province of Canada supplying its own market with lawful reprints proved a harsh awakening to the realities of the province's colonial circumstances.

In its intransigence, the imperial government may have missed an opportunity to realize more auspicious outcomes for itself and the Province of Canada, guided as it was by a determination to protect

---

95  See LAC Index of Copyright Registrations, Province of Canada 1841–1868, RG 105, vols. 378–9. The 1847 amendment required that the copyright notice after the title page of the publication include detailed information about the local printer and publisher.

96  *An Act to Amend the Law relating to International Copyright,* 7 & 8 Vict., c. 12 (UK).

the British publishing industry and its views of colonialism and the privileges of empire. The need for colonists to procure unauthorized reprints from the United States might have been obviated if the British had allowed colonial printing and publishing of British copyright works. Of course, British authors and copyright holders would have to have confidence in the capacity of the colonial book trade to fulfil their printing and publishing requirements, but British government endorsement of the Province of Canada's initiative would have gone a long way toward supporting the colonial book trade and, with it, the United Kingdom's loyal provincial subjects. Instead, the British chose to favour the Americans.

The 1847 provincial copyright amendment could have been a positive, transformative moment in Anglo-Canadian colonial relations. Its rejection became the harbinger of a string of legislative disappointments that would be emblematic of Canada's copyright history for the rest of the century, as the province and, later, the Dominion sought unsuccessfully to shore up the printing and publishing industry through domestic copyright policy. The relationship with the empire became strained as domestic and colonial copyright laws and policies increasingly collided. Copyright became a litmus test for provincial legislative independence as well as the site from which provincial policies on cultural identity and nationalism could be advanced.

As it turned out, the British solution was no solution at all. American reprints continued to circulate, smuggled across the border by defiant individuals and booksellers. Colonial customs officials had little incentive to actively enforce the law, claiming that the costs of enforcement were far greater than the duties collected.[97] The records show that between 1851 and 1856, only £687 10s 8 ½d were collected in the Province of Canada.[98] However, as a direct result of the legislative actions and reactions that arose between 1842 and 1850, the public narrative in the Province of Canada and, later, the Dominion of Canada became galvanized around the injustice of imperial copyright policy, which "taxed

---

97   Statement from the Canadian Custom House in 1855, as discussed in Seville, *The Internationalisation of Copyright Law*, 88.

98   Seville, *The Internationalisation of Copyright Law*, 88. See also United Kingdom, *Return of Amounts Received*, showing a total amount of £5,278 9s for the period 1877 to 1895. In one dramatic example, a certain Archbishop Trench received the sum of eleven pence, or a penny a year, representing the full amount levied by Canadian customs at the border, "although it is well known that Dr. Trench's books had during this period a large and constant sale in Canada." See Moss, "Copyright in Canada."

knowledge," inhibited the growth of domestic publishing, and stifled the development of a national literature. The mixed messages from the imperial government only increased the frustration. The Province of Canada had achieved responsible government and was expected to be more economically self-sufficient. Yet when it came to copyright, the Province of Canada remained very much under the imperial yoke. Henry Boulton's expostulations in 1850 about Downing Street dictating copyright policy for the province continued to resonate decades later. In 1897, Canadian publisher J. Ross Robertson wrote: "We can legislate with intelligence in all other subjects, but when it comes to copyright the governor general has standing orders to refuse his assent to all copyright acts without special permission from Downing Street."[99]

Francis Hincks, who had convinced the legislature to acquiesce to the import duty in 1850 as a temporary measure because of "the book trade being at the time insignificant in extent," later regretted his actions.[100] According to a newspaper article in *The Globe* published in the early 1870s, Hincks had done much in the intervening years to correct what many perceived to have been a mistake. Indeed, when the matter of protecting British copyright interests resurfaced in 1870, Hincks, who was then the Minister of Finance in the Dominion of Canada, declared unequivocally that domestic printing and publishing requirements were non-negotiable: "There is no probability of the Dominion Parliament consenting to any measure for enforcing British copyright in Canada, unless it provides for local publication."[101] As the final chapter will illustrate, nineteenth-century post-Confederation Canadian copyright policy was uncompromising in imposing domestic printing and publishing requirements on non-resident authors in support of the country's socio-economic and cultural objectives.

The lessons learned from the period from 1842 to 1850 shaped the Province of Canada's approach to copyright and the circulation of print material as the nineteenth century progressed. The next chapter examines the copyright registration data for the period 1841 to 1867 to provide a deeper understanding of the impact of copyright on the advancement of the province's education and cultural objectives. In addition, the Assembly's treatment of book petitions and its support of works of "native talent" foreshadowed more ambitious actions by the Dominion of Canada to foster an independent Canadian cultural identity.

99   Cited in Poulton, *The Paper Tyrant*, 106.
100   Alfred Hutchinson Dymond, *The Globe*, 14 May 1872.
101   Memorandum, Francis Hincks and Christopher Dunkin, 30 November 1870, in
     United Kingdom, *Colonial Copyright*. On Francis Hincks (1807–1885), see DCB.

# Chapter Nine

# Copyright and Canadian Content in the Province of Canada

The geopolitical tumult over the importation of foreign reprints spurred greater cultural protectionism in the Province of Canada. The dearth of appropriate schoolbooks remained a copyright concern. However, the policy discourse expanded to include the role copyright played in promoting "Canadian" content, irrespective of the genre. The province's dual history shaped its search for identity, as can be discerned in the copyright registration data. In English Canada, copyright-protected books and other works on patriotic themes fostered a nationalist pride that grew over time, especially as Confederation neared. For French Canadians, the anxiety over safeguarding their history, their language, and their laws can be gleaned from the registered material.

These two communities were not entirely isolated solitudes, however. Some practices of accommodation and mutual understanding emerged despite the minority status of French Canadians and their concern over their linguistic and cultural assimilation. As this chapter will demonstrate, the themes of education and cultural identity, both French Canadian and English Canadian, can be traced in the copyright registration data and in the actions of the Assembly. The deeply entrenched narrative of the two founding peoples – French Catholic and English Protestant – meant that Indigenous peoples and religious or racialized minorities were ignored in copyright policies and practices, just as they were within the province's book and print culture as a whole.[1]

## Copyright Registrations, 1841–1867

A longitudinal review of the copyright registry from 1841 to 1867 elicits patterns of registration that serve as proxies for overall trends in

---

1  See for example, Warkentin, "In Search of 'The Word of the Other.'"

authorship and printing and publishing. It also captures the priorities and preoccupations of the province's two largest linguistic, religious, and cultural communities.

The process for reviewing the provincial registration data was considerably easier than for Lower Canada given the survival of official records from 1841 onwards. I relied primarily on the indexes of copyright registrations that recorded in abbreviated form the titles of the works, the names of the registrants, the dates of registration, and the registration numbers. However, these records are not entirely accurate and contain errors and omissions. In addition, the brevity of the entries meant that some works could not be identified. The data from these indexes should have been cross-referenced with the entries in the original copyright registries themselves. These copyright registries provided the full titles of the works, the full names of the registrants and their places of residence, often the names of the printers and publishers, and whether the claimants were authors or proprietors. These copyright registries were available early in the project but, unfortunately, they later became inaccessible.[2] In the absence of these key records and to capture the data as fully as possible, I cross-referenced the titles collected from the indexes with other primary and secondary sources for more complete bibliographical details. I also verified each registered title against any copyright notices contained in the physical copies of the protected works themselves. The results are sufficiently exact to document the trends and patterns discussed in this chapter.

Like its Lower Canadian predecessor, the Province of Canada's 1841 Copyright Act did not lead to a surge in copyright registrations relative to overall publications.[3] Although registrations increased steadily over the period, the numbers were still low and fluctuated until the 1860s, when a marked increase occurred. After 1860, registration numbers fluctuated between the high forties or low fifties; the highest number of registrations was recorded in 1864, with fifty-eight entries. However, it is difficult to attribute this increase to any mounting enthusiasm over copyright on the part of authors or the book trade, given that the

---

2  See Appendix 3.

3  As a rough guide, between 1841 and 1851 there were eighty-one copyright registrations. This is to be contrasted with the roughly 226 pamphlets, journals, and reports printed and published in the province during that same period according to Canada, *Catalogue of Pamphlets Journals and Reports in the Public Archives of Canada 1611–1867*, 2nd ed. (Ottawa: J. de L. Taché, 1916). This catalogue does not include books, musical works, or other printed matter such that the total number of books, pamphlets, and other material was significantly greater than the number protected by copyright.

Copyright registrations, Province of Canada, 1841–1867

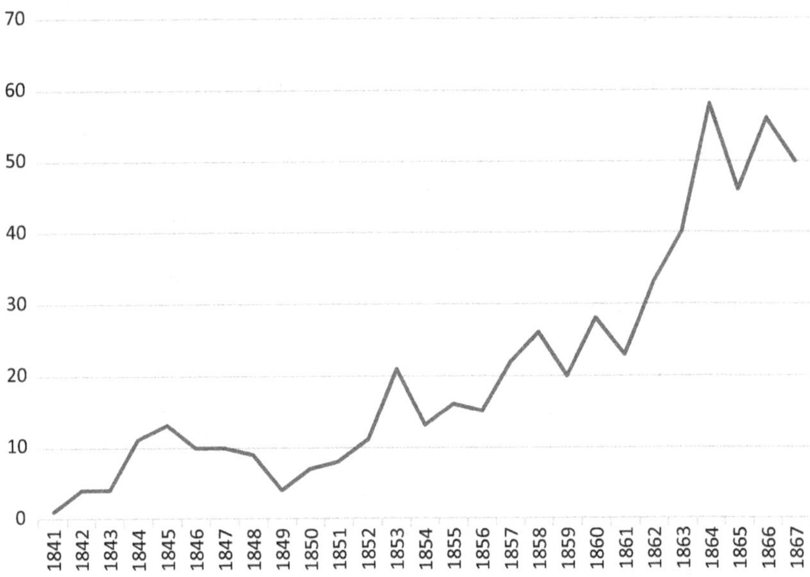

growth in registrations was consistent within an increase in population. Between 1842 and 1861, the number of inhabitants in the province doubled from around 1.2 million to 2.5 million.[4]

The copyright records provide an illuminating snapshot of the political, cultural, and economic development of the province. Assessing the copyright registrations from the Lower Canadian period to that of the Province of Canada confirms that the society's book and print culture evolved apart from the availability of copyright. The relative disregard of provincial copyright is especially striking if one considers the political fall-out that arose from the passage of the UK Copyright Act 1842, discussed in the previous chapter. The heightened rhetoric over reducing provincial dependence on American reprints or expensive British or French imports did not lead to greater copyright take-up in practice.

Of the works registered under the 1841 Copyright Act, the largest proportion remained didactic and instructional in nature, useful books that included schoolbooks, maps, directories, and almanacs. However, works of literature, such as novels, poetry, plays, memoirs, and

---

4  See census data for 1842 and 1861, Canada, *Censuses of Canada 1665 to 1871*.

autobiographies began to figure among the works protected during this period. The registration records of this period also bear witness to the introduction of new technologies, such as photography, that were not expressly contemplated within the statute.

Copyright encouraged the dissemination of works that were intrinsically "Canadian" in content and sensibility and emblematic of the French-Canadian and English-Canadian communities. This is not surprising since copyright was only available to resident authors (or British subjects resident the United Kingdom who printed and published in the province). Provincial authors were the ones most inclined to explore themes of local interest. These copyright-protected works evince English Canada's search for identity and French Canada's struggle for survival.

*Copyright Registrations: Genres, Patterns, and Trends*

The linguistic breakdown of the registrations for books and other textual material reveals that English-language works vastly outnumbered their French-language equivalents. Of 435 registrations for books, pamphlets and printed sheets, guides, directories, almanacs, music (excluding maps, photographs, engravings, lithographs, and unidentifiable material), 309 or 71 per cent were in English and 124 or 28 per cent were in French, with three bilingual books counted once for each language.[5] There were two books printed in German. These percentages were roughly equal to the population of each of the two major demographic groups. In 1861, French Canadians accounted for approximately 33 per cent of the population.[6]

Law books and treatises were by far the most popular genres of copyright-protected works, accounting for seventy-eight registrations.

---

5   These totals include two bilingual books and one trilingual work in English, French, and Latin, each counted once for English and French. I have included registrations that were later called into question or cancelled by the provincial registrar, because they remained uncorrected in the index of registrations. There was only one instance where the index of registrations recorded a cancellation, and I excluded that work from the final tally. In addition, there were 127 entries that I did not consider. These works consisted of maps, photographs, and similar material to which a specific language could not be ascribed, and otherwise unidentifiable material.

6   In 1861, the population of Canada East was approximately 1,110,664 with 847,320 being French Canadian or roughly 75 per cent. The population in Canada West was 1,396,091, with a much smaller percentage of francophones.

Copyright registrations by genre, 1841–1867

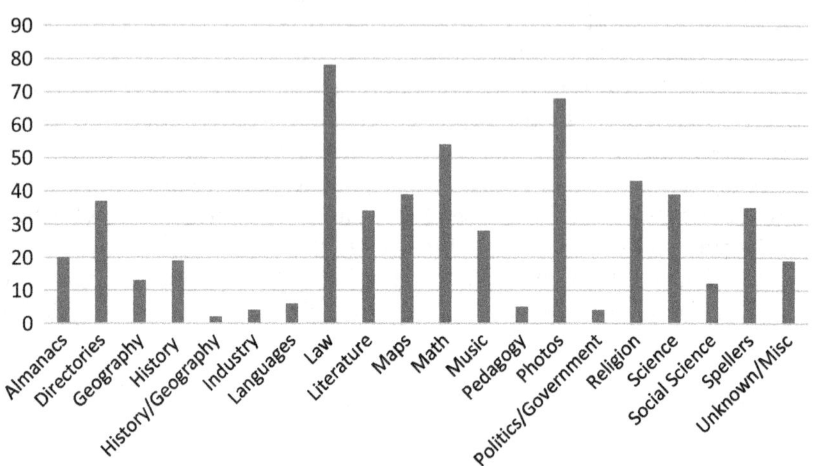



Note: *Almanacs* include sheets, charts, circulars and calendars; *Directories* includes guides and manuals; *Industry* includes commerce and banking; *Literature* includes novels, plays, poetry, biographies, memoirs, and travelogues; *Maps* includes plans, prints, engravings, and lithographs; *Math* includes arithmetic, tables, and reckoners; *Music* includes sacred and religious music; *Religion* includes morals (temperance); *Science* includes agriculture, natural science, medicine, and archaeology; *Social Science* includes statistical analyses and descriptions of colonial society; *Spellers* includes primers, readers, grammars, and writing.

These books were practice-oriented and consisted mainly of descriptive commentary on specific provincial laws, reports of judicial decisions, rules and court practices, or magistrates' manuals. Most of them were written in English for the legal profession in Canada West.

Despite the colonial history of the province, only two legal treatises focused on British or French law. Toronto lawyer Alexander Leith registered his copyright in a treatise on Blackstone's *Commentaries on the Laws of England applicable to Real Property*, which he had adapted for use in Canada West.[7] Montreal lawyer Thomas Kennedy Ramsay wrote a compendium of the sixteenth-century French customary laws, which his printers and publisher Beauchemin & Valois registered for copyright in 1863. *Notes sur la coutume de Paris indiquant les articles encore en force* was written in anticipation of the ambitious civil law codification

---

7   Blackstone, *Commentaries on the Laws of England applicable to Real Property by Sir William Blackstone Knt*. Copyright registered by Leith on 19 May 1864.

project that would be launched in 1857.[8] Ramsay was briefly involved in assisting the members of the codification commission that had been established to rationalize, synthesize, clarify, and consolidate the laws of Lower Canada.[9]

Historian Brian J. Young described the civil law codification project as "a building-block of state formation" that could only have been made possible because of an educated public. He described it as "a simple, written code, theoretically accessible and understandable by all citizens, [that] coincided with the implementation of universal education."[10] So it is apt that Augustin-Norbert Morin was one of three judges appointed as commissioners to lead the codification effort. The last surviving member of the Lower Canadian copyright champions, Morin was appointed to the Court of Queen's Bench in 1855 after a long and distinguished political career. The codification project was to be his final contribution to public life. He died on 27 July 1865, a couple of months before the new civil code received Royal Assent.[11]

The Civil Code of Lower Canada was brought into force on 1 August 1866. Four contemporaneous legal treatises on the new code were registered, three having been written for anglophone jurists. Thomas Mc-Cord, a Montreal lawyer and secretary to the codification commission, registered his copyright on 23 July 1866 in *Synopsis of the Changes in the Law effected by the Civil Code of Lower Canada*.[12] McCord also wrote *The Civil Code of Lower Canada*, which his printers and publishers Dawson Brothers registered for copyright in August 1867.[13] Moses Hart wrote an *Index to the Matters contained in Civil Code of Lower Canada* and claimed his copyright on 1 December 1866.[14] The sole French-language publication was Edouard Lefebvre de Bellefeuille's *Code civil du Bas-Canada : d'après le rôle amendé déposé dans le bureau du greffier du Conseil législatif, tel que prescrit par l'acte 29 Vict., chap. 41, 1865*, in which printers and publishers Beauchemin & Valois claimed copyright in September 1866.[15]

---

8   Ramsay, *Notes sur la coutume de Paris*. Copyright registered 9 November 1863.

9   See Young, *Politics of Codification*; Girard, Phillips, and Brown, *A History of Law in Canada*.

10   Young, *Politics of Codification*, 6.

11   The Civil Code of Lower Canada was given Royal Assent on 18 September 1865 and came into force on 1 August 1866. Morin died on 27 July 1865.

12   McCord, *Synopsis of the Changes*.

13   McCord, *The Civil Code of Lower Canada*.

14   Hart, *Index to the Matters*. Moses O. Hart worked for the codification commission for a time and was a notary by profession.

15   De Bellefeuille, *Code civil du Bas-Canada*. Copyright registered 18 September 1866.

The proposed union of the Province of Canada, Nova Scotia, and New Brunswick to form the Dominion of Canada was a significant transformative event for the British North American provinces. Despite this political and constitutional reorganization, however, the registry contains only one contemporaneous legal treatise on the implications of Canadian Confederation, namely John Gooch's *Manual or Explanatory Development of the Act of the Union of Canada, Nova Scotia and New Brunswick in one Dominion under the name of Canada.*[16] However, the prospect of Canadian Confederation was celebrated in other genres of print material, especially in sheet music. The first copyright registrations for sheet music appeared in the 1850s as music publishing firms like Carey Brothers and A. & S. Nordheimer opened their establishments in Montreal and Toronto respectively.[17] Unlike the hymns, sacred songs, and canticles that were characteristic of French Canadian music publishing, the sheet music registered in the latter half of the century was composed mainly for English Canadians. Many of the songs evoked military and patriotic themes – for example, *The Canadian National Air* (1858)[18] and the *Grand Canadian Military March* (1867).[19] As Confederation neared, expressions of nationalistic pride increased, with songs like *For Canada and Right* (1866),[20] *Canadian National Anthem: God Bless our New Nation* (1867),[21] and *This Canada of Ours* (1867).[22]

The copyright records also capture the introduction of new technologies like photography that provided visual representations of the lives and experiences of provincial Canadians. Even though they had not been contemplated within the copyright statute, photographs were accepted for registration starting in 1859. Indeed, they became the

---

16  Gooch, *Manual or Explanatory Development.* Copyright registered by Gooch on 16 October 1867.

17  In total, there were twenty-eight registrations, which included sheet music, hymn books, and song books. For insights into early Canadian music publishing, see Calderisi, *Music Publishing in the Canadas.*

18  Printed and published by A. & S. Nordheimer, Toronto. Lyrics by Mrs William Mathews, music by Martin Lazare. The copyright was registered to William Mathews on 24 April 1858.

19  Composed by Edwin Gledhill and printed at the Christian Guardian Office in Toronto. Copyright registered by Gledhill on 2 February 1867.

20  Music by Frank Wodehouse Alexander, lyrics by Ogle R.G. Buchanan. Printed in Toronto by R.E. Buttand. Copyright registered 23 August 1866 by Alexander.

21  Copyright registered by Michael Byrne, HMS *Aurora*, Quebec, 15 August 1867.

22  Music by Elizabeth Harriet Ridout, lyrics by James David Edgar, printed, published, and registered by A. & S. Nordheimer, Toronto, 12 September 1867.

second-largest genre of protected works, supplanting prints, engravings and lithographs. Sixty-eight photographs were registered between 1859 and 1867, as professional photographers like Antoine Bazinet and William Notman from Montreal and the Livernois firm in Quebec City began to ply their trade. Antoine Bazinet was the most prolific copyright holder during this period, registering sixteen photographs between 1863 and 1867. The Livernois family, especially Elise Livernois, the widow of the founder, were also active, with ten registrations.[23] In contrast, the internationally renowned William Notman registered only three of his photographs.[24]

The registered photographs depicted scenes of provincial life, chronicled affairs of the day, or captured the images of prominent people, monuments, and buildings. The technology brought these incidents, sites, and individuals to life for provincial Canadians who were unlikely to experience them in person. Perhaps the most stirring example of the impact of photography as a visual record of current events was a series of five images registered by Antoine Bazinet that captured the immediate aftermath of a railway accident at Beloeil Bridge in 1864 in which ninety-nine people perished.[25]

Photography enabled visual artists to expand their audience and secure some protection over their paintings, since the law did not extend to artistic works like paintings or sculptures.[26] In 1864, artist Cornelius Krieghoff registered photographic representations of thirteen of his paintings. These depicted quintessentially provincial scenes, as in "Crossing in Canoe Quebec Winter," "Canadians in Sleigh," and "Old French Canadian Winter Costume," and the daily lives of Indigenous people, as in "Indian Hunter Winter" and "Indian Woman Summer."[27]

Portrait photography was also represented in the copyright registry. On 19 April 1865, Antoine Bazinet registered copyright in a photograph of John Wilkes Booth. Booth had assassinated American

---

23  On Jules-Isaïe Benoît *dit* Livernois (1830–1864), the founder of the firm, see his entry at DCB. See also Lessard, *Les Livernois photographes*. Elise Livernois (1827–1896) ran the business after his death and trained her sons and son-in-law, who succeeded her.

24  On William Notman (1826–1891), see his entry in DCB.

25  Antoine Bazinet, "Railway Accident Beloeil Bridge," 1–5. Five separate copyright registrations on 2 July 1864 in Bazinet's name. The photographs can be found at LAC Fonds Canadian Intellectual Property Office, negative C-003285. On Bazinet, see brief entry in Karel, *Dictionnaire des artistes*.

26  The Copyright Act of 1868 was the first to specifically refer to "artistical works."

27  Copyright registered in each photograph by Krieghoff on 28 April 1864.

president Abraham Lincoln five days before Bazinet secured his copyright. Booth, a stage actor, was a frequent visitor to Montreal and had performed at the city's Theatre Royal in the early 1860s. He returned in October 1864 for more nefarious purposes. During the American Civil War, Montreal had become a haven for American anti-abolitionists who opposed Lincoln's anti-slavery policies. It is believed that Booth met with some of these individuals to plot the assassination.[28] He also seems to have found the time to sit for his portrait at Bazinet's studio on the corner of rue St-Vincent and rue Notre Dame. Bazinet was an astute entrepreneur. He registered the photograph a few days after the Lincoln assassination, presumably because he recognized that the value of the photograph would increase and he wanted full control over its reproduction and dissemination.

Some significant events, like Royal visits, were commemorated in copyright clusters. From July to November 1860, the Prince of Wales toured British North America and the United States.[29] In anticipation of the visit, poet and lyricist Edouard Sempé and composer Charles Sabatier wrote a cantata in the prince's honour. On 26 June 1860, Sempé registered his copyright in what the index of copyright registrations recorded as a "Song in Honour of the Prince of Wales' Visit to Canada."[30] On 6 September 1860, William Notman registered a photograph of the prince during his stay in Montreal.[31] Finally, a book by Henry J. Morgan titled *The Tour of H.R.H. the Prince of Wales Through British America and the United States* was registered on 20 November 1860, not long after the prince's departure from North America.[32]

Compendia of local information, such as almanacs and directories, ranked high in numbers of registrations. There were fifty-seven registrations for works of this genre. Equally popular were books that provided statistical, demographic, geographic, political, and societal descriptions of the province, such as *Le Canada, ses institutions ressources, produits, manufactures* (1855)[33] and *Eighty Years Progress of British*

---

28   See, in this regard, Booth, *Right or Wrong*.
29   Albert Edward (1841–1910), eldest son of Queen Victoria. He succeeded her in 1901 (King Edward VII).
30   Sabatier and Sempé, *Cantata*; conductor, Charles Wugk Sabatier, music by C.W. Sabatier; words by W.E. Sempé. French title: *Cantate en l'honneur de Son Altesse royale le prince de Galles à l'occasion de son voyage au Canada.*
31   William Notman, "Photographic Picture of H.R. Highness the Prince of Wales and Suite Montreal." Copyright registered by Notman on 6 September 1860.
32   Morgan, *The Tour of H.R.H. the Prince of Wales.* Copyright registered by Morgan.
33   Langevin, *Le Canada.* Copyright registered by Langevin on 10 July 1855.

*North America* (1863).[34] These sorts of books, twelve of which were registered for copyright, were often written as informational guides for prospective immigrants. Notable among them was Catharine Parr Traill's *The Female Emigrant's Guide*, which provided insights about women's experiences of settler life.[35] The importance placed on this kind of demographic and statistical information is underscored by the actions of Stanislas Drapeau, the author and copyright holder in *Études sur les développements de la colonisation du Bas-Canada* (1863). He issued an open licence to provincial newspapers to reprint portions of his book to ensure the wide dissemination of its contents. The blanket licence appeared in the book after the copyright notice: "Avis à la Presse: Nonobstant l'enregistrement du droit de propriété littéraire chez le Régistrateur de la Province, les Editeur et Auteur de ce livre en permettent la reproduction libre dans les journaux du pays, pour le plus grand avantage de l'oeuvre qui s'y trouve concernée."[36]

This statement of permission suggests a level of sophistication among provincial copyright holders regarding third-party uses of their works and is reminiscent of today's Creative Commons licences.[37]

Useful books formed the bulk of copyright registrations in the Province of Canada, but by now works of literature such as novels, poetry, plays, memoirs, biographies, and travelogues were also beginning to appear in the registry. There were thirty-four entries in this category. English-language poetry that evoked provincial themes and sentiments was the most prevalent genre, with eleven registrations. The first to be registered was *Niagara Falls: A Poem in Three Cantos* by James K. Liston, who secured his copyright in 1843.[38] There was one anthology of poetry titled *Selections from Canadian Poets*, compiled by Edward Hartley Dewart in 1864 to "rescue from oblivion some of the floating pieces of Canadian authorship worthy of preservation in a more permanent form; and to direct the attention of my fellow-countrymen to the claims

---

34  Hind et al., *Eighty Years Progress*. Copyright was registered by Lovell on 26 May 1863.

35  Traill, *The Female Emigrant's Guide*. Traill was one of Canada's most celebrated early writers. See entry for Traill (1802–1899) in DCB and in CEWW.

36  Drapeau, *Études sur les développements*. [Notice to the Press: Notwithstanding the registration of copyright with the Provincial Registrar, the publisher and author of this book give permission to freely reproduce its contents in the newspapers in this country for the greater benefit of the work.]

37  A Creative Commons licence enables authors to set, up-front, the terms and conditions for making their works freely available online.

38  James K. Liston, *Niagara Falls: A Poem in Three Cantos* (Toronto: Guardian Office, 1843). Copyright registered by Liston on 23 May 1843.

of Canadian poetry."[39] Like many of his contemporaries in literary and policy circles, Dewart believed that a "national literature [was] an essential element in the formation of national character."[40] Registered French Canadian poetry was in the form of lyrics to songs that marked current events, an example being Edward Sempé's cantata for the Prince of Wales. Similarly, French poet and chansonnier Antoine Grosperrin registered his copyright in the lyrics of his song *Complainte du Condamné*, which marked the execution of convicted murderer John Meehan in Quebec City in 1864.[41]

Memoirs, biographies, and travel adventures were popular. Some were military reminiscences, while others recorded the lives and exploits of adventurers – or political exile, as in the case of Léandre Ducharme, whose *Journal d'un exilé politique aux terres australes* recounted his life in Australia after he was banished from Lower Canada for his participation in the rebellions.[42] In 1847, John Richardson registered *Eight Years in Canada* and its sequel *Guards in Canada or the Point of Honor*, which provided accounts of his life and military experiences.[43] John Henry Wilton, a British soldier stationed in Montreal, secured his copyright in 1848 in *Scenes in a Soldier's Life, a narrative of the principal events in Scinde, Bellochistan, and Afghanistan*.[44] In 1853, Okah Tubbee registered his copyright in his life story *A sketch of the life of Okah Tubbee, (called) William Chubbee, son of the head chief, Mosholeh Tubbee, of the Choctaw nation of Indians*, which was printed and published in Toronto.[45] Tubbee arrived in Toronto in the early 1850s and remained in the province for only a few years before returning to the United States. In 1861, Catherine Stahl registered copyright as proprietor in respect of her husband's autobiography, published posthumously in 1861.[46] Finally, printer and

---


39   Dewart, *Selections from Canadian poets*, preface. Copyright registered by Revd E.H. Dewart on 16 May 1864.

40   Dewart, *Selections from Canadian poets*, ix.

41   The song was included in *Éxécution de John Meehan*. Copyright registered by Grosperrin on 28 March 1864.

42   Ducharme, *Journal d'un exilé politique*. Copyright registered by Durcharme on 29 December 1845.

43   Richardson, *Eight Years in Canada*; Richardson, *The Guards in Canada*. Richardson registered his copyright in the books on 1 March 1847 and 24 December 1847 respectively.

44   Wilton, *Scenes in a Soldier's Life*. Copyright registered by Wilton on February 8, 1848.

45   Tubbee, *A sketch in the life*. Copyright registered by Tubbee on 24 October 1853.

46   Mayerhoffer, *Twelve years a Roman Catholic priest*. Copyright registered in the name of Mrs Mayerhoffer on 28 February 1861. The copyright was registered in the United States as well.

publisher L.M. Darveau registered copyright in 1862 in Louis Peltier's memoirs of his seafaring adventures.[47]

Biographies of politicians and other important public figures also figured in the registry. Charles Lindsey registered his biography of his father-in-law William Lyon Mackenzie in 1862, a year after the politician's death.[48] That same year, Henry J. Morgan registered his *Sketches of Celebrated Canadians, and persons connected with Canada, from the earliest period in the history of the province down to the present time*.[49] In 1865, William Notman registered *Portraits of British Americans with biographical sketches*, which consisted of the biographies and photographs of prominent provincial and imperial individuals.[50] French Canadian novelist and lawyer Philippe-Joseph Aubert de Gaspé wrote his memoirs in 1866, with copyright registered by his printers and publishers G. & E. Desbarats.[51] Additionally, De Gaspé's novel *Les Anciens Canadiens* and its English translation titled *Canadians of Old* were registered by the Desbarats firm in 1863 and 1865 respectively.[52]

The registry records two other works of French-language fiction, Pierre-Joseph-Olivier Chauveau's novel of manners *Charles Guérin*, registered in 1853 by the printer and publisher George Hyppolite Cherrier,[53] and Napoleon Bourassa's historical work *Jacques et Marie Souvenirs d'un peuple dispersé*, registered by the author in 1866.[54] English-language novels and other works of fiction accounted for five registrations and included William Kirby's *The U.E.: A Tale of Upper Canada* (1859).[55] Two plays were also registered: poet and playwright Charles Heavysege registered his copyright in his verse play *Count Filippo or the Unequal Marriage: A Drama in Five Acts* on 30 June 1860.[56] In 1865 a posthumous publication of French Canadian playwright Pierre Petitclair's

---

47  Peltier, *Voyage de Louis Peltier.* Copyright registered by Darveau on 15 November 1862.

48  Lindsey, *The life and times of Wm. Lyon Mackenzie.* See Lindsey's entry in DCB. Copyright registered by the author on 5 September 1862.

49  Morgan, *Sketches of Celebrated Canadians.* Copyright registered 18 January 1862.

50  Notman, *Portraits of British North Americans.* Copyright registered 13 May 1865.

51  De Gaspé, *Mémoires.*

52  De Gaspé, *Les Anciens Canadiens*; de Gaspé, *Canadians of Old.*

53  Chauveau, *Charles Guérin.* Copyright registered by Cherrier on 28 October 1853.

54  Bourassa, *Jacques et Marie.* Copyright registered by Bourassa on 9 October 1866.

55  Kirby, *The U.E.* Copyright registered by Kirby on 26 November 1859.

56  Charles Heavysege, *Count Filippo or the Unequal Marriage: A Drama in Five Acts* (Montreal: n.p, 1860). Heavysege's poem, *Jephthah's Daughter*, was registered a few years later, on 6 December 1864, by Dawson Brothers.

*Une Partie de Campagne: Comedie en deux actes* was registered by printer and publisher Joseph Savard.[57]

Henry J. Morgan's bibliographical work *Bibliotheca Canadensis or A manual of Canadian literature* was registered by Ottawa printer and publisher G.E. Desbarats within months of Confederation.[58] Morgan described his work as "a compendious record or history of Canadian Bibliography or Literature, from the time of the Conquest of Quebec down to the present year."[59] In compiling his bibliography, Morgan sought

> to render some slight aid to the nascent Literature of our native country, by exhibiting to the rising youth of the New Dominion the extent of our intellectual development as evinced in the literary efforts which have from time to time been made in the country, and which would serve as examples and an incentive to those in the same field.

He continued:

> There is just now, and has been for some years past, a perceptible movement on the part of the two great branches, French and English, which compose our New Nationality, and principally amongst the younger men, to aid the cause of Canadian Literature by their own contributions to the Literature.[60]

Morgan's work is an important example of the imperative to encapsulate the intellectual and creative achievements of provincial Canadians, at least those who fell within the "two great branches, French and English." These branches also dominated the copyright records. Those who were not white, male, and French Catholic or English Protestant were largely absent from the registry. Still, some diversity can be found.

The copyright index records the fact that on 9 April 1845, "Israel C.M. Lewis" registered *The Youth's Guard Against Crime*.[61] The author, a formerly enslaved African American, co-founded the Wilberforce Settlement for Black Americans near London, Canada West.[62] Okah Tubbee,

---

57   Petitclair, *Une Partie de Campagne*. Copyright registered by Savard on 9 December 1865.

58   Morgan, *Bibliotheca Canadensis*. Copyright registered 23 November 1867.

59   Morgan, *Bibliotheca Canadensis*, vii.

60   Morgan, *Bibliotheca Canadensis*, viii.

61   Lewis, *A Class Book*.

62   See Steward, *Twenty-Two Years a Slave*.

who registered copyright in his autobiography in 1853, identified himself as a member of the Choctaw tribe of the southern United States, although it appears he was African American.[63] Five members of the province's Jewish community also appear in the records, including Toronto music printers and publishers Abraham and Samuel Nordheimer. Jacob Meir Hirschfelder, lecturer in Hebrew at King's College in Toronto, registered his copyright in *A Key to German Conversation* in 1845.[64] Finally, three members of the prominent Hart family of Trois-Rivières and Montreal were copyright holders.[65] Constance Hannah Hatton Hart registered her copyright in *Household Recipes or Domestic Cookery* in 1865.[66] Her husband, Adolphus M. Hart, held copyright in *Practical Suggestions on Mining Rights and Privileges* in 1867,[67] and their nephew Moses O. Hart registered his book on the civil code of Lower Canada in 1866.[68]

Women wrote and published books and other print material in the province, but few registered their copyright. Even where copyright was secured, the right was generally held by their printers and publishers as in the case of Jennet Roy's schoolbook, for which copyright was registered by Thomas Campbell of Montreal.[69] The Act implicitly considered authorship a male preserve, in that the statute explicitly provided that the renewal of the copyright of deceased authors passed to the author's widow. Nevertheless, women were able to claim copyright in their own right, and some did.

Between 1841 and 1867, eleven women, including Constance Hart and Catharine Parr Traill, and one Catholic congregation, the Reverend Ladies of Notre Dame de Montreal, registered their copyright in

---

63  In his memoir, Tubbee claimed to be a member of the Choctaw tribe who had been kidnapped as a child and raised by an enslaved black woman in Mississippi. However, recent scholarship suggests that that he was an enslaved African American and he assumed the persona of an Indigenous person later in life. See Hudson, *Real Native Genius.*

64  Hirschfelder, *A Key to German Conversation.* Copyright was registered on 16 June 1845. Hirschfelder was of German-Jewish descent and later converted to Anglicanism. See Speisman, *The Jews of Toronto.*

65  See generally, Vaugeois, *Les premiers Juifs d'Amérique.*

66  Hart, *Household Recipes. In the tradition of the time, in addition to culinary recipes, the book included instructions for preparing hair oil, cough remedies, and varnish for violins.*

67  Hart, *Practical Suggestions on Mining Rights and Privileges.* Copyright registered on 13 May 1867.

68  Moses O. Hart's father Aaron was Adolphus's brother. See "Obituary Record," *Montreal Gazette,* 9 April 1918, 10.

69  Roy, *History of Canada.* Copyright registered by Campbell on 18 November 1858.

Women copyright holders in the Province of Canada as recorded in the index of copyright registrations, 1841–1867

| Registration Date | Copyright Holder | Title of Work |
| --- | --- | --- |
| 16 June 1845 | Mrs. Fleming | Exercises on the English Language |
| 24 January 1850 | L. Eliza McNally | Book of "Skeleton Maps" |
| 29 May 1850 | L. Eliza McNally | Key to "Skeleton Maps" |
| 27 April 1855 | Mrs. C.P. Traill | The Female Emigrant's Guide |
| 18 October 1856 | Mrs. J. C. Sheppard | Chants Canadiens |
| 13 March 1857 | Mrs Col. Savage | Watch the Prophecy of the Scripture |
| 2 November 1859 | Augusta Baldwyn | Poems |
| 28 February 1861 | Mrs. Mayerhoffer | Autobiography of Rev'd V.P. Mayerhoffer |
| 13 May 1865 | Rev. Ladies of Notre Dame de Montréal | Mois de Marie Desolée |
| 29 December 1865 | C. Hannah | Household Recipes or Domestic Cookery |
| 11 May 1866 | Mrs. J. B. Livernois | Galerie des Contemporains |
| 25 February 1867 | Margaret Robertson | Shenac's Work at Home |
| 13 April 1867 | H. Louisa Whitcomb | First Canadian Arithmetic |
| 26 April 1867 | Madame J. B. Livernois and Louis Bienvenu | Photographie du Mosaïque des Prêtres du Diocèse de Québec |

fourteen different works spanning a variety of genres from novels to photographs. Ten of the registrants were the authors or compilers of the material in which they claimed rights. The Reverend Ladies of Notre Dame de Montreal and Caroline Stahl (Mrs Mayerhoffer) held copyright as proprietors for books written by others.

The first woman to hold copyright as an author in British North America was Montreal schoolteacher Ann Cuthbert Rae Knight Fleming. She registered copyright in her schoolbook *Progressive Exercises on the English Language* in the Province of Canada on 16 June 1845.[70] Fleming was born in Scotland in 1788 and settled in Montreal around 1815. An accomplished poet, author and schoolteacher, she had previously obtained a British copyright for *A Year in Canada and other poems*, which

---

70   Fleming, *Progressive Exercises*. See Dufour, "Les premières enseignantes."

she registered at Stationers' Hall in 1816.[71] Fleming was also the first woman to write schoolbooks in the province and the only woman to have petitioned the Assembly for financial aid to print and publish a book, as will be discussed later in this chapter. In another first, the entrepreneurial Elise Livernois, who had taken over her husband's photography studio after his death, was the first woman to hold copyright in a photograph.[72] Catharine Parr Traill's *The Female Emigrant's Guide* was the first and only book she registered under provincial law. As a general rule, the prolific English Canadian author preferred to secure a British copyright in her books.[73]

For these women, claiming their copyright was a public affirmation of their identities as authors in an arena assumed to be male. They were asserting their legitimacy to claim legal rights and their agency over the conditions under which their books would be disseminated.[74] Nevertheless, they remained subject to gender distinctions regarding the ways in which they described themselves or were described by others in the public records.[75] Women were captive to the conventions of their time that tied their identities to their marital status, as the attributions in their books and the names recorded in the indices attest. Whether these authors were directly involved in the registration process or, more likely, were represented by male agents or relatives, the registry indexes frequently identified them by their married names with first name or initials omitted, as with Mrs Mayerhoffer. Similarly, Ann Cuthbert Fleming registered her copyright and identified herself in her books as Mrs Fleming. Madame J.B. Livernois was referred to by her husband's initials. Others, like Mrs Col. Savage, claimed their spouse's social status.[76] In contrast, Catharine Parr Traill and Josette Desbarats Sheppard used their own initials and were registered as Mrs C.P. Traill

---

71   Knight, *A Year in Canada*.

72   Copyright in "Galerie des Contemporains," 1866. Thereafter, she held the business in partnership with her son-in-law, Louis Bienvenu, and they registered the copyright jointly.

73   Traill's most famous work was *The Backwoods of Canada*. Copyright was secured in the UK by the Committee for the Promotion of Useful Knowledge, and the author received £110 for her rights. See Traill, *I bless you in my heart*.

74   On American women authors, see Homestead, *American Women Authors*. Copyright and married women's property rights are beyond the scope of this book.

75   On feminist book history, see Ozment, "Rationale for Feminist Bibliography." See as well Gerson, *Canadian Women in Print*.

76   Mary Ann Savage, spouse of John Morris Savage, who was a retired colonel with the British Royal Artillery. See her entry in CEWW.

and Mrs J.C. Sheppard respectively.[77] The unmarried women were registered under their full first and last names without a prefix: Augusta Baldwyn, Margaret Murray Robertson, and H. Louisa Whitcomb.[78] I have been unable to determine precisely who L. Eliza McNally, was but I am presuming that she too fell within this category.[79] Only Constance Hart appears to have eschewed convention, if one can assume that the index to the copyright registry accurately recorded her true intentions. Both the registry and the copyright notice in the cookbook identify her by her first initial and middle name, which suggests a desire for anonymity, since many would not have associated C. Hannah with Constance Hannah Hatton Hart or Mrs Aldolphus Hart. In addition, the attribution of authorship on the title page of the cookbook said only that it was written "by a Montreal lady."

*Copyright in Schoolbooks*

The centrality of schoolbooks in British North American constructions of copyright can be mapped in the province's registration data. Even though the take-up was still only a small proportion of overall schoolbook printing and publishing, the data suggest that the law was achieving its objective of encouraging greater domestic schoolbook production, especially in the case of French Canada. As a class, schoolbooks and other educational material accounted for roughly 22 per cent (124 out of 559 works) of all material registered from 1841 to 1867. If one excludes the registrations of maps, engravings, lithographs, photographs and uncategorized miscellany, the percentage of schoolbook registrations rises to 28 per cent (124 out of 433 registered books, pamphlets, printed sheets, music, directories, and almanacs). Of these 124 protected schoolbooks and related educational materials, there were thirty books of arithmetic and mathematics (including reckoners and book-keeping), thirteen geography and eleven history books, two books that combined history and geography, and thirteen science books (especially agriculture). In terms of language and literacy, there were thirteen spellers, primers, and readers, ten grammars, ten

---

77   Sheppard, *Chants Canadiens*. Printed by J. & O. Crémazie in 1856.

78   Biographies of Baldwyn and Robertson can be found in CEWW. In 1896, Whitcomb documented her early experiences as a teacher and was referred to as "Miss Whitcomb." See Hodgins, *Documentary History of Education in Upper Canada*, vol. 5, 276.

79   The copyright holder may have been the Irish-born schoolteacher Eliza Lucinda McNally, referred to in Smith, *Seen but Not Seen*. If this is indeed the case, McNally was unmarried at the time her books were published.

dedicated to writing and epistolary arts, and six in language studies (French, English, and German, including one English and German, one French and English and one book entirely in German). Finally, there were five books on pedagogy, five works on religion and morality, the latter being mostly on temperance, two law books, one on politics and government, one of music theory, one almanac, and one directory.

Schoolbook registrations were steady throughout the period under review with greater take-up for French-language schoolbooks than for English-language publications. These schoolbooks and other pedagogical material served the educational and sociocultural imperatives of the predominant ethnic and linguistic communities in the province. The data relating to copyright works in the French language are particularly revealing. Schoolbooks represented more than half of the entire portfolio of protected French-language publications. There were sixty-four schoolbook registrations (including one in both English and French, counted for each language) out of a total of 124 French-language registrations (including three in English and French, which were counted for each language).[80] In contrast, of the 309 English-language items protected by copyright (including three in English and French, which were counted once for each language), sixty titles were schoolbooks (including one in French and English). This represented only 19 per cent of the total English-language publications registered between 1841 and 1867. There was one schoolbook printed entirely in German.

Additionally, the number of French-language schoolbooks was slightly more than half of the total number of schoolbooks registered in the province. Sixty-four of the 124 schoolbooks were printed and published in French. This percentage was proportionately higher than the total French-Canadian population in Canada East, which stood at roughly 33 per cent in 1861.[81] It is difficult to draw any firm conclusions as to what caused this high proportion of French-language

---

80  Paul Aubin has noted that with the creation of Superintendent of Education in 1841 and a Council on Public Instruction in 1856, the printing of schoolbooks in Canada East climbed to an average of 73.5 books per year (from 3.6 books before 1840). See Aubin, *300 ans de manuels scolaires au Québec*.

81  In 1861 the population of Canada East was approximately 1,110,664, of whom 847,320 were French Canadian or roughly 75 per cent. Canada West had a population of 1,396,091, including Franco-Ontarians, who were not considered to be *Canadiens* from Lower Canada. Francophones in Canada West (Franco-Ontarians) were not considered in this analysis of French-language schoolbooks. In any case, during the period under review, no Franco-Ontarian author secured copyright in French in Canada West.

Schoolbooks by Genre and Language, 1841–1867

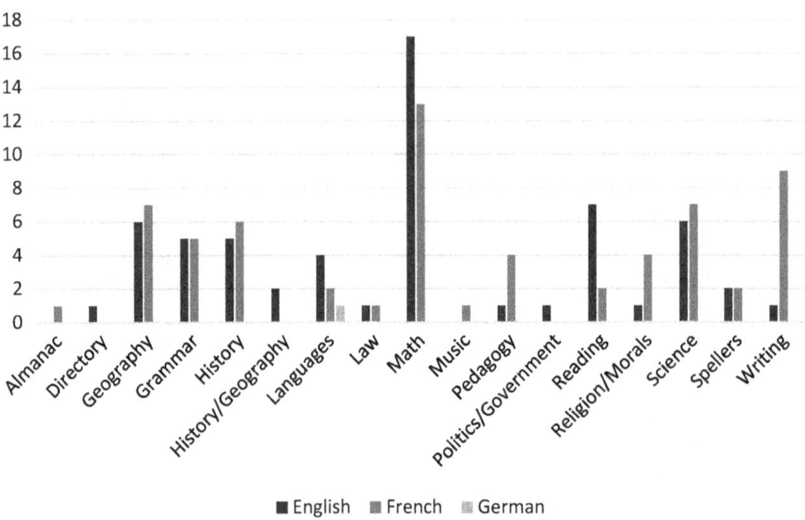


registrations, although it could be surmised that the number was indicative of the heightened importance of education and schoolbooks to a community that felt itself under threat. For French Canadians living in Canada East, survival as a distinct people within the province meant teaching future generations about the features and characteristics that distinguished them from English Canadians, on the one hand, and the British on the other. Indeed, French Canada's anxiety over its future can be discerned in the breakdown of the genres of protected schoolbooks.

Maintaining French literacy and language was a paramount concern. Copyright was registered in respect of twenty-four spellers, readers, writing and epistolary works, grammars, and material on French-language education. Only two of these books were intended to teach English to French Canadian children, one of which offered bilingual instruction on English and French pronunciation.[82] Similarly, farming and rural life were closely connected to community and a sense of belonging in French Canada. According to historian Peter Russell, "agriculture has been integral to the self-understanding of Quebec. It has been intimately tied to French Canada's sense of its own identity from

---

82   Meilleur, *Nouvelle grammaire anglaise*; Gouin, *A New System of French*.

the Conquest to the mid-twentieth century."[83] In light of this, it is not surprising that six of the seven schoolbooks on science concerned agricultural science.

The history of Canada meant something quite specific in the mid-nineteenth century – the term "Canadian" meant *Canadiens* of Lower Canada. French Canadian schoolchildren learned their history through books written within a broader political, religious, and sociocultural context. Book historian Leslie Howsam has explained that "history books are embedded within the book culture of the period when they are written and published."[84] The six copyright-protected schoolbooks were written, printed, and published in Canada East and described the histories of New France (1535 to 1763) and Lower Canada (1763–1840).[85] In content, they never ventured past the date of the union of the Canadas in 1840, conveying, symbolically at least, a sense that French Canadians lost their history after the dissolution of Lower Canada. For example, Michel Bibaud's two-volume history of Canada, *Histoire du Canada sous la Domination Française* and *Histoire du Canada et des Canadiens sous la Domination Anglaise*, covered New France and Lower Canada up to 1830, with a brief addendum chronicling the period of the rebellions up to 1837.[86] *Abrégé de l'histoire sainte, de l'histoire de France et de l'histoire du Canada*, by Les Frères de Écoles Chrétiennes, devoted the first 117 pages to the histories of France and New France and relegated to the remaining nine pages a discussion of the entire period of British rule from 1763 to the union of Lower Canada and Upper Canada.[87]

These schoolbooks also established the characteristics of those who could legitimately write French Canada's history. For example,

---

83  Russell, *How Agriculture Made Canada*, 36. See also Jarrell, *Educating the Neglected Majority*.

84  Howsam, *Past into Print*, 2.

85  The six history books consisted of four separate titles; two were issued in two volumes that were registered separately. For a critical analysis of exclusion and racism in early history books, see D'Almeida, "La présence des noirs au Québec." See also Larochelle, *L'école du racisme*.

86  The first volume was first issued in 1837 with copyright registered by Bibaud under the Lower Canadian Act: Michel Bibaud, *Histoire du Canada sur la Domination Française*. In 1844, Bibaud released and registered for copyright in the Province of Canada a revised edition of volume 1 and the first edition of volume 2: Michel Bibaud, *Histoire du Canada et des Canadiens sur la Domination Anglaise*. On Bibaud (1782–1857), see his entry in DCB.

87  Les Frères de Écoles Chrétiennes, *Abrégé de l'histoire sainte*. Copyright registered by the Frères de Écoles Chrétiennes on 25 April 1845.

Catholic priest Jean-Baptiste Antoine Ferland wrote a two-volume *Cours d'histoire du Canada*, focusing exclusively on French rule up to 1763. The books were published in 1861 and 1865, and copyright was registered by the printer and publisher Augustin Côté & Co.[88] In the preface, Ferland declared that as a "Canadien par la naissance et par le coeur, et catholique avant tout, nous avons étudié l'histoire du Canada et nous l'avons traité comme Canadien et comme catholique."[89] The same printer and publisher Augustin Côté & Cie conveyed similar sentiments directly to readers in its preface to François-Xavier Garneau's *Abrégé de l'Histoire du Canada depuis sa découverte jusqu'à 1840*.[90] It undertook to offer "des livres d'écoles *écrits* par des Canadiens, *au point de vue* canadien, *édités* et *imprimés* par des Canadiens."[91]

Despite the importance of the Catholic Church to French Canadian society, only two schoolbooks on religious themes were registered over the twenty-six years of recorded registration data. In contrast, there had been thirteen religious schoolbooks registered under the Lower Canadian Copyright Act. Nevertheless, copyright remained important for French-language religious texts in general. Religious works were the largest category of protected material in terms of total French-language copyright registrations. In addition to the two schoolbooks, there were twenty-one books and other materials on Catholicism and moral themes (temperance), and an additional seven musical works that consisted mainly of hymnals and books of sacred music.

English-language schoolbook registrations were slightly fewer than their French counterparts. These schoolbooks also represented a small proportion of the total number of protected English-language publications. English-language schoolbooks in the Province of Canada (including two bilingual books, English/French and English/German) represented 48 per cent of all registered schoolbooks and 19 per cent of

---

88   The two volumes were published in 1861 and 1865 by Augustin Côté & Cie, which held the copyright. According to the index of copyright registrations, the registration dates were 1861 and 1867, but the latter date does not correspond to the bibliographical data. A search in the actual volume (digital version) reveals a copyright registration notice dated 1865.

89   Ferland, *Cours d'histoire du Canada* vol. 1, xi. [As a *Canadien* by birth and in our heart, and above all a Catholic, we have studied the history of Canada and have addressed it as a *Canadien* and as a Catholic.]

90   Garneau, *Abrégé de l'Histoire du Canada*. Copyright registered by Côté & Cie on 28 November 1856.

91   Garneau, *Abrégé de l'Histoire du Canada*, iv. [Schoolbooks *written* by *Canadiens, from the point of view* of the *Canadiens, printed and published* by *Canadiens*.]

all protected English-language titles (60 out of 124 schoolbooks and 60 out of 308 total English-language works).[92]

Of the English-language schoolbooks, many, like Alexander Davidson's *The Canada Spelling Book*, exhibited a nationalist ethos characterized by unapologetic anti-American tropes or by proud proclamations of a distinct British North American identity. For instance, in the preface to his schoolbook on constitutional government, *The Every Boy's Book or Digest of the British Constitution*, John George Bridges explained that he had written the book "to counteract the dangerous tendency of those publications advocating republican institutions, with which the Provinces are inundated."[93] For his part, John George Hodgins wrote *Geography and History of British America and of the other colonies of the Empire* because "until a very recent period, the pupils in our public and private schools were left either to glean a scanty knowledge of their own and the sister Provinces through the often uncertain and inaccurate medium of an European geography; or to adopt the foreigner's unfriendly interpretation of our colonial institutions and laws."[94] There was some interest in introducing schoolchildren in Canada West to the history of French Canada. Jennet Roy wrote *History of Canada for the use of Schools and Families* upon discovering that there was no English-language history of French Canada. In her prefatory address to teachers, Roy explained that she "ventured to put forth this little work, pleading, as her excuse, the absolute necessity of providing such a source of information for British American Youth."[95] The book covered New France and Lower Canada up to the union. It was initially published in 1847 and was reissued in six subsequent editions, including the 1858 copyright version.

*Printers and Publishers*

Authors (including creators of works of visual arts) and non-printer proprietors held most of the copyright registrations in the Province of

---

92  There were seventeen books of arithmetics and mathematics, seven reading, six science, six geography, five history, five grammar, four language (one book in English and French counted for each language), two history and geography, two spellers, one writing, one law, one politics and government, one directory, one religious, one pedagogy.

93  Bridges, *The Every Boy's Book*, preface. Copyright registered by the author.

94  John George Hodgins, *Geography and History of British America*, preface. Copyright in the book was registered by the author.

95  Roy, *History of Canada*, Preface: "To Teachers."

Canada. Of the 559 registrations, 347 were registered in the names of authors (including editors, compilers, translators, engravers, lithographers, and photographers) or non-printer/publisher proprietors (usually relatives of the creators). Only 173 registrations were held by printers/publishers, including those who were also creators or compilers of publications (usually directories or almanacs). The status of thirty-nine registrants is unknown. The Lovell firm (Lovell & Gibson, and later John Lovell) of Montreal held the largest copyright portfolio by far. Toronto bookseller Henry Rowsell was the second most prolific but held roughly half the number of registrations of Lovell. According to Eric Leroux, there were 752 individuals involved in different aspects of the book trade in 1851; twenty years later, the sector had grown to more than 4,000.[96] Most continued to identify themselves primarily as printers rather than publishers, who would have been more inclined to claim some commercial stake in the work. The relative dearth of copyright registrations in the names of printers and publishers was consistent with this nature of the book trade throughout the period. Even during the period of accelerated growth in the industry, the number of registrations was disproportionately low. Between 1860 and 1867, printers and publishers registered only 105 works compared to 204 for authors (with 25 of unknown status). Regardless of the nature of the registrants, Canada East – especially Montreal – was the largest centre for printing and publishing in the province. There were 325 copyright works printed in Canada East, 195 in Canada West, 7 outside the province, and 32 location unknown. As Confederation neared, copyright registrations for works printed in Canada West slightly overtook registrations from Canada East.

English was the predominant language of the printed textual material (including maps and sheet music but excluding lithographs, engravings, and photographs) regardless of place of publication. French-language printing and publishing was done exclusively in Canada East, save for Philippe Aubert de Gaspé's *Mémoires*, which was printed and published in Ottawa by George-Édouard Desbarats, who had established an office there in 1864.[97]

Most of the printing done outside the province was handled in the United States, but there were some works printed in London and Paris as well. It will be recalled that eligibility for copyright was dependent

---

96   See Leroux, "Printers: From Shop to Industry," in HBC, vol. 2, 75.
97   De Gaspé, *Mémoires*. Copyright registered by Desbarats on 11 July 1866.

## Place of Printing and Publishing Canada East and Canada West

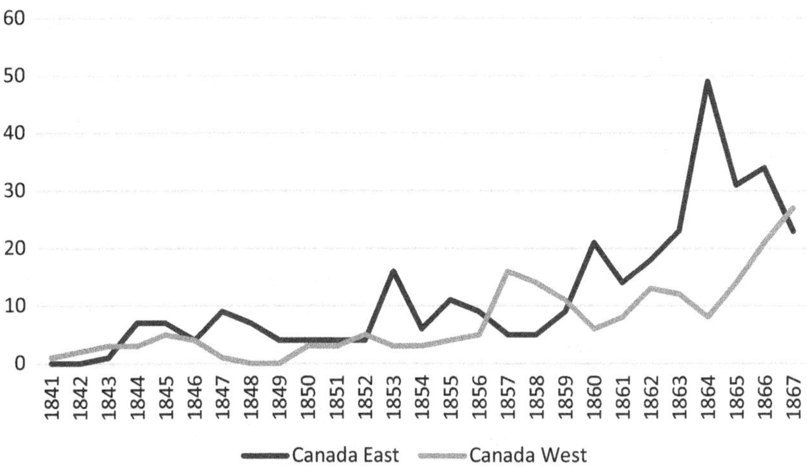



on the author's residence in the province rather than domestic printing and publishing (unless the author was a British subject residing in the United Kingdom). The registrar of copyright was strict in this regard. For example, as evidenced from the index to the copyright registry, on 15 August 1864, Dewey K. Warren registered copyright in *The Household Physician for the use of Families, Planters, Seamen and Travellers*, which was printed and published in the United States. The Montreal firm Dawson Brothers was Warren's agent in the copyright registration process. On 19 August, it received an inquiry from the provincial registrar William Kent as to Warren's place of residence. Upon learning that Warren lived in the United States, Kent rejected the application, returned the two deposited copies of the book, and reimbursed the registration fees.[98]

Despite the growth in the provincial population and an educated readership, book production remained a challenging endeavour for printers and publishers, and the industry's plight was often described

---

98  Provincial Registrar William Kent to Dawson Brothers, 16 August 1864, 19 August 1864, and 4 October 1864, in LAC, *Provincial Secretary Letter Books: 1857–1864*, vol. 3, 373, 375, 382. *The Household Physician* was written by Ira Warren, Dewey Warren's uncle. This example also illustrates the inaccuracy of the copyright registration index since the entry in the copyright index was never expunged. Because this title remained in the books, it is included in the registration data.

in the books themselves. For example, in the publisher's preface to Pierre-Joseph-Olivier Chauveau's novel *Charles Guérin*, George Hyppolite Cherrier referred to his "act of courage" in assuming all the publishing risks in support of French Canadian literature:

> Les choses n'en sont pas encore rendues au point que nos auteurs puissent faire exclusivement leur métier d'auteur... Dans l'état actuel des choses, nous croyons donc avoir fait un acte de courage et de bon exemple, en achetant les premiers une oeuvre littéraire, en offrant à un de nos écrivains une remunération assurée, si mince qu'elle soit, pour son travail, en lui épargnant les risques et les ennuis de la publication... Nous avons par la assuré à notre littérature naissante un des premiers, sinon le premier roman de mœurs canadiennes, qui ait paru jusqu'à présent.[99]

In his introductory remarks to *A history of Canada and the other British provinces in North America*, its author J. George Hodgins praised his printer and publisher John Lovell for his "patriotic purpose of keeping within the country large sums of money to promote its own industry, which were sent, year after year, to the United States and England, to pay the artisan and publisher in those countries for books which were in use among us, and which were either ill adapted to our peculiar circumstances or inimical to our institutions."[100]

Actions taken in the United States and the United Kingdom loomed large for the English-language book trade in the province. In at least one instance, the geopolitics of copyright justified a very public act of rebellion. In 1856, Montreal printer and publisher Edmund Pickup reprinted without permission American author Harriet Beecher Stowe's anti-slavery novel *Dred*.[101] Stowe's London publishers Sampson Low & Co. held the British copyright and offered to settle the matter if Pickup paid a royalty for the permission to print. Instead, Pickup printed his correspondence with the publishers in *The Gazette* (Montreal) and *The*

---

99   Chauveau, *Charles Guérin*, v. Copyright registered by Cherrier on 28 October 1853. [Things have not yet reached the stage where authors can devote themselves exclusively to their writing. Because of this state of things, we think we have acted with courage and are leading by example by being the first to buy a literary work and providing guaranteed remuneration, albeit meagre, to one of our authors for his work and saving him the risks and burdens of publishing. We have therefore secured to our nascent literature one of the first, if not the first *Canadien* novel of manners to have been produced thus far.]

100   Hodgins, *A History of Canada*. Copyright registered by Lovell 30 July 1866.

101   Stowe, *Dred*.

*Globe* (Toronto) and advised his friends and allies that he "declined all compromise ... and will stand or fall on the real merits of the case."[102] Pickup drew a distinction between the British copyright of a British author and the British copyright of an American author. Sampson Low & Co. were merely the "British assignees of an American authoress, with interests antagonistic to the advocates of international copyright." Pickup considered that his refusal to settle the claim was justified, and he was "quite satisfied to leave the question before the tribunal of public opinion." It appears that Pickup was able to rely on the tribunal of public opinion to avoid a trial.[103]

### To Foster Native Talent: The Provincial Assembly, Printing Petitions, and Tariffs on Imported Schoolbooks

The copyright registrations provide a rich and highly illuminating profile of the province through the intermediary of its book and print culture. Read in conjunction with the actions of the Assembly, a more precise picture emerges of the ways in which both law and policy contributed to the advancement of learning, the development of national cultural identity and the encouragement of the provincial book trade. Sixty-nine petitioners sought some form of legislative assistance in respect of ninety-one separate books and other print materials (some petitioned for different works at different periods in time, some works were individual volumes of multivolume works). Copyright and legislative aid were not mutually exclusive; the Assembly supported twenty-one of thirty-four requests involving registered works.[104] Petitions from authors formed the bulk of the requests to the legislature. However, for

---

102  "The Copyright of 'Dred' and Mr. Pickup," *The Globe*, 10 November 1856, 2. Reprinted from the *Gazette* (Montreal). All Pickup quotations are from this article.

103  Editorials in local newspapers expressed support for Pickup and framed the copyright dispute as raising the much larger question of the extent to which provincial Canadians should be forced to adhere to British laws. The *Quebec Gazette* of 8 October 1856 provided a detailed explanation of the claim and argued that Pickup's actions were lawful. The editorial concluded that "the public will support Mr. Pickup in his spirited attempt to ascertain what our rights as Canadians are." An editorial in the *Montreal Herald and Daily Commercial Gazette* for 20 October 1856 suggested that Pickup had a lot of public sympathy. I could find no subsequent discussion of the case in the press. However, Pickup continued to advertise the sale of his Montreal edition as late as December 1856. There is also no reported judicial decision involving the parties so it is unclear if and how the dispute was resolved.

104  This number includes Doucet's *Fundamental principles of the laws of Canada*, which was registered in 1840 in Lower Canada.

the first time on record in British North America, printers and publishers petitioned in respect of books authored by others. The only other petition by a printer and publisher was made in Upper Canada in 1839 when the Toronto firm of Charles Fothergill & Co. asked the legislature for financial support for an almanac it had compiled. Finally, consistent with the principle adopted by the legislatures of Nova Scotia and the former Lower Canada, the Assembly would not generally entertain petitions for works not already in print. In rejecting Walter Crofton's petition for his parliamentary manual in 1854, the committee reviewing his request affirmed that it would not "recommend appropriations on behalf of works which are not already in print, unless special reasons exist to the contrary."[105] The legislature supported commendable works by subscribing for copies instead of subsidizing the printing costs.

*Schoolbook Petitions*

Eight schoolbook petitions were presented to the legislature between 1841 and 1858. Only three were successful. The others were either ignored after their introduction or stalled after being referred to a parliamentary committee for consideration. This pattern was consistent with the data from Lower Canada and Nova Scotia, where schoolbook petitions were generally rejected after the introduction of copyright legislation. The first petition was Ann Cuthbert Knight Fleming's, introduced in the parliamentary session of 1844–5. The petition for an aid to permit her to "publish certain Elementary works on the English language" was read on 9 January 1845 but did not proceed any further.[106] We do know, however, that *Progressive Exercises on the English Language* was printed and published and that Fleming registered her copyright on 16 June 1845. In that same legislative session, E.L. Hayden of William Henry (Sorel, Quebec) asked for funds to stereotype his book on English grammar. He also sought to be "remunerated for his labour ... and for his copyright."[107] The intention here was for the province to purchase the copyright and with it, the right to print, publish, and reprint the work. The petition met with the same fate as Fleming's, but there is no record of Hayden's schoolbook having been printed or published. In 1855 and again in 1856, French Canadian historian Michel Bibaud submitted petitions "to enable him to publish the continuation of his work on the History of Canada."[108]

---

105  Journals of the Legislative Assembly of the Province of Canada, 1854, 18 Vict., 473.
106  Journals of the Legislative Assembly of the Province of Canada, 1844–1845, 8 Vict., 100.
107  Journals of the Legislative Assembly of the Province of Canada, 1844–1845, 8 Vict., 52.
108  Journals of the Legislative Assembly of the Province of Canada, 1855, 18 Vict. Part II, 705, and 1856, 19 Vict., 24.

These petitions never proceeded beyond their introduction. Bibaud's existing works, *Histoire du Canada sur la Domination Française* and *Histoire du Canada et des Canadiens sur la Domination Anglaise* had already been published, and copyright was secured by the author. Bibaud never continued his oeuvre; his health declined, and he died in 1857.

The five schoolbook petitions that proceeded beyond their introduction related to materials on agriculture and botany. In 1847, an instruction was given by the legislature to the Standing Committee of Contingencies to "consider the propriety of purchasing 200 copies" of *The Canadian Agricultural Reader*, but the matter seems to have ended there.[109] The book had been printed, published, and registered for copyright by John Simpson & Co. the year before.[110] In 1849, printer and publisher William Ruthven successfully petitioned for funds for an English translation of Napoleon Aubin's *Chimie Agricole*.[111] In the 1852–3 session, printer and publisher Stanislas Drapeau appealed to the legislature for support for *Le Cultivateur, ou Traité Élémentaire sur l'Agriculture Pratique, destiné à l'usage des Écoles dans le Bas-Canada*. The petition was referred to the Joint Committee of the Library and received a favourable response. However, no specific financial commitment appears to have been made, and there is no evidence that this work was ever published.[112] In 1852, French agronomist Frédéric Ossaye submitted a petition for "aid to enable him to publish a Work relating to Agriculture."[113] The teacher of agricultural science sought public support for *Les veillées canadiennes*, which the Superintendent of Education for Canada East, Jean-Baptiste Meilleur, had recommended both as a book on agricultural practices and as a reading primer for elementary schoolchildren.[114] The Assembly subscribed for the purchase of 250 copies.[115] The work was printed and published by Augustin Côté in 1852, and

---

109　Journals of the Legislative Assembly of the Province of Canada, 1847, 10 Vict., 212.

110　*The Canadian agricultural reader.* "By a Vice-President of the Niagara District Agricultural Society … published for the proprietors."

111　Journals of the Legislative Assembly of the Province of Canada, 1849, 13 Vict., 307. The legislature agreed to subscribe for two hundred copies.

112　Journals of the Legislative Assembly of the Province of Canada, 1852–1853, 16 Vict., pt. 1, 715, and pt 2, 1084.

113　Journals of the Legislative Assembly of the Province of Canada, 1852–1853, 16 Vict., pt. 1, 714.

114　Ossaye, *Les veillées canadiennes.* Meilleur's endorsement can be found after the title page of the book. The book was also endorsed by the Agricultural Society of Lower Canada. François-Marie-Frédéric Ossaye was the director of the first experimental farm in the province.

115　Journals of the Legislative Assembly of the Province of Canada, 1852–1853, 16 Vict., pt. 2, 1078.

Ossaye registered his copyright in 1853. Finally, in 1859, the Assembly subscribed for 300 copies of Reverend L. Provancher's schoolbook *Traité élémentaire de botanique à l'usage des maisons d'éducation* to enable the author to sell the book at a reasonable price.[116]

*With a View to Fostering Native Talent / Avec le désir de protéger le talent national*

The catastrophic fire that decimated the Parliamentary Library in 1849 led to a redoubling of efforts to rebuild the collection after 1850. To facilitate this work, the Legislative Assembly and the Legislative Council established a Joint Committee for the Direction of the Library of Parliament to oversee the purchase and donations of books and other material.[117] Most of the book and printing petitions presented to the legislature after 1850 were referred to this committee, and many of the allocations made by the legislature were directed to the purchase of books for the library. The collection was also enhanced through the mandatory library deposit under the 1841 Copyright Act, but as we have already seen, compliance rates were low. The year 1850 also marked provincial acquiescence to British demands to impose duties on foreign reprints. As discussed in the previous chapter, the outrage at British and American actions provoked a nationalist response, one that can also be discerned from the joint committee's review of book petitions. Indeed, during the 1852–3 parliamentary session, the joint committee made its operating principles clear: allocations of public funds were to be made with a view to fostering "native talent, when directed to matters of historical research, or practical utility."[118] The Assembly went to great lengths to encourage useful works that were "of public interest," "of commendable character," and "deserving of encouragement" or of "special excellence and utility."

The aim of fostering native talent was both an inward- and outward-looking exercise. The joint committee, and by extension the legislature, supported internal interests when it granted petitions to rebuild the Parliamentary Library collection and to encourage provincial authors to write useful books for a domestic audience. However, the

---

116  Journals of the Legislative Assembly of the Province of Canada, 1859, 22 Vict., 526; Provancher, *Traité élémentaire de botanique*. Copyright was not registered.

117  Journals of the Legislative Assembly of the Province of Canada, 1850, 13 Vict., 50, 58.

118  Journals of the Legislative Assembly of the Province of Canada, 1852–1853, 16 Vict., pt. 2, 1078.

legislature also looked beyond provincial borders by recognizing its critical role in showcasing native talent to the outside world. The joint committee proudly championed works that were firsts of their kind. Reverend L. Provancher's schoolbook on Canadian botany was worthy of an allocation from public funds because it was "the first attempt to depict the floral products of our woods and fields."[119] In 1866, the joint committee supported what it described as the "first Treatise upon Medical Science that has been written by a native Upper Canadian" by recommending the purchase of 50 copies of Dr William Canniff's book *A Manual of the Principles of Surgery*, which was printed and published in the United States with copyright secured there.[120] In the same session, Alpheus Todd was lauded for having produced a book of "great utility to all Statesmen and politicians throughout the British Empire: and they deem it a matter of congratulation to Canada that the first practical treatise that has ever appeared on Parliamentary Government should emanate from this Province."[121] The sense of satisfaction at being the first jurisdiction in the British Empire to produce such a book is palpably evident.

The legislature also offered small awards for works of poetry and literary anthologies, these being emblematic of an emergent Canadian literature. As Henry Morgan wrote in *Bibliotheca Canadensis*, "no nation can be considered truly great which does not possess some literary power and excellence."[122] In 1863, the joint committee recommended the purchase of twelve copies of each of Charles Sangster's two volumes of poetry, *The St-Lawrence and the Saguenay* and *Hesperus and Other Poems*.[123] Sangster was regarded as one of the most significant pre-Confederation poets, and his work was the first to explore Canadian themes. In similar vein, in 1866 a recommendation for the subscription of fifty copies of Leon-Pamphile Le May's *Essais Poétiques* was made on the basis that the book was a "very commendable contribution to the literature of Lower

---

119   Journals of the Legislative Assembly of the Province of Canada, 1859, 22 Vict., 526.
120   Journals of the Legislative Assembly of the Province of Canada, 1866, 29 Vict., 213. Canniff, *A Manual of the Principles of Surgery*. The book was registered for copyright by the publishers in the United States.
121   Alpheus Todd, *On Parliamentary Government in England*.
122   Morgan, *Bibliotheca Canadensis*, "Introductory Remarks."
123   Journals of the Legislative Assembly of the Province of Canada, 1863, 26 Vict., 125. Sangster, *The St-Lawrence and the Saguenay*; Sangster, *Hesperus and Other Poems*. The books have copyright notices after the title pages but are not listed in the index of copyright registrations. On Sangster (1822–1893), see his entry in DCB.

Canada."[124] Finally, copies of James Huston's *Le répertoire national, ou Recueil de littérature canadienne* were purchased "as an encouragement to the Author for his commendable design of collecting, in a shape for preservation, the fugitive literature of Eastern Canada."[125]

Works of historical interest were especially prized, and many received generous grants from the legislature, especially for works issued in multiple volumes. Narratives of the War of 1812 elicited legislative encouragement, at least in the early years of the new provincial Parliament. In 1842, John Richardson was awarded £250 to "encourage the publication of the 'War of 1812.'"[126] His ambition was to produce three volumes, but at the time of the petition, he had only completed the first instalment, and he never finished the remaining two. Richardson registered his copyright in the existing publication on 12 October 1842, the same day the legislature approved his grant. In contrast, William Coffin did not receive similar favourable consideration when, in 1865, he asked the legislature to subscribe for copies of his book *1812: The War and Its Morals – A Canadian Chronicle*, which he had registered for copyright the year before.[127]

Treatises on the history of Lower Canada also garnered legislative interest. In 1849, F.X. Garneau was awarded £250 to assist him with his three-volume treatise *Histoire du Canada depuis sa découverte jusqu'à nos jours*.[128] During the 1852–3 session, the joint committee recommended the purchase of thirty copies of the second edition of Garneau's book. Garneau petitioned again in 1859, and a subscription for 150 copies of the third edition was approved on the basis that the author had been unable to print and publish the previous editions without legislative assistance.[129] In an analogous example, in 1849, the Assembly purchased

---

124  Journals of the Legislative Assembly of the Province of Canada, 1866, 29 Vict., 251; Le May, *Essais Poétiques*.

125  Journals of the Legislative Assembly of the Province of Canada, 1851, 15 Vict., 249; Huston, *Le répertoire national*.

126  Journals of the Legislative Assembly of the Province of Canada, 1842, 6 Vict., 126.

127  William Coffin, *1812: The War and Its Morals*. See Journals of the Legislative Assembly of the Province of Canada, 1865, 28 Vict., 119. The petition never proceeded beyond its introduction.

128  François-Xavier Garneau, *Histoire du Canada depuis sa découverte jusqu'à nos jours*. See Journals of the Legislative Assembly of the Province of Canada, 1849, 13 Vict., 342. Garneau did not register copyright in this work, which was printed and published in Quebec by N. Aubin. However, his schoolbook, *Abrégé de l'histoire du Canada*, was registered by the printer and publisher A. Côté in 1856.

129  Journals of the Legislative Assembly of the Province of Canada, 1859, 22 Vict., 937.

150 copies of the first volume of Robert Christie's *A History of the Late Province of Lower Canada*, which was printed and published in six volumes from 1848 to 1855.[130] In 1851, additional copies of volumes 1 to 4 were subscribed for along with 150 copies of the *Supplementary volume to the History of the Late Province of Lower Canada*.[131] When Christie returned in 1854 claiming losses in respect of the supplementary volume, the joint committee set aside £250 for the purchase of 1,000 copies.[132] Charles Roger was not as fortunate. He was rebuffed three times in respect of his proposed two-volume *The Rise of Canada from Barbarism to Wealth and Civilization*.[133] The first volume was printed and published in 1856, and copyright was registered by the printer and publisher.[134] Roger never completed the second volume.

Some historical subject-matter was more controversial than others. In 1846, a select committee recommended a subscription of twenty-five copies of Alfred Hawkins's plan of the military and naval operations in Quebec City in 1759. The map was printed in the United Kingdom in 1841 and Hawkins registered his copyright in the Province of Canada in 1842.[135] The journals of the Assembly described the work as "illustrative of that interesting portion of history, so memorable in the progress of the British Arms, and characterised by the death in the moment of victory of the illustrious Wolfe."[136] For the French Canadian members of the legislature, however, it was a painful reminder of the defeat of the French forces and the surrender of New France to the British. Not surprisingly, the journals record that the members of the Assembly were divided on the purchase.

The Assembly recognized that book production costs remained a disincentive to the circulation of works of native talent. At times, the

---

130  Journals of the Legislative Assembly of the Province of Canada, 1849, 13 Vict., 307.

131  Journals of the Legislative Assembly of the Province of Canada, 1851, 15 Vict., 294, 1077–8; Christie, *Interesting Public Documents*.

132  Journals of the Legislative Assembly of the Province of Canada, 1854, 18 Vict., 474.

133  Journals of the Legislative Assembly of the Province of Canada, 1857, 21 Vict., 64; Journals of the Legislative Assembly of the Province of Canada, 1858, 22 Vict., 938. In considering Roger's third petition, the Joint Committee of the Library concluded that since his application in respect of volume 1 "was not favorably entertained," there was no reason to change course in relation to the subsequent volume; Journals of the Legislative Assembly of the Province of Canada, 1864, 27 Vict. 392.

134  Roger, *The Rise of Canada*. Copyright registered 6 March 1856.

135  Hawkins, *Plan of the military & naval operations*. Copyright registered 13 October 1842.

136  Journals of the Legislative Assembly of the Province of Canada, 1846, 9 Vict., 336. Hawkins first petitioned in 1845 for the patronage of the legislature in support of his map. It was referred to a committee but nothing more was decided during that session.

legislature increased its original contribution when petitioners came forward to explain that the original grant was insufficient. For example, in 1851, 100 copies of the fourth volume of James Huston's *Le répertoire national, ou Recueil de littérature canadienne*, were purchased because of the work's "historical value and intrinsic merits."[137] Huston came forward the following year to explain that the allocation was not sufficient and that he had suffered considerable losses. The joint committee awarded him an additional £50 to "carry out their original intentions of assisting him in his literary labors" after "having satisfied themselves by a certificate from the printer of the book, that Mr. Huston could derive no benefit from their vote of last year, but [would] actually sustain considerable pecuniary loss."[138] In the case of author W.H. Smith, copyright and a subscription for copies from the legislature were insufficient to cover the printing and publishing costs of *Canada: Past, Present and Future*, a book that provided statistical and demographic information about the province. In 1851, the legislature had purchased copies to the value of £50; Smith had secured his copyright that same year.[139] Smith returned to the Assembly in the 1852–3 session advising that the allocation had been "absorbed into cost of publication, and that ... the Author had received little or no pecuniary benefit from his literary labors."[140] The joint committee agreed to an additional subscription for £50 on the basis that the work was "one of public interest, and of commendable character, and ... that its circulation in Europe might prove beneficial in disseminating accurate and interesting information to intending Emigrants."[141]

Deputy Surveyor General Joseph Bouchette Jr, the son of the late Lower Canadian Surveyor General Joseph Bouchette, suffered similar financial misfortunes as his father in printing and publishing his maps. His *Map of the Provinces of Canada, New Brunswick, Nova Scotia, Newfoundland and Prince Edward Island* was printed in the United States at

---

137   Journals of the Legislative Assembly of the Province of Canada, 1850, 14 Vict., 275. The book was published in four volumes from 1848 to 1850 by Lovell & Gibson, Montreal. Copyright was not registered.
138   Journals of the Legislative Assembly of the Province of Canada, 1851, 15 Vict., 294.
139   Journals of the Legislative Assembly of the Province of Canada, 1851, 15 Vict., 293. Smith, *Canada; Past, Present and Future*.
140   Journals of the Legislative Assembly of the Province of Canada, 1852–1853, 16–17 Vict., 714.
141   Journals of the Legislative Assembly of the Province of Canada, 1852–1853, 16–17 Vict., 714–15.

great expense. Bouchette, who had registered both a provincial and an American copyright in 1846, turned to the legislature for "an aid to enable him to sustain the heavy expenses incurred in [its] compilation."[142] The Assembly agreed to purchase twenty-five copies in 1847. Bouchette returned to the Assembly in 1851 to appeal for more financial help because the copper plates of the map, which were pledged to the engraver, were "in danger of being sacrificed and passing into foreign hands."[143] He received no response to this request, perhaps because the Assembly judged that it had already contributed its share to the endeavour.

Requests for aid from printers and publishers were met with some solicitude, but the actual results were mixed. In 1860, John Lovell came before the legislature proposing to publish a four-volume English translation of the *Relations des Jésuites*, a compilation of the correspondence sent by the Jesuit missionaries in New France to the French authorities between 1632 and 1672. Augustin Côté had printed and published the original French-language work two years before.[144] The joint committee reviewed passages from the English translation and concluded that "the general interest evinced by the English portion of the community in this curious and entertaining work, replete with interest to the student of early Canadian history, has induced the Committee to recommend a large subscription to this edition."[145] The recommendation was for the purchase of 572 copies of the work, but Lovell spent months waiting in vain for the funds to be disbursed and eventually abandoned the project.[146]

In 1849, Quebec City printer and publisher William Ruthven successfully obtained Assembly support to produce an English translation of Napoleon Aubin's schoolbook on agricultural chemistry. He had printed and published the original French text *Chimie Agricole* in 1847 and secured its copyright.[147] However, Ruthven's fortunes changed when he returned to the Assembly a few years later requesting financial aid to distribute the work. Asking for public funds to support the public circulation and sale of a book was a novel request, and it was rejected. The Assembly had already supported this publication through the purchase of copies, and it was thought inadvisable "to encourage

---

142   Journals of the Legislative Assembly of the Province of Canada, 1847, 11 Vict., 214.
143   Journals of the Legislative Assembly of the Province of Canada, 1851, 15 Vict., 78.
144   Bois, *Relations des Jésuites*.
145   Journals of the Legislative Assembly of the Province of Canada, 1860, 23 Vict., 350.
146   Charland, "À qui devons-nous."
147   Aubin, *La chimie agricole*.

indiscriminate applications of this nature or to make appropriations on [behalf of the public] unless in the case of works of special excellence and utility."[148] However, the petition underscores the fact that the publishing pathway from typesetting to sales was financially onerous even where, as in this case, the publishers held the copyright in the original French edition.

*Provincial Tariffs on Imported Books*

The rule that the legislature would only subscribe for copies of an existing publication may have been sound policy from a public accountability perspective, but, as evidenced from the petitions, reliance on copyright alone was insufficient to address the challenges associated with book production. Many publications were simply not commercially viable on the strength of copyright and sales alone, even with the guarantee of purchases by the legislature. The province's objective of showcasing native talent to the world could not be achieved without a viable printing and publishing industry. In the late 1850s, the provincial Parliament turned to tariffs as the policy lever to support the domestic book trade.

As explored in the previous chapter, imperial duties on British books imported directly from the United Kingdom were abolished in 1846. The only imperial importation duties that remained were those on foreign books (7%) and on unauthorized foreign reprints of British books, which were taxed at 12.5 per cent *ad valorem*.[149] The Province of Canada had imposed an import duty of its own but had eliminated its levies on books, periodicals, and pamphlets in 1849.[150] The tide turned a decade later, when a convergence of fiscal necessity and a more protectionist legislature revived the use of tariffs in the province. In 1859 a provincial duty of 10 per cent a*d valorem* was imposed on printed books "not being reprints of British copyrights nor Blank Account or Copy Books or Books to be written or drawn upon."[151] The tariff applied to all imported books, including British books, with the exception of foreign reprints of British copyright

---

148  Journals of the Legislative Assembly of the Province of Canada, 1852–1853, 16–17 Vict., 714. There appears to be no bibliographical record of an English translation even though the petition suggests that the book was in print.

149  *An Act for repealing and consolidating the present Duties of Customs in this Province,* 1847, 10 & 11 Vict., c. 31.

150  *An Act to Amend the Law relative to Duties of Customs,* 1849, 12 Vict., c. 1.

151  *An Act to Amend the Act relating to Duties of Customs,* 1859, 22 Vict., c. 2.

works, which were subject to a higher statutory duty.[152] The use of tariffs on British books appears to have been partly designed to achieve indirectly what could not be achieved directly, given the failure of the 1847 copyright amendment to satisfy imperial expectations regarding foreign reprints. The provincial tariff raised the cost of British imports, making them even more unaffordable to the average provincial reader. The chill on the market might have provided greater incentives for British authors to engage directly with the local book trade. However, the question of tariffs on books was contentious. Most members of the Assembly objected to the measure as a tax on knowledge.[153] George Brown, the founder of *The Globe* newspaper and a member of the legislature, "thought that there should be no duty upon books at all, because they strived to address the educational interests of the country."[154] His Assembly colleague, John Lorn MacDougall, noted that " the revenues to be derived from a duty on books would be very small indeed, and the duty would only have the effect of preventing the diffusion of knowledge."[155] When Thomas D'Arcy McGee expressed his concern that the measure would harm provincial importers and booksellers, Finance Minister Alexander Galt, who had initiated the tariff, reportedly countered with the view that "there was another establishment in the country… that of [printer and publisher] Mr. Lovell … who told him that the absence of a duty on books did him a great deal of injury."[156] Sydney Robert Bellingham from Canada East concurred because "he knew from experience that many of our best printers had been forced to give up their business for want of employment. We ought by all means assist and encourage our own establishments, and if these could not compare with those of the States, he believed, at any rate, that Mr Lovell's establishment was competent enough, considering the general state of the country."[157]

---

152  *An Act to Amend the Act relating to Duties of Customs*, 1859, 22 Vict., c. 2, section 2.

153  "House of Assembly: Executions against Homesteads Destitution," *The Globe*, 19 March 1859, 2: under "The Tariff"; George Brown, "The Tax on Books," *The Globe*, 8 March 1859, 2. This editorial, presumably written by Brown, referred to the "the hostility of the Government to the diffusion of knowledge among the people."

154  See entry for George Brown (1818–1880) in DCB. On Brown's parliamentary career see J.M.S. Careless, *Brown of the Globe*.

155  "House of Assembly: Executions against Homesteads Destitution," *The Globe*, 19 March 1859, 2.

156  "House of Assembly: Executions against Homesteads Destitution," *The Globe*, 19 March 1859, 2. See also John Lovell's letter to the editor of the *Gazette* (Montreal), 3 September 1858, reproduced in *Canadian Manufactures*.

157  "House of Assembly: Executions against Homesteads Destitution," *The Globe*, 19 March 1859, 2.

The Assembly debates make it clear that the tariff was levied in support of domestic printing and publishing. The tariff would have made business circumstances more difficult for provincial importers and booksellers, but it would also have strengthened the position of the precarious and underdeveloped printing and publishing industry. The levy was also imposed as a reciprocal measure since the United States taxed imports of books printed in Canada. Robert Harwood, the elected representative from Vaudreuil, suggested that "as the United States charged a duty on books printed in Canada, we should have a duty protecting our publishers."[158] John Lovell had been vocal in arguing for parity between American and Canadian printers and publishers: "All we say is, Put us on an equality with the United States. They will not alter their policy. We must remodel ours; otherwise it will be impossible for Canada ever to boast of extensive publishing-houses, or to bring out the talent that is latent in the country."[159] Not every member of the book trade was in favour of the tariff, however. Andrew Armour of the firm Armour & Ramsay demurred. In an opinion piece published in the *Globe*, he argued that the tariff would do more harm than good. He concluded by stating that "the real grievance under which publishers in Canada suffer, is the operation of the ... Imperial Copyright Law, which places the Canadian printer in a worse position than his American neighbour."[160]

The British authorities and the British book trade mounted a pressure campaign to urge the province to reconsider the tariff. The Board of Trade argued that the levy on British books was a betrayal of the province's commitments under the Foreign Reprints Act because it diminished "by two-thirds the amount of protection hitherto enjoyed by British authors entitled to copyright; and as this protection was given in lieu of the monopoly which they previously possessed in the Colonial market, my Lords would submit that it constitutes a departure from the understanding upon which Her Majesty was advised to give effect the Canadian Act ... by Her Order in Council of the 12th December 1850, which was issued on the ground that the Act in question afforded a reasonable compensation of British authors for the loss of their monopoly."[161]

---

158   See "Legislative Assembly: First Readings ... duty on books," *The Globe*, 25 April 1860.

159   John Lovell, letter to the editor of the *Gazette* (Montreal), 8 March 1858.

160   Andrew H. Armour, "The Book Duty," *The Globe*, 14 March 1859, 2.

161   Duke of Newcastle to Colonial Governor, Sir Edmund Head, 5 November 1859, "Enclosing a report from the Office of the Committee of Privy Council for Trade dated October 20, 1859." United Kingdom, *Customs duties (Canada)*, 9–10.

The choice for provincial readers was to buy British copyright works directly from the United Kingdom free of imperial duties or procure reprints from the United States and pay the importation duty on foreign reprints. The Lords never considered the third possibility, namely that British authors might voluntarily print and publish their works in the province because the new colonial tariff made imported editions unaffordable and they preferred that option over the foreign reprints system.

In 1860, the front-page editorial in *The Publishers' Circular*, the British periodical of British and foreign literature, announced with some exultation:

> We have good news from Canada. In reply to a quiet, well-organised agitation, accompanied by a petition which the booksellers induced all their customers to sign, an intimation has been received from the government that the recent infliction of an import duty on English printed books will be relinquished. We trust that any other English possessions which may have contemplated following the example set by Canada a year since, will now abandon the idea for ever; for we learn that the result of the experiment was a great falling off in the importation of English books, and as a natural consequence, the measure completely failed to benefit the revenue.[162]

The provincial legislature had eliminated the general tariff. The government insisted it was acting independently and had not capitulated to British demands. Minister Galt said that the imperial government "only referred to the subject as affecting the copyright question."[163] In other words, a tariff could be imposed as long as it did not undermine the foreign reprints system. In the end, the Assembly retained an import duty on "school books or other books which now are or hereafter may be printed in this Province."[164] Schoolbooks were, once again, the battleground for the educational and cultural ambitions of this developing society and its rising generation.

The revised tariff was narrow in that it only applied to imported schoolbooks that competed directly with those that were actually printed in the province, not necessarily those that were domestically authored, or those of a kind that might be printed and published in

---

162  *The Publishers Circular*, 1 May 1860, 1.
163  "Legislative Assembly: First Readings ... duty on books," *The Globe*, 25 April 1860.
164  *An Act respecting certain Duties of Customs*, 1860, 23 Vict., c. 18 (19 May 1860).

future.[165] Nevertheless, the measure was intended to level the field for provincial schoolbook production by increasing the cost of imports, especially those originating in the United States. It was clearly protectionist in nature despite protestations to the contrary by the government of the day. As an editorial in *The Globe* wryly observed: "What a curious commentary it is on the statement of Mr. Galt, that the Government has not adopted a protective policy."[166] In fact, as the concluding chapter will illustrate, protectionist approaches to printing and publishing were the defining feature of Canada's post-Confederation policy to the end of the century as parliamentary focus shifted from tariffs back to copyright.

---

165  *The Globe* reproduced the announcement in the Canada Gazette by Robert Shore. Milnes Bouchette, Commissioner of Customs, "Notice to Printers and Publishers in Canada" outlining the procedure for the imposition of the tariff on foreign school and other books: *The Globe*, 1 June 1860. The French notice "Avis aux Imprimeurs et Éditeurs Au Canada" appeared in newspapers like *Le Canadien* (Monday, 4 June 1860, 5).

166  "Alteration in the Tariff," *The Globe*, 1 June 1860.

# Chapter Ten

# The Imprint of the Province of Canada on Copyright Law and Policy in the Dominion of Canada, 1867–1924

Copyright law and policy in post-Confederation Canada has been the subject of important scholarly research and will not be revisited here in any great detail.[1] Instead, the intent behind this concluding chapter is to demonstrate the extent to which the events in the Province of Canada, especially imperial interference through the Copyright Act 1842 and the Foreign Reprints Act, informed Canada's actions well into the twentieth century. Memories were long.

On 1 July 1867, the self-governing Dominion of Canada, a confederation of the provinces of New Brunswick, Nova Scotia, Ontario, and Quebec, was established under the British North America Act.[2] The uneasy union between English Canada and French Canada ended when the Province of Canada was divided into Ontario and Quebec, effectively reinstating the former provinces of Upper Canada and Lower Canada. Legislative powers were divided between federal and the provincial parliaments. The Parliament of Canada, which consisted of the Crown, an elected House of Commons, and an appointed Senate, was entrusted with matters of national scope.

As demonstrated in the previous chapter, copyright remained the preferred instrument for the encouragement of learning, especially in relation to schoolbook production, but policy-makers became increasingly preoccupied with promoting Canadian voices through the agency of print, whether through schoolbooks or otherwise. This intersection

---

1  For scholarship on post-Confederation copyright law from a Canadian perspective, see especially the work of Sara Bannerman, Ysolde Gendreau, Eli MacLaren, Pierre-Emmanuel Moyse, Meera Nair, and George Parker.

2  *An Act for the Union of Canada, Nova Scotia, and New Brunswick, and the Government thereof; and for Purposes connected therewith*, 30 & 31 Vict., c. 3 (UK) ("The British North America Act 1867").

between book production and national cultural identity meant that legislative jurisdiction over copyright was assigned to the federal Parliament, as a matter of common interest throughout the country, even though education itself, as in schools, teachers, and school curricula, became a provincial priority.[3]

However, the friction at the centre of the imperial–colonial copyright relationship did not magically disappear after 1867. The new confederation remained as subordinate on matters of copyright as the individual British North American provinces had been, and the lessons learned by the Province of Canada drove the Canadian narrative. Imperial actions from 1842 onward had repercussions long after they were implemented and left an indelible stain on imperial–colonial relations. British refusal to entertain the province's preferred solution to the question of unauthorized American reprints remained ever-present in the minds of politicians, the book trade, and the public long after the Province of Canada ceased to exist. In 1914, lawyer John H. Moss observed of the period: "On account of its bringing into prominence ... the question of Canadian autonomy, the subject of copyright acquired for a short time a public interest which it would otherwise not have achieved."[4] The politics of copyright galvanized Canadians, who were affronted by the injustice of Canada's subordination and by Britain's indulgence of American obduracy.

There was much at stake for this new nation and its position in the world. In a speech to the Royal Society of Canada in 1883, novelist William Kirby expressed a commonly held view:

> A country not known by its literature loses half its prestige, and prestige is power, wealth and influence in the modern world, which more than ever is governed by ideas. Intellect is everywhere supplanting rude force, and those nations which have the clearest and most vital ideas expressed in a vigorous and noble literature are precisely those which rule the world.
>
> The literary and moral forces of Britain are pre-eminently of that sort – those of the United States, speaking the same language and vitalized by kindred ideas, are growing daily in magnitude and power. How then, it may be asked, does it happen that Canada, standing between these two nations and the recipient of all that is best and most valuable in the

---

3   Section 91(23) of the British North America Act 1867 (now the Constitution Act) gives the federal Parliament exclusive legislative jurisdiction over "Copyright." Section 93 confers exclusive jurisdiction over education to the provincial legislatures.

4   Moss, "Copyright in Canada," 7.

literature of each of them, finds its own literature in a state of decay and as far as the publishing in Canada of Canadian books is concerned, almost extinct.[5]

Kirby's despondency expressed the widespread belief that the creation and circulation of works of Canadian literature, such as novels and poetry, were dependent on the strength of domestic printing and publishing. As matters stood, the Canadian market was insufficient to provide the industry with scale and volume, and copyright was an inadequate commercial lever for many printers and publishers. This reality is borne out by the registration data discussed in the previous chapter, which demonstrated that the members of the book trade were underrepresented as copyright registrants in the Province of Canada. In addition, regardless of who held the copyright, didactic works remained the mainstay for the industry because there was an established internal market for these kinds of publications.

The new Dominion turned its attention to copyright to drive the development of a viable industry. However, its actions were hampered by its colonial status. Indeed, a series of Canadian and imperial judicial decisions and legislative actions reinforced Canada's weak position in matters of copyright. These events, spanning the remaining decades of the nineteenth century, ensured that Canada's copyright law would remain largely parochial and closely circumscribed well into the next century. Almost immediately after it was constituted, the federal Parliament passed the Copyright Act of 1868 to extend copyright protection throughout the country. This statute was an updated version of the 1841 Act of the Province of Canada, which was repealed along with Nova Scotia's copyright legislation. The Province of Canada's 1847 amendment allowing a British subject resident in the United Kingdom to secure a domestic copyright was carried forward in the new Act and, in modified form, in the Copyright Act of 1875.[6] At the same time, Parliament enacted an *Act to impose a duty on foreign reprints of British copyright works* to comply with the Foreign Reprints Act, but, like the legislature of the former Province of Canada, it did so grudgingly.[7] Canadian lawmakers remained intent

---

5   Kirby, "Mr. Kirby on Copyright."

6   The Copyright Act of 1875 eliminated the requirement that the foreign author had to be resident in Great Britain or Ireland.

7   *Act to impose a duty on foreign reprints of British copyright works*, 1868, 31 Vict., c. 56 (22 May 1868). French Title: *Acte pour imposer un droit sur les ré-impressions étrangères des ouvrages britanniques soumis au droit de propriété littéraire.* On 7 July 1868, the requisite British order-in-council was issued pursuant to the Foreign Reprints Act enabling

on curtailing the American reprint trade in favour of domestic printing and publishing. Indeed, as the duty on foreign reprints bill was making its way through Parliament, the Senate of Canada petitioned the imperial authorities to allow Canadian printers and publishers to reprint British copyright works upon payment of an amount equivalent to the 12.5 per cent *ad valorem* tariff. The upper chamber sought "to impress upon her Majesty's Government the justice and expediency of extending the privileges granted by the [Foreign Reprints Act] so that … Colonial reprints of British copyright works shall be placed on the same footing as foreign reprints in Canada, by which means British authors will be more effectually protected in their rights, and a material benefit will be conferred on the printing industry of this Dominion."[8]

The British government rejected the request, arguing that the foreign reprints scheme was only intended as an exceptional and provisional measure until a copyright treaty could be entered into with the United States. Progress on this front would be impeded if the Canadian Senate's proposal were entertained.[9] Yet again, the imperial authorities refused to consider whether they had any responsibility or role to play in encouraging the book trade in the colonies and Dominions or, indeed, in the optics of tenaciously preferring American reprinting over Canadian.

Within days of this refusal, the British House of Lords rendered a decision that enlarged the scope of those who could claim British copyright protection.[10] In *Routledge v. Low*, the court held that foreign authors could obtain a British copyright by residing temporarily in any part of the British dominions while their books were being published in the United Kingdom. This generous interpretation of British law supported the British publishing industry (since first publication had to occur in Britain) and was a boon to American authors, who now had an easy path to securing their copyright in the United Kingdom and North America. Prior to this decision, American authors had to be resident in the United Kingdom at the time of publication. Many took advantage of this new opportunity, including American author and satirist Samuel Clemens (Mark Twain), who visited Montreal on several occasions in

---

the importation of foreign reprints that had been prohibited under the UK Copyright Act 1842. See United Kingdom, *British and Foreign State Papers 1874–1875*, vol. 66, 549–50.

8  Journals of the Senate of Canada, first session, first Parliament 1867–1868, 31 Vict., 290. (15 May 1868).

9  *The Globe*, "The Copy-Right Question," 29 April 1869, 2.

10  *Routledge v Low*, (1868) 3 L.R 3 H.L 100: Judgment reported 28 May 1868.

the 1880s to secure a British copyright in his books.[11] An editorial in the *New Brunswick Morning Journal* conveyed the general feeling among Canadians about the implications of the *Routledge* judgment: "we cannot admire either the morality or decency of the farce so often gone through, of coming for a few days to this side of the lines under the make-believe of becoming a resident, in order to secure a pecuniary advantage."[12] Canadian printers and publishers, especially members of the English-speaking book trade, had little leverage to pursue their own arrangements with American authors. Why would American authors go through the trouble when a British copyright would guarantee them the Canadian market, and the only hardship they would have to endure was a brief sojourn across the border?

In the face of these challenges, the English-language printing and publishing industry took its plight to the Dominion Parliament. The book trade was already influential in policy circles, as evidenced by the survey of importers and booksellers conducted by the Assembly of the Province of Canada in 1843. In addition, the struggles of individual printers and publishers had frequently been raised by members of the legislature of the Province of Canada in their debates over copyright and tariffs on imported books. Montreal printer and publisher John Lovell was outspoken about the challenges faced by the trade, and his views were frequently invoked by members of the Assembly. The fact that Lovell laboured to stay afloat under the prevailing circumstances signalled that legislative intervention was necessary. The convergence of interests between the new federal Parliament and the English-language printing and publishing industry provided a united front from which to contest the actions of the imperial authorities.

The chosen strategy involved introducing a compulsory licence provision into the copyright statute. A compulsory licence was a measure that enabled domestic printers and publishers to reprint any work that had not already been printed and published in Canada by the copyright holder. A government authority would grant the licence to reproduce the work. The copyright holder had no discretion to refuse but was entitled to a royalty fixed by statute. This measure was designed to support domestic industry, but it offered the additional benefit of

---

11  See Hill, *Mark Twain's Letters*. See also Roper, "Mark Twain and his Canadian Publishers"; Roper, "Mark Twain and his Canadian Publishers: A Second Look."

12  *The Globe*, 12 October 1868, 2, under the heading: "We Learn from the New Brunswick Morning Journal." It appears that American author Reverend Albert Barnes spent time in Saint John, New Brunswick, for the purpose of securing his British copyright.

supplying Canadian readers with affordable British books, and it ensured that American printers and publishers would no longer be rewarded for their reprinting practices. The first legislative salvo occurred in 1872 with an amendment to the Copyright Act of 1868 to introduce a compulsory licensing provision.[13] The preamble to the 1872 statute conveyed the bitter history of the foreign reprints debacle:

> Whereas it is expedient to make provision for securing and protecting in Canada the rights of authors in works wherein the copyright is subsisting in Great Britain ... and whereas Her Majesty has seen fit ... to act upon the authority conferred upon Her, and foreign reprints of British copyright works are now permitted to be imported into Canada ... but, nevertheless, reprints in Canada of such British copyright works have not heretofore been permitted; and whereas by the British North America Act, 1867, express power is given to the Parliament of Canada to legislate upon the subject of copyright; and whereas provision for securing and protecting authors of British copyright works can be much more effectually made by authorizing the reprinting and publication of such works in Canada on the terms in this Act contained; and *whereas it is but just that Her Majesty's subjects in Canada should be allowed, on such conditions as will sufficiently protect and secure the authors of such copyright works, the advantages accorded to aliens and foreigners in respect of the reprinting of British copyright works.* [emphasis added]

The provision would have allowed Canadian printers and publishers to reprint British copyright works without permission should British authors or their assigns fail to print and publish their books in Canada within a stipulated time frame. British authors would, however, be entitled to receive a royalty payment set at 12.5 per cent *ad valorem*, this being the same amount as the foreign reprints import duty. Once a compulsory licence was issued, American reprints of the licensed material would be denied entry into the country. In effect, the 1872 legislative initiative was a mandatory version of what had been intended by the Province of Canada's 1847 amendment, had the British allowed it to redirect the reprinting of British copyright works to the Canadian trade. What the 1847 amendment sought to encourage voluntarily, the

---

13  *An Act to Amend the Act respecting Copyrights*, 1872 (passed by Parliament of Canada, 14 June 1872): The text of this failed statute can be found in Solberg, *Copyright in Canada and Newfoundland*, 72–5. Note that the UK Copyright Act 1842 had a compulsory licensing provision, but it was limited to circumstances where the author had died and the copyright holder refused to republish the work.

1872 initiative purported to make compulsory. It is therefore fitting that it was Canada's finance minister, Francis Hincks, who steered the 1872 Copyright Bill through Parliament. It will be recalled from chapter 8 that Hincks had been very active on the foreign reprints file as a member of the legislature of the Province of Canada. He had been instrumental in convincing his Assembly colleagues to impose a duty on foreign reprints in 1850 instead of insisting that they hold fast to their initial solution under the 1847 amendment, a position he later renounced.

However, Canada was bound by the British Colonial Laws Validity Act 1865, which prohibited the federal Parliament from enacting copyright legislation that was repugnant to imperial laws.[14] Colonial reprinting of British copyright works was absolutely prohibited under the UK Copyright Act 1842. The import duty on foreign reprints was the only means by which Canadian readers could acquire affordable copies of British books. The system preserved the absolute authority of British authors and publishers to control the market for books throughout the British empire. A compulsory licence system under Canadian copyright law would have usurped the British copyright holder's discretion over colonial reprinting and undermined the Foreign Reprints Act.[15] Royal Assent was refused.[16]

Three years later, the federal Parliament successfully passed the Copyright Act of 1875, which for the first time, imposed an obligation to print and publish in Canada as a prerequisite to copyright protection.[17] However, the new Act did not include the much-coveted compulsory licensing mechanism that would have permitted republication in Canada without the author's consent. Even so, the new legislation raised similar constitutional concerns as its predecessor in that it purported to exclude the operation of imperial laws in respect of foreign reprints where a British author had obtained a Canadian copyright. It was unclear whether the Dominion Parliament had the constitutional

---

14  *An Act to Remove Doubt about the Validity of Colonial Laws*, 1865, 28 & 29 Vict., c. 63.

15  The British book trade was also concerned that cheaper Canadian editions would make their way to England and undercut their market.

16  I believe that this was the only instance in Canadian legislative history that Royal Assent was refused for legislation that had been duly passed by a federal or provincial Parliament. Later expressions of Crown displeasure took the form of a refusal to proclaim the legislation into force. This softer approach was used in the case of the 1889 Canadian Copyright Act, discussed later in this chapter. On the constitutional implications of the 1872 Act, see Miller, "'Political imagination.'"

17  Section 2: "That the condition for obtaining such copyright shall be that the said literary, scientific or artistic works be printed and published or reprinted and republished in Canada." This Act repealed the Copyright Act of 1868.

authority to supplant British law in this way. To remove any doubt on the subject, the British Parliament statutorily endorsed the Canadian legislation.[18]

Some members of the Canadian book trade, like Toronto printers and publishers Belford Brothers, believed that the imperial validation of the Canadian statute meant that Canadian copyright law had displaced the operation of British law in Canada.[19] The Belfords tested this hypothesis before the Ontario courts in the case of *Smiles v. Belford*.[20] The *Smiles* decision involved the publication in England of Samuel Smiles's popular book *Thrift*.[21] Having secured his British copyright, Smiles argued that he was protected throughout the British dominions and therefore had the sole right to authorize the printing or reprinting of his work throughout the empire. The Belford Brothers reprinted *Thrift* without the author's permission, arguing that the Canadian Act of 1875 rendered British laws on copyright inoperative within the Dominion. Since Smiles had not complied with the Canadian statute by having his book reprinted and republished in the country, he could do nothing to prevent the Belfords' actions. But the Ontario Court of Appeal rejected the Belfords' claim: Canada's Parliament did not have the authority to override British copyright law. British copyright holders could exercise their rights on Canadian soil without registering their copyright there. Justice Thomas Moss nevertheless recognized the harm that the decision caused to Canadian printers and publishers:

> I confess that it is not without reluctance that I have arrived at the same conclusion. I fear that the state of the law which we find inflicts a hardship on the Canadian publisher, while it confers no very valuable benefit upon the British author. Its effect, if I rightly understand the matter, is to enable the British author to give an American publisher a Canadian copyright. It is no very violent assumption that every American publisher, who treats

18   *An Act to Give Effect to an Act of the Parliament of the Dominion of Canada respecting Copyright*, 1875, 38 & 39 Vict., c. 53 (U.K). The preamble explained that there was concern that the Canadian statute was in conflict with the British Order-in-Council allowing the importation of foreign reprints. The British statute giving effect to the Canadian Act also contained a provision prohibiting parallel importation of cheaper Canadian editions into the United Kingdom.

19   Charles, Robert, and Alexander Belford established their printing and publishing firm in 1872. On Charles Belford (1837–1880), see his entry in DCB. See also MacLaren, *Dominion and Agency*.

20   *Smiles v. Belford*, [1877] 1 O.A.R. 436.

21   Samuel Smiles, *Thrift*.

with a British author for advance sheets of his work, will stipulate for the use of the author's name to restrain a Canadian reprint. By this arrangement he will be enabled to secure the practical monopoly of the Canadian market, for which he may be induced to pay the author some consideration; but however small this consideration may be, I apprehend it will be found sufficient to induce the author to concede the privilege rather than secure Canadian copyright by treating with the Canadian publisher.[22]

The Copyright Act of 1875 did nothing to change the status quo for Canadian printers and publishers. They remained barred from reprinting British books, leaving British authors and American publishers to carve up the Canadian market for themselves. Some incensed Canadian printers and publishers, like John Lovell and the Belford Brothers, took matters into their own hands. They set up printing establishments in the United States for the purpose of reprinting British copyright works, which they could lawfully import into Canada upon payment of the duty on foreign reprints.[23] The Belfords were particularly sanctimonious about their activism, especially in relation to reprinting the works of American authors, like Mark Twain, who had secured their British copyright. They justified their actions to a sympathetic Canadian readership in a lengthy preface to their unauthorized reprint of Twain's *The Prince and the Pauper*:[24]

The Importers of this cheap edition ... do not disguise their motive in placing it on the Canadian market. Their object ... is to show, by its importation into, and sale in Canada, *as a foreign reprint of a work which has secured British copyright*, how anomalous is the present law of Literature in the Colonies, and how injuriously, and in an especial degree this affects Canadian printing and publishing industries ...

... had the Act of 1872, which our Parliament desired to place on our Statute Books, not been vetoed by the Imperial Parliament, Mr. Clemens would not have had the privilege in our market, which his British copyright unjustly secures him.

---

22  *Smiles v. Belford*, 446.
23  Roy, "Discours présidentiel de la propriété littéraire," claimed that Lovell had 500 employees when he set up his operations in the United States. See also MacLaren, *Dominion and Agency*.
24  Mark Twain had obtained a British copyright in *The Prince and The Pauper* under the rule in *Routledge v. Low*, by having spent a brief time in Canada while his book was being published in London. Dawson Brothers published the authorized Canadian edition of *The Prince and the Pauper* (Montreal: Dawson Brothers, 1881).

The action we have now taken … nullifies in great measure, the benefit which Imperial copyright affords … and this course we feel justified in adopting, so long as the United States government refuse [*sic*] to accord to British or Colonial authors reciprocal legislation, and while American publishers are free to flood Canadian markets with reprints of English books.[25]

It was not just the Belford Brothers, whom Twain referred to as "Canadian thieves," who were frustrated.[26] Samuel Dawson, whose firm was the authorized Canadian printer and publisher of *The Prince and Pauper*, was equally critical of the status quo: "In many respects Mr. Clemens is entitled to sympathy… But then the Americans have the remedy in their own hands. The moment an International Treaty is made they will come under our Statute … They cannot hoodwink the Canadians as they do the English people, and I am sure they will never get from the Canadian Parliament anything but reciprocal rights."[27]

Canadians would not allow themselves to be hoodwinked by the Americans. This grievance narrative fuelled the Canadian discourse around identity and self-determination.

In 1889, the Parliament of Canada tried once again to enact a compulsory licence provision in its copyright statute.[28] This time, the measure received Royal Assent, but it was never proclaimed into force. In the aftermath of yet another legislative failure, justice minister John Thompson sardonically observed:

I think we have the right to legislate in respect of this subject irrespective of any Statute of the Imperial Parliament passed before the British North America Act was passed. The Act which declared that Colonial Statutes were invalid if they were repugnant to Imperial Statutes was passed in 1865. Two years after that, we received the ample gift of powers which the British North America Act contains. In the exercise of those powers, we

---

25  Belford Brothers, preface to Mark Twain, *The Prince and the Pauper* (emphasis Belford Bros.)

26  "Belford Bros., Canadian thieves, are flooding America with a cheap pirated edition of Tom Sawyer … This piracy will cost me $10,000, and I will spend as much more to choke off those pirates." Mark Twain to Moncure D. Conway, 2 November 1876, in Hill, *Mark Twain's Letters*, 105.

27  Dawson, *Copyright in Books*. Dawson's expertise in copyright law led to his appointment as adviser to the Canadian delegate Sir Leonard Tilley at the International Copyright Conference 1881–1882, held in Washington, DC. See Aach, *Impressions*.

28  *An Act to amend The Copyright Act Chapter sixty-two of the Revised Statutes*, 1889, 52 Vict., c. 29. French title: *Acte modifiant l'Acte concernant les droits d'auteur*.

have repealed, sometimes by implication, and sometimes directly, scores of Imperial enactments, in addition to volumes of the Common Law of the United Kingdom; and, if the objection were sustained in regard to the exercise of our powers on the question of copyright it would strike off at least one-half of the Revised Statutes.[29]

The fact that the Canadian Parliament had unilaterally repealed "scores of Imperial enactments" did not matter insofar as copyright was concerned.

In 1890, Thompson wrote to Lord Knutsford, the Secretary of State for the Colonies, requesting that the 1889 Act be brought into force. One passage in this lengthy letter is particularly noteworthy. Thompson reminded the British government of the promise made by Earl Grey in 1847 that the British North American legislatures would have sole discretion to decide how to implement the Foreign Reprints Act. Thompson stated:

> Your Lordship cannot then be surprised that after *Earl Grey's promise of more than forty years ago*, and after more than twenty-two years of agitation on the part of Canada, by addresses from both branches of our Parliament, by memoranda from our Ministers of Finance and Agriculture, by Minutes of Council, and by Statutes passed unanimously in both Houses, introduced by three successive Governments, representing opposite political opinion, and with encouragements held out at every stage of the agitation to expect a reasonable and favourable consideration of our representations by her Majesty's Government, the Canadian Parliament believed in 1889, that the Act then passed, to give effect to what had so often been asked for … should receive a favourable consideration at the hands of Her Majesty's Government. [emphasis added][30]

That the British had ostensibly reneged on Earl Grey's undertaking had never been forgiven or forgotten. The consequences of that single act of betrayal festered decades later as a symbol of colonial subjugation. The Canadian Parliament's single-minded pursuit of compulsory licensing was the result of this one portentous action. The Dominion of

---

29  As cited in Hopkins, *The Life and Work*, 388: The situation was entirely different with other forms of intellectual property. The Canadian Parliament did not encounter the same interference when it came to its patent, trademark, and industrial design legislation.

30  Letter from Sir John Thompson to Lord Knutsford, London, 14 July 1890 (London: s.n., 1890), 21.

Canada, like the Province of Canada before it, remained burdened by the intransigence of the British and by the colonial strictures to which it was bound. By the late 1880s, the international copyright environment was evolving in a manner that only compounded the inequity. The United States Congress amended the copyright statute to enable British authors to secure copyright in the United States as long as their books were typeset and printed there.[31] The new Chace Act 1891 made it even less likely that a British author would deal directly with a Canadian printer and publisher. American printers and publishers could now supply the Canadian market with authorized editions of British copyright works by negotiating for the North American market in their publishing agreements with British authors. Furthermore, under the *Routledge* rule, American authors could benefit from British copyright protection in Canada without having to print and publish their works there.

In 1894, John Thompson, now Canada's newly elected fourth prime minister, sailed to London to take this matter up with the British government.[32] In a tragic turn of events in the ongoing imperial–colonial copyright saga, Thompson died on that journey without having arrived at a resolution, although contemporaneous accounts suggest that he had come close to settling the matter in Canada's favour.[33] A year later, the Canadian legislature attempted yet again to enact a compulsory licence provision as an amendment to the Copyright Act of 1875. This time, the compulsory licence was limited to cases where the copyright holder failed to reproduce the work "in sufficient numbers and in such manner as to meet the demand in Canada."[34] The narrower scope did not save the provision, and it too failed to become law.

The Canadian Parliament had more success in 1900 when it introduced a measure to enable British copyright holders to voluntarily enter into a licence with a Canadian printer and publisher to reproduce the work for the Canadian market.[35] It was not a compulsory scheme. Instead, it was a compromise put forward by the newly formed Canadian

---

31  *An act to amend title sixty, chapter three, of the Revised Statutes of the United States, relating to copyrights*, 1891, 26 Stat. 1106 (3 March 1891) ("the Chace Act").

32  Sir John Sparrow David Thompson (1845–1894). See his entry in DCBO.

33  Hopkins, *The Life and Work*, 436. See also Nair, "The Copyright Act of 1889."

34  *An Act to amend the Copyright Act*, 1895, 58–59 Vict., c. 37 (22 July 1895). French title: *Acte modifiant l'Acte concernant les droits d'auteur.*

35  *An Act to amend the Copyright Act*, 1900, 63 & 64 Vict., c. 25 (18 July 1900). French title: *Acte modifiant l'Acte concernant les droits d'auteur.* See also Morang, *The Copyright Question.*

Authors' Society, which had been established in 1899 to promote the interests of Canadian authors.[36] This was the first instance of an authors' group successfully lobbying Parliament, and it demonstrated the increased visibility of authors as an important copyright constituency. In an address to the Royal Society of Canada in 1892, the president of the University of Toronto, Daniel Wilson, discussed the role of authors in framing copyright policy:

> The passing of the Copyright Act in 1889 almost without attracting the notice of Canadian authors and those specifically interested in science and letters is significant. Our legislators appear to have welcomed advice from the book trade, but to have wholly ignored the representatives of the "manufacturer" of books. But brief as is the interval, Canadian authorship has already assumed a more aggressive status, and the small but growing number of Canadian authors may find it worth their while to look at the question from another point of view.[37]

Wilson declared that "an honest Canadian Copyright Act will place the author's rights foremost."[38]

The ascendance of authors as an organized class in Canadian copyright policy emerged in step with international developments. In 1886 the United Kingdom and France led the negotiations toward the successful conclusion of the first multilateral copyright treaty, the *Berne Convention for the Protection of Literary and Artistic Works*, an agreement generally regarded as author-centric in its orientation.[39] The United Kingdom signed the treaty on behalf of its colonies, possessions, and dominions but agreed to denounce membership at the behest of the Canadian government if the Dominion chose to pursue that route. Immediately, questions were raised as to whether membership in the Berne Convention was in Canada's best interests. In 1888, the Copyright Association of Canada, comprised of leading members of the book trade, urged the Canadian government to renounce its participation in the treaty. The fear was that the Berne Convention would "practically

---

36  See James Mavor's contemporaneous account of the establishment of the society. Mavor, "Canadian Copyright." Mavor was a member of the society and delivered remarks on its behalf at the third international congress of publishers, organized by the Publishers' Association of Great Britain and Ireland, held in London in 1899.
37  Wilson, "Canadian Copyright," 12.
38  Wilson, "Canadian Copyright," 17.
39  *Berne Convention for the Protection of Literary and Artistic Works.* UK ratification was by Order-in-Council, 28 November 1887.

emasculate the entire trades in this Dominion in connection with books, and that the publishers would be ruined."[40] However, Parliamentary opinion was divided, and Canada remained a party to the treaty despite having twice signified its intent to withdraw.[41] Communication policy scholar Sara Bannerman has studied Canada's engagement with the Berne Convention and has captured this period in vivid detail, so the specifics need not be revisited here.[42] What is important to highlight, however, is that for the first time since the enactment of the UK Copyright Act 1842, Canadian parliamentary disagreements arose in relation to defining the country's own national and international copyright policy rather than as a direct response to actions taken by the British or the Americans.

In 1911 the United Kingdom overhauled its copyright legislation to consolidate and modernize its statute and to adhere to the terms of the Berne Convention. The UK Copyright Act 1911 was a significant departure from its nineteenth-century predecessors.[43] It introduced a post-mortem duration of copyright (author's life plus fifty years) and recognized copyright limitations and exceptions such as fair dealing for the purposes of private study, research, criticism, review, and newspaper summary. The 1911 Act was also an imperial statute in that it sought to harmonize copyright law throughout the empire. British colonies and possessions were automatically within its purview. In contrast, self-governing Dominions like Canada were free to chart their own course, although the United Kingdom exerted persuasive pressure to encourage conformity. The adoption of a statute that was substantially similar to the British legislation had the advantage of ensuring Berne Convention compliance. Following the British lead would enable

---

40   Copyright Association of Canada, "Interviewing the Cabinet."

41   The Canadian Authors Association was established in 1921 by prominent Canadian authors, including Stephen Leacock. See Harrington, *Syllables of Recorded Time*. The association represented English Canadian and French Canadian authors and had a self-governing French Canadian section. One of the most active members was Louvigny de Montigny, who worked for the Justice Department in Ottawa. De Montigny played an influential role on matters relating to copyright and Berne Convention compliance. See Luneau, *Louvigny de Montigny*. On the influence of authors' and publishers' associations, see, for example, Parker, "Authors and Publishers on the Offensive."

42   Bannerman, *The Struggle for Canadian Copyright*. See also Bannerman, "Canadian Copyright."

43   *An Act to amend and consolidate the Law relating to copyright*, 1911, c. 46 (16 December 1911). On the 1911 UK Act, see, generally, Suthersanen and Gendreau, *A Shifting Empire*; and Birnhack, *Colonial Copyright*.

Canadian authors to benefit from copyright protection throughout the British Empire and in Berne member-countries. It was a defining moment for Canada.

In 1921, Canada enacted its new Copyright Act.[44] A close approximation of the UK Copyright Act 1911, this statute is the antecedent of the copyright legislation that continues to govern Canadians to this day. The Canadian Parliament turned away from American copyright models and harmonized its law with the United Kingdom and other members of the British Commonwealth. The Act repealed the existing Canadian copyright statute along with all the imperial copyright legislation that had applied in the country, thereby ending the dual copyright system and the colonial conditions that enabled it. Copyright emancipation was achieved at long last.

In order to comply with the international norms under the Berne Convention, the Canadian statute eliminated its domestic printing and publishing requirements.[45] However, the legislation retained compulsory licensing provisions, which the Canadian Parliament was now at liberty to enact without imperial veto. It was unclear whether their inclusion would affect Canada's membership in the Berne Convention, and the provisions were harshly criticized. One particularly disparaging commentator suggested that "a more retrograde step has never disfigured any Copyright Act."[46] The statute was not proclaimed into force.[47] Canada eventually compromised. It invoked the 1914 *Protocol Additionel* to the Berne Convention that enabled Berne member-countries to impose restrictions on non-member countries whose level of protection for foreign authors was deemed insufficient.[48] In 1923, the copyright statute was amended to limit the compulsory licence

---

44  *An Act to Amend and Consolidate the Law Relating to Copyright* S.C. 1921 11 & 12 Geo. 5, c. 24.

45  The 1908 Berlin revision of the Berne Convention stated that treaty countries could not impose any formalities on authors as prerequisites to securing their rights. The United States remained the outlier in the international arena. It retained mandatory manufacturing formalities in its copyright legislation for most of the twentieth century before finally abandoning them to join the Berne Convention in 1989. *The Berne Convention Implementation Act of 1988,* H.R. 4262, 100th Cong. (1988): Came into force 1 March 1989.

46  "The New Canadian Copyright Act," *The Musical Times (UK),* 1 July 1921, vol. 60, no. 94, 497.

47  See Bannerman, *The Struggle for Canadian Copyright,* for extensive discussion on the question of Berne compliance and the delays in proclaiming the 1921 Act in force.

48  *Additional Protocol to the Revised Berne Convention,* signed 20 March 1914 and ratified 20 April 1915.

provisions to Canadian authors who printed and published their works outside of Canada or authors from non-Berne Convention countries, like the United States.[49] This amendment was consistent with the international treaty and ushered in a new chapter in Canada's copyright story. The amended Copyright Act was proclaimed into force on 1 January 1924, 100 years after François Blanchet first rose in the Lower Canadian House of Assembly to introduce his *Bill for the Encouragement of Learning*.

49  *An Act to Amend the Copyright Act 1921*, 1923, 13 & 14 Geo. 5 c. 10 (13 June 1923). The intention was that licences could be issued against Canadian authors who first published in the United States, but the clause implied that even publication in a Berne member country could trigger a licence against a Canadian author. See "Copyright Act Amendment," Hansard, *House of Commons Debates* (30 April 1923), 2343–6. Canadian authors complained at being placed at a disadvantage as compared to their Berne Convention peers. The president of the Canadian Authors Association Lawrence J. Burpee characterized the compromise as "humiliating to the Canadian-born artist. After all, the poor devil of a Canadian writer is made the victim, while the mantle of justice is thrown over authors of France and England, Italy and Spain." See Harrington, *Syllables of Recorded Time*, 37.

# Epilogue

To return to the initial question that prompted this examination of Canada's nineteenth-century copyright history: What is Canada's copyright tradition? Does Canada follow the French "droit d'auteur" model as Justices Décary and Gonthier described it? Or does it adhere to the British copyright system, placing the publisher's economic right at the forefront, as per Justice Binnie? This book demonstrates the deficiencies in the characterization of copyright in terms of silos of authors or publishers – or, indeed, of users. Compartmentalizing copyright in this way is not helpful in that it assumes that one statutory text or body of law cannot embrace the interests of creators, users, and industry at the same time. It obscures the more complex reality that copyright encompasses and combines all those interests and that its ultimate objective is broader than any one of those communities.

Copyright can only be fully understood through a multidisciplinary lens that begins with the legal record but that must necessarily expand to include archival and bibliographical materials that reveal its textured nature. The law did not arise in a vacuum, nor does copyright continue to exist in isolation. On their own, the tools of legal inquiry cannot fully capture the breadth of copyright's many facets. Indeed, I began this study by turning to conventional legal research methods but quickly found myself at an impasse since nineteenth-century legal material was very scant – there was no systematic recording of parliamentary debates, no jurisprudence, and no doctrinal commentary for the period under review. In addition, written records frequently did not survive the passage of time, the Lower Canadian copyright registries being a case in point. Furthermore, my starting point was to approach copyright as a form of intellectual property and to study it exclusively within that legal categorization. As the book illustrates, this assumption was flawed. While there was clearly a close connection between copyright and patents in the nineteenth century, copyright had a unique history of its own. It was only once I broadened the scope of my inquiry to engage more fully with the research methods of book history that an unanticipated and more complete picture emerged. Examining copyright legal history from the perspective of book history uncovered new insights about the law and the way it manifested itself in the communities it affected. It revealed a rich copyright history imbued with distinctly Canadian patterns and characteristics. The research findings challenged conventional assumptions about copyright law in general and about Canada's experience more specifically. This methodology at the intersection of law and book history lays the foundation for further inquiry by copyright legal scholars and book historians.[1] This kind of historical examination facilitates greater reflection on how the past has influenced the present and how it might inform future actions. Some of these reflections are offered here.

## The Importance of Evidence-Based Approaches to Copyright Law, Policy, and Practice

Lawmakers set policy and implement that policy through legislation. However, systematic assessments of whether the law has fulfilled its policy objectives are not an integral part of the process. Studying the copyright registration records, the archives of printers and publishers and early lawmakers, and the agreements between authors and the book trade, among other documentary material, introduced an evidence-based understanding of the larger context in which the law was operationalized. The findings demonstrate that the policy objectives that led to the enactment of the law were not necessarily realized in practice, whether the intent was to encourage schoolbook production or to advance national cultural imperatives. Recognizing that the stated policy did not align with the empirical realities required a deeper understanding of the way copyright law was practised, especially by those outside the legal profession. The relationships between educators and learners, and authors and the book trade, influenced the way the law evolved on the ground. Although copyright's behaviour is more difficult to capture today because of the absence of mandatory registration requirements, this finding from the past should cause current lawmakers to pause and question their assumptions about the law's impact in the absence of empirical evidence.

---

1   See further, Tawfik, "Copyright History as Book History."

## The Importance of Knowing Copyright's "Origin Story": Echoes of the Past in the Present

*Copyright and Education Policy*

In 1924, Quebec law professor Antonio Perrault delivered a speech to the Royal Society of Canada in which he described copyright as an evolutionary process that began with exclusive privileges conferred on printers and publishers and ended with authors being granted exclusive rights over their works. He suggested that this was a universal pattern and implied that the recognition of authors' rights was the apogee of enlightened thinking on the law: "L'histoire de la législation révéle qu'en tous pays il y eut évolution relativement aux droits des écrivains sur les oeuvres. On concède d'abord un privilège aux éditeurs, puis aux auteurs; plus tard l'on substitue un droit d'auteur au privilège. A la fin du 19ᵉ siècle, le droit d'auteur obtient un rayonnement plus considérable et est reconnu par des conventions internationales."[2]

If, as Perrault suggested, copyright evolves over time, his analysis did not look back far enough to the law's origins or, indeed, to its prehistory. It is clear from this book that copyright in British North America did not directly concern itself with domestic printing and publishing in the first half of the nineteenth century. Indeed, the statutes did not mandate domestic printing and publishing until 1875. Furthermore, the early history demonstrates that authors were only considered to the extent that they were teachers writing schoolbooks. The Lower Canadian experience provides the purest and most authentic example of copyright as education policy, without the distractions of industry or creator lobbies that were characteristic of later periods. The law's primary concern was the learner and the advancement of learning through the medium of print.

Antonio Perrault's position was consistent with twentieth-century thinking on copyright that saw only two dichotomous interests – creators and industry – jockeying for position within copyright policy. Indeed, as copyright became more closely tied to cultural policy, copyright reform in the last century alternated between legislative

---

2 Perrault, *La propriété littéraire et artistique*, 54. [The history of the legislation reveals that in every country there was an evolution regarding the rights of authors over their works. At the beginning, one conceded a privilege to publishers, then to authors. Later, authors' rights were substituted for the author's privilege. At the end of the nineteenth century, *le droit d'auteur* was given a larger scope and was recognized in international treaties.]

amendments to bolster industry and measures to support authors. The interests of users of copyright works were marginalized on the assumption that they had no independent stake in the law. The interventions by user rights groups, generally drawn from the public education and library sectors, were frequently ignored and sometimes scorned. Some Members of Parliament went so far as to vilify advocates of user rights for being radical extremists and pro-user zealots.[3]

Taking the long view on copyright is important. Historical explorations are essential in the legal context because unsubstantiated assumptions about the law risk being passed down from generation to generation to (mis)inform the approaches taken by lawyers, judges, and legal scholars. Similarly, biases about the dichotomous nature of copyright – as either a creator's right or a publisher's right – arise in the field of book history as well, which tends to study copyright at its margins without fully exploring its legal intricacies and nuances. Closer integration between these two disciplines would offer greater awareness about the law's influence on authors, publishers, and readers and the ways in which book and print culture helped to shape the law.

In the twenty-first century, learners have recaptured their place in the policy discourse. The concept of fair dealing has been defined as a user's right by the Supreme Court of Canada. This characterization has provided copyright user groups with a policy platform that is distinct from that of creators or industry. Recognizing fair dealing as a user's right has also reaffirmed the educational function of copyright, in other words, the policy interest that dominated the law at its genesis. Indeed, echoes of Canada's immutable copyright past remain. In holding that teachers could, without seeking prior permission, make copies of excerpts of copyright works for classroom use, Justice Abella of the Supreme Court of Canada explained in 2012: "Teachers have no ulterior motive when providing copies to students ... the teacher's purpose in providing copies is to enable the students to have the material they need for the purpose of studying."[4]

We are reminded of schoolmaster William Morris's plight in 1832: "I lay before the Committee a Manuscript Book containing a treatise on Arithmetic and practical Geometry ... I am of opinion that if my work was printed and put into practice, children could learn all the rules that it contains in one year."

---

3  See for example, Tawfik, "History in the Balance."
4  *Alberta (Education) v. Canadian Copyright Licensing Agency (Access Copyright)*, 2012 SCC 37 at para. 23.

While it is true that the text of the statute has changed over the centuries, and that the legal framework enabling teachers to reproduce works for their students has been markedly transformed, the imperative is the same. Fair dealing, which was introduced in the Copyright Act 1921, is borne of the recognition that as copyright rights expanded over time, they needed to be tempered by limitations and exceptions to facilitate access to knowledge. Indeed, many of the permissible uses that fall within fair dealing are grounded in activities related to learning such as private study, research, criticism, and the category of fair dealing for education, which was introduced into the Canadian statute in 2012. Without the long view, policy-makers risk giving too much weight to arguments raised by copyright groups that seek to restrict or limit the scope of fair dealing. The same impetus that gave rise to copyright in nineteenth-century Lower Canada, namely the desire to provide students with schoolbooks to learn from, is at the heart of contemporary constructions of fair dealing.

In this sense then, my initial objective in embarking on this work has been fulfilled. History provides an evidentiary foundation for addressing contemporary legal problems. In the recent decision of *York University v. Canadian Copyright Licensing Agency (Access Copyright)*, the Supreme Court of Canada relied, in part, on my historical findings to confirm that "[c]reators' rights and users' rights are mutually supportive of copyright's ends."[5] In other words, copyright has an end of its own, separate and apart from the specific interests of creators, industry, or users.

This methodology can also provide opportunities for scholarly reflection on systemic biases within the law. The historical record can tease out implicit or explicit assumptions about the kinds of works that were eligible for copyright or the individuals or groups deemed worthy of claiming rights. There is much to be explored in terms of the way copyright law and its practices were (and still are) experienced by Indigenous people, women, and racialized minorities. Understanding systemic exclusion from the vantage point of history provides a basis upon which to evaluate our current structural injustices. Scholarship at the intersection of critical legal studies and critical book and bibliographical studies would undoubtedly yield instructive insights.

---

5 *York University v. Canadian Copyright Licensing Agency (Access Copyright)* 2021 SCC 32 at paragraph 94, citing Tawfik, "History in the Balance."

*Copyright and Culture*

This book argues that in the nineteenth century, especially prior to Confederation, the reading and education needs of *Canadiens* were accommodated by the legislature in its policies and practices. It would be fruitful to consider in greater detail the role played by French Canada in the development of Canadian copyright law. How did the law advance or inhibit the literary, cultural, and educational aspirations of French Canadians? What influence did francophone authors, members of the book trade, politicians, jurists, and social reformers have in shaping the law? For example, largely at the insistence of French Canadian politicians, Canada was the first among its British Commonwealth peers to enact a moral rights provision in its copyright law in order to comply with Berne Convention obligations. Does nineteenth-century history provide a way of interrogating the extent of this Canadian distinctiveness?

This book also illustrates that Canadian protectionism over the domestic printing and publishing industry was a direct consequence of British intervention in 1842. Canada's colonial status and its proximity to the United States created the circumstances that led to a series of actions and reactions, including the determined pursuit of compulsory licensing. We know that compulsory licence provisions were included in the Copyright Act 1921, but these were rarely if ever invoked, as Canadian publishers pursued alternative strategies.[6] A study of the impact of compulsory licensing, especially in encouraging publishers to work around the law, would enhance our understanding of the alignment or misalignment of policy with the reality on the ground. This would enable more nuanced and evidence-based assessments of other government actions in support of the publishing industry. In 1993 and 1994 the federal Parliament repealed the compulsory licensing provisions in the Copyright Act to comply with Canada's international trade obligations.[7] At the same time, the federal government successfully negotiated an exemption in its trade agreements with the United States to

---

6   George O'Halloran, writing in 1928, referred to two applications for licences that were never granted because the authors in question voluntarily undertook to issue Canadian editions instead. O'Halloran, "Copyright in Canada." George Parker says that no successful licences were ever issued. See Parker, "Authors and Publishers on the Offensive."

7   See *An Act to Implement the North American Free Trade Agreement*, 1993, 40–41–42 Eliz. II, c. 44; and *An Act to Implement the Agreement Establishing the World Trade Organization*, 1994, 42–43 Eliz. II, c. 47.

shield Canada's cultural industries, including the publishing industry, from the full impact of liberalized trade.[8] This measure to safeguard Canada's cultural industries represents another echo of the past. Canadian policy-makers in the latter half of the twentieth century were driven by the same overarching concern as their nineteenth-century counterparts to protect domestic publishing in an international copyright context that threatened Canada's national cultural sovereignty. Whether this mechanism, which operates independently and is not expressly tied to copyright, has been more successful than the compulsory licence provisions in achieving Canada's cultural objectives would be an interesting subject for further scholarly examination.

If the nineteenth century was, for Canada, the colonial copyright period with all its strictures and geopolitical tensions, and the twentieth century represented the international copyright era with its expansionist tendencies, what will Canada's next 100 years of copyright look like? Canada is, after all, at the cusp of its third century of copyright and in the midst of the Fourth Industrial Revolution. The advent of new digital technologies has been as transformative as the invention of the printing press was centuries ago. This new technological frontier will inevitably influence the direction of international and domestic copyright developments and will continue to pose new policy challenges. I hope this book will help liberate Canadian copyright law and policy from the burdens of an unexamined past so that this next chapter in Canada's copyright story will be marked by greater independence of purpose and informed resolve, if ever.

---

8  The exemption was first introduced in the *Canada–United States Free Trade Agreement* (1988) and was carried forward in the *North American Free Trade Agreement* (1993) and in the *Canada-United States-Mexico Free Trade Agreement* (2020).

# Methodology Employed in Chapter 6 to Determine Copyright Registrations in Lower Canada from 1832 to 1841

The 1832 Copyright Act of Lower Canada required that a number of formalities be fulfilled for copyright to be secured. These included the deposit of a printed copy of the title page of the work in the "Clerk's office of the Superior Court of Original Jurisdiction in the District in which the author or proprietor shall reside," which in 1832 signified the judicial districts of Quebec, Montreal, Trois-Rivières and St-Francis. In addition, a notice of the copyright registration was to be printed after the title page of the work itself, and the title of the work was to be recorded in an official registry book. Finally, a copy of the entire work was to be deposited with the Clerk of the Court within three months of publication. In turn, the Clerk of the Court was to transmit to the Provincial Secretary, on an annual basis, a certified list of registrations as well as any copies of books or other material received as a result of the registration process.

The most comprehensive official data would be found in the registry books for the various judicial districts or in the certified lists held by the Provincial Secretary. Despite rigorous searching, the copyright registries for the most important districts, of Quebec and Montreal, have not been located.[1] Given that Quebec and Montreal were the most important publishing centres, those particular records would have yielded a

---

1 Some archivists at LAC and BAnQ suggest that these registries might still surface at some point because some material in their collections remains uncatalogued. However, others wonder whether they may have been destroyed in the fire at the Parliamentary Library in 1848. If and when the registries for the districts of Montreal and Quebec come to light, they may tell a different story. I am grateful to Evelyn Kolish and Ghislain Roussel at BAnQ for their attempts to locate the registries and for having found the one for Trois-Rivières. Patricia Kennedy at LAC also provided indispensable help and guidance.

rich body of information from which to develop theories about rates of registration and registration practices. Only the registry for the district of Trois-Rivières has been located at present. Even this copyright registry appears to be inaccurate, however, in that it only provides entries for the years 1832 (three registrations), 1847 (one registration), and 1855 (one registration). In its current state, the register does not include the registration of James Russell's *Matilda or the Indian's Captive: A Canadian Tale Founded on Fact*, printed by George Stobbs in 1833. According to the notice on the title page of the book itself, copyright was registered by the author in 1833. It was either the case that official record-keeping was poor, that the registration formalities for Russell's *Matilda* were never fully completed, or that there are pages missing from the registry. It was impossible to determine which of these possibilities was factually correct. I was not able to look at the actual registry and relied on digital images obtained from BAnQ, which are inconclusive. It is also true that copyright records were not always accurately maintained, so the registrar may have inadvertently omitted the record, but there is limited corroborating evidence to indicate whether Russell had completed all the requisite formalities. The records of the Provincial Secretary, to whom the various prothonotaries were to send their lists of copyright registrations as well as the requisite book deposits, are also missing or unavailable. The only official record I could uncover was the Provincial Secretary's letter book for 1832, which records the receipts from Trois-Rivières for that year, but the record does not identify the specific books deposited.

As a result of the fragmentary nature of the existing records, I have scoured a multitude of bibliographical records to develop as comprehensive a list as possible of titles printed and published in Lower Canada between 1832 and 1841. The statute was premised on the residence of the author rather than place of publication; however, most books by resident authors were in fact printed locally. To compile this list, I relied on a number of contemporaneous bibliographies, including G.B. Faribault, *Catalogue d'ouvrages sur l'histoire de l'Amérique, et en particulier sur celle du Canada, de la Louisiane, de l'Acadie, et autres lieux; avec des notes bibliographiques, critiques et littéraires* (Quebec: William Cowan, 1837); François-Maximilien Bibaud, *Bibliothèque canadienne, ou annales bibliographiques* (Montreal: Cérat & Bourguignon, 1858); and Philéas Gagnon, *Essai de bibliographie canadienne: inventaire d'une bibliothèque comprenant imprimés, manuscrits, estampes, etc. relatifs à l'histoire du Canada et des pays adjacents avec des notes bibliographiques* (Quebec: A. Côté, 1895). I cross-referenced these early bibliographical entries with online databases like Paul Aubin's Manuels Scolaires (ManScol), and the University of Alberta's Internet Archive, which are searchable by year. I then determined each publication's copyright status based on the notice after the title page of the book itself, which I reviewed either in hard copy, in microform, or in online digitized format, and through a smattering of individual registration certificates found in the John Neilson, Neilson & Cowan and Duvernay archives.

This methodology assumes that the printed copyright notice after the title page of the publication is evidence that the copyright had been perfected, although it is conceivable that the author or publisher failed to fulfil the other registration formalities. Because the statute imposed a penalty for anyone who printed a copyright notice fraudulently, I am presuming this would have been an effective deterrent. In some cases, the notice after the title page reproduced the actual text of the copyright registration itself. For these publications, at least, the evidence of a perfected copyright is unassailable. Other than those recorded in the registry at Trois-Rivières, or where the notice after the title page happened to provide the necessary details, relying on notices in the books as the only evidence of the copyright raised a further difficulty in terms of establishing the chronological order of registrations. The statute only required that the notice after the title page identify the year of registration rather than the day and month as well, so it was difficult in many cases to pinpoint a precise registration date.

Appendix 2 provides my reconstructed list of copyright registrations. I recognize that absolute accuracy cannot be guaranteed from the data I have compiled. Nevertheless, my findings are sufficiently comprehensive to offer a reliable picture of copyright registration patterns in Lower Canada, at least until the copyright registries for the districts of Montreal, Quebec, and St-Francis are recovered, if ever.

# Reconstructed Copyright Registrations in Lower Canada from 1832 to 1841 in Order of Registration Date

**1832: Nine Registrations**

David Chisholme, *Observations on the Rights of the British Colonies to representation in the Imperial Parliament* (Three-Rivers: George Stobbs, 1832). Copyright registered 22 March 1832 by Chisholme.

I. Pigott, *The Canadian Mechanic's Ready Reckoner, or, Tables for converting English lineal, square and solid measures into French* (Three-Rivers: George Stobbs, 1832). Copyright registered 17 May 1832 by Stobbs.

Jean Holmes, *Nouvel abrégé de géographie moderne suivi d'un appendice, et d'un abrégé de géographie sacrée, à l'usage de la jeunesse* (Quebec: Neilson & Cowan, 1832). Copyright registered 23 May 1832 by Neilson & Cowan.

Henri Des Rivières-Beaubien, *Traité sur les lois civiles du Bas-Canada* (Montreal: Ludger Duvernay, 1832). Copyright registered 6 July 1832 by Duvernay.

Hugues Heney, *Commentaire ou Observations sur l'Acte de la 31è année du Règne de Geo. III. chap. 31, communément appelé Acte Constitutionnel du Haut et Bas Canada* (Trois-Rivières: G. Stobbs, 1832). Copyright registered 11 August 1832 by Heney. Unable to find a record of his book having been published.

*Petit manuel des cérémonies romaines; à l'usage du diocèse de Québec* (Quebec: Chez Fréchette & Cie, 1832). Copyright registered 13 August 1832 by Jean-Baptiste Fréchette & Etienne Parent.

Hugues Heney, *Commentaire ou Observations sur l'Acte de la 31è année du Règne de Geo. III. chap. 31, communément appelé Acte Constitutionnel du Haut et Bas Canada* (Montreal: Leclère & Jones, 1832). Copyright registered 20 October 1832 by Leclère & Jones.

Neilson & Cowan, *Calendrier de Québec pour l'année 1833* (Quebec: Neilson & Cowan, 1832). Copyright registered 5 November 1832 by Neilson & Cowan.

Ludger Duvernay, *Calendrier de Montréal pour l'année 1833* (Montreal: Ludger Duvernay, 1832). Copyright registered 23 November 1832 by Duvernay.

## 1833: Twelve Registrations

Jean-Baptiste Boucher, *Recueil de cantiques à l'usage des missions, retraites et catéchismes*, dixième edition (Quebec: Neilson & Cowan, 1833). Copyright registered 7 May 1833 by Neilson & Cowan.

John MacDonald, *The Christian's Pocket Library in four parts*, 2nd ed. (Quebec: Neilson & Cowan, 1833). Copyright registered 17 May 1833 by Neilson & Cowan.

Joseph-François Perrault, *Abrégé de l'histoire du Canada en quatre parties*, première partie, 2nd ed. (Quebec: P. & W. Ruthven, 1832). Copyright registered 21 May 1833 by Peter and William Ruthven.

Joseph-François Perrault, *Abrégé de l'histoire du Canada en quatre parties*, troisième partie (Quebec: P. & W. Ruthven, 1833). Copyright registered 21 May 1833 by Peter and William Ruthven.

Joseph-François Perrault, *Abrégé de l'histoire du Canada en quatre parties*, quatrième partie (Quebec: P. & W. Ruthven, 1833). Copyright registered 21 May 1833 by Peter and William Ruthven.

*Le grand Catéchisme à l'usage du diocèse de Québec* (Quebec: T. Cary & Cie, 1833). Copyright registered 19 July 1833 by Cary. Assuming registration based on the copyright notice in the 1836 third edition. Unable to locate this volume.

Jean Holmes, *Nouvel abrégé de géographie moderne suivi d'un appendice, et d'un abrégé de géographie sacrée, à l'usage de la jeunesse*, seconde partie (Quebec: Neilson & Cowan, 1833). Copyright registered 7 August 1833 by Neilson & Cowan.

Ludger Duvernay, *Calendrier de 1834 pour Montréal* (Montreal: Ludger Duvernay, 1833). Copyright registered 20 September 1833 by Duvernay.

Neilson & Cowan, *Calendrier de Québec pour l'année 1834* (Quebec: Neilson & Cowan, 1833). Copyright registered 7 November 1833 by Neilson & Cowan.

Francois-Xavier Noiseux, *Liste chronologique des évêques et des prêtres, tant séculiers que réguliers, employés au service de l'église du Canada depuis l'établissement de ce pays* (Quebec: T. Cary & Cie, 1834). Copyright registered 6 December 1833 by Cary & Co.

James Russell, *Matilda, or, the Indian's Captive: A Canadian tale founded on fact* (Trois-Rivières: George Stobbs, 1833). Copyright registered in 1833 by Russell.

Jean Holmes, *Nouvel abrégé de géographie moderne suivi d'un appendice, et d'un abrégé de géographie sacrée, à l'usage de la jeunesse*, 2nd ed. (Quebec: Neilson & Cowan, 1833). Contains notice of original 1832 copyright registration by Neilson & Cowan.

## 1834: Nine Registrations

*Lower Canada Farmers' and Mechanics' Almanack* (Quebec: Neilson & Cowan, 1834). Copyright registered 22 January 1834 by Neilson & Cowan.

Edouard Moreau, *Instructions sur l'art des accouchemens pour les sages-femmes de la campagne* (Montreal: Fabre & Perrault, 1834). Copyright registered 8 April 1834 by Moreau.

*The Canada Commercial Register, or Montreal Counting-House Directory for 1834* (Montreal: Andrew H. Armour & Co., 1834). Copyright registered 12 May 1834 by Robert Armour, Robert Armour Jr., and Andrew Harvie Armour.

Leclère & Jones, *Calendrier de 1835, pour Montréal* (Montreal: Leclère & Jones, 1834). Copyright registered 28 July 1834 by Leclère & Jones.

Alfred Hawkins, *Hawkins's Pictures of Quebec with historical recollections* (Quebec: Neilson & Cowan, 1834). Copyright registered 5 August 1834. Registrant not identified but likely Hawkins.

Andre Jobin & Adolphus Bourne (lithographer), *Carte de l'Île de Montréal* (Montreal: 1834). Copyright registered in 1834 by Jobin.

Andre Jobin & Adolphus Bourne (lithographer), *Map of the City of Montreal* (Montreal: 1834). Copyright registered in 1834 by Jobin.

John Bruce, Charles Secretan, James Prendergast, *The Quebec Commercial List* (Quebec: T. Cary, 1834). Assuming registration in 1834 by Bruce, Secretan, Prendergast.

Neilson & Cowan, *Calendrier de Québec pour l'annee 1835* (Quebec: Neilson & Cowan, 1834). Assuming registration in 1834 by Neilson & Cowan.

## 1835: Fourteen Registrations

Joseph Vincent Quiblier, *Abrégé chronologique d'histoire sacrée et profane à l'usage du Collège de Montréal* (Montreal: Leclère & Jones, 1835). Copyright registered 8 January 1835 by Quiblier.

Joseph Vincent Quiblier, *Cours abrégé de rhétorique à l'usage du Collège de Montréal* (Montreal: Leclère & Jones, 1835). Copyright registered 9 January 1835 by Quiblier.

Alfred Hawkins, *Plan of the city of Quebec respectfully inscribed to the Mayor* (Quebec: 1835). Copyright registered April 1835. Registrant not identified but likely Hawkins.

John Bruce, Charles Secretan, James Prendergast, *The Quebec Commercial List* (Quebec: T. Cary & Co., 1835). Copyright registered 27 May 1835 by Bruce, Secretan, Prendergast.

William Evans, *A Treatise on the Theory and Practice of Agriculture adapted to the Cultivation and Economy of the Animal and Vegetable Productions of Agriculture in Canada* (Montreal: Fabre & Perrault, 1835). Copyright registered 9 July 1835 by Evans.

Jérôme Demers, *Institutiones philosophicae ad usum studiosae juventutis* (Quebec: Cary & Cie, 1835). Copyright registered 22 August 1835 by Cary & Cie.

Jean Holmes, *Abridgment of Modern Geography with an appendix and an Abridgment of Sacred Geography adapted for Youth, Part I, comprising America and Europe* (Quebec: Cary & Co., 1836). Copyright registered 26 September 1835 by Cary & Co.

Neilson & Cowan, *Calendrier de Québec pour l'Année Bissextile 1836* (Quebec: Neilson & Cowan, 1835). Copyright registered 22 October 1835 by Neilson & Cowan.

Neilson & Cowan, *Quebec Sheet Almanac for 1836* (Quebec: Neilson & Cowan, 1835). Copyright registered 4 December 1835 by Neilson & Cowan. Print copy of almanac unavailable for confirmation. Relying on copy of official copyright registration, LAC Fonds Collection Neilson.

Jean Antoine Bouthillier, *Traité d'arithmétique pour l'usage des écoles*, 3rd ed. (Quebec: Neilson & Cowan, 1835). Copyright registered in 1835 by Neilson & Cowan.

*Map of Lower Canada* (St-Francis: Walton & Gaylord, 1835). Copyright registered in 1835 by Walton & Gaylord.

George Okill Stuart, *Reports of cases argued and determined in the Courts of King's Bench and in the Provincial Court of Appeals of Lower Canada, with a few more important cases in the Court of Vice Admiralty* (Quebec: Neilson & Cowan, 1834). Copyright registered in 1835 by Stuart. Neilson & Cowan issued a new state of the book sometime in 1834 or 1835. The copyright notice can be found at the back just before the Index.

Zadock Thompson, *Geography and History of Lower Canada designed for the use of schools* (St-Francis: Walton & Gaylord). Copyright registered in 1835 by Walton & Gaylord.

Ludger Duvernay, *Calendrier de l'Année Bissextile 1836, pour Montréal* (Montreal: Ludger Duvernay, 1835). Contains notice of original copyright registered 20 September 1832 by Duvernay.

## 1836: Eleven Registrations

John Bruce, Charles Secretan, James Prendergast, *The Quebec Commercial List* (Quebec: Cary & Co., 1836). Copyright registered 23 May 1836 by Bruce, Secretan, Prendergast.

William Evans, *Supplementary Volume to A Treatise on the Theory and Practice of Agriculture adapted to the Cultivation and Economy of the Animal and Vegetable Productions of Agriculture in Canada* (Montreal: Louis Perrault, 1836). Copyright registered 8 July 1836 by Evans.

Casimir Ladreyt, *Nouvelle arithmétique raisonnée ou Cours complet de calcul théorique et pratique, à l'usage des élèves des collèges et des maisons d'éducation de l'un et l'autre sexe* (Montreal: Imprimé pour l'auteur, 1836). Copyright registered 14 July 1836 by Ladreyt.

Joseph-François Perrault, *Abrégé de l'histoire en cinq parties – cinquième partie* (Quebec: P. & W. Ruthven, 1836). Copyright registered 1 September 1836 by William Ruthven.

*Extrait du rituel de Québec contenant l'administration des sacremens [sic] de baptême, de la confirmation, de pénitence, de l'eucharistie, de l'extrême-onction et de mariage: et aussi les bénédictions et diverses formes d'actes* (Quebec: Cary & Cie, 1836). Copyright registered 2 September 1836 by Cary & Cie.

Samuel Neilson, *Calendrier de Québec pour l'année 1837* (Quebec: Samuel Neilson, 1836). Copyright registered 19 October 1836 by Neilson.

*Le livre des enfans [sic], Nouvel alphabet français*, 2nd ed. (Quebec: Samuel Neilson, 1836). Copyright registered 29 November 1836 by Neilson. Unable to locate record of book having been published. Relying on copy of official copyright registration, LAC Fonds Collection Neilson.

*Map of Upper Canada* (St-Francis: Walton & Gaylord, 1836). Copyright registered in 1836 by Walton & Gaylord.

Ludger Duvernay, *Calendrier de Montréal pour l'année 1837* (Montreal: Ludger Duvernay, 1836). Contains notice of original copyright registered 20 September 1832 by Duvernay.

*Le grand Catéchisme à l'usage du diocèse de Québec*, 3rd ed. (Quebec: Cary & Cie, 1836). Contains notice of original copyright registered in 1833 by Cary & Cie.

Neilson & Cowan, *Lower Canada Farmers' and Mechanics' Almanack* (Quebec: Neilson & Cowan, 1836). Contains notice of original copyright registered in 1834 by Neilson & Cowan.

## 1837: Fourteen Registrations

Jean Larkin, *Eklekta Muthistorias* (Montreal: John Jones, 1837). Copyright registered 9 January 1837 by Joseph Vincent Quiblier. In Greek and French.

Joseph Laurin, *Traité d'arithmétique contenant une claire et familière explication de ses principes et suivi d'un traité d'algèbre* (Quebec: Fréchette & Cie, 1836). Copyright registered 4 February 1837 by Laurin.

*Nouvel abrégé de l'histoire de la France depuis Pharamond jusqu'à nos jours; à l'usage de la jeunesse* (Quebec: Cary & Cie, 1837). Copyright registered 21 February 1837 by Cary & Cie.

*Notice sur l'oeuvre de la propagation de la foi pour le diocèse de Québec* (Quebec: Fréchette & Cie, 1837). Copyright registered 27 February 1837 by Fréchette & Cie.

*Sketch of the Association for the Propagation of the Faith in the Diocese of Quebec* (Quebec: Samuel Neilson, 1837). Copyright registered 6 March 1837 by Neilson.

Francois-Xavier Paradis, *New Ready Reckoner: for the Use of Merchants, Masters of Ships and Measurers of Timber, comprising deals and staves of all sizes, reduced to Quebec standard, with several useful comparative results respecting lumber* (Quebec: William Cowan, 1837). Copyright registered 6 March 1837 by Paradis.

Joseph Laurin, *Livre destiné à l'instruction de l'enfance ou nouvel alphabet français à l'usage des enfans* [*sic*] (Quebec: P. Ruthven, 1837). Copyright registered 9 March 1837 by Ruthven.

George-Barthélemy Faribault, *Catalogue d'ouvrages sur l'histoire de l'amérique, et en particulier sur celle du Canada, de la Louisiane, de l'Acadie et autres lieux, ci-devant connus sous le nom de Nouvelle-France* (Quebec: William Cowan, 1837). Copyright registered 17 April 1837 by Faribault.

Jean Larkin, *Grammaire grecque, à l'usage du Collège de Montréal*, 1st ed. (Montreal: John Jones, 1837). Copyright registered 6 July 1837 by Joseph Vincent Quiblier.

*Armour & Ramsay's Interest Tables: Tables Shewing the Interest at Six per centum of any Sum from One Pound to One Thousand Pounds, from One Day to Three Hundred & Sixty-Five Days and from One Month to Twelve Months* (Montreal: Armour & Ramsay, 1837). Copyright registered 16 September 1837 by Armour & Ramsay.

Michel Bibaud, *Histoire du Canada, sous la domination française* (Montreal: John Jones, 1837). Copyright registered 18 September 1837 by Bibaud.

William Neilson, *Calendrier de Québec pour l'année 1838* (Quebec: William Neilson, 1837). Copyright registered 5 November 1837 by Neilson.

Henry Hughes, *A Treatise on Hydrophobia* (Montreal: Herald Office, 1837). Copyright registered by Hughes.

John Bruce, Charles Secretan, James Prendergast, *The Quebec Commercial List* (Quebec: T. Cary, 1837). Contains notice of original copyright registered in 1836 by Bruce, Secretan, Prendergast.

## 1838: One Registration

William Neilson, *Calendrier de Québec pour l'année 1839* (Quebec: William Neilson, 1838). Contains notice of original copyright registered 5 November 1837 by Neilson.

## 1839: Seven Registrations

Newton Bosworth, *Hochelaga Depicta – The Early History and Present State of the City and Island of Montreal* (Montreal: William Greig, 1839). Copyright registered 15 February 1839 by Greig.

Walter Henry, *Trifles from my Portfolio, or Recollections of Scenes and Small Adventures during Twenty-Nine Years' Military Service in the Peninsular War and Invasion of France, the East Indies, Campaign in Nepaul [sic], St. Helena during the Detention and until the Death of Napoleon, and Upper and Lower Canada* (Quebec: William Neilson, 1839). Copyright registered 28 September 1839 by Neilson.

John Lovell, *The Lower Canada Almanack and Montreal Commercial Directory for 1840* (Montreal: John Lovell, 1839). Copyright registered 19 October 1839 by Lovell.

Joseph-François Perrault, *Traité d'agriculture adapté au climat du Bas-Canada* (Quebec: Fréchette & Cie, 1839). Copyright registered 29 November 1839 by Fréchette & Cie.

Jean Holmes, *Nouvel Abrégé de Géographie Moderne suivi d'un appendice, et d'un Abrégé de géographie sacrée, à l'usage de la jeunesse*, 3rd ed. (Quebec: William Neilson, 1839). Contains notice of original copyright registered in 1832 by Neilson & Cowan.

Louis Perrault, *Calendrier de Montréal pour l'année bissextile 1840* (Montreal: L. Perrault, 1839). BAnQ has hard copy, but I was unable to view it. I assume registration by Perrault based on practice in 1841.

William Neilson, *Calendrier de Québec pour l'année 1840* (Quebec: William Neilson, 1839). I have not been able to locate a record of this particular calendar but I am assuming that Neilson issued it and that it contained a notice of the earlier registration in 1837, similar to the 1839 and 1841 calendars, which are available online.

## 1840: Nine Registrations

John Richardson, *The Canadian Brothers; or, the Prophecy Fulfilled: A Tale of the Late American War* (Montreal: Armour & Ramsay, 1840). Copyright registered 2 January 1840 by Richardson.

Nicolas Benjamin Doucet, *Fundamental Principles of the Laws of Canada as they existed under the natives, as they were changed under the French Kings, and as they were modified and altered under the domination of England* (Montreal: John Lovell, 1841). Copyright registered 14 February 1840 by Doucet.

Joseph-Vincent Quiblier, *Cours abrégé de belles lettres à l'usage du collège de Montréal* (Montreal: C.P Leprohon, 1840). Copyright registered 21 March 1840 by Quiblier.

Luke Burke, *Phrenological Enquiries Parts I & II* (Quebec: William Cowan, 1840). Copyright registered 6 August 1840 by Burke.

*Neuvaine en forme de litanies, en l'honneur du bienheureux Alphonse Rodriguez, frère coadjuteur temporel de la Compagnie de Jesus béatifié le 12 juin 1825, par la Sainteté Léon XII, et dont la fête a été fixée par le Saint Siège au 30 Octobre* (Quebec: Louis Perrault, 1840). Copyright registered 8 October 1840. Registrant not identified. I assume registration by Perrault.

Alfred Hawkins, *This Plan of the City of Quebec* (Quebec: 1840). Copyright registered April 1840. Registrant not identified. Assume Hawkins.

William Neilson, *Calendrier de Québec pour l'année 1841* (Quebec: William Neilson, 1840). Contains notice of earlier copyright registration in 1837 by Neilson.

*Notice sur l'oeuvre de la propagation de la foi pour le diocèse de Québec* (Quebec: Fréchette & Cie,1840). Contains notice of original copyright registered in 1837 by Fréchette & Cie.

Amable-Daniel Duchaine, *Calendrier de l'année 1841, pour Montréal* (Montreal: Louis Perrault, 1840). BAnQ has a hard copy but I have been unable to view it. I assume registration by Perrault based on the practice in 1841.

**1841: Seven Registrations**

*Petit manuel de l'Archiconfrérie du très-saint et immaculé coeur de Marie, établie dans l'Eglise Cathédrale de Montréal, le 7 Février 1841* (Montreal: Bureau des Mélanges Religieux, 1841). Copyright registered 16 February 1841. Registrant not identified. I assume registration by Mélanges Religieux.

*An Easy and Concise Introduction to Modern Geography, containing an enlarged account of the British North American Colonies, particularly Lower and Upper Canada, for the use of Canadian Schools* (Quebec: William Cowan, 1841). Copyright registered 23 February 1841 by Cowan.

*Cours d'histoire contenant 1) L'Abrégé de l'Histoire Sainte, 2) L'Abrégé de l'Histoire des principaux peoples du monde et 3) L'Histoire abrégée du Canada précédée d'un précis de l'Histoire de France, à l'usage des écoles chrétiennes* (Montreal: Louis Perrault, 1841). Copyright registered 30 April 1841 by Perrault.

*Chemin de la croix appelé communément via crucis* (Quebec: Fréchette & Cie, 1841). Copyright registered 14 June 1841 by Fréchette & Cie.

Amable-Daniel Duchaine, *Calendrier de l'année 1842 pour Montréal* (Montreal: Louis Perrault, 1841). Copyright registered 19 November 1841 by Perrault.

Robert C. Greggie, *Practical Guide to a right understanding of the prefixes and affixes in the English Language, in two parts (for the use of schools)* (Quebec: William Neilson, 1841). Copyright registered 24 November 1841 by Greggie.

Joseph Cauchon, *Notions élémentaires de physique, avec planches, à l'usage des maisons d'éducation* (Quebec: Fréchette & Cie, 1841). Copyright registered 9 December 1841 by Cauchon.

# Methodology Employed in Chapter 9 to Determine Copyright Registrations in the Province of Canada from 1841 to 1867

The data relied on were drawn primarily from the indexes to the copyright registries held at Library and Archives Canada (LAC).[1] Reliance on the indexes alone for official registration data was unfortunate because they are not entirely accurate. The ability to review the actual copyright registries, which provided more accurate information and factual details, would have resolved many questions and gaps in my records. I was able to consult the full text copyright registries from 1841 to 1867, which were available at LAC when I first began this research. Unfortunately, by the time I embarked on chapter 9 and the data analysis, the copyright registries had become unavailable as they had been transferred to the Canadian Intellectual Property Office and temporarily lost. While LAC has since retrieved many of the records, the copyright registries for the Province of Canada remained unaccounted for at the time of writing. It will be important to reconcile the indices with the full text of each copyright registration.

I discovered many books with copyright notices in the publications that were not recorded in the indices. I excluded them from consideration on the assumption that the copyright had never been fully perfected, but it is equally likely that the indexes themselves are incorrect. For example, in the report of the Parliamentary Librarian for the year 1869 there is mention of a copyright deposit for G. Doutre, *Les lois de la procédure civile* (Montreal: Eusèbe Sénécal, 1867). There is a copyright notice in the book itself as well, but this title does not appear in the index, strongly suggesting an error in the index rather than an unperfected copyright.

Another discrepancy can be found in a parliamentary report commissioned in 1859 in anticipation of the consolidation of the statutes of

---

1  LAC, RG 105 vol. 378 (1 December 1841–26 April 1865); RG 105, vol. 379 (1865–1868).

the Province of Canada. This report suggests that Robert Christie regis-tered *A History of the Late Province of Canada* before Alexander Davidson. However, the record also indicated that Christie did not complete all the necessary formalities – the record stated "Incomplete, only two volumes deposited."[2] The bibliographical records of this work show that it was published in six volumes from 1848 to 1855. The notices included in the first two volumes claimed that the book was entered in the copyright registry in 1841, but these notices were dated February 1848 and June 1848 respectively. The latter dates are consistent with the year of publication of these volumes. Since the statute required the deposit of the book at the time of registration, Christie could not have lawfully registered his copyright in 1841, which suggests that the reference to 1841 in the notices may have been a misprint. Further, I was able to consult the official handwritten registration at LAC, which identified Davidson as the first and only registrant in 1841. In addition, William Riddell's paper "The First Copyrighted Book in the Province of Canada," published in 1929, is exclusively about Davidson and the *Canada Spelling Book*. Until such time as more conclusive evidence surfaces about Christie's copyright, I am assuming that Davidson was the first registrant in the Province of Canada.

As a final remark, the early copyright archives provide an invalua-ble resource for legal scholars, book historians, and cultural historians, among others. It is my fervent wish that these archives can be fully restored and made readily available to future copyright researchers.

---

2  See *Return to an Address from the Legislative Assembly, dated 11th April, of Books published and copyrighted in Canada under the Act 4th and 5th Victoria, cap. 60 (1841), showing the number of registered in each year, names of Authors and Proprietors, by whom and where printed, and other information required...*, Appendix to the Journals of the Legislative Assembly of the Province of Canada, 1859, 22 Vict., Appendix no. 60.

# Bibliography

**Archives**

American Antiquarian Society Library, Joseph Lancaster Papers, Worcester, MA (JLP)

American Philosophical Society. Benjamin Smith Barton Papers. Section 1: Correspondence

Archives of Richard Bentley & Son 1829–1898 (Cambridge: Chadwyck-Healey, 1976)

Archives of the House of Longman 1794–1914 (Cambridge: Chadwyck-Healey, 1978)

Bibliothèque et Archives nationales du Québec (BAnQ)

    BAnQ (Québec), Fonds Imprimerie Neilson

    BAnQ (Québec), Fonds Famille Neilson

    BAnQ (Vieux-Montréal), Fonds Ludger Duvernay

Collection du Centre d'Histoire de Saint-Hyacinthe, Saint-Hyacinthe, Québec. Fonds Augustin-Norbert Morin

Library and Archives Canada (LAC)

    Canada East: Provincial Secretary Letterbooks, Quebec, Lower Canada and Canada East

    Civil Secretary's Correspondence Quebec, Lower Canada and Canada East (1760–1863)

    Civil Secretary's Letter Books Lower Canada

    Civil Secretary and Provincial Secretary Applications for Licenses, Bonds and Certificates, Quebec, Lower Canada and Canada East (1763–1867)

    Collection Joseph-François Perrault

    Copyright Registries, Province of Canada (1841–68)

    Fonds Canadian Intellectual Property Office

Fonds James Kempt
Fonds Wilfrid Laurier, Family Papers
Fonds Denis-Benjamin Viger
Index to Copyright Registries, Province of Canada (1841–68)
Neilson Collection
Register of Commissions for Notaries, Advocates and Land Surveyors,
    Land Surveyor for the City of Quebec, District of Quebec
University of Toronto, Thomas Fisher Rare Book Library, Canadian Pamphlets
    and Broadsides Digital Collection

**Case Law**

*British North America and Canada*

*Alberta (Education) v. Canadian Copyright Licensing Agency (Access Copyright)*,
    2012 SCC 37.
*Boucher v. Casgrain* K.B.Q. 1810.
*CCH Canadian Ltd. v. Law Society of Upper Canada*, 2004 SCC 13.
*Fraser v. Peltier* K.B.Q. 1816.
*Langlois v. Vincent* (1874) 18 Lower Canada Jurist 160.
*Smiles v. Bedford*, [1877] 1 O.A.R. 436.
*Smith v. Binet* K.B.Q. 1821.
*Tele-Direct (Publications) Inc. v. American Business Information Inc* [1998] 2 F.C 22.
*Théberge v. Galerie d'art du Petit Champlain inc.*, 2002 SCC 34.
*York University v. Canadian Copyright Licensing Agency (Access Copyright)* 2021
    SCC 32.

*United Kingdom (and Great Britain)*

*Beckford v. Hood* (1798) 7 D. & E. 620.
*Donaldson v. Becket*, Hansard, 1st ser. 17 (1774): 953–1003.
*Jefferys v. Boosey* (1854) 4 H.L.C 815.
*Hime (or Hine) v. Dale*, 1803, 2 Camp. 27.
*Routledge v Low,* (1868) L.R 3 H.L.100.

*United States*

*Stowe v. Thomas* 23 F. Cas. 201 (1853).
*Wheaton v. Peters* 33 U.S 591 (1834).
*Georgia v. Public.Resource.org Inc.* 140 S.Ct. 1498 (2020).

## Legislation

*British North America*

LOWER CANADA

*An Act for the Encouragement of Elementary Education,* 1829, 9 Geo. 4, c. 46.

*An Act for the Establishment of Free Schools and the Advancement of Learning in this Province,* 1801, 41 Geo. 3, c. 17.

*An Act for the Protection of Copy Rights,* 1832, 2 Will. 4, c. 53.

*An Act to Appropriate Certain Sums of Money therein Mentioned to the Encouragement of Education in this Province,* 1832, 2 Will. 4, c. 30.

*An Act to Authorize the purchase of a certain number of the Topographical Map and Statistical Tables to be Published by Joseph Bouchette, Esq,* 1829, 9 Geo. 4, c. 68.

*An Act to grant an Aid towards printing in the French Language, the Treatise on Agriculture written by William Evans,* 1836, 6 Will. 4, c. 44.

*An Act to grant to Jean Baptiste Bedard the exclusive Right and Privilege of erecting Bridges in this Province, according to the models therein mentioned,* 1807, 47 Geo. 3, c. 15.

*An Act to make further provision for the Encouragement of Education in this Province,*1831, 1 Will. 4, c. 7.

*An Act to Promote the Progress of Useful Arts in this Province,* 1824, 4 Geo. 4, c. 25.

*An Act to provide for the distribution of certain copies of the Topographical Map and Statistical Tables published by Joseph Bouchette Esquire,* 1832, 2 Will. 4, c. 52.

*An Act to Provide for the publication of certain Laws and for the Printing and distributing of certain Persons, for the purpose of public information, all Laws that have been or shall be passed in the Legislature of this Province under the present Constitution,* 1793, 33 Geo. 3, c. 1.

NEW BRUNSWICK

*An Act for encouraging and extending Literature in this Province,* 1805, 45 Geo. 3, c. 12.

*An Act to Provide for Reporting and Publishing the Decisions of the Supreme Court,* 1836, 6 Will. 4, c. 14.

*Judicature Act,* Revised Statutes of New Brunswick 1973, c. J-2.

NOVA SCOTIA

*An Act for applying certain Monies therein mentioned for the service of the year of our Lord One Thousand Eight Hundred and Forty, and for other purposes therein specified,* 1840, 3 Vict. c. 1.

*An Act for Securing Copy Rights,* 1839, 2 Vict. c. 36.

*Title XXXI: Of the Law of Copyright*, R.S, 1851, c. 119.
*To Appoint a New Board of Governors of Dalhousie College*, 1840, 3 Vict. c. 7.

## British North America: Province of Canada

*An Act to Amend the Act relating to Duties of Customs*, 1859, 22 Vict., c. 2.
*An Act to amend the Charter of the University established at Toronto by His late Majesty King George the Fourth, to provide for the more satisfactory government of the said University, and for other purposes connected with the same, and with the College and Royal Grammar School forming an appendage thereof*, 1849, 12 Vict., c. 82.
*An Act to Amend the Law relative to Duties of Customs*, 1849, 12 Vict. 1.
*An Act to amend the Laws relating to the University of Toronto, by separating its functions as a University from those assigned to it as a College, and by making better provision for the management of the property thereof and that of Upper Canada College*, 1853, 16 Vict. c. 89.
*An Act to Consolidate and Amend the Laws of Patents for Inventions in this Province*, 1849, 12 Vict., c. 24.
*An Act to extend the Provincial Copy-right Act to persons resident in the United Kingdom, on certain conditions* 1847, 10 & 11 Vict., c. 28.
*An Act for granting Provincial Duties of Customs*, 1845, 8 Vict., c. 3.
*An Act to impose a duty on Foreign re-prints of British Copyright Works*, 1850, 13 & 14 Vict., c. 6.
*An Act for the Protection of Copy Rights in this Province*, 1841, 4 & 5 Vict. c. 61.
*An Act to Provide for the Indemnification of Parties in Lower Canada whose Property was Destroyed during the Rebellion in the years 1837 and 1838*, 1849, 12 Vict., c. 58.
*An Act to provide for the translation into the French Language of the Laws of this Province*, 1841, 4 & 5 Vict., c. 11.
*An Act to repeal certain Acts therein mentioned and to make provision for the establishment and maintenance of Common Schools throughout the Province*, 1841, 4 & 5 Vict., c. 18.
*An Act for repealing and consolidating the present Duties of Customs in this Province*, 1847, 10 & 11 Vict., c. 31.
*An Act Respecting Copyright*, R.S 1859, 22 Vict., c. 31.
*An Act respecting certain Duties of Customs*, 1860, 23 Vict., c. 18.

UPPER CANADA

*An Act to make Permanent and Extend the Provisions of the Laws now in force for the Establishment and Regulation of Common Schools throughout this Province and for granting to His Majesty a Further Sum of Money to Promote and Encourage Education within the Same.* 1824, 4 Geo 4 c. 8.

*An Act Providing for the publication of reports of the decisions of His Majesty's Court of King's Bench in this Province*, 1823, 4 Geo. 4, c. 3.

*An Act to Repeal Certain Parts of an Act Passed in the fourteenth year of His Majesty's Reign, entitled "An Act for making more effectual provisions for the Government of the Province of Quebec in North America" and to introduce the English Law as the Rule of Decision in all matters of controversy relating to Property and Civil Rights*, Statutes of Upper Canada, 1792, 32 Geo. 3, c. 1.

*Canada*

*An Act to Amend the Act respecting Copyrights*, 1872 (Royal Assent refused).

*An Act to amend The Copyright Act Chapter sixty-two of the Revised Statutes*, 1889, 52 Vict., c. 29. (not proclaimed)

*An Act to amend the Copyright Act*, 1895, 58–59 Vict., c. 37. (not proclaimed)

*An Act to amend the Copyright Act*, 1900, 63 & 64 Vict., c. 25.

*An Act to Amend the Copyright Act 1921*, 1923, 13 & 14 Geo. 5.

*An Act to amend and consolidate the Law relating to Copyright*, 1921, 11–12 Geo. 5, c. 24 (assented to in 1921, amended in 1923 13 & 14 Geo. 5 and proclaimed into force in 1924).

*An Act Respecting Copyrights*, 1868, 31 Vict., c. 54.

*An Act respecting Copyrights*, 1875, 38 Vict., c. 88.

*An Act respecting Copyrights*, R.S 1886, 49 Vict., c. 62.

*An Act to impose a duty on foreign reprints of British copyright works*, 1868, 31 Vict., c. 56.

*An Act to Implement the Agreement Establishing the World Trade Organization*, 1994, 42–43 Eliz. II, c. 47.

*An Act to Implement the North American Free Trade Agreement*, 1993, 40–41–42 Eliz. II, c. 44.

*Copyright Act* R.S.C 1985 c. C-42.

*Library and Archives Canada Act*, S.C. 2004, c. 11.

*France*

*Décret de la Convention Nationale du dix-neuf juillet 1793 relatif aux droits de propriété des Auteurs d'écrits en tout genre, des Compositeurs de musique, des Peintres et des Dessinateurs.*

*Great Britain and United Kingdom*

*An Act to Amend and Consolidate the Law relating to Copyright*, 1911, c. 46.

*An Act to Amend the Copyright Act*, 1842, 5 & 6 Vict., c. 45.

*An Act to Amend the Laws Relating to Customs*, 1842, 5 & 6 Vict., c. 47.

*An Act to Amend the Law relating to International Copyright*, 1844, 7 & 8 Vict., c. 12.

*An Act to amend the Law relating to the Protection in the Colonies of Works entitled to Copyright in the United Kingdom*, 1847, 10 & 11 Vict., c.95.

*An Act to Amend the Laws for the Regulation of the Trade of the British Possessions Abroad*, 1842, 5 & 6 Vict., c. 49.

*An Act to amend the several Acts for the Encouragement of Learning, by securing the Copies and Copyright of Printed Books, to the Authors of such Books or their Assigns...*, 1814, 54 Geo. 3, c. 156.

*An Act for the Encouragement of Learning, by Vesting the Copies of Printed Books in the Authors or Purchasers of such Copies, during the Times therein mentioned*, 1710, 8 Ann., c. 21.

*An Act for the further Encouragement of Learning, in the United Kingdom of Great Britain and Ireland, by securing the Copies and Copyright of printed Books to the Authors of such Books, or their Assigns for the Time herein mentioned*, 1801, 41 Geo.III, c.107.

*An Act for the General Regulation of the Customs*, 1833, 3 & 4 Will. 4, c. 52.

*An Act to Give Effect to an Act of the Parliament of the Dominion of Canada respecting Copyright*, 1875, 38 & 39 Vict., c. 53.

*An Act to Make Temporary Provision for the Government of Lower Canada*, 1838, 1 Vict., c. 9.

*An Act for Making More Effectual Provision for the Government of the Province of Quebec in North America*, 1814, 14 Geo. 3, c. 83.

*An Act for Preventing Abuses in Printing Seditious, Treasonable, and Unlicensed Books and Pamphlets, and for Regulating of Printing and Printing Presses 1662*, 3 & 4 Car.II, c. 33.

*An Act for the Union of Canada, Nova Scotia, and New Brunswick, and the Government thereof; and for Purposes connected therewith*, 1867, 30 & 31 Vict., c. 3 .

*An Act to Regulate the Trade of British Possessions Abroad*, 1845, 8 & 9 Vict., c. 93.

*An Act to Remove Doubt about the Validity of Colonial Laws*, 1865, 28 & 29 Vict., c. 63.

*An Act to Repeal certain parts of an Act passed in the fourteenth year of His Majesty's Reign, entitled, 'An Act for making more effectual provision for the Government of the Province of Quebec in North America' and for making further provision for the Government of the said Province*, 1791, 31 Geo. 3, c. 31.

*An Act to Repeal so much of an Act of the Third and Fourth Years of Her present Majesty, to re-unite the Provinces of Upper and Lower Canada, and for the Government of Canada, as relates to the Use of the English Language in Instruments relating to the Legislative Council and Legislative Assembly of the Province of Canada*, 1847–1848, 11–12 Vict., c. 56.

*An Act to Reunite the Provinces of Upper and Lower Canada, and for the Government of Canada*, 1840, 3 & 4 Vict., c. 35.

*Ordinance further to continue, for a limited time, certain Acts therein mentioned* 1840, 3 Vict., c. 15.

*United States*

An Act to amend the Several Acts Respecting Copy Rights, 1831, c. 16, 21st
  Congress, 2d Session. 4 Stat 436.
An act to amend title sixty, chapter three, of the Revised Statutes of the United States,
  relating to copyrights, 1891, 26 Stat. 1106.
An Act for the Encouragement of Learning, by securing the copies of maps, charts
  and book to the authors and proprietors of such copies during the times therein
  mentioned, 1790, 1 Statutes at Large 124.
An Act to Establish the Smithsonian Institution for the Increase and Diffusion of
  Knowledge among Men, 1846, c. 178, 29th Congress, 1st Session I, chapter 178
  (1846).
An Act supplementary to an act, entitled "An act for the encouragement of learning, by
  securing the copies of maps, charts, and books to the authors and proprietors of such
  copies during the times therein mentioned" and extending the benefits thereof to the arts
  of designing, engraving, and etching historical and other prints, 2 Stat. 171 (1802).
Berne Convention Implementation Act of 1988, H.R. 4262, 100th Cong. (1988).
Patent Act of 1793, Ch 11, 1 Stat. 318–323.

## International Treaties

Berne Convention, Additional Protocol to the Revised Berne Convention (signed 20
  March 1914, and ratified on 20 April 1915).
Berne Convention for the Protection of Literary and Artistic Works 331 U.N.T.S 217
  (1886).
Convention between Her Majesty and the French Republic for the Establishment of
  International Copyright (signed at Paris, 3 November 1851, ratified 8 January
  1852) Parliamentary Papers 1851 Paper No. 1432, LIV., 103.

## Parliamentary Proceedings

All the legislative Journals of the British North American provinces (House
  of Assembly and Legislative Council) and the Dominion of Canada as well
  as the Appendixes to the Journals, as cited in the footnotes, can be found
  online at www.canadiana.ca.

## Books and Pamphlets

Aach, Hana K. *Impressions: Stories of the Nation's Printer – Early Years to 1900.*
  Canada: Department of Supply and Services, 1990.
Abbott, Maude A. *History of Medicine in the Province of Quebec.* Montreal:
  McGill University, 1931.

Ajzenstat, Janet. *The Canadian Founding: John Locke and Parliament*. Montreal and Kingston: McGill-Queen's University Press, 2007.

Alexander, Isabella. *Copyright Law and the Public Interest in the Nineteenth Century*. London: Bloomsbury, 2010.

American Philosophical Society. *Transactions of the American Philosophical Society held at Philadelphia for Promoting Useful Knowledge*. Volume 5. Philadelphia: printed by Budd & Bartram for Thomas Dobston, 1802.

Amory, Hugh, and David D. Hall, eds. *History of the Book in America*, vol. 1: *The Colonial Book in the Atlantic World*. Chapel Hill: University of North Carolina Press, 2007.

Armour, Robert. *The Montreal Almanack, or Lower Canada Register for 1829*. Montreal: H.H. Cunningham, 1828.

Aubin, Napoléon. *La chimie agricole mise à la portée de tout le monde*. Quebec: Ruthven, 1847.

Aubin, Paul, ed. *300 ans de manuels scolaires au Québec*. Quebec: Bibliothèque et Archives Nationales du Québec et Les Presses de l'Université Laval, 2006.

Australia. Copyright Law Review Committee (Australia), *The Importation Provisions of the Copyright Act 1968 – A Historical and Comparative Analysis*, Appendix D. Canberra: Australian Government Publishing Services, 1988.

Baillie, Thomas. *An Account of the Province of New Brunswick; Including a Description of the Settlements, Institutions, and Climate of that Important Province, with Advice to Emigrants*. London: J.G. & F. Rivington, 1832.

Bannerman, Sara. *International Copyright and Access to Knowledge*. Cambridge: Cambridge University Press, 2016.

– *The Struggle for Canadian Copyright: Imperialism and Internationalism 1842–1971*. Vancouver: UBC Press, 2013.

Barnes, D.G. *A History of Corn Laws: From 1660–1846*. London: Routledge, 2006.

Barnes, James J. *Authors, Publishers, and Politicians: The Quest for an Anglo-American Copyright Agreement 1815–1854*. Columbus: Ohio State University Press, 1974.

Barrington-Partridge, R.C. *The History of the Legal Deposit of Books throughout the British Empire*. London: Library Association, 1938.

Barry, John. *The Philadelphia Spelling Book, Arranged upon a Plan Entirely New*. Philadelphia: John James, 1790.

Beadie, Nancy. *Education and the Creation of Capital in the Early American Republic*. Cambridge: Cambridge University Press, 2010.

Bédard, Éric. *Les Réformistes: Une génération canadienne-française au milieu du XIXè siècle*. Montreal: Éditions du Boréal, 2009.

– *Survivance: Histoire et mémoire du xixè siècle canadien-français* Montreal: Éditions du Boréal, 2017.

Bernard, Philippe. *Amury Girod: Un Suisse chez les patriotes du Bas-Canada*. Quebec: Septentrion, 2001.

Bibaud, Michel. *Histoire du Canada et des Canadiens sous la Domination Anglaise.* Montreal: Lovell & Gibson, 1844.

– *Histoire du Canada sous la Domination Française.* Montreal: John Jones, 1837.

Birnhack, Michael. *Colonial Copyright: Intellectual Property in Mandate Palestine.* Oxford: Oxford University Press, 2012.

Birrell, Augustine. *Seven Lectures on the Law and History of Copyright in Books.* New York: G.P. Putnam's Sons, 1899. Reprint, New York: Augustus M. Kelley, 1971.

Blackstone, Sir William. *Commentaries on the Laws of England* [1765–70]. 4 vols. Oxford: Clarendon Press, 2016.

– *Commentaries on the Laws of England applicable to Real Property by Sir William Blackstone, Knt; adapted to the present state of the law in Upper Canada by Alexander Leith of Osgoode Hall, Barrister at Law.* Toronto: W.C. Chewett, 1864.

Blanchet, François. *Recherche sur la médecine, ou l'application de la chimie à la médecine.* New York: Imprimerie Parisot, 1800.

– *Appel au Parlement impérial et aux habitans des colonies angloises, dans l'Amérique du Nord, sur les prétentions exorbitantes du gouvernement exécutif et du Conseil législatif de la province du Bas-Canada.* Quebec: Flavien Villerand, 1824.

Blanchet, Renée, and Léo Beaudoin. *Jacques Viger: une biographie.* Montreal: VLB, 2009.

Bois, Louis-Édouard. *Relations des Jésuites: contenant ce qui s'est passé de plus remarquable dans les missions des pères de la Compagnie de Jésus dans la Nouvelle-France.* Quebec: Augustin Côté, 1858.

Booth, John Wilkes. *Right or Wrong: God Judge Me, The Writings of John Wilkes Booth.* Edited by John Rhodehamel and Louise Taper. Champaign: University of Illinois Press, 1997.

Boswell, James. *Life of Johnson: An Edition of the Original Manuscript in Four Volumes.* 2 vols. Edited by Bruce Redford and Elizabeth Goldring. Edinburgh: Edinburgh University Press; New Haven: Yale University Press, 1998.

Bouchard, Gérard, and Yvan Lamonde, eds. *Québecois et Américains: La culture québécoise au XIXè et XXè siècles.* Quebec: Fides, 1995.

Bouchette, Joseph. *The British Dominions in North America, or a Topographical and Statistical Description of the Provinces of Lower & Upper Canada, New Brunswick, Nova Scotia, the Islands of Newfoundland, Prince Edward and Cape Breton, including considerations on Land-granting and Emigration – To which are annexed, statistical Tables and Tables of Distances etc,* 2 vols. London: Longman and Co., 1832.

– *A Topographical Description of the Province of Lower Canada: with remarks upon Upper Canada, and on the relative connexion of both provinces with the United States of America.* London: William Faden, 1815.

- A *Topographical Dictionary of the Province of Lower Canada*. London: Longman and Co., 1832.

Bouchette, Robert S.M. *Mémoires de Robert S.-M. Bouchette 1805–1840 receuillis par son fils Errol Bouchette et annotés par A.-D. Decelles*. Montreal: La cie de publication de la revue canadienne, 1904.

Boulton, Henry John. *A Short Sketch of the Province of Upper Canada, for the Information of the Labouring Poor throughout England: To Which is Prefixed Thoughts on Colonization, Addressed to the Labouring Poor, the Clergy, Select Vestries, and Overseers of the Poor, and Other Persons, Interested in the Administration of Parish Relief in the Different Parishes in England*. London: J. Murray, 1826.

Bourassa, Napoléon. *Jacques et Marie: Souvenirs d'un people dispersé*. Montreal: Eusèbe Sénécal, 1866.

Bourinot, John George. *Parliamentary Procedure and Practice in the Dominion of Canada*. Montreal: Dawson Bros, 1884.

- *The Intellectual Development of the Canadian People: An Historical Review*. Toronto: Hunter, Rose & Co., 1881.

Bridges, John George. *The Every Boy's Book or Digest of the British Constitution*. Ottawa: Ottawa Advocate Office, 1842.

British and Foreign School Society. *Report of the British and Foreign School Society 1815 with an Appendix and List of Subscribers and Benefactors*. London: Richard & Arthur Taylor, 1815.

*The British North American Arithmetic containing Elementary Lessons for the Younger Classes in Common Schools, prepared expressly for the British Provinces by a Teacher*. Stanstead: Walton & Gaylord, 1833.

Bruce, John, Charles Secretan, and James Pendergast. *The Quebec Commercial List*, vol. 22. Quebec City: T. Cary, 1837.

Brymner, Douglas. *Report on Canadian Archives*. Ottawa: S.E. Dawson, 1899.

Buckingham, James S. *Canada, Nova Scotia, New Brunswick and the other British Provinces in North America with a plan of National Colonization*. London: Fisher, Son & Co, 1843.

Buschman, John, and Gloria J. Leckie, eds. *The Library as Place: History, Community, and Culture*. Westport: Libraries Unlimited – Greenwood Press, 2007.

Cadavid, Jhonny Antonio Pabón. *De los privilegios a la propriedad intelectual: La protección en Colombia a las Obras Literarias, Artísticas y Científicas en el Siglo XIX*. Bogotá: Universidad Externado de Colombia, 2010.

Calderisi, Maria. *Music Publishing in the Canadas 1800–1867 / L'édition musicale au Canada*. Ottawa: National Library of Canada, 1981.

Canada. *Catalogue of Pamphlets, Journals and Reports in the Public Archives of Canada 1611–1867*, with index. 2nd ed. Ottawa: J. de L. Taché, 1916.

- Censuses of Canada 1665 to 1871: Statistics of Canada. Ottawa: J.B. Taylor, 1876.

– *Sessional Papers of the Dominion of Canada*, Session 1914, vol. 25. Ottawa, 1914.

*The Canadian agricultural reader, designed principally for the use of schools.* Niagara: John Simpson, 1845.

*Canadian Manufactures.* Montreal: John Lovell, 1858.

Canniff, William. *A Manual of the Principles of Surgery, based on Pathology for Students.* Philadelphia: Lindsay & Blakiston, 1866.

Careless, J.M.S. *Brown of the Globe*, vol. 1: *The Voice of Upper Canada 1818–1859.* Toronto: Macmillan, 1959.

Castonguay, Stéphane, and Camille Limoges. *François Blanchet*, vol. 1: *L'étudiant et le savant.* Montreal: VLB, 2005.

Chapdelaine, Pascale. *Copyright User Rights: Contracts and the Erosion of Property.* Oxford: Oxford University Press, 2017.

Chauveau, Pierre-Joseph-Olivier. *Charles Guérin: Roman de moeurs canadiennes.* Montreal: G.H. Cherrier, 1852.

– *François-Xavier Garneau, sa vie et ses œuvres.* Montreal: Beauchemin & Lavoie, 1883.

Christie, Robert. *A History of the Late Province of Lower Canada, Parliamentary and Political, from the Commencement to the Close of Its Existence as a Separate Province*, in 6 volumes. Quebec: T. Cary & Co, 1848–1866.

– *Interesting Public Documents, and Official Correspondence, Illustrative of, and Supplementary to the History of Lower Canada.* Montreal: John Lovell, 1855.

Coffin, William. *1812: The War and Its Morals – A Canadian Chronicle.* Montreal: John Lovell, 1864.

Colgate, William. *Nahum Mower: An Early Printer of Montreal.* Toronto: North York Herald, 1964.

Copyright Association of Canada. "Interviewing the Cabinet, The Copyright Association lay their case before the Government." Toronto, 1888.

Craig, Carys. *Copyright, Communication, and Culture: Towards a Relational Theory of Copyright Law.* Cheltenham: Edward Elgar, 2011.

Craig, Gerald M., Janet Ajzenstat, and Guy Laforest, eds. *An Abridgment of Report on the Affairs of British North America by Lord Durham.* Montreal and Kingston: McGill-Queen's University Press, 2006.

Curtis, Bruce. *Ruling by Schooling Quebec: Conquest to Liberal Governmentality – A Historical Sociology.* Toronto: University of Toronto Press, 2012.

Davidson, Alexander. *The Canada Spelling Book.* Toronto: Henry Rowsell, 1840.

Davidson, Cathy N. *Revolution and the Word: The Rise of the Novel in America.* New York: Oxford University Press, 2004.

Davies, Richard A. *Inventing Sam Slick: A Biography of Thomas Chandler Haliburton.* Toronto: University of Toronto Press, 2005.

Dawson, Benjamin. *A Catalogue of Books, Stationery and Miscellaneous Articles for Sale by B. Dawson.* Montreal: Lovell & Gibson, 1849.

Dawson, Samuel Edward. *Copyright in Books. An Inquiry into Its Origin and an Account of the Present State of the Law in Canada*. Montreal: Dawson Brothers, 1882.

Deazley, Ronan. *On the Origin of the Right to Copy: Charting the Movement of Copyright Law in Eighteenth Century Britain (1695–1775)*. Oxford: Hart, 2004.

de Bellefeuille, Édouard Lefèbvre. *Code civil du Bas-Canada*. Montreal: Beauchemin & Valois, 1866.

de Gaspé, Philippe A. *Canadians of Old*. Translated by Georgiana M. Pennée. Quebec: G. & G.E. Desbarats, 1865.

– *Les Anciens Canadiens*. Quebec: Desbarats & Derbyshire, 1863.

– *Mémoires*. Ottawa: G.E. Desbarats, 1866.

de Tocqueville, Alexis. *Regards sur le Bas-Canada*. Montreal: Éditions Typo, 2003.

Dewart, Edward Hartley. *Selections from Canadian poets: with occasional critical and biographical notes and an introductory essay on Canadian poetry*. Montreal: John Lovell, 1864.

Dickson, Daniel. *A Guide to Town Officers, Shewing their Appointments, Duties, Liabilities and Privileges: According to the Laws of the Province*. Pictou: The Bee Office, 1835.

Doucet, Benjamin. *Fundamental principles of the Laws of Canada as they existed under the natives, as they were changed under the French Kings, and as they were modified and altered under the domination of England*. Montreal: John Lovell, 1841.

Doutre, G., and P.B.E. Lareau. *Le droit civil canadien suivant l'ordre établi par les codes précédé d'une histoire générale du droit Canadian*. Montreal: A. Doutre, 1872.

Drahos, Peter. *A Philosophy of Intellectual Property*. Aldershot: Dartmouth, 1996.

Drapeau, Stanislas. *Études sur les développements de la colonization du Bas-Canada depuis dix ans (1851 à 1861)*. Quebec: L Brousseau, 1863.

Drone, Eaton S. *A Treatise on the Law of Property in Intellectual Productions in Great Britain and the United States: Embracing Copyright in Works of Literature*. Boston: Little, Brown & Co., 1879.

Ducharme, Léandre. *Journal d'un exilé politique aux terres australes*. Montreal: F. Cinq Mars, 1845.

Dunlop, William. *Statistical Sketches of Upper Canada*. London: John Murray, 1832.

Eamon, Michael. *Imprinting Britain: Newspapers, Sociability, and the Shaping of British North America*. Montreal and Kingston: McGill-Queen's University Press, 2015.

Evans, William. *Supplementary Volume to a Treatise on Agriculture[:] the Theory and Practice of Agriculture, adapted to the Cultivation and Economy of the Animal and Vegetable Productions of Agriculture in Canada*. Montreal: L. Perrault, 1836.

– *A Treatise on the Theory and Practice of Agriculture: adapted to the Cultivation and Economy of the Animal and Vegetable Productions of Agriculture in Canada.* Montreal: Fabre & Perrault, 1835.

– *Traité théorique et pratique de l'agriculture: adapté à la culture et l'économie des productions animales et végétales de cet art en Canada.* Montreal: L. Perrault, 1836.

Everton, Michael J. *The Grand Chorus of Complaint: Authors and the Business Ethics of American Publishing.* Oxford: Oxford University Press, 2011.

*Exécution de John Meehan.* Quebec: Le Canadien, 1864.

*Extrait du rituel du Québec contenant l'administration des sacremens [sic] de baptême, de la confirmation, de pénitence, de l'eucharistie, de l'extrême-onction et de mariage: et aussi les bénédictions et diverses formes d'actes.* Quebec: Cary & Desbarats, 1836.

Faribault, G.B. *Catalogue d'ouvrages sur l'histoire de l'Amérique, et en particulier sur celle du Canada, de la Louisiane, de l'Acadie, et autres lieux, ci-devant connus sous le nom de Nouvelle-France; avec des notes bibliographiques, critiques et littéraires.* Quebec: W. Cowan, 1837.

Fauteux, Aegidius. *The Introduction of Printing into Canada.* Montreal: Rolland Paper Company Ltd., 1930.

Feather, John. *Publishing, Piracy, and Politics: An Historical Study of Copyright in Britain.* London: Mansell, 1994.

Febvre, Lucien, and Henri-Jean Martin. *L'Apparition du Livre.* Paris: Les Éditions Albin Miche, 1958.

Ferland, Jean-Baptiste Antoine. *Cours d'histoire du Canada.* Quebec: Augustin Côté & Cie, 1861.

Fleming, Ann Cuthbert Rae Knight. *Progressive Exercises on the English Language, to correspond with "the Prompter."* Montreal: Lovell & Gibson, 1845.

Fleming, Patricia Lockhart, Gilles Gallichan, Yvan Lamonde, Fiona A. Black, Carole Gerson, and Jacques Michon. *History of the Book in Canada.* 3 vols. Toronto: University of Toronto Press, 2004.

Francoeur, Louis-Benjamin. *Le dessin linéaire d'après la méthode de l'enseignement mutuel.* Paris: L. Colas, 1819.

Freame, John. *Scripture Instruction: Digested into Several Sections, by Way of Question and Answer [...].* London: Printed and Sold by the Assigns of J. Sowle, 1713.

Les Frères de Écoles Chrétiennes. *Abrégé de l'histoire sainte, de l'histoire de France et de l'histoire du Canada.* Montreal: Lovell & Gibson, 1846.

Gagnon, Philéas. *Essai de bibliographie canadienne: inventaire d'une bibliothèque comprenant imprimés, manuscrits, estampes, etc. relatifs à l'histoire du Canada et des Pays Adjacents avec des notes bibliographiques.* Quebec: Imprimé pour l'auteur, 1895.

Galarneau, Claude, and Maurice Lemire. *Livre et lecture au Québec (1800–1850).* Quebec: Institut québécois de recherche sur la culture; Saint-Laurent: Diffusion Prologue Inc., 1988.

Gallichan, Gilles. *Livre et politique au Bas-Canada 1791–1849*. Sillery: Septentrion, 1991.

Garneau, François-Xavier. *Abrégé de l'Histoire du Canada depuis sa découverte jusqu'à 1840*. Quebec: Augustin Côté & Cie, 1856.

– *Histoire du Canada depuis sa découverte jusqu'à nos jours*. 3 vols. Quebec: N. Aubin, 1845–52.

Gerson, Carole. *Canadian Women in Print, 1750–1918*. Waterloo: Wilfrid Laurier University Press, 2010.

Girard, Philip, Jim Phillips, and R. Blake Brown. *A History of Law in Canada*, vol. 1: *Beginnings to 1866*. Toronto: University of Toronto Press, 2018.

Girod, Amury. *Conversations sur l'agriculture par un habitans [sic] de Varennes*. Quebec: Fréchette & Cie 1834.

– *Notes diverses sur le Bas-Canada*. St-Jean-sur-Richelieu: De Boucher Belleville, 1835.

Gleason, Thomas Henry. *The Quebec Directory for 1822 containing an alphabetical list of the Merchants, Traders, and House Keepers etc within the City*. Quebec: Neilson & Cowan, 1822.

Godson, Richard. *A Practical Treatise on the Law of Patents for Inventions and of Copyright*. London: Saunders & Benning, 1832.

Gooch, John. *Manual or Explanatory Development of the Act of the Union of Canada, Nova Scotia and New Brunswick in one Dominion under the name of Canada*. Ottawa: G.E. Desbarats, 1867.

Gouin, L.J. *A New System of French and English Pronunciation*. Montreal: John Lovell, 1860.

Goulson, Cary F. *A Source Book of Royal Commissions and Other Major Governmental Inquiries in Canadian Education, 1787–1978*. Toronto: University of Toronto Press, 1981.

Gross, Robert A., and Mary Kelley, eds. *A History of the Book in America*, vol. 2: *An Extensive Republic: Print, Culture, and Society in the New Nation, 1790–1840*. Chapel Hill: University of North Carolina Press, 2010.

Hackenburg, Michael, ed. *Getting the Books Out*: *Papers of the Chicago Conference on the Book in 19th Century America*. Washington: Center for the Book, Library of Congress, 1987.

Haliburton, Thomas Chandler. *An Historical and Statistical Account of Nova Scotia*. Halifax: J. Howe, 1829.

Hamilton, James. *The History, Principles, Practice, and Results of the Hamiltonian System*. London: W. Aylott & Co., 1831.

Harrington, Lyn. *Syllables of Recorded Time: The Story of the Canadian Authors Association 1921–1981*. Toronto: Simon & Pierre, 1981.

Hart, Adolphus M. *Practical Suggestions on Mining Rights and Privileges*. Montreal: Lovell, 1867.

Hart, Constance Hannah Hatton. *Household Recipes or Domestic Cookery*. Montreal: A.A. Stevenson, 1865.

Hart, Michael. *A Trading Nation: Canadian Trade Policy from Colonialism to Globalization*. Vancouver: UBC Press, 2002.

Hart, Moses. *Index to the Matters contained in Civil Code of Lower Canada*. Montreal: John Lovell, 1866.

Hawkins, Alfred. *Plan of the military & naval operations, under the command of the immortal Wolfe, & Vice Admiral Saunders, before Quebec*. London: James Wyld, 1841.

Heavysege, Charles. *Count Filippo or the Unequal Marriage: A Drama in Five Acts*. Montreal: n.p, 1860.

– *Jephthah's Daughter*. Montreal: Dawson Brothers, 1864.

Hill, Hamlin, ed. *Mark Twain's Letters for his Publishers 1867–1894*. Berkeley: University of California Press, 1967.

Hind, H.Y, T.C. Keefer, J.G. Hodgins, Charles Robb, M.H. Perley, and W.M. Murray. *Eighty Years Progress of British North America*. Montreal: Lovell, 1863.

Hirschfelder, Jacob Meir. *A Key to German Conversation consisting of familiar dialogues and calculated to facilitate the acquisition of that language*. Toronto: H.W. Rowsell, 1845.

Hodgins, J. George. *Geography and History of British America and of the other colonies of the Empire*. Toronto: Thomas Maclear, 1857.

– *A history of Canada and the other British provinces in North America*. Montreal: John Lovell, 1866.

Hodgins, J. George, ed. *Documentary History of Education in Upper Canada from the Passing of the Constitutional Act of 1791 to the Close of the Reverend Doctor Ryerson's Administration of the Education Department in 1876*. Toronto: Department of Education, 1895.

Hogg, Peter W. *Constitutional Law of Canada*, 5th ed. Scarborough: Thomson Carswell, 2007.

Holmes, Jean. *Nouvel abrégé de géographie moderne suivi d'un appendice et d'un Abrégé de géographie sacrée à l'usage de la jeunesse*. Quebec: J. & O. Crémazie, 1854.

Homestead, Melissa J. *American Women Authors and Literary Property, 1822–1869*. Cambridge: Cambridge University Press, 2005.

Hopkins, J. Castell. *The Life and Work of the Right Hon. Sir John Thompson*. Brantford: Bradley, Garretson & Co, 1895.

Houston, Susan E., and Alison Prentice. *Schooling and Scholars in Nineteenth-Century Ontario*. Toronto: University of Toronto Press, 1988.

Howsam, Leslie. *Past into Print: The Publishing of History in Britain 1850–1950*. Toronto: University of Toronto Press, 2009.

Howsam, Leslie, ed. *The Cambridge Companion to the History of the Book*. Cambridge: Cambridge University Press, 2015.

Howsam, Leslie, and James Raven, eds. *Books between Europe and the Americans: Connections and Communities 1620–1860*. Basingstoke: Palgrave Macmillan, 2011.

Hudson, Angela Pulley. *Real Native Genius: How an Ex-Slave and a White Mormon Became Famous Indians.* Chapel Hill: University of North Carolina Press, 2015.

Hulse, Elizabeth. *A Dictionary of Toronto Printers, Publishers, Booksellers, and the Allied Trades 1798–1900.* Toronto: Anson-Cartwright Editions, 1982.

Huston, James. *Le répertoire national, ou Recueil de littérature canadienne.* 4 vols. Montreal: Lovell & Gibson, 1848–1850.

Inglis, John. *A Charge Delivered to the Clergy of His Diocese.* London: J.G. & F. Rivington, 1831.

Jarrell, Richard A. *Educating the Neglected Majority: The Struggle for Agricultural and Technical Education in Nineteenth-Century Ontario and Quebec.* Montreal and Kingston: McGill-Queen's University Press, 2016.

Jolois, Jean-Jacques. *Joseph-Francois Perrault (1753–1844) et les origines de l'enseignement laïque au Bas-Canada.* Montreal: Presse de l'Université de Montréal, 1969.

Kaplan, Benjamin. *An Unhurried View of Copyright.* New York: Columbia University Press, 1967.

Karel, David. *Dictionnaire des artistes de langue française en Amérique du Nord.* Laval: Musée du Québec, Les Presses de l'Université Laval, 1992.

Keighren, Innes M., Charles W.J. Withers, and Bill Bell. *Travels into Print: Exploration, Writing And Publishing with John Murray 1773–1859.* Chicago: University of Chicago Press, 2015.

Kendall, Joshua. *The Forgotten Founding Father: Noah Webster's Obsession and the Creation of an American Culture.* New York: G.P. Putnam's Sons, 2010.

Khan, Zorina. *The Democratization of Invention: Patents and Copyrights in American Economic Development (1790–1920).* Cambridge: Cambridge University Press, 2005.

Kirby, William. *The U.E.: A Tale of Upper Canada.* Niagara: The Mail Office, 1859.

Knight, Ann Cuthbert. *A Year in Canada and other Poems.* London: Baldwin, Cradock and Co., 1816.

Lamonde, Yvan. *Allégeances et dépendances: L'histoire d'une ambivalence identitaire.* Quebec: Éditions Nota Bene, 2001.

– *Histoire sociale des idées au Québec.* Montreal: Fides, 2000.

Lamonde, Yvan, and Claude Corbo, eds. *Le rouge et le bleu: une anthologie de la pensée politique au Québec de la Conquête à la Revolution tranquille.* Montreal: Les Presses de l'Université de Montréal, 2009.

Lamonde, Yvan, and Claude Larin, eds. *Louis-Joseph Papineau. Un demi-siècle de combats: interventions publiques.* Anjou: Éditions Fides, 1998.

Lamonde, Yvan, and Sophie Montreuil, eds. *Lire au Québec au XIXè Siècle.* Montréal: Éditions Fides, 2003.

Lancaster, Joseph. *Epitome of some of the Chief Events and Transactions in the Life of Joseph Lancaster.* New Haven: Baldwin & Peck, 1833.

– *Hints and Directions for building fitting-up and arranging schoolrooms on the British system.* London: Darnton & Harvey, 1809.

– *Improvements in Education, as it Respects the Industrious Classes of the Community.* London: Darnton and Harvey, 1803.

– *Improvements in Education, as It Respects the Industrious Classes of the Community: With a Brief Sketch of the Life of Joseph Lancaster*, 3rd ed. London: Darnton & Harvey, 1805.

– *Improvements in Education; Abridged, Containing a Complete Epitome of the System of Education Invented and Practiced by the Author.* London: J. Lancaster, 1808.

– *The Lancasterian System of Education with Improvements.* Baltimore: W.O. Niles, 1821.

– *Letters on National Subjects Auxiliary to Universal Education and Scientific Knowledge.* Washington: Jacob Gideon, 1820.

– *New method of Lancasterian education: Brief outline of the result of an experiment, to ascertain in how short a time, it was possible to teach eight ignorant boys, to read the first chapter of John; by a new and simple process in education, invented by Joseph Lancaster.* Montreal: s.n., 1829.

– *Oppression and Persecution, or a Narrative of a Variety of Singular Facts That Have Occurred in the Rise, Progress, and Promulgation of the Royal Lancasterian System of Education.* Bristol: John Evans & Co. 1816.

– *Report of the Singular Results of Joseph Lancaster's New Discoveries in Education made at Montreal, from the commencement in 1832 to complete development of systematic principle in 1833.* Montreal: n.p., 1833.

– *Scripture Instruction in the form of Questions and Answers as taught in the Royal Lancasterian Schools ... originally compiled by John Freame (1713)*, 6th ed. London: Darnton and Harvey, 1813.

Lancefield, Richard T. *Notes on Copyright – Domestic and International.* Hamilton: Canadian Literary Bureau, 1896.

Langevin, Hector. *Le Canada, ses institutions ressources, produits, manufactures.* Quebec: Lovell & Lamoureux, 1855.

Larkin, Jean. *Eklekta muthistorias.* Montreal. John Jones, 1837.

– *Grammaire grecque, à l'usage du Collège de Montréal*, 1st ed. Montreal: John Jones, 1837.

Larochelle, Catherine. *L'école du racisme: La construction de l'altérité à l'école québécoise (1830–1915).* Montreal: Les Presses de l'Université de Montréal, 2021.

Lebrun, Isidore. *Tableau statistique et politique des deux Canadas.* Paris: Treuttel & Würtz, 1833.

Lebrun, Monique. *Le manuel scolaire: d'ici et d'ailleurs, d'hier à demain.* Quebec: Presse de l'Université du Québec, 2007.

*Le grand catéchisme, à l'usage du diocese de Québec.* Quebec: Cary & Desbarats, 1836.

Lemire, Maurice, ed. *La vie littéraire au Québec*, vol. 2: *1806–1839*. Sainte-Foy: Les Presses de l'Université Laval, 1992.

Lessard, Michel. *Les Livernois photographes*. Quebec: Musée du Québec, 1987.

Lewis, Francis. *The Toronto Directory and Street Guide for 1843–44*. Toronto: H & W Rowsell, 1844.

Lewis, Israel. *A Class Book for the use of common schools and families in the United Canadas entitled the Youth's Guard Against Crime*. Kingston: Atheneum Printing Office, 1844.

L'Homond, Charles-François. *Élemens de la grammaire française*. Quebec: John Neilson, 1800.

Lindsey, Charles. *The life and times of Wm. Lyon Mackenzie: with an account of the Canadian rebellion of 1837, and the subsequent frontier disturbances, chiefly from unpublished documents*. Toronto: P.R. Randall, 1862.

Liston, James K. *Niagara Falls: A Poem in Three Cantos*. Toronto: Guardian Office, 1843.

Le May, Léon-Pamphile. *Essais poétiques*. Quebec: G.E. Desbarats, 1865.

Lower Canada. *Report from the Select Committee on the Civil government of Canada; ordered by the House of Commons to be printed 22 July 1827*. Quebec: Reprinted by order of the House of Assembly of Lower Canada, 1829.

Luneau, Marie-Pier Luneau. *Louvigny de Montigny: A la défense des auteurs*. Montreal: Lémeac, 2011.

MacLaren, Eli. *Dominion and Agency: Copyright and the Structuring of the Canadian Book Trade 1867–1918*. Toronto: University of Toronto Press, 2011.

Maugham, Robert. *A Treatise on the Laws of Literary Property, Comprising the Statutes and Cases Relating to Books, Manuscripts, Lectures* […]. London: Longman, Rees, Orme, Brown, and Green, Paternoster Row, 1828.

May, Christopher, and Susan K. Sell. *Intellectual Property Rights: A Critical History*. Boulder: Lynne Rienner, 2006.

Mayerhoffer, Vincent Philip. *Twelve years a Roman Catholic priest, or, the autobiography of the Rev. V.P. Mayerhoffer, M.A., late military chaplain to the Austrian army, and grand chaplain of the orders of freemasons and Orangemen, in Canada, B.N.A., containing an account of his career as military chaplain, monk of the order of St. Francis, and clergyman of the Church of England in Vaughan, Markham and Whitby, C.W.* Toronto: Rowsell & Ellis, 1861.

McCord, Thomas. *The Civil Code of Lower Canada*. Montreal: Dawson Brothers, 1867.

– *Synopsis of the Changes in the Law effected by the Civil Code of Lower Canada*. Ottawa: G.E. Desbarats, 1866.

McFarlane, W.G. *New Brunswick Bibliography: The Books and Writers of the Province*. St. John: Press of the Sun Printing Co. Ltd, 1895.

McGill, Meredith L. *American Literature and the Culture of Reprinting, 1834–1853*. Philadelphia: University of Pennsylvania Press, 2003.

McKay, George L. *A Register of Artists, Engravers, Booksellers, Bookbinders, Printers and Publishers in New York City 1633–1820.* New York: New York Public Library, 1942.

McKay, Robert W. Stuart. *The Montreal Directory for 1842–1843.* Montreal: Lovell & Gibson, 1843.

McLeod, Jane. *Licensing Loyalty: Printers, Patrons, and the State in Early Modern France.* University Park: Pennsylvania State University Press, 2011.

Meilleur, J-B. *Nouvelle grammaire anglaise en deux parties, suivies d'une série de thèmes.* Montreal: J.B. Rolland, 1854.

Micklethwait, David. *Noah Webster and the American Dictionary.* Jefferson: McFarland, 2000.

Milton, John. *Areopagitica; A Speech of Mr. John Milton for the Liberty of Unlicensed Printing, To the Parliament of England.* London, 1644.

Monière, Denis. *Ludger Duvernay et la révolution intellectuelle au Bas-Canada.* Montreal: Éditions Québec-Amérique, 1987.

Morang, George N. *The Copyright Question: A Letter to the Toronto Board of Trade.* Toronto: George N. Morang & Co. Ltd., 1902.

Moreau, Édouard. *Instructions sur l'art des accouchemens [sic] pour les sages-femmes de la campagne.* Montreal: E. Fabre & L. Perrault, 1834.

Morgan, Henry J. *Bibliotheca Canadensis: A Manual of Canadian Literature.* Ottawa: J.E. Desbarats, 1867.

– *Sketches of Celebrated Canadians, and persons connected with Canada, from the earliest period in the history of the province down to the present time.* Quebec: Hunter, Rose & Co., 1862.

– *The Tour of H.R.H. the Prince of Wales Through British America and the United States.* Montreal: John Lovell, 1860.

Morin, Augustin Norbert. *Lecture prononcée par L'Hon. A.N Morin, devant l'Institut Canadien.* Montreal: Lovell & Gibson, 1846.

Morris, William. *The Accountant's Guide for Elementary Schools in Canada.* Quebec: Published by the authority of the Parliament of Lower Canada, 1833.

Moustalon, M. *Abrégé de mythologie à l'usage des maisons d'éducation.* Quebec: Neilson & Cowan, 1832.

Murdoch, Beamish. *Epitome of the Laws of Nova Scotia.* 3 vols. Halifax: Joseph Howe, 1833.

Murray, Heather. *Come, Bright Improvement! The Literary Societies of Nineteenth-Century Ontario.* Toronto: University of Toronto Press, 2002.

Murray, Lindley. *The English Spelling Book.* Montreal: Nahum Mower, 1811.

Myers, Robin. *Records of the Worshipful Company of Stationers, 1554–1920.* Cambridge: Chadwyck-Healey, 1985.

Myers, Robin, and Michael Harris, eds. *The Stationers' Company and the Book Trade 1550–1990.* New Castle: Oak Knoll Press, 1997.

Myers, Robin, Michael Harris, and Giles Mandelbrote, eds. *Libraries and the Book Trade: The Formation of Collections from the Sixteenth to the Twentieth Centuries*. New Castle: Oak Knoll Press, 2000.

Nish, Elizabeth, ed. *Debates of the Legislative Assembly of United Canada*. Montreal: Presses de L'École de Hautes Études Commerciales, 1970.

Noiseux, François-Xavier. *Liste chronologique des évêques et des prêtres, tant séculiers que réguliers employés au service de l'Église du Canada*. Quebec: T. Cary, 1834.

Notman, William. *Portraits of British Americans with biographical sketches*. Montreal: John Lovell, 1865.

Nowell-Smith, Simon. *International Copyright Law and the Publisher in the Reign of Queen Victoria*. Oxford: Clarendon Press, 1968.

Oleson, Alexandra., and Sanborn C. Brown, eds. *The Pursuit of Knowledge in the Early American Republic: American Scientific and Learned Societies from Colonial Times to the Civil War*. Baltimore: Johns Hopkins University Press, 1976.

Ossaye, Frédéric. *Les veillées canadiennes: traité élémentaire d'agriculture à l'usage des habitants franco-canadiens*. Quebec: Augustin Côté, 1852.

Palairet, Jean. *Nouvelle méthode pour apprendre à bien lire*. Quebec: La Nouvelle Imprimerie, 1821.

Paradis, Jean-Marc. *Augustin-Norbert Morin, 1803–1865*. Sillery: Septentrion, 2005.

Parizeau, Gérard. *La vie studieuse et obstinée de Denis-Benjamin Viger*. Montreal: Fides, 1980.

Parker, George L. *The Beginnings of the Book Trade in Canada*. Toronto: University of Toronto Press, 1985.

Patry, William F. *Copyright Law and Practice*. Washington, DC: Bureau of National Affairs, 1994.

Patterson, L. Ray. *Copyright in Historical Perspective*. Nashville: Vanderbilt University Press, 1968.

Patterson, L. Ray, and Stanley W. Lindberg. *The Nature of Copyright: A Law of Users' Rights*. Athens: University of Georgia Press, 1991.

Peltier, Louis. *Voyage de Louis Peltier par terre et par mer: comprenant le récit de son voyage à la pêche à la baleine et de ses excursions en Afrique*. Quebec: Bureau de "La Réforme," 1862.

Perrault, Joseph-François. *Abrégé de l'histoire du Canada*. Quebec: P. & W. Ruthven, 1832–36.

– *Biographie de Joseph-François Perrault, protonotaire de la cour du Banc du Roi pour le district de Québec, écrite par lui-même, à l'âge de quatre-vingts ans, sans lunettes, à la suggestion du Lord Aylmer Gouverneur en Chef du Bas-Canada*. Quebec: Thomas Cary & Cie, 1834.

– *Code rural à l'usage des habitants tant anciens que nouveaux du Bas-Canada: concernant leurs devoirs religieux et civils, d'après les lois en force dans le pays*. Quebec: Fréchette, 1832.

– *Cours d'éducation élémentaire à l'usage de l'école gratuite établie dans la cité de Québec en 1821*. Quebec: Nouvelle Imprimerie, 1822.

– *Dictionnaire portatif et abrégé des loix et règles du Parlement provincial de Bas Canada: depuis son établissement par l'acte de la 31ème année du règne de Sa Trés Gracieuse Majesté George III, Ch. XXXI jusques et compris l'an de Notre Seigneur 1805*. Quebec: John Neilson, 1806.

– *Moyens de conserver nos institutions, notre langue, nos lois*. Quebec: Fréchette, 1832.

– *Nouvelle méthode pour apprendre la langue angloise [sic] avec facilité, expédition et économie, introduite dans l'École Gratuite à Québec*. Quebec: Le François, 1823.

– *Rural Code for the Old and New Inhabitants of Lower Canada concerning their religious and civil duties*. Quebec: Thomas Cary & Co, 1832.

– *Traité d'agriculture adapté au climat du Bas-Canada*. Quebec: Fréchette, 1831, 1839.

– *Traité d'agriculture pratique, publié sous le patronage de la Chambre et des sociétés d'agriculture du Bas-Canada* par J. Perrault. Montreal: n.p, 1865.

Perrin, John. *The Elements of French Conversation: With Familiar and Easy Dialogues*, 10th ed. Montreal: printed by Nahum Mower for H.H. Cunningham, 1810.

*Petit manuel des cérémonies romaines; à l'usage du diocèse de Québec*. Quebec: Fréchette & Parent, 1832.

Petitclair, Pierre. *Une partie de campagne: Comédie en deux actes*. Québec. Joseph Savard, 1865.

Phillips, William. *A New and Concise System of Arithmetic, Calculated to Facilitate the Improvement of Youth in Upper Canada*. York: Printed for Eastwood and Skinner, 1833.

Piggott, I. *The Canadian Mechanic's Ready Reckoner or Tables for Converting English, Lineal, Square and Solid Measures into French, and the Contrary*. Three-Rivers: G. Stobbs, 1832.

Porter, Roy. *Enlightenment: Britain and the Creation of the Modern World*. London: Penguin Books, 2000.

Poulton, Ron. *The Paper Tyrant: John Ross Robertson of the Toronto Telegram*. Toronto: Clarke, Irwin, 1971.

Provancher, Léon. *Traité élémentaire de botanique à l'usage des maisons d'éducation*. Quebec: St Michel et Darveau, 1858.

Québec (Province), *Rapport de l'archiviste de la province de Québec pour 1926–1927*. Quebec: L. Amable Proulx, 1927.

Québec (Province), Ministère de L'Instruction Publique. *Journal de l'instruction publique*. Montreal: Dept. de l'instruction publique, 1863.

Ramsay, Thomas Kennedy. *Notes sur la coutume de Paris indiquant les articles encore en force avec tout le texte de la coutume à l'exception des articles relatifs aux fiefs et censives, les titres du retrait lignager et de la garde noble et bourgeoise*. Montreal: Beauchemin & Valois, 1863.

Rauch, Alan. *Useful Knowledge: The Victorians, Morality, and the March of Intellect*. Durham: Duke University Press, 2001.

Richardson, John. *The Canadian Brothers or the Prophecy Fulfilled: A Tale of the Late American War*. Montreal: A. H. Armour & H. Ramsay, 1840.

– *The Canadian Brothers Or, The Prophecy Fulfilled: A Tale of the Late American War*. Edited by Donald Stephens. Ottawa: Carleton University Press, 1992.

– *Eight Years in Canada: Embracing a Review of the Administrations of Lords Durham and Sydenham, Sir Chas. Bagot, and Lord Metcalfe; and Including Numerous Interesting Letters from Lord Durham, Mr. Chas. Buller, and Other Well-Known Public Characters*. Montreal: H.H. Cunningham, 1847.

– *The Guards in Canada; or, the Point of Honor: being a sequel to Major Richardson's "Eight Years in Canada."* Montreal: H.H. Cunningham, 1848.

Robertson, John Ross. *Copyright in Canada; The Question Discussed Practically and Constitutionally*. Toronto: J. Ross Robertson, 1879.

Roger, Charles. *The Rise of Canada from Barbarism to Wealth and Civilization*. Quebec: P. Sinclair, 1856.

Roldán Vera, Eugenia. *The British Book Trade and Spanish American Independence*. Abingdon: Routledge, 2016.

Rolph, Thomas. *A Brief Account, Together with Observations, Made During a Visit in the West Indies, and a Tour Through the United States of America: In Parts of the Years 1832–3; Together with a Statistical Account of Upper Canada*. Dundas, U.C.: Heyworth Hackstaff, Printer, 1836.

Rose, Mark. *Authors and Owners: The Invention of Copyright*. Cambridge, MA: Harvard University Press, 1993.

Roy, Jean-Louis. *Édouard Raymond Fabre: libraire et patriote canadien (1799–1854) contre l'isolement et la sujétion*. Montreal: Hurtubise HMH (Collection Histoire et Documents d'Histoire), 1974.

Roy, Jennet. *History of Canada for the use of Schools and Families*. Montreal: Armour & Ramsay, 1847.

Royal Acadian School. *Report of the Royal Acadian School instituted in 1813, incorporated 1840*. Halifax: Royal Acadian School, 1851.

Russell, Peter A. *How Agriculture Made Canada*. Montreal and Kingston: McGill-Queen's University Press, 2012.

Sabatier, C.W., and W.E. Sempé. *Cantata composed in honor of H.R.H. the Prince of Wales' visit to Canada sung by the Montreal Musical Union, at the grand musical festival*. Montreal: John Lovell, 1860.

Salmon, David. *Joseph Lancaster*. London: Longmans, Green & Co., 1904.

Sangster, Charles. *Hesperus and Other Poems*. Montreal: J. Lovell, 1860.

– *The St-Lawrence and the Saguenay*. Kingston: J. Creighton & J. Duff, 1856.

Saunders, David. *Authorship and Copyright*. London: Routledge, 1992.

Schonhardt-Bailey, Cheryl. *From the Corn Law to Free Trade: Interests, Ideas, and Institutions in Historical Perspective*. Cambridge, MA: MIT Press, 2006.

Scobie & Balfour. *A Catalogue of books, now on sale by Scobie and Balfour, booksellers and stationers, printers, engraver, lithographers, and bookbinders.* Toronto: Scobie & Balfour, 1850.

Seville, Catherine. *The Internationalisation of Copyright Law: Books, Buccaneers and the Black Flag in the Nineteenth Century.* Cambridge: Cambridge University Press, 2006.

– *Literary Copyright Reform in Early Victorian England: The Framing of the 1842 Copyright Act.* Cambridge: Cambridge University Press, 1999.

Sheppard, Josette Charlotte Desbarats. *Chants canadiens avec accompagnement de piano.* Quebec: J. & O. Crémazie, 1856.

Sher, Richard B. *The Enlightenment and the Book.* Chicago: University of Chicago Press, 2006.

Sherman, Brad, and Lionel Bently. *The Making of Modern Intellectual Property Law: The British Experience, 1760–1911.* Cambridge: Cambridge University Press, 1999.

Slauter, Will. *Who Owns the News: A History of Copyright.* Stanford: Stanford University Press, 2019.

Smiles, Samuel. *Thrift.* London: John Murray, 1875.

Smith, Donald B. *Seen but Not Seen: Influential Canadians and the First Nations from the 1840s to Today.* Toronto: University of Toronto Press, 2021.

Smith, W.H. *Canada; Past, Present and Future: Being a Historical, Geographical, Geological and Statistical Account of Canada West.* 2 vols. Toronto: T. Maclear, 1851.

Solberg, Thorvold. *Copyright in Canada and Newfoundland.* Washington, DC: Library of Congress – Government Printing Office, 1903.

Southey, Robert. *The Origin, Nature and Object of the New System of Education.* London: Printed for John Murray, 1812.

Sparks, Jared, ed. *The Writings of George Washington.* 7 vols. Boston: American Stationers' Company, 1837.

Speisman, Stephen A. *The Jews of Toronto: A History to 1937.* Toronto: McClelland and Stewart, 1979.

Spoo, Robert E. *Without Copyrights: Piracy, Publishing, and the Public Domain.* Oxford: Oxford University Press, 2013.

Steward, Austin. *Twenty-Two Years a Slave and Forty Years a Freeman: Embracing a Correspondence of Several Years while President of Wilberforce Colony, London, Canada West.* Rochester: William Alling, 1857.

Stowe, Harriet Beecher. *Dred: A Tale of the Great Dismal Swamp.* London: Sampson Low, 1856.

Stuart, Charles. *An Emigrant's Guide to Upper Canada.* London: Longman, 1820.

Stuart, George Okill. *Reports of cases argued and determined in the courts of King's Bench and in the provincial Court of Appeals of Lower Canada, with a few of the more important cases in the Court of Vice Admiralty and on Appeals from Lower Canada Before the Lords of the Privy Council.* Quebec: Neilson & Cowan, 1834.

348  Bibliography

St Clair, William. *The Reading Nation in the Romantic Period.* Cambridge: Cambridge University Press, 2004.

Suthersanen, Uma, and Ysolde Gendreau, eds. *A Shifting Empire: 100 Years of the Copyright Act 1911.* Cheltenham: Edward Elgar, 2013.

Talbot, Edward Allen. *Five Years Residence in the Canadas: Including a Tour through Part of The United States of America, in the Year 1823.* 2 vols. London: Longman, 1824.

Taylor, Barbara, and Sarah Knott. *Women, Gender, and Enlightenment.* Basingstoke: Palgrave Macmillan, 2005.

Taylor, Joyce. *Joseph Lancaster: The Poor Child's Friend: Educating the Poor in the Early Nineteenth Century.* Kent: Campanile Press, 1996.

Tebbel, John. *A History of Book Publishing in the United States: The Creation of an Industry 1630–1865.* New York: R.R. Bowker, 1972.

Thomas, Isaiah. *The Diary of Isaiah Thomas 1805–1828*, vol. 1. In *Transactions and Collections of the American Antiquarian Society*, vol. 9. Worcester: American Antiquarian Society, 1909.

Todd, Alpheus. *On Parliamentary Government in England: Its Origin, Development, and Practical Operation*, 2 vols. London: Longman & Green, 1867 (vol. 1), 1869 (vol. 2).

Tomlinson, James. *L'Imprimerie Neilson.* Montreal: Faculté des Études Supérieures, École de Bibliothéconomie, Université de Montréal, 1972.

Torno, Barry. *Crown Copyright in Canada: A Legacy of Confusion.* Ottawa: Supply and Services Canada, 1981.

Traill, Catharine Parr. *The backwoods of Canada: being letters from the wife of an emigrant officer, illustrative of the domestic economy of British America.* London: C. Knight, 1836.

– *I Bless You in My Heart: Selected Correspondence of Catharine Parr Traill.* Edited by Carl Ballstadt, Elizabeth Hopkins, and Michael A. Peterman. Toronto: University of Toronto Press, 1996.

– *The Female Emigrant's Guide and Hints on Canadian Housekeeping.* Toronto: MacLearn, 1855.

Trudel, Marcel. *L'influence de Voltaire au Canada*, vol. 1: *De 1760 à 1850.* Montreal: Éditions Fides, 1945.

Tubbee, Okah. *A sketch of the life of Okah Tubbee, (called) William Chubbee, son of the head chief, Mosholeh Tubbee, of the Choctaw nation of Indians, which was printed and published in Toronto.* Toronto: Printed for O. Tubbee by H. Stephens, 1852.

Twain, Mark. *The Prince and the Pauper.* Montreal: Dawson Brothers, 1881.

– *The Prince and the Pauper.* Toronto: Belford Brothers, 1882.

Unger, Harlow G., and Dale Williams. *Encyclopedia of American Education.* Berkeley: University of California Press, 1996.

United Kingdom. *British and Foreign State Papers 1874–1975*, vol. 66. London: W. Ridgway, 1882.

United Kingdom. *Colonial Copyright, return to an address of the Honourable the House of Commons*, dated 12 April, 1872, for "Copies or extracts of correspondence between the Colonial Office, the Board of Trade, and the Government of Canada, which preceded the passing of the Act 10 and 11 Vict. c. 95"; "and, of any recent correspondence on the subject of that act and of proposals for amending or extending the same, including the letter of the 27th day of July, 1869, no. 687–69." London: HMSO, 1872.

– *Customs duties (Canada). Return to an address of the Honourable the House of Commons, dated 5 May 1864, for, "A copy of any correspondence between the Colonial Office and the authorities in Canada, on the subject of the removal or reduction of the duties charged on British goods entering Canada."* London: HMSO, 1864.

– Her Majesty's High Commissioner. *Report on the Affairs of British North America (Durham Report) by Earl of Durham.* Toronto: Examiner Office, 1839.

– *Report of the Royal Commission on Copyright Commission.* London: Eyre and Spottiswoode, 1878.

– *Return of Amounts Received from Canada since 1877 as duties collected on foreign reprints of British copyright works.* London: Eyre & Spottiswoode, 1895.

– *Timber Duties &.: Return to an Address to the Honourable the House of Commons, dated 25 August 1841, for copies of any correspondence between the secretary of state for the Colonial Department and the Governors of the British Possessions in North America relative to the Proposed Alteration in the Duties on Timber etc…* London: HMSO, 1841.

United States. *Copyright Law Revision. Deposit of Copyright Works. Studies prepared for the Subcommittee on Patents, Trademarks, and Copyrights of the Committee of the Judiciary United States Senate, eighty-sixth Congress, second session.* Studies 20: Deposit of Copyright Works. Washington, DC: Government Printing Office, 1960.

– *Copyright Law Revision, Studies prepared for the Subcommittee on Patents, Trademarks, and Copyrights of the Committee of the Judiciary United States Senate, eighty-sixth Congress, second session,* Studies 32–34, Study 33: Copyright in Government Publications. Washington, DC: Government Printing Office, 1961.

– *Judicial Committee Report,* 21st Congress, 2nd Session (1830) House of Representatives, Rep. No. 3 "Copy-Right" 1830 at p. 2. 17 December 1830.

Vallée, Jacques. *Tocqueville au Bas-Canada.* Montreal: Les Éditions du Jour, 1973.

Vaugeois, Denis. *Les Premiers Juifs d'Amérique 1760–1860 – L'extraordinaire histoire de la famille Hart.* Quebec: Les Éditions Septentrion, 2011.

Vaughan, Edgar. *Joseph Lancaster en Caracas (1824–1827): y sus relaciones con El Libertador Simón Bolívar*, 2 vols. Translated by Héctor D. Mago Rodríguez. Caracas: Editiones del Ministerio de Educación, 1987–89.
– *Joseph Lancaster in Caracas* (unpublished manuscript). Joseph Lancaster Papers. American Antiquarian Society Library. Worcester, Mass.
Verrette, Michel. *L'alphabétisation au Québec, 1660–1900: En marche vers la modernité culturelle*. Quebec: Septentrion, 2002.
Vinovskis, Maris, ed. *Education, Society, and Economic Opportunity: An Historical Perspective on Persistent Issues*. New Haven: Yale University Press, 1995.
Warfel, Harry R. *Noah Webster, Schoolmaster to America*. New York: Octagon Books, 1966.
Watson, Fiona M. *A Credit to This Province: A History of the Ontario Legislative Library and Its Predecessors, 1792–1992*. Ontario: Legislative Library, 1993.
Webster, Noah. *The American Spelling Book: containing an easy standard of pronunciation*. Boston: Isaiah Thomas and Ebenezer T. Andrews, 1793.
– *On the Education of Youth in America*. Boston: Isaiah Thomas & Ebenezer T. Andrews, 1790.
Webster, Noah, ed. *A Collection of Papers on Political, Literary and Moral Subjects*. New York: Webster & Clark, 1843.
Wedderburn, Alexander. *Statistical and Practical Observations relative to the province of New Brunswick*. Saint John: H. Chubb, 1835.
Wilcocke, Samuel Hull. *History of the Session of the Provincial Parliament of Lower Canada for 1828–29*. s.l, s.n. 1830?
Willinsky, John. *The Intellectual Properties of Learning*. Chicago: University of Chicago Press, 2017.
Wills, Elizabeth Carter, and James Gilreath. *Federal Copyright Records 1790–1800*. Washington, DC: Library of Congress, 1987.
Willis, John Howard. *Scraps and Sketches, or, the Album of a Literary Lounger*. Montreal: H.H. Cunningham, 1831.
Wilson, J. Donald, Robert M. Stamp, and Louis-Philippe Audet. *Canadian Education: A History*. Toronto: Prentice-Hall, 1970.
Wilton, John Henry. *Scenes in a Soldier's Life, a narrative of the principal events in Scinde, Bellochistan, and Afghanistan*. Montreal: R. & C. Chalmers, 1848.
Winship, Michael. *American Literary Publishing in the Mid-Nineteenth Century: The Business of Ticknor and Fields*. Cambridge: Cambridge University Press, 1995.
Wood, Samuel Simpson. *An Apology for the Colonial Clergy of Great Britain specifically for those of Lower and Upper Canada*. London: Hatchard & Son, 1828.
Woodmansee, Martha, and Peter Jaszi, eds. *The Construction of Authorship: Textual Appropriation in Law and Literature*. Durham: Duke University Press, 1994.

Young, Brian J. *The Politics of Codification: The Lower Canadian Civil Code of 1866.*
   Montreal and Kingston: McGill-Queen's University Press for the Osgoode
   Society for Canadian Legal History, 1994.

**Chapters in Books or in Edited Collections**

Adeney, Elizabeth. "Moral Rights in Canada: An Historical and Comparative
   View." In *An Emerging Intellectual Property Paradigm: Perspectives from Canada,*
   edited by Ysolde Gendreau. 163–96. Cheltenham: Edward Elgar, 2008.
Alexander, Isabella. "*Sayre v. Moore (1785).*" In *Landmark Cases in Intellectual
   Property Law,* 1st ed, edited by Jose Bellido, 59–86. London: Hart, 2017.
Aubin, Paul. "Books of Instruction in New France, Quebec, and Lower
   Canada." In *History of the Book in Canada,* vol. 1: *Beginnings to 1840,* edited
   by Patricia Lockhart Fleming, Gilles Gallichan, and Yvan Lamonde. Toronto:
   University of Toronto Press, 2004.
Black, Fiona A. "Importation and Book Availability." In *History of the Book
   in Canada,* vol. 1: *Beginnings to 1840,* edited by Patricia Lockhart Fleming,
   Gilles Gallichan, and Yvan Lamonde, 116–24. Toronto: University of Toronto
   Press, 2004.
Brouillete, Sarah. "Books of Instruction in Upper Canada and the Atlantic
   Colonies." In *History of the Book in Canada,* vol. 1: *Beginnings to 1840,* edited
   by Patricia Lockhart Fleming, Gilles Gallichan and Yvan Lamonde, 259–62.
   Toronto: University of Toronto Press, 2004.
Darnton, Robert. "What Is the History of Books?" In *The Kiss of Lamourette:
   Reflections in Cultural History,* edited by Robert Darnton, 107–35. New York:
   W.W. Norton, 1990.
Ducharme, Isabelle. "L'offre de titres littéraires dans les catalogues de la
   bibliothéque de collectivités à Montréal (1797–1898)." In *Lire au Québec au
   XIXè Siècle,* edited by Yvan Lamonde et Sophie Montreuil, 237–77. Saint-
   Laurent: Fides, 2003.
Galarneau, Claude. "The Desbarats Dynasty in Quebec and Ontario." In
   *History of the Book in Canada: 1840–1918,* vol. 2, edited by Yvan Lamonde,
   Patricia Lockhard Fleming, and Fiona A. Black, 87–9. Toronto: University of
   Toronto Press, 2005.
Gallichan, Gilles. "Parliamentary and Professional Libraries." In *History of
   the Book in Canada,* vol. 1: *Beginnings to 1840,* edited by Patricia Lockhart
   Fleming, Gilles Gallichan and Yvan Lamonde, 151–7. Toronto: University of
   Toronto Press, 2004.
Girard, Philip. "British Justice, English Law, and Canadian Legal Culture."
   In *Canada and the British Empire,* edited by Philip Buckner, 259–78. Oxford:
   Oxford University Press, 2008.

Goff, F.R. "The First Decade of the Federal Act for Copyright 1790–1800."
In *Essays Honoring Lawrence C. Wroth*, edited by Frederick R. Goff, 113–28.
Portland: Anthoensen, 1951.

Green, James N. "The Rise of Book Publishing in America, 1782 to 1830." In *A
History of the Book in America*, vol. 2: *An Extensive Republic: Print, Culture, and
Society in the New Nation, 1790–1840*, 1st ed., edited by Robert A. Gross and
Mary Kelley, 75–127. North Carolina: University of North Carolina Press,
2010.

Gross, Robert A. "Building a National Literature: The United States 1800–
1890." In *A Companion to the History of the Book*, edited by Simon Eliot and
Jonathan Rose, 315–28. Oxford: Wiley-Blackwell, 2007.

Hare, John, and Jean-Pierre Wallot. "The Business of Printing and Publishing."
In *History of the Book in Canada*, vol. 1: *Beginnings to 1840*, edited by Patricia
Lockhart Fleming, Gilles Gallichan, and Yvan Lamonde, 71–7. Toronto:
University of Toronto Press, 2004.

Hare, John, and J.P. Wallot. "Le Livre au Québec et la Librarie Neilson au
tournant du XIXè Siècle." In *Livre et Lecture au Québec (1800–1850)*, edited by
Claude Galarneau and Maurice Lemire, 93–112. Quebec: Institut Québecois
de Recherche sur la Culture, 1988.

Hobbins, James H. "Shaping a Provincial Learned Society: The Early History
of the Albany Institute." In *The Pursuit of Knowledge in the Early American
Republic: American Scientific and Learned Societies from Colonial Times to the
Civil War*, edited by Alexandra Oleson and Sanborn C. Brown, 117–50.
Baltimore: Johns Hopkins University Press, 1976.

Judge, Elizabeth. "Crown Copyright and Copyright Reform in Canada." In
*In the Public Interest, the Future of Canadian Copyright Law*, edited by Michael
Geist, 550–94. Toronto: Irwin Law, 2005.

Lamonde, Yvan "La lecture et 'le livre de l'histoire' chez Amédée Papineau
(1835-1845)." In *Lire au Québec au XIXè siècle*, edited by Yvan Lamonde and
Sophie Montreuil, 69–93. Quebec: Édition Fides, 2003.

Lamonde, Yvan, and Andrea Rotundo. "The Book Trade and Bookstores." In
*History of the Book in Canada*, vol. 1: *Beginnings to 1840*, edited by Patricia
Lockhart Fleming, Gilles Gallichan, and Yvan Lamonde, 124–37. Toronto:
University of Toronto Press, 2004.

Laurence, Gérard. "The Newspaper Press in Quebec and Lower Canada." In
*History of the Book in Canada*, vol. 1: *Beginnings to 1840*, edited by Patricia
Lockhart Fleming, Gilles Gallichan, and Yvan Lamonde, 233–8. Toronto:
University of Toronto Press, 2004.

Leroux, Eric. "Printers: From Shop to Industry." In *History of the Book in
Canada*, vol. 2: *1840–1918*, edited by Yvan Lamonde, Patricia Lockhart
Fleming, and Fiona A. Black, 75–6. Toronto: University of Toronto Press,
2004.

Love, James. "Anti-American Ideology and Education Reform in 19th Century Upper Canada." In *An Imperfect Past: Education and Society in Canadian History*, edited by J. Donald Wilson, 170–80. Vancouver: UBC Press, 1984.

Macdonald, Mary Lu. "Subscription Publishing." In *History of the Book in Canada*, vol. 1: *Beginnings to 1840*, edited by Patricia Lockhart Fleming, Gilles Gallichan, and Yvan Lamonde, 78–80. Toronto: University of Toronto Press, 2004.

Melançon, François. "Print and Manuscript in French Canada under the Ancien Régime." In *Books between Europe and the Americas: Connections and Communities 1620–1860*, edited by Leslie Howsam and James Raven, 83–103. Basingstoke: Palgrave Macmillan, 2011.

Monette, Isabelle. "L'offre de titres littéraires dans les catalogues de la librarie montréalaise (1816–1879)." In *Lire au Québec au XIXè Siècle*, edited by Yvan Lamonde and Sophie Montreuil, 201–35. Saint-Laurent: Fides, 2003.

Moyse, Pierre-Emmanuel. "Canadian Colonial Copyright: The Colony Strikes Back." In *An Emerging Intellectual Property Paradigm: Perspectives from Canada*, edited by Ysolde Gendreau, 107–38. Cheltenham: Edward Elgar, 2008.

Murray, Heather. "Readers and Society." In *History of the Book in Canada*, vol. 1: *Beginnings to 1840*, edited by Patricia Lockhart Fleming, Gilles Gallichan, and Yvan Lamonde, 178–82. Toronto: University of Toronto Press, 2004.

Ouellet, Fernand. "Inventaire de la Saberdache de Jacques Viger." In *Rapport de l'Archiviste de la Province de Québec pour 1955–1956 et 1956–1957*, 33–176. Quebec: Secrétariat de la Province, Imprimeur de sa Majesté la Reine, 1957.

Pfister, Laurent. "Author and Work in the French Print Privileges System: Some Milestones." In *Privilege and Property: Essays on the History of Copyright*, edited by R. Deazley, M. Kretschmer, and L. Bently, 115–36. Cambridge: Open, 2010.

Reiter, Eric H. "From Shaved Horses to Aggressive Churchwardens: Social and Legal Aspects of Moral Injury in Lower Canada." In *Essays in the History of Canadian Law: Quebec and the Canadas*, edited by G. Blaine Baker and Donald Fyson, 460–502. Toronto: Osgoode Society for Canadian Legal History, 2013.

Rotundo, Andrea. "Les catalogues et leur contribution à une histoire des pratiques de lectures au Québec." In *Lire au Québec au XIXè Siècle*, edited by Yvan Lamonde and Sophie Montreuil, 153–8. Saint-Laurent: Fides, 2003.

Suarez, Michael S.J. "To What Degree Did the Statute of Anne (8 Anne c. 19, [1709]) Affect Commercial Practices of the Book Trade in Eighteenth-Century England? Some Provisional Answers about Copyright, Chiefly from Bibliography and Book History." In *Global Copyright: Three Hundred Years Since the Statute of Anne, from 1709 to Cyberspace*, edited by Lionel Bently, Uma Suthersanen, and Paul Torremans, 54–69. Cheltenham: Edward Elgar, 2010.

Tawfik, Myra J. "Copyright History as Book History: The Law in Multidisciplinary Context." In *Research Handbook on Copyright*, 2nd ed., edited by Paul Torremans, 31–56. Cheltenham: Edward Elgar, 2017.
– "History in the Balance: Copyright and Access to Knowledge." In *From "Radical Extremism" to "Balanced" Copyright and the Digital Agenda*, edited by Michael Geist, 69–89. Toronto: Irwin Law, 2010.
Weatherall, Kimberley. "The Emergence and Development of Intellectual Property Law in Australia and New Zealand." In *The Oxford Handbook of Intellectual Property Law*, edited by Rochelle Dreyfuss and Justine Pila, 291–314. Oxford: Oxford University Press, 2018.
Webster, Noah. "Origin of the Copyright Laws in the United States." In *A Collection of Papers on Political, Literary, and Moral Subjects*, edited by Noah Webster, 173–8. New York: Webster & Clark, 1843.

**Journal Articles**

Abrams, Howard B. "The Historic Foundation of American Copyright Law: Exploding the Myth of Common Law Copyright." *Wayne Law Review* 29, no. 3 (1982–83): 1119.
Ailwood, Sarah, and Maree Sainsbury. "The Imperial Effect: Literary Copyright in Colonial Australia." *Law, Culture and the Humanities* 12, no. 3 (2016): 716–40.
Alston, Sandra. "Canada's First Bookseller's Catalogue." *Papers of the Bibliographical Society of Canada / Cahiers de la Société bibliographique du Canada* 30, no. 1 (1992): 7–26.
Ardagh, W.D., and Robert A. Harrison, eds. *The Upper Canada Law Journal*, vol. 8. Toronto: W.C. Chewett & Co., 1862.
Asher, Gordon. "The Development of the Patent System in Canada since 1767." *Canadian Patent Reporter* 43 (1965): 56–75.
Audet, Francis J. "John Neilson." *Proceedings and Transactions of the Royal Society of Canada / Délibérations et mémoires de la Société royale du Canada* 22, no. 3 (1928): 81–97.
Banks, Kenneth J. "Communications and 'Imperial Overstretch': Lessons from the Eighteenth-Century French Atlantic." *French Colonial History* 6 (2005): 17–32.
Bannerman, Sara. "Canadian Copyright: History, Change, and Potential." *Canadian Journal of Communication* 36 (2011): 31–49.
Bently, Lionel. "The 'Extraordinary Multiplicity' of Intellectual Property Laws in the British Colonies in the Nineteenth Century." *Theoretical Inquiries in Law* 12, no. 1 (2011): 161–200.
Bernatchez, Ginette. "La société littéraire et historique de Québec (The Literary and Historical Society of Quebec) – 1824–1890." *Revue d'histoire de l'Amérique française* 35, no. 2 (September 1981): 179–92.

Bernier, Jacques, "François Blanchet et le mouvement réformiste en médecine au début du XIXè siècle." *Revue d'histoire de l'Amérique Française* 34, no. 2 (September 1980): 223–44.

Black, Fiona. "'Horrid Republican Notions' and Other Matters: School Book Availability in Georgian Canada." *Paradigm: Journal of the Textbook Colloquium* 2, no. 3 (July 2001): 7–18.

Boileau, Gilles. "L'histoire de la fameuse carte de Joseph Bouchette." *Histoire Québec* 10, no. 2 (2004): 36–8.

Bracha, Oren. "The Adventures of the Statute of Anne in the Land of Unlimited Possibilities: The Life of a Legal Transplant." *Berkeley Technology Law Journal* 25, no. 3 (Summer 2010): 1427–74.

– "The Ideology of Authorship Revisited: Authors, Markets, and Liberal Values in Early American Copyright." *Yale Law Journal* 118, no. 2 (2008): 186–271.

Bruckner, Martin. "Lessons in Geography: Maps, Spellers, and Other Grammars of Nationalism in the Early Republic." *American Quarterly* 51, no. 2 (June 1999): 311–43.

Burn, D.L. "Canada and the Repeal of the Corn Laws." *Cambridge Historical Journal* 2, no. 3 (1928): 252–72.

Burns, James. "From 'Polite Learning' to 'Useful Knowledge,' 1750–1850." *History Today* 36 (April 1986): 21–9.

Charland, Thomas. "À qui devons-nous la réédition des Relations des Jésuites?" *Revue d'histoire de l'Amérique française* 3, no. 2 (September 1949): 210–26.

Chauveau, Pierre-Joseph-Olivier. "Bibliographie Canadienne – William Evans L'Agronome." *Journal de L'Instruction Publique* 1, no. 2 (February 1857): 33–4.

Chisick, Harvey. "On the Margins of the Enlightenment: Blacks and Jews." *The European Legacy: Towards New Paradigms* 21, no. 2 (2016): 127–44.

Conrad, Sebastian. "Enlightenment in Global History: A Historiographical Critique." *American Historical Review* 117, no. 4 (2012): 999–1027.

Cormier, Louis-P. "Quatre lettres inédites de Joseph-François Perrault." *La Revue de l'Université Laval* 17, no. 6 (February 1963): 508–19.

Côté, Jean E. "The Reception of English Law." *Alberta Law Review* 15, no. 1 (1977): 29–92.

Curtis, Bruce. "Joseph Lancaster in Montreal *bis*: Monitorial Schooling and Politics in a Colonial Context." *Historical Studies in Education/Revue d'histoire de l'éducation* 17, no. 1 (Spring/printemps 2005): 1–27.

– "Schoolbooks and the Myth of Curricular Republicanism: The State and the Curriculum in Canada West, 1820–1850." *Histoire Sociale-Social History* 16, no. 32 (1983): 305–29.

– "Tocqueville and Lower Canadian Educational Network." *Encounters on Education* 7 (Fall 2006): 113–30.

Dallon, Craig W. "The Problem with Congress and Copyright Law: Forgetting the Past and Ignoring the Public Interest." *Santa Clara Law Review* 44 (2004): 365–455.

Deazley, Ronan. "The Myth of Copyright at Common Law." *Cambridge Law Journal* 62, no. 1 (March 2003): 106–33.

Dmitrieva, Irina Y. "State Ownership of Copyright in Primary Law Materials." *Hastings Communications and Entertainment Law Journal* 23 (2000): 81–119.

Donner, Irah. "The Copyright Clause of the US Constitution: Why Did the Framers Include It with Unanimous Approval?" *American Journal of Legal History* 36 (1992): 361–78.

"Dossier Jacques Labrie." *Revue d'histoire de l'Amérique française* 1, no. 3 (December 1947): 408–18.

Dufour, Andrée. "Les premières enseignantes laïques au Québec. Le cas de Montréal, 1825–1835." *Histoire de l'éducation* 109 (2006): 3–32.

Emblidge, David. "Isaiah Thomas Invents the Bookstore Chain." *Publishing Research Quarterly* 28, no. 1 (March 2012): 53–64.

Feather, John. "The Book Trade in Politics: The Making of the Copyright Act of 1710." *Publishing History* 8 (1980): 19–44.

– "Publishers and Politicians: The Remaking of the Law of Copyright in Britain 1775–1842, pt 1: Legal Deposit and the Battle of the Library Tax." *Publishing History* 24 (1988): 49–76.

– "Review of the Origin of the Right of Copy by Ronan Deazley." *English Historical Review* 120 (2005): 842.

– "From Rights in Copies to Copyright: The Recognition of Authors' Rights in English Law and Practice in the Sixteenth and Seventeenth Centuries." *Cardozo Arts and Entertainment Law Journal* 10 (1992): 455.

Fingard, Judith. "Attitudes towards the Education of the Poor in Colonial Halifax." *Acadiensis* 2, no. 2 (Spring 1973): 15–42.

– "English Humanitarianism and the Colonial Mind: Walter Bromley in Nova Scotia, 1813–1825." *Canadian Historical Review* 54, no. 2 (1973): 123–51.

Fontaine-Bernard, Steven. "Le Bas-Canada dans la presse française de 1830 à 1838." *Bulletin d'histoire politique* 13, no. 2 (2005): 171–90.

Fraser, Angus. "John Murray's Colonial and Home Library." *Papers of the Bibliographical Society of America* 91, no. 3 (September 1997): 339–408.

Gagnon, Hervé. "Pierre Chasseur et l'émergence de la muséologie scientifique au Québec 1824–1838." *Canadian Historical Review* 75, no. 2 (1994): 205–38.

Galarneau, Claude. "Le Métier du livre à Québec (1764–1859)." *Les Cahiers des Dix* 43 (1983): 143–65.

– "Samuel Neilson (1800–1837)." *Les Cahiers des Dix* 50 (1995): 79–116.

Gallichan, Gilles. "Les débats parlementaires du Québec (1792–1964) ou la mémoire des mots." *Papers of the Bibliographical Society of Canada/Cahiers de la Société bibliographique du Canada*, 27, no. 1 (1988): 38–79.

Gendreau, Ysolde. "De l'importance d'être constant." *La revue du notariat* 96 (1993): 129–42.

Gerriets, Marilyn, and Gwyn, Julian. "Tariffs, Trade, and Reciprocity: Nova Scotia, 1830–1866." *Acadiensis* 25, no. 2 (Spring 1996): 62–82.

Gilchrist, John. "Copyright Deposit: Legal Deposit or Library Deposit: The Government's Role as Preserver of Copyright Material." *Queensland University of Technology Law Justice Journal* 5, no. 2 (2005): 177–94.

Ginsburg, Jane C. "The US Experience with Copyright Formalities: A Love/Hate Relationship." *Columbia Journal of Law and the Arts* 33, no. 4 (2010): 311–48.

Gómez-Arostegui, H. Tomás. "What Is the Point of Copyright History: Reflections on *Copyright At Common Law in 1774*." CREATe Working Paper 2016/4.

Hare, John, et Jean-Pierre Wallot. "Les entreprises d'imprimerie et d'édition en Amérique du Nord Britannique, 1751–1840." *MENS Revue d'histoire intellectuelle et culturelle* 5, no. 2 (Spring 2005): 307–44.

Hart, Lawrence. "Joseph-François Perrault (1753–1844) and Admissibility to the Bar." *McGill Law Journal* 8 (1960–61): 270–83.

Harvey, D.C. "Early Public Libraries in Nova Scotia." *Dalhousie Review* 14 (1934–35): 429–43.

Hayhurst, William. "Intellectual Property Laws in Canada: The British Tradition, the American Influence, and the French Factor." *Intellectual Property Journal* 10 (1996): 265.

Hesse, Carla. "Enlightenment Epistemology and the Laws of Authorship in Revolutionary France, 1777–1793." *Representations* 30 (Spring 1990): 109–37.

– "The Rise of Intellectual Property, 700 BC–AD 2000: An Idea in the Balance." *Daedalus* 131, no. 2 (Spring 2002): 26–45.

Hofmeyer, Isabel. "Colonial Copyright Customs and Port Cities: Material Histories and Intellectual Property." *Comparative Literature* 70, no. 3 (2018): 264–77.

Howsam, Leslie. "What the Victorian Empire Learned: A Perspective on History, Reading, and Print in Nineteenth-Century Textbooks." *Journal of Victorian Culture* 25, no. 1 (2020): 47–62.

Huzzey, Richard. "Petitions, Parliament, and Political Culture: Petitioning the House of Commons, 1780–1918." *Past and Present* 248, no. 1 (2020): 123–64.

Kennedy, Patricia. "What Marie Tremaine Did Not Find: An Exploration of Archival Back Rooms." *Papers of the Bibliographical Society of Canada / Cahiers de la Société bibliographique du Canada* 30, no. 1 (Spring 1992): 27–51.

Kharem, Haroon. "The African Free Schools: A Black Community's Struggle against Cultural Hegemony in New York City 1820–1850." *Taboo: The Journal of Culture and Education* 4, no. 2 (2000): 27–36.

Khong, Dennis W.K. "The Historical Law and Economics of the First Copyright Act." *Erasmus Law and Economics Review* 2, no. 1 (2006): 35–69.

Kirby, William. "Mr. Kirby on Copyright." Speech delivered to Royal Society of Canada, 1883. Newspaper clipping of speech available at Toronto Public Library.

Laurence, W.H. "'Never Been a Very Promising Speculation': Requests for Financial Assistance from Authors of Non-Fiction Books to the Nova Scotia House of Assembly, 1800–1850." *Papers of the Bibliographical Society of Canada / Cahiers de la Société bibliographique du Canada* 39, no. 2 (2001): 45–78.

Leblond, Silvio, "Pioneers of Medical Teaching in the Province of Quebec." *Journal of the American Medical Association* 200 (1967): 843–8.

Levin, Salmond S. "The Origins of the Jews' Free School." *Transactions (Jewish Historical Society of England)* 19 (1955–59): 97–114.

Li, Xing, Megan MacGarvie, and Petra Moser. *Dead Poets' Property: How Does Copyright Influence Price? RAND Journal of Economics* 49, no. 1 (March 2018): 181–205.

Love, James H. "Cultural Survival and Social Control: The Development of a Curriculum for Upper Canada's Common Schools in 1846." *Social History* 15, no. 30 (November 1982): 357–82.

Macdonald, Mary Lu. "The Montreal Non-Tea Party; or, American Printings of British Copyright Material Imported into Canada East in 1849–1850." *Epilogue* 10, no. 1–2 (1995): 1–24.

– "Three Early Canadian Poets." *Canadian Poetry* 17 (Fall–Winter 1985). http://canadianpoetry.org/volumes/vol17/macdonald.html.

Magnan, C-J. "Le centenaire du premier traité de pédagogie publié au Canada (1822–1922)." *l'Enseignement Primaire* (1922): 273.

Mahé, Yvette T.H. "La Survivance: Discourses and the Curriculum in French-Speaking Communities in North America 1840–1960." *Journal of Educational Thought / Revue de la Pensée Éducative* 38, no. 2 (Autumn 2004): 183–207.

Matte, Raymond, and Leo Gagné. "'Nos institutions, notre langue, nos lois': La Société Saint-Jean-Baptiste de Québec." *Cap-Aux Diamants* 29 (1992): 24–7.

Mavor, James. "Canadian Copyright." *University of Toronto Monthly* (1901): 139–45.

McCadden, Joseph J. "Joseph Lancaster and Philadelphia." *Pennsylvania History* 4, no. 1 (January 1937): 6–20.

– "Joseph Lancaster in America." *Social Studies* 28, no. 2 (1937): 73–7.

McLaren, Scott. "Anti-British in Every Sense of the Word? Methodist Preachers, School Libraries, and the Problem of American Books in Upper Canada, 1820–1860." *Historical Papers of the Canadian Society of Church History* (2013): 55–76.

Migneault, Gaëtan. "La pratique du droit en français au Nouveau-Brunswick." *Ottawa Law Review/Revue de Droit d'Ottawa* 44, no. 3 (2013): 529–60.

Mignault, P.B. "La propriété littéraire." *La Thémis* 10, no. 2 (1880): 289.

Miller, Bradley. "'Political imagination, in its most fervid and patriotic flights': Copyright and Constitutional Theory in Post-Confederation Canada." *Journal of the Canadian Historical Association* 20, no. 1 (2009): 85–105.

Monotti, A. "Nature and Basis of Crown Copyright in Official Publications." *European Intellectual Property Review* 14 (1992): 305–16.

Moss, John H. "Copyright in Canada." *University Magazine*, April 1914.

Nair, Meera. "The Copyright Act of 1889: A Declaration of Independence." *Canadian Historical Review* 90 (2009): 1–28.

Nash, Margaret. "Contested Identities: Nationalism, Regionalism, and Patriotism in Early American Textbooks." *History of Education Quarterly* 49, no. 4 (October 2009): 417–41.

Nickless, Joseph. "On Literary and Historical Societies." *Canadian Magazine and Literary Repository* 2, no. 8 (1824): 111–13.

Ochoa, Tyler T., and Mark Rose. "The Anti-Monopoly Origins of the Patent and Copyright Clause." *Journal of the Patent and Trademark Office Society* 84 (2002): 909–40.

O'Halloran, George F. "Copyright in Canada." *Canadian Bar Review* 11 (1928): 109–14.

Oliar, Dotan. "Making Sense of the Intellectual Property Clause: Promotion of Progress as a Limitation on Congress's Intellectual Property Power." *Georgetown Law Journal* 94 (2006): 1771–846.

O'Neill, Mora Dianne. "William Eagar: Artist and Gentleman." *Journal of the Royal Nova Scotia Historical Society* 6 (2003): 65–91.

Ozment, Kate. "Rationale for Feminist Bibliography." *Textual Cultures* 13, no.1 (Spring 2020): 149–78.

Parizeau, Gérard. "Joseph Bouchette: l'homme et le haut fonctionnaire." *Proceedings and Transactions of the Royal Society of Canada/Mémoires et compte-rendus de la Société royale du Canada* 9, no. 4 (1971): 95–126.

Parker, George L. "Authors and Publishers on the Offensive: The Canadian Copyright Act 1921 and the Publishing Industry 1920–1930." *Papers of the Bibliography Society of Canada / Cahiers de la Société Bibliographique du Canada* 50, no. 2 (2012): 131–84.

Pelanda, Brian Lee. "Declarations of Cultural Independence: The Nationalistic Imperative behind the Passage of Early American Copyright Laws, 1783–1787." *Journal of the Copyright Society of the USA* 58 (2011): 431–54.

Perrault, Antonio. "La propriété littéraire et artistique" (1924). *Proceedings and Transactions of the Royal Society of Canada/Délibérations et mémoires de la Société royale du Canada*, 49–71.

Perrault, Joseph-François. "Plan raisonné d'éducation générale et permanente le plus propre à faire la prospérité du Bas-Canada, en égard à ses circonstances actuelles," vol. 2: Original Series. Quebec: *Transactions of the Literary and Historical Society of Quebec*, 1831.

Plant, Arnold. "The Economic Aspects of Copyright in Books." *Economica* 1, no. 2 (May 1934): 167–95.

Pollack, Malla. "What Is Congress Supposed to Promote? Defining 'Progress' in Article 1, Section 8, Clause 8 of the US Constitution or Introducing the Progress Clause." *Nebraska Law Review* 80 (2002): 754.

"Proceedings in Congress during the Years 1789 and 1790, Relating to the First Patent and Copyright Laws." *J. Pat. Off. Society* 22 (1940): 243–88.

"Proceedings of the Royal Lancasterian Institute for 1812." *Scots Magazine and Edinburgh Literary Miscellany* 75, no. 2 (September 1813): 680–1.

Radin, Margaret Jane. "Property and Personhood." *Stanford Law Review* 34 (1982): 957–1015.

Rayman, Ronald. "Joseph Lancaster's Monitorial System of Instruction and American Indian Education 1815–1838." *History of Education Quarterly* 21, no. 4 (Winter 1981): 395–409.

Reese, R. Anthony. "Innocent Infringement in US Copyright Law: A History." *Columbia Journal of Law and the Arts* 30, no. 2 (2007): 133–84.

Remer, Rosalind. "Preachers, Peddlers, and Publishers: Philadelphia's Backcountry Book Trade, 1800–1830." *Journal of the Early Republic* 14, no. 4 (1994): 497–522.

Riddell, William Renwick. "The First Copyrighted Book in the Province of Canada." *Ontario Historical Society: Papers and Records and Ontario History* 25 (1929): 405–14.

Roderick, Gordon W., and Michael D. Stephens. "The Role of Nineteenth Century Provincial Literary and Philosophical Societies in Fostering Adult Education." *Journal of Educational Administration and History* 5, no. 1 (1973): 28–33.

Roper, Gordon. "Mark Twain and His Canadian Publishers." *American Book Collector* 10, no. 10 (1960): 13–29.

– "Mark Twain and His Canadian Publishers: A Second Look." *Papers of the Bibliographical Society of Canada / Cahiers de la Société bibliographique du Canada* 5, no.1 (1966): 30–89.

Rose, Mark. "The Author as Proprietor: *Donaldson v. Becket and* the Genealogy of Modern Authorship." *Representations*, no. 23 (Summer 1988): 51–85.

– "Nine-Tenths of the Law: The English Copyright Debates and the Rhetoric of the Public Domain." *Law and Contemporary Problems* 66 (Winter 2003): 75–88.

– "The Public Sphere and the Emergence of Copyright: Aeropagitica, the Stationers' Company, and the Statute of Anne." *Tulane Law Journal of Technology and Intellectual Property* 12 (2009–10): 123–44.

Rosen, Zvi S., and Richard Schwinn. "An Empirical Study of 225 Years of Copyright Registrations." *Tulane Law Review* 94 (2020): 1003.

Ross, Terence P. "Copyright Corner: Copyright Registration in the Early Republic: A Bibliographic Note." *Journal of the Copyright Society of the USA* 59 (2011–12): 711–21.

Ross, Terence P., and William J. Maher. "Copyright Term, Retrospective Extension, and the Copyright Law of 1790 in Historical Context." *Journal of the Copyright Society USA* 49 (2002): 1021–39.

Ross, Trevor. "Copyright and the Invention of Tradition." *Eighteenth-Century Studies* 26 (1992): 1–27.

Roy, J. Edmond. "Discours présidentiel de la propriété littéraire." Appendix A, *Proceedings and Transactions of the Royal Society of Canada / Mémoires et compte-rendus de la Société royale du Canada*, Third series, *1909–1910*, vol. 3 (1910): 83–119.

Sadler, John. "Maritime Entrepreneurism: The History of Law Reporting in New Brunswick and Prince Edward Island." *Canadian Association of Law Libraries* 18 (1993): 106–17.

Sherman, Brad. "Remembering and Forgetting: The Birth of Modern Copyright Law." *Intellectual Property Journal* 10 (1995): 1.

Smith, Karen. "Early Libraries in Halifax." *Journal of the Royal Nova Scotia Historical Society* 7 (2004): 1–14.

Spragge, George. "Joseph Lancaster in Montreal." *Canadian Historical Review* 22, no. 1 (March 1941): 35–41.

Sternberg, Ilse. "The British Museum Library and Colonial Copyright Deposit." *The British Library Journal* 17, no. 1 (Spring 1991): 61–82.

Tawfik, Myra J. "Copyright as *droit d'auteur*." *Intellectual Property Journal* 17, no. 1 (2003): 59–81.

Tessier, François-Xavier. "A la mémoire du docteur François Blanchet" *L'Observateur* 25, no. 1 (1830): 393.

Tessier, Yves. "Ludger Duvernay et les débuts de la presse périodique aux Trois-Rivières (suite et fin)." *Revue d'histoire de l'Amérique Française* 18, no. 4 (1965): 566–81.

"The New Canadian Copyright Act," *Musical Times* (UK), 1 July 1921, vol. 60, no. 94, 497.

Tunis, Barbara, "Medical Education and Medical Licensing in Lower Canada: Demographic Factors, Conflict, and Social Change." *Social History* 14, no. 27 (1981): 67–91.

Vaver, David. "Copyright Defences as User Rights." *Journal of the Copyright Society of the USA* 60, no. 4 (2013): 661–72.

Wallot, Jean-Pierre. "Frontière ou fragment du système atlantique: Des idées étrangères dans l'identité bas-canadienne au début du XIXè siècle." *Historical Papers / Communications historiques* 1 (1983): 1–29.

Walsh, Patrick. "Education and the 'Universalist' Idiom of Empire: Irish National School Books in Ireland and Ontario." *History of Education* 37, no. 5 (2008): 645–60.

Warkentin, Germaine. "In Search of 'The Word of the Other': Aboriginal Sign Systems and the History of the Book in Canada." *Book History* 2 (1999): 1–27.

Willinsky, John. "When the Law Advances Access to Learning: Locke and the Origins of Modern Copyright." *KULA: Knowledge Creation, Dissemination, and Preservation Studies* 1, no. 1 (2017): 1–10.

Wilson, Daniel. "Canadian Copyright." Paper read before the Royal Society of Canada, May 31, 1892, *Proceedings and Transactions of the Royal Society of Canada/Délibérations et mémoires de la Société royale du Canada*, Volume 10, Section 2 (1893): 3–17.

Wilson, Donald J. "Common School Texts in Use in Upper Canada Prior to 1845." *Papers of the Bibliographical Society of Canada / Cahiers de la Société bibliographique du Canada* 9 (1970): 36–53.

Winearls, Joan. "The Printing and Publishing of Maps in Ontario before Confederation." *Papers of the Bibliographical Society of Canada / Cahiers de la Société bibliographique du Canada* 31, no. 1 (1993): 57–79.

**Dissertations**

Bateson, Nora. "John Neilson of Lower Canada (1818–1828)." Master's thesis, McGill University, 1933.

Black, Fiona. "Book Availability in Canada, 1752–1820, and the Scottish Contribution." PhD diss., Loughborough University, 1999.

D'Almeida, Augustin Roland. "La présence des noirs au Québec: état des lieux et examen de quatre manuels d'enseignement de l'histoire au XIXè siècle." Masters' thesis, Université Laval, 2010.

Ellis, Charles Calvert. "Lancasterian Schools in Philadelphia." PhD diss., University of Pennsylvania, 1909.

Fens-de Zeeuw, Lyda. "Lindley Murray (1745–1826): Quaker and Grammarian." PhD diss., Leiden University, 2011.

Hagerman, Marion. "John Neilson: His Political Activities in Lower Canada 1818–1834." Master's thesis, University of Saskatchewan, 1937.

Kominek, Helen Isabel. "The Royal Institution for the Advancement of Learning: An Examination of its Educational Agenda in Lower Canada 1818–1833." PhD diss., University of Calgary, 2008.

Koropchak, Shannon Clark. "The Love of Learning in the Industrial Age: Useful Knowledge, Imagination, and the Education of the Nineteenth-Century British Working Classes." PhD diss., Graduate School of Arts and Sciences of Washington University, 2013.

McGarry, Kevin John. "Joseph Lancaster and the British and Foreign School Society: The Evolution of an Educational Organization from 1798–1846." PhD diss., University of Wales, 1985.

Neilson, John Gilbert. "Constitutionalism and Nationalism in Lower Canada." Master's thesis, Acadia University, 1982.

O'Brien, Gary. "Pre-Confederation Parliamentary Procedure: The Evolution of Legislative Practice in the Lower Houses of Central Canada, 1792–1866." PhD diss., Carleton University, 1988.

Spragge, George. "Monitorial Schools in the Canadas 1810–1845." PhD diss., University of Toronto, 1935.

Wall Jr., Edward Flavin. "Joseph Lancaster and the Origins of the British and Foreign School Society." PhD diss., Columbia University, 1966.

**Online Databases**

Canada's Early Women Writers (CEWW), https://cwrc.ca/project/canadas-early-women-writers

Dictionary of Canadian Biography (DCB), http://www.biographi.ca/en/index.php

Les Manuels Scolaires Québécois (ManScol), https://www.bibl.ulaval.ca/ress/manscol/

# Index

*The bibliography contains full bibliographical details of legislation cited in the volume. Key pieces of legislation also appear as entries in the index.*

# Studies in Book and Print Culture

General Editor: Leslie Howsam

Benjamin C. Withers, *The Illustrated Old English Hexateuch, Cotton Ms. Claudius B.iv: The Frontier of Seeing and Reading in Anglo-Saxon England*

Mary Ann Gillies, *The Professional Literary Agent in Britain, 1880–1920*

Lisa Surwillo, *The Stages of Property: Copyrighting Theatre in Spain*

Janet Friskney, *New Canadian Library: The Ross-McClelland Years, 1952–1978*

Elspeth Jajdelska, *Silent Reading and the Birth of the Narrator*

Dean Irvine, *Editing Modernity: Women and Little-Magazine Cultures in Canada, 1916–1956*

Elizabeth Driver, *Culinary Landmarks: A Bibliography of Canadian Cookbooks, 1825–1949*

Willa Z. Silverman, *The New Bibliopolis: French Book-Collectors and the Culture of Print, 1880–1914*

Martyn Lyons, *Reading Culture and Writing Practices in Nineteenth-Century France*

Janice Cavell, *Tracing the Connected Narrative: Arctic Exploration in British Print Culture, 1818–1860*

Robert A. Davidson, *Jazz Age Barcelona*

Gail Edwards and Judith Saltman, *Picturing Canada: A History of Canadian Children's Illustrated Books and Publishing*

Miranda Remnek, ed., *The Space of the Book: Print Culture in the Russian Social Imagination*

Bonnie Mak, *How the Page Matters*

Adam Reed, *Literature and Agency in English Fiction Reading: A Study of the Henry Williamson Society*

Eli MacLaren, *Dominion and Agency: Copyright and the Structuring of the Canadian Book Trade, 1867–1918*

Ruth Panofsky, *The Literary Legacy of the Macmillan Company of Canada: Making Books and Mapping Culture*

Archie L. Dick, *The Hidden History of South Africa's Book and Reading Cultures*

Darcy Cullen, ed., *Editors, Scholars, and the Social Text*

James J. Connolly, Patrick Collier, Frank Felsenstein, Kenneth R. Hall, and Robert Hall, eds., *Print Culture Histories Beyond the Metropolis*

Kristine Kowalchuk, *Preserving on Paper: Seventeenth-Century Englishwomen's Receipt Books*

Ian Hesketh, *Victorian Jesus: J.R. Seeley, Religion, and the Cultural Significance of Anonymity*

Kirsten MacLeod, *American Little Magazines of the Fin de Siècle: Art, Protest, and Cultural Transformation*

Emily Francomano, *The Prison of Love: Romance, Translation and the Book in the Sixteenth Century*

Kirk Melnikoff, *Elizabethan Publishing and the Makings of Literary Culture*

Amy Bliss Marshall, *Magazines and the Making of Mass Culture in Japan*

Scott McLaren, *Pulpit, Press, and Politics: Methodists and the Market for Books in Upper Canada*

Ruth Panofsky, *Toronto Trailblazers: Women in Canadian Publishing*

Martyn Lyons, *The Typewriter Century: A Cultural History of Writing Practices*

Marina Balina and Serguei Alex. Oushakine, eds., *The Pedagogy of Images: Depicting Communism for Children*

Alison Hedley, *Making Pictorial Print: Media Literacy and Mass Culture in British Magazines, 1885–1918*

Myra Tawfik, *For the Encouragement of Learning: The Origins of Canadian Copyright Law*